SCAR

Frontispiece. An artist's impression of the Vikings landing in Orkney.
Copyright David Simon.

SCAR

A VIKING BOAT BURIAL
ON SANDAY, ORKNEY

Olwyn Owen and Magnar Dalland

with contributions from
*Anne Allen, Michél Carlsson, Stephen Carter, Amanda Clydesdale, Dianne Dixon
Thea Gabra-Sanders, Chris Gaffney, John Gater, Daphne Home Lorimer,
Roderick McCullagh, Kim Nissan, Andrea Smith, William Thomson, Paul Watson,
Richard Welander and Paul Wilthew*
and with illustration by
Sylvia Stevenson and *Christina Unwin*
and artefact photography by
Michael Brooks

TUCKWELL PRESS

In association with

HISTORIC SCOTLAND

First published in Great Britain in 1999
by Tuckwell Press
The Mill House
Phantassie
East Linton EH40 3DG
Scotland

ISBN 1 86232 080 2

British Library Cataloguing in Publication Data

A catalogue record for this book is available on request from the British Library

Designed by Design Associates

Printed and bound by Zure, Spain

CONTENTS

6   THE MAN'S EQUIPMENT   103

ILLUSTRATIONS

(all copyright of Historic Scotland, unless otherwise stated
in the caption)

For Ben

The start of it all…

Towards the north end of Burness in Sanday lies Scar, one of the larger farms on this northern Orkney island. The farm, on gently undulating grazing land, faces a wide bay with sandy beaches and rocky shores. One day in 1985, as the farmer John Deerness was walking along the beach after a storm, he discovered some bones sticking out of the low sea-eroded cliff section, at a place called The Crook, about 1 km north-east of the farmhouse. The bones looked human and he reckoned that they belonged to a foreign sailor who had died at sea and been buried on the shore. As the farmer looked more closely, he discovered a round lead object, roughly the size of a pound coin, lying in the washed-out sand in front of the section. He showed it to his neighbour who thought it was part of a car battery. Nevertheless, Mr Deerness took it home and kept it safe. The next time he was in Kirkwall he took the object to show Dr Raymond Lamb, then the Orkney Archaeologist; but Dr Lamb was out of the office that day. John Deerness sadly died a few years later not knowing the importance of his discovery.

In September 1991, Julie Gibson, then Historic Scotland's monument warden for Orkney, visited Ruth Gosney, an archaeologist living on Sanday, who had heard about the bones at Scar. Ms Gibson examined the sandy section containing the bones and found a couple of rusty lumps of iron that looked like rivets. On her way back from the site, she called on Caroline Deerness to ask about the discovery of the bones. Mrs Deerness remembered the object her husband had found years earlier, and showed it to Julie Gibson who recognised it as an archaeological find.

Back in Kirkwall, the object was identified as a Viking lead bullion weight, used for weighing gold and silver on balance scales. Julie Gibson and Raymond Lamb believed that, if the lead weight found on the beach near the skeletal remains was associated with the bones, then there could be a Viking burial at Scar. Furthermore, the two rusty lumps of iron looked very much like boat rivets, perhaps indicating that this was the site of a Viking boat burial – rarely discovered in Britain. The last boat burial discovered in Orkney was excavated in 1980, at Westness in the island of Rousay.

A few days later, Raymond Lamb visited the site. The skeletal remains were clearly visible and Dr Lamb came across further corroded boat rivets. Some ten years earlier, during a general survey of the area, Dr Lamb had recorded a mound immediately inshore from the exposed bones; but, at that time, no archaeological remains were exposed on the seaward side of the mound. Although the evidence was scant, both Julie Gibson and Raymond Lamb were now convinced that the bones at Scar were from a Viking boat burial.

By then it was the end of September, and the first autumn gales would hit the island at any time. Strong winds combined with high tides could easily damage or even completely remove the archaeological remains. There was probably very little time to record the site before it was washed away by the sea.

Olwyn Owen and Patrick Ashmore of Historic Scotland visited the site soon afterwards and agreed to organise a rescue excavation. Funding was provided by Historic Scotland with support from Orkney Islands Council, and a team of five archaeologists from Historic Scotland's then excavation unit, Archaeological Operations and Conservation, started to plan and prepare for the fieldwork.

But before the archaeologists could reach the site, the first autumn gales hit Orkney. The team flew to Sanday as the wind was too severe for the boat to sail from Kirkwall. Once on Sanday, there was a further five days of waiting until the equipment arrived by boat. Luckily, the wind direction during the storms had been favourable to the site and there was no damage. By the end of October, just over a month after the site was discovered, the team, led by Magnar Dalland, was in place – ready to rescue the extraordinary Viking boat burial falling out of the low sandy cliff at Scar …

1. Human bones eroding out of the low sandy cliff at Scar in 1991. The human bones, lying on small stone slabs, can be seen as a dark stripe in the low section to the right of the ranging pole. With these few scant clues – the eroding bones, a handful of rusty boat rivets and a lead bullion weight – local archaeologists recognised that this could be the site of a Viking boat burial.

CHAPTER 1

VIKING AGE SANDAY

THE SETTING

Magnar Dalland & Olwyn Owen

> *On a map the North Isles lie like the scattered pieces of a jigsaw puzzle that no one could reassemble, cut by the altogether freakish forces of geology and the pounding sea. Sanday looks like a fossilized gigantic bat …*

(Eric Linklater 1980, 140)

The Orkney Islands are separated from the northern coast of the Scottish mainland by the Pentland Firth, at its narrowest only about 10km wide. The island group extends for 80km from north to south and 47km west to east, and comprises about ninety islands and skerries of which fourteen are inhabited. Sanday is one of the biggest and most populous of the north isles of Orkney. It is about 21km long from north-east to south-west and 1–3km wide, and is largely composed of gently inclined sedimentary rocks of Middle Old Red Sandstone age. The site of the Scar boat burial lies on the exposed north coast of the peninsula of Burness, facing out towards the Atlantic Ocean. The peninsula of Burness projects from the main line of the island and forms a well-defined district, which is one of Sanday's three parishes. The northern part of Sanday is very flat and, from a distance, is barely visible above the horizon. During a bad storm in 1953 the sea level rose so high that it cut Sanday into three parts, turning the peninsula of Burness temporarily into an island itself. Nowadays Burness consists of well-cultivated agricultural land, fringed by sand dunes and low reefs, with shingle ridges and spectacular beaches. Its low-lying terrain and sandy soils produce a distinctive topography quite different from most parts of Orkney.

Most of the area to the north-east of Scar farmhouse lies less than 10m above sea level. Calcareous sandy soils deriving from windblown sand cover the area. Although some areas along the shore have been eroded by high winds, there are no large dune formations, and the terrain is gently undulating with few features higher than 2 metres.

In common with everywhere else in the Orkney islands, the place-names of Sanday are overwhelmingly Scandinavian in origin—some 99%. Many Orkney names include a characteristically Scandinavian element, such as: skaill (Old Norse *skáli,* a hall); bu (O.N. *bú,* farmstead, estate etc); -by (O.N. *boer,* a farm settlement); garth (O.N. *garðr,* a farm etc); bister (O.N. *bólstaðr,* a farm settlement); and quoy (O.N. *kví,* cattle-fold or place where animals assembled), all referring to settlements of varying type, age and significance. Other common Scandinavian name elements refer to topographical features such as: ness (O.N. *nes,* a headland); wick (O.N. *vík,* a bay); or howe (O.N. *haugr,* a mound). The name 'Sanday' itself is one of these 'nature-names',

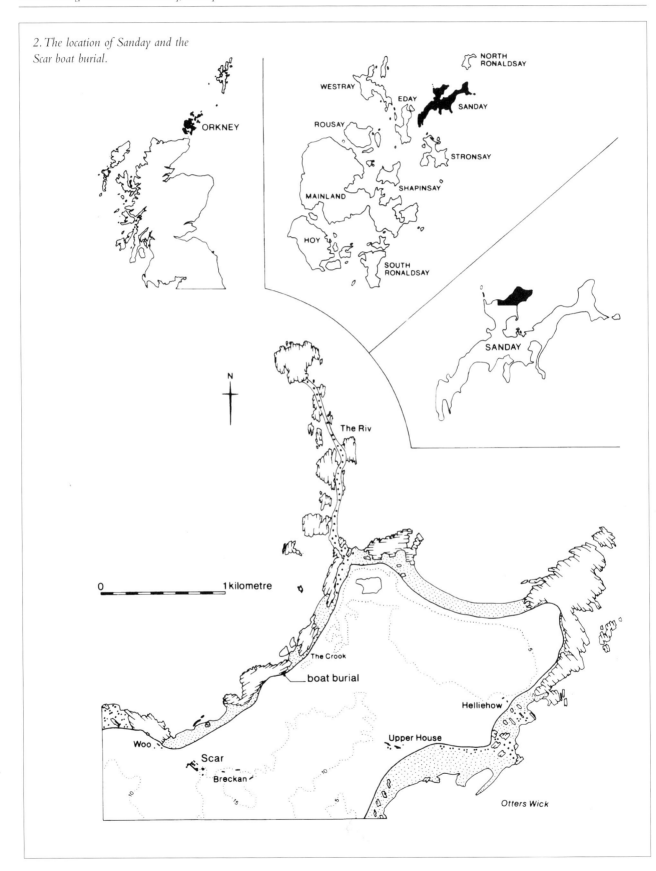

2. The location of Sanday and the
Scar boat burial.

3. The Scar boat burial lay on the exposed north coast of Burness peninsula, facing out towards the Atlantic.

meaning literally 'Sand-isle' (Marwick 1952, 6). The origins of the name 'Scar', however, are uncertain.

Sanday as a whole stands out in Orcadian history for the abnormally high valuation for skat (tax) purposes imposed on the island in Norse times. Whereas modern Orcadian agriculture concentrates on the production of beef cattle and the main crop for human consumption is potatoes, the ancient wealth of Sanday arose from its suitability for growing barley. There is no doubt that, in the Viking period, Sanday was incomparably the wealthiest of Orkney's northern isles. Taking mere area into account, that scale of early taxation was about three times what might have been expected which, Marwick (1952, 6) suggests, might indicate that the island was already extensively cultivated when Norsemen first arrived.

THE LANDSCAPE OF BURNESS IN THE VIKING AGE

William P L Thomson

In attempting to discover what Burness was like in the ninth and tenth centuries, we need to be clear about the limitations of the evidence. Written information contemporary with the site is entirely lacking, and the *Orkneyinga Saga* (written c 1200) contains only a scattering of references to Sanday, all of which relate to the twelfth century and are therefore too late to be of any use; there is only one place in Sanday which the saga mentions by name, 'Volunes', and its location cannot be identified (Taylor 1938, 241, 254, 307, 315, 324–5). The few other medieval documents are even later in date and are equally unhelpful. These sources do not contain a single piece of information which deals specifically with Burness.

Nearer the relevant date than anything in *Orkneyinga Saga* is the story in *Flateyjarbók* about Úlfr Illi ('Wolf the Bad'), a great chief who lived in Sanday in the time of Earl Sigurd Hlodversson, apparently before Earl Sigurd's conversion to Christianity in AD 995 (Nordal 1944, IV, 242–5; Dasent 1894, 369–73). We are told that 'Wolf the Bad … lived up to his name'; when his offer to buy an estate in North Ronaldsay was rejected, he killed the owner and seized the property. Although Earl Sigurd disapproved of the killing, such was Úlf's power that the earl's attempts at mediation failed, and Úlf escaped retribution. The story contains some fabulous elements, and Úlf's wickedness is perhaps emphasised as a contrast to the Christian virtues of his victim's grandson who had annual encounters with St Peter and became a bishop in Ireland. Yet the story may correctly reflect certain aspects of tenth-century society. In later records we find that the northern isles of Orkney consisted of a series of fairly large properties, with only a little udal or privately owned land. Sanday is likely to have been a society dominated by unruly magnates rather than inhabited by independent peasant farmers (Thomson 1993).

Much of the following reconstruction is based on rentals dating from 1502 and 1595 (Peterkin 1820, I and II). These rentals not only record the pennylands, landownership, skat (tax) and rent payments for each township, but are the earliest source of all the main place-names. At one time this kind of evidence would have been confidently used to reconstruct the Viking Age landscape, despite being more than half a millennium later in date. Scholars such as Hugh Marwick assumed that the system of tax assessment based on the valuation of land in ouncelands and pennylands stretched back virtually unchanged to the days of King Harald Fairhair, c AD 900 (H Marwick 1952, 210–12). This reasoning also led Marwick to date the creation of most of the important Norse place-names to the same period. However, we now know that taxation based on land-assessment is unlikely to be as early as he supposed, and it is also becoming increasingly clear that place-names with generics such as *boer, skáli, bólstaðr, staðir, land,* garth *(garðr),* setter *(sætr)* and quoy *(kví)* are not necessarily Viking Age, and cannot be used as an automatic mechanism to establish a chronology of settlement (Thomson 1995). Landscape reconstruction must therefore be more tentative, yet settlement patterns do seem to have been remarkably stable and, when treated with care, rentals can still reveal information which relates to an early period.

The first piece of useful information to emerge from the rentals is Sanday's quite extraordinarily large number of pennylands. Orkney had a total of about 3,667 pennylands, and of these about 668 pennylands were in Sanday, about 18% of the Orkney total. In recent times Sanday has had only 4% of Orkney's population, 4% of the rateable value, and about 8% of the arable land. Although the valuation in pennylands is unlikely to be as early as the burial, the large number can nevertheless be taken as a measure of the high value which was placed on Sanday in early times. Burness had 129 pennylands and, because they were so numerous, pennylands were unusually small in size, averaging only 2–3 acres of arable land exclusive of associated pasture (Peterkin 1820, I, 93–6; *Burness map*).

Eighteen pennylands made the little district known as the *urisland* or *ounceland,* and in Burness the urisland structure was unusually complete. The urislands corresponded to a series of large townships separated by turf dykes which were still in existence in 1750 when Murdoch Mackenzie's charts were published. However, it is not obvious how the site of the boat burial is related to these townships, since the site is in an isolated position, apparently on or near the boundary between Sand and Braebister. An old map of Burness, encrusted with layers of wallpaper from Scar house where it was at one time pasted to a wall, shows marvellous detail of the pre-improvement landscape, but only part of the map survives; unfortunately the portion which shows the Sand-Braebister boundary is missing *(Burness map).*

The large number of pennylands reflects the attractiveness of an environment where light soils were easily cultivated by primitive ploughs, and where values were enhanced by long lengths of coastline amazingly rich in the seaweed on which the manuring of the corn land depended; there was easy access to fishing grounds, and there were abundant supplies of cockles and 'spoots' (razor-fish), the importance of which is attested by the many shells in the huge midden deposits exposed by coastal erosion at Langskaill (R G Lamb 1980, 17, no 81). Despite its low altitude and light soils, only

4. Murdoch Mackenzie's chart of Sanday, 1750. Reproduced by permission of the Trustees of the National Library of Scotland.

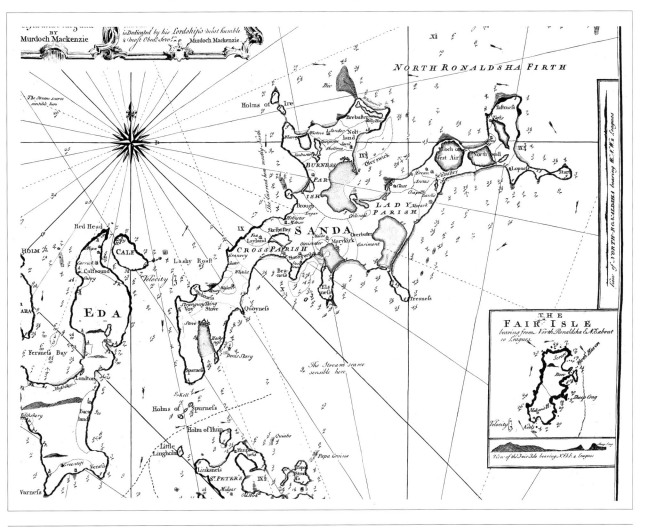

21% of Burness was cultivated prior to nineteenth-century improvement. In the absence of subsoil drainage, low-lying areas were often waterlogged, and lochs were more extensive than at present (Mackenzie 1750; *Burness map*). According to the *New Statistical Account,* written in 1842 when reclamation had already begun, a fourth part of the parish consisted of 'sandy downs and links', and a similar proportion was moorland which, towards the boundary with Cross parish, presented 'a most barren and forbidding appearance' (*NSA,* 84, 85).

An earlier even more widespread pastoral use is preserved in some of the place-names. Stangasetter contains the setter element used for grazing areas, milking places and home-shielings, often at no great distance from the parent farm, which in this case was presumably at Scar. Kirkisetter, another setter-name, was in a similar relationship to Westove. The name 'Noltland' also suggests pastoral use (O.N. *naut(a)-land,* 'cattle-land'), and indeed it seems that 'Noltland' was almost a technical term; this Noltland, the other Sanday Noltland which lies in Lady Parish, and the two Noltlands in Westray all lie on brown calcareous soils derived from shell-sand with shallow rooting zone. The fine grasses and good drainage of this links land provided grazing which could be used in the wet conditions of late autumn and early spring, and this must have been particularly valuable in an agricultural economy where winter fodder was invariably scarce (*Soil Survey;* Thomson 1990).

The destruction of arable land from sand-blow was a recurring danger, particularly in the townships of Sand, Braebister (Brybist), Helliehow and Noltland where the soils were derived from shell-sand. An interesting feature of the 1502 rental is the extent of the devastation at that time. Half of the land in Sand was described as 'blawin waist', in Braebister two of its nine pennylands had been lost, and a quarter of Helliehow and a third of Noltland were similarly eroded or else overblown by sand. The same destruction is recorded on other sandy land in Orkney's north isles, but we do not know whether the sands broke loose from natural causes, or whether the reason was damage to the protective vegetation cover caused by an extension of cultivation, over-grazing or the introduction of rabbits (Peterkin 1820, I, 93–6; Thomson 1996, xiii–xiv). No doubt there were other periods of sand-blow when agriculture was in retreat, as well as times when farming prospered. The light soils of Burness may have been attractive to early farmers, but they were a fragile environment with specific problems not usually encountered elsewhere in Orkney.

Besides its high value in pennylands, the other indication of the early importance of Sanday is the number of great earldom farms. The Norse earls of Orkney based their power, not on a single centre, but on large farms located throughout the islands, often distinguished by a Bu-name (Bu = large farm) and by *bordland* status (exemption from skat or tax). Three of these farms, the Bu of Walls, the Bu of Tofts and the Bu of Lopness, were situated together at the north-east extremity of Sanday, and they no doubt originally formed a single, very large 54–pennyland manor farm on a headland location, almost cut off from the rest of the island. Other Sanday bordland consisted of the Bu of Tresness (18 pennylands), the Bu of Brough (18 pennylands), the Bu of Hacksness (18 pennylands) and Grindally (6 pennylands). No other part of Orkney had such a number of earldom bordlands.

Although the earl's Sanday bordlands were extensive, there was no bordland in Burness. The greater part of Burness was described in the 1502 rental as 'pro rege' (belonging to the king). Clouston interpreted the term 'pro rege' as indicating 'kingsland', the former estates of the Norwegian crown (Clouston 1923–4). It is commonly believed that much of this kingsland was property forfeited to King Sverre when the defeated islanders failed to redeem it after their disastrous intervention in Norway's civil wars and their defeat in 1194 at Florvåg (Sephton 1899, 156–7). However, Burness was not necessarily one of these forfeited estates. Despite what Clouston wrote, it is clear that the rental often uses 'pro rege' to indicate all the land which was in the hands of the King of Scots, and by 1502 this was mainly the former earldom estate which James III had acquired in 1470 when he bought out Earl William Sinclair (Thomson 1996, xix). There is reason to believe that Burness had latterly been in the possession of the Orkney earls rather than the Norwegian-Danish crown. However, it was not skat-free bordland, and so it was presumably a late addition to the earldom estate.

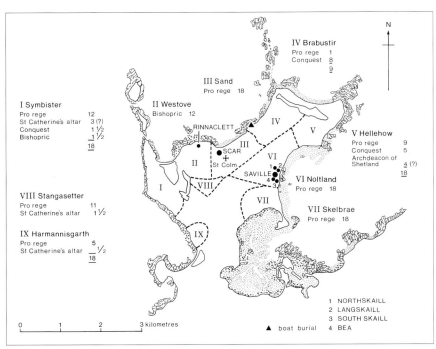

5. *Landownership and urislands, 1502. The 'pro rege' land formed a single important estate which at an unknown date appears to have passed into the hands of the Orkney earls. Presumably the various church lands had once been part of this estate. The 'conquest' lands had been udal, probably in the hands of a number of owner-occupiers, but these properties without exception were acquired by William Sinclair, Earl of Orkney 1434–70. (Based on information from Peterkin 1820; Mackenzie 1750; Burness map [nd]; and Miller & Hebden 1872.)*

Whether Burness was Norwegian kingsland or an addition to the Orkney earldom estate does not materially affect the interpretation of its early history. It was a single, cohesive estate of a kind not commonly found in Orkney where property was often fragmented and dispersed to an extent which people unfamiliar with the islands find hard to imagine. With 92½ pennylands (more if the church endowments had once been part of it), the Burness 'pro rege' land was considerably bigger than any of the Sanday bordlands, and indeed nearly as big as all of them put together. It was one of the most important properties in Sanday and, prior to its acquisition by the earl or king, it was presumably in the hands of a single owner. It was the kind of estate which could have formed a power-base for a chieftain such as 'Wolf the Bad'.

Within this property block, the main centre lay in the urisland of Sand or Sander (18 pennylands) which contains the mansion house of Scar. Sand is a topographic name of a simple kind often associated with early settlement on prime sites, whereas Scar is probably a relatively minor name promoted to importance when the mansion house was built. The way in which other urislands are named according to their position relative to Sand indicates its pre-eminence. Two *bólstaðr* (bister) names can be seen, Symbister and Braebister, one on either side of this nucleus. As is often the case, *bólstaðr*-names were used to indicate sub-divisions of a larger unit. Symbister, the south *bólstaðr*, was 'south' in relation to the centre at Scar. A further *bólstaðr*-name, Kirkabuster, is now lost (Barclay 1977, no 151); perhaps Kirkabuster was the original name for Westove which was bishopric property and so might readily be described as 'the church *bólstaðr*'. Westove is another directional name relative to Sand; it was first recorded in 1595 as 'Be-west ow' from its location west of the stream which divided it from Sand (H Marwick 1952, 14). However, the present form shows that people wrongly assumed that 'West á' was a 'stove'-name deriving from *stofa*, a high status name associated with prestigious buildings on big farms. The designation 'of Westove', rather than 'of Scar', was used by eighteenth- and nineteenth-century lairds of Burness.

The memory of an impressive farm in this area is preserved in a Sanday legend, first recounted by Walter Traill Dennison. According to the story, the family of Cok lived at Rinnaclett in Westove, immediately to the west of Scar. The 'Cock of the North', as he was remembered, was so wealthy that, when his cattle were put out to graze, the last animal was leaving the byre as the first reached the 'grind' (gate) in the hill-dyke, almost half a mile away (Craven 1897, 74–5; H Marwick 1923, 29). Despite Hugh Marwick's belief that the long procession of cattle echoed events in *Laxdæla Saga,* the story is unlikely to be particularly early. The Coks were first recorded in 1551, and the Sanday connection may date from 1585 when James Cok was admitted as Chancellor in St Magnus Cathedral and minister of Lady parish, Sanday (*O & S Recs,* I, 266; Craven 1897, 74; Smith 1907, 266–7). Westove presumably came into his hands when, like other cathedral clergy in the post-Reformation period, he succeeded in converting a bishopric property into a private estate.

The parish church of St Colm, sometimes attributed to St Columba, is located in Sand 'under the shadow' of the mansion house of Scar (Tulloch 1995, 39). It occupies a position characteristic of many early Orkney churches, immediately adjacent to the centre of temporal power. St Colm was a Pictish saint, but it would be unwise to interpret the dedication as sufficient evidence for a pre-Norse church and pre-Norse power-centre. There are numerous Orkney dedications to this obscure Aberdeenshire saint but they may be of late medieval origin rather than genuinely early. It is possible that religion of a different kind is indicated by 'Helliehow' (O.N.

helighaugr, 'holy mound'). Tradition records that the mound was inhabited by a hogboon who caused such annoyance that the people in the farm resolved to leave and live elsewhere (H Marwick 1923, 28; E Marwick 1975, 42). Vestiges of heathenism are interesting in view of a possible connection with the boat burial, but folklore and place-names are difficult to connect with genuine heathenism, of which there are remarkably few traces in Orkney.

If Scar in the urisland of Sand was a centre of importance, Saville in the urisland of Noltland was another. The importance of the location is attested by a group of high status names, Northskaill, Langskaill and South Skaill, which indicate the division of the lands of a single Norse *skáli* (hall), and the name 'Bea' (*boer*) is found in this same cluster (G Lamb 1992, 16, map 23). Marwick regarded *boer*-names as 'great original settlements', but Gillian Fellows-Jensen has more recently suggested that they may have come into existence when a big settlement disintegrated. That explanation fits exactly with the division of the land of the *skáli*, and its replacement by a relatively minor name, Saville, 'the corn field' or perhaps 'the sea-field' (Fellows-Jensen 1984, 155; H Marwick 1952, 21; G Lamb 1992, 57). However, the location of all of these names within an urisland which has a pastoral name (Noltland, 'cattle land') suggests that we ought to look to Scar, rather than Saville, as the principal centre within Burness.

The later history of the estate may be briefly told: Westove passed into the hands of the Traill family following the marriage of James Traill to Jean Cok in 1668 (Traill 1883, 37). The Traills were gradually able to add to their property until eventually they owned the entire parish except for 24 acres. In the nineteenth century the Burness part of the Westove estate extended to 2,259 acres; there were about sixty tenant farmers, and two mansion houses, one at Scar and the other at Saville (*NSA,* 91; Miller & Hebden 1872). The estate was overdependent on help, and Thomas Traill was bankrupted when prices collapsed. He was eventually succeeded by Colonel George Horwood; then, after Horwood's death, the estate was sold off in 1919, mainly to sitting tenants.

To summarise, then, the evidence of rentals, place-names and folk-tradition points to an important and cohesive estate in the Viking Age which comprised all but small portions of Burness, centred on the general vicinity of the present mansion house of Scar. Although much of the evidence is impossible to date, there is an impression of continuity, and reason to believe that the estate was important at an early period. The site of the Scar boat burial, however, although lying within this major settlement unit, is some distance away from the primary centre at Scar. Indeed, it is not closely associated with any farm which can be identified from historical records.

THE VIKING AGE ARCHAEOLOGY OF SANDAY

Olwyn Owen

The probable intensity and longevity of the Norse presence on Sanday has recently been highlighted by three archaeological studies: firstly, by the work of Dr Raymond Lamb whose inventory of the archaeological sites and monuments of Sanday (1980) drew attention to a number of probable Norse sites; secondly, by the fieldwork of Professor John Hunter and Steven Dockrill (1982, 570–6; Hunter, Dockrill, Bond and Smith, forthcoming), who examined three of these sites in more detail and carried out large-scale excavations at one of them (Pool); and thirdly, by Dr Donald Davidson and colleagues (1983; 1986) who have examined the phenomenon of some fifteen 'farm mounds' on the island.

Amongst the almost 200 sites and monuments of all periods recorded by Lamb in 1980, the 'most striking peculiarity … is the prominent mounds on

6. Sanday, showing the location of all sites mentioned in the text.

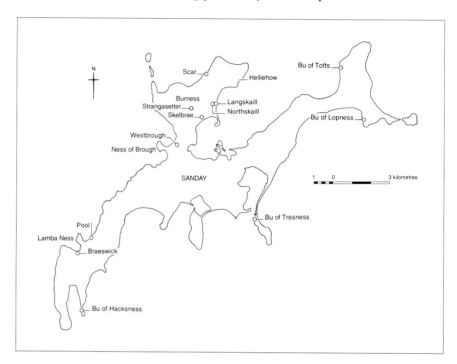

the summits of which many of the largest and oldest-established farms are built' (Lamb 1980, 7). These farm mounds vary in diameter from 50m to 205m, with deposits sometimes more than 4m thick. Lamb characterised them as 'veritable tells', built up over several millennia of continuous occupation. Although most of the mounds originated before the Viking period, the names of the farms on their summits often indicate that they were used by the Norse colonisers as primary settlements. Interestingly, name elements such as 'how' (O.N. *haugr*, mound) demonstrate that most of the mounds already existed at the time of the Norse colonisation in the ninth and tenth centuries.

At first it was thought that these farm mounds must consist largely of building debris and sand-blow, but preliminary surveys in 1981 of three mounds at Westbrough, Langskaill and Skelbrae (Davidson, Lamb & Simpson 1983) showed that stone buildings, where present at all, account for only a small proportion of the immense volume of a farm mound, the bulk of which is composed of soils and organic matter. It was suggested that the variability between the three mounds in sediment type and stratigraphic complexity reflected their long evolution with the foci of accumulation moving about over them (*ibid.* 43). It seemed likely that the mounds grew by extension of their summit areas—of which Viking-period activity was but one episode. Further analyses (Davidson, Harkness & Simpson 1986) have suggested that these organic soils accumulated from the ash of domestic hearths as well as from the residues of bedding materials from the byres, including cut and dried turves. Davidson, Harkness and Simpson suggest that the inherent fertility of the island may have made it unnecessary for the farmers to spread the dung over the fields, which in turn would explain why there is such a concentration of farm mounds on Sanday—an island notable in earlier times precisely for its fertile soils.

More recently, excavations at St Boniface, a farm mound in the neighbouring island of Papa Westray, have shown that the mound there

7. *The cliff section at St Boniface, Papa Westray, during archaeological sampling and recording, showing typical Norse farm mound deposits.*

actually consists of two distinct accumulations of material, separated by a long-standing soil (Lowe 1998, 187–99). A depth of about 1m of fuel ash, derived primarily from the burning of turves and mixed with domestic refuse, developed just before the Viking Age (between roughly AD 500 and 750). From then until about AD 1100, a soil supporting a heath vegetation existed on its surface. But in the twelfth century, in the space of a few decades at most, a further colossal depth of some 3m of material accumulated on the mound, this time consisting of fuel ash derived from the burning of turf and other organic sediments, mixed with abundant fish-processing waste and a little domestic refuse. The twelfth-century inhabitants of St Boniface seem to have been engaged in a specialist fishing enterprise, processing freshly caught white fish to produce wind-dried fillets (stock fish). The fuel ash came from fires probably used to render down the fish livers for oil.

Similar farm mounds occur in Norway north of the Arctic Circle (Bertelsen 1979), where they seem to be composed primarily of turf, perhaps from the repeated construction and disintegration of turf-built structures. Evidently, there is no one explanation for the development of farm mounds in Viking and medieval Orkney and Norway. Research into their formation processes is continuing, but, in Orkney's northern isles, including Sanday, they clearly indicate intensive Viking Age and later settlement and activities.

Hunter and Dockrill concentrated their efforts on the sites at Lamba Ness, the Ness of Brough and Pool, all in the south-west of the island, and all close to the reputed findspots of previously discovered Viking artefacts or definite Viking graves. Two Viking burials are recorded from the vicinity of Lamba Ness. One was a female grave containing two bronze oval brooches, a penannular brooch, a jet armlet and an amber bead (Grieg 1940, 86–8; Shetelig 1954, 70; R G Lamb 1980, no. 131); and the other probably a male grave with a double-edged iron sword and iron spearhead (Grieg 1940, 88; Shetelig 1954, 70; R G Lamb 1980, no. 130). Both graves are thought to be tenth century in date, but their precise findspots are unknown. Another presumed Viking grave, containing an axe and a spear, was found in Sanday as early as c 1750; its precise findspot is also not recorded (James Graham-Campbell, personal communication).

At the Ness of Brough, four mounds are sited on the tip of a headland at a place known as the Styes of Brough (R G Lamb 1980, nos. 132, 248–9). These mounds, damaged in antiquity, now vary in diameter from 15m to 30m and, in height, from less than 0.5m to over 2m. Hunter and Dockrill (1982, 576) speculated that they were Norse on the basis of a number of Viking artefacts recovered from the area, including an iron sword (Grieg 1940, fig. 86) reportedly found 'in a tumulus at Sties' (Anderson 1874, 172); and an iron axe and 'cauldron' (Grieg 1940, 172: the supposed 'cauldron', first described as a 'helmet', was most probably a shield boss; it is now lost). Although the precise findspots of these artefacts are unknown, Hunter & Dockrill (1982, 576) suggested that it was 'not altogether implausible' that the finds and the mounds are associated. In 1997, trenches were dug in all four mounds for a programme in Channel 4's *Time Team* series, and showed that they were all prehistoric sites; but a disturbed boat-shaped stone setting was found inserted into Mound 2, together with a fragment of human bone, and may well have been the site of a Viking burial (Bond, Dockrill, Gibson & Owen forthcoming).

8. The Styes of Brough from the air during the Time Team's 1997 investigations. Copyright Mick Aston.

At Braeswick, a short distance to the south of Pool, a possible female burial of the Viking period yielded a bronze oval brooch and beads of glass and amber (Grieg 1940, 2, 88; Wainwright 1962, 148; R G Lamb 1980, no. 129); while a Viking bone comb appears to have been found in the same vicinity (Hunter & Dockrill 1982, 571). Hunter and Dockrill's survey of the site at Pool (R G Lamb 1980, no. 84), traditionally thought to be a Viking harbour, confirmed that the site was extensive, multi-period and of considerable archaeological importance—and that it was eroding alarmingly fast.

The survey at Pool was therefore followed by large-scale excavations of this eroding settlement mound during the mid-1980s which uncovered extensive Neolithic deposits and a later Iron Age structural horizon,

9. *Excavations at Pool revealed that the Vikings re-used earlier buildings. Here we see a Late Iron Age roundhouse, but the Vikings had paved over the Pictish hearth and cut new steps into earlier deposits. Copyright University of Bradford & Historic Scotland.*

underlying the Viking and later Norse settlement (Hunter *et al* 1993, 272–84; and forthcoming). Thus, the Viking presence at Pool, and probably elsewhere, appears as part of a long process of cultural development rather than as a disconnected interval of Viking colonisation. There is a clearly identifiable period of overlap between the thriving pre-Norse farming community, probably dating from the fourth century AD onwards, and the Viking presence, identified by a 'series of observable shifts in structural morphology, material culture and subsistence economics' (Hunter *et al* 1993, 275). Indeed, several of the fifth- and sixth-century structural components were still being used more than five hundred years later. Radiocarbon dates from the earliest, securely Viking, cultural contexts (calibrated to AD 671–788 (GU-2004); AD 681–852 (GU-2002); and AD 882–1004 (GU-1807): Hunter *et al* 1993, 280) indicate a significantly early primary occupation, in advance of the creation of the Earldom in the later part of the ninth century.

From the very earliest phase of Viking settlement, Pool was a well-founded settlement with houses, outbuildings and activities. Economically, perhaps the most important developments in the early Viking period were the introduction of flax cultivation; the breeding of horses, apparently not for heavy labour but perhaps for eating and other purposes; and the use of carbonised seaweed, the function of which has not yet been adequately explained but which is often found on Norse settlement sites in the Northern Isles. These developments took place alongside more traditional farming methods: the growing of six-rowed hulled barley or 'bere' and of a cultivated form of oat, and husbandry of cattle and sheep.

There is every reason to suppose that this picture of a peaceful continuum of a thriving later Iron Age and early Viking farming community at Pool is replicated at other sites in Orkney and on Sanday, including perhaps at the north end of the island, probably somewhere in the general vicinity of the Scar boat burial.

10. A reconstruction painting of life on a Viking farm in the Northern Isles. Copyright David Simon.

CHAPTER 2

SURVEY AND EXCAVATION

THE SURVEY

The topographical survey

Magnar Dalland

The topography of the area next to the site is largely determined by the thickness of the sandy soils on top of bedrock or basal till, and the mounds and ridges seen on the surface could be entirely made up from sand, created by wind erosion and deposits in the past. Since the presence of stone structures is likely to affect the pattern of sand accumulation and erosion, however, the present topography may indicate where stone structures are buried; and so it was decided to undertake a topographical survey of the area next to the boat burial, to look for evidence of a settlement or further graves.

The topographical survey was centred on the area along the coast to the south-west of the boat burial. An area measuring 250m along the coast and 50–90m inland was covered. Two features were surveyed in detail: the mound next to the grave and an irregular rectangular platform some 80m to the south-west. A second mound (40m in diameter and 3m high) lies about 230m to the north-east. The area along the coast between the two mounds shows no distinct topographical features, except for a wide, shallow depression behind the sandy beach ridge running along the shore.

The mound next to the excavation area was surveyed on a 0.5m grid, and the survey data were used to create a contour map of the mound at 5cm contour intervals (a copy is with the site archive in the National Monuments Record of Scotland). The map shows the eroded north face of the mound with a shelf in front of the sea-eroded cliff face. The summit of the mound is elongated north-west to south-east, reflecting the line of a stone wall running through the middle of the mound. On the south side of the mound there is a 1.5m wide groove which has been eroded into the surface by the track. The contour map shows how the erosion from the track has created a round mound from what used to be a more irregular ridge aligned with the wall. The stone wall could be traced on the ground surface running SSE inland from the shore: the visible remains suggest that it is at least 25m long. Since only a short section of the wall was excavated, it was not possible to determine its nature. The linear nature of the feature as seen on the surface suggests that it was a boundary wall. The possible remains of a right angle turn of the wall towards the west, however, may indicate that it is part of a building. The collection of cattle and sheep bones found amongst the stone rubble against the wall clearly indicates human occupation contemporary with the wall, in this area.

A rectangular feature is situated some 80m south-west of the boat burial. It is a low platform, 38m long and 12m wide, and is aligned NNW to SSE,

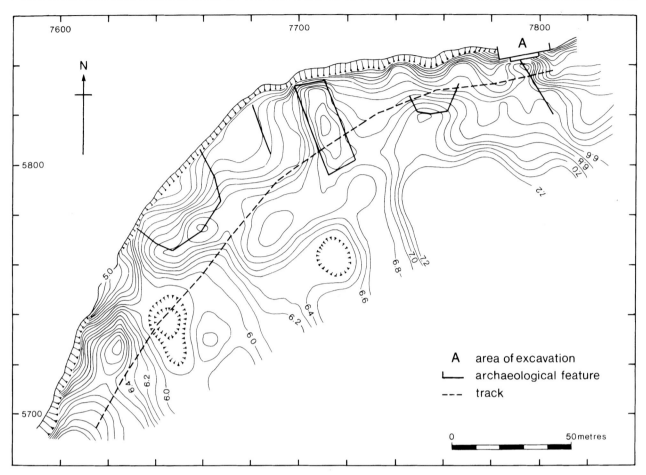

11. The results of the topographical survey along the coast by the Scar boat burial.

roughly at right angles to the shore line. The west side is well defined, as is the south-west corner. At the northern end it runs into the steep grassy slope at the edge of the beach. The low cliff edge is stable in this area and there are no stones protruding through the turf, nor any other evidence of archaeological features. The east side of the platform is less well defined. The surface of the platform is horizontal but undulating. Although there are no visible remains of walls on the surface, the feature could be the collapsed remains of a long rectangular building, possibly, from its shape, a Viking long house.

Several other topographical features were noted in the survey area but not mapped in detail. About 40m south-west of the boat burial is a curving bank, 0.1 to 0.4m high and shaped as a broad angled ridge. The bank forms a splayed U, with the west side running south from the shore at roughly right angles to the beach. It then curves round towards the east and then north towards the shore where it fades out. About 100m further along the shore to the west lies a second U-shaped bank, facing the sea. This bank is better preserved than the bank to the east. The west side is up to 0.6m high, and the east side is less prominent but clearly visible. The bank extends about 22m in from the coast and encloses an area of almost 800m². The two curving banks have a very similar form, and might have served a similar function. They are situated in an area called Quoy-banks. 'Quoy' stems from the old Norse word *kví* which means enclosure. It is possible that these two U-shaped structures are remains of enclosures which gave the area its name.

About 110m west of the boat burial is a linear feature which can be traced for about 20m in from the shore. The feature was seen as a small but marked step in a gentle slope on the west side of the rectangular platform, running parallel to, and 20m away from, the west side of the platform. There were no visible remains of the feature in the eroded section along the shore and no clear indications of its nature, but it may indicate the line of a stone wall, similar and almost parallel to the wall next to the grave.

Some 40m to the south-west of the larger enclosure was an elongated mound, 26m long, 14m wide and up to 1m high, and aligned roughly north to south. Stone settings are exposed at the surface of the mound, and it is likely that the mound contains archaeological features, possibly a rectangular building.

In addition to the features mentioned above, the area contains many smaller hollows and mounds. While several of these may be artificial, others might be the result of rabbit burrowing and wind erosion. Along the beach ridge to the east of the boat burial are several stone-lined pits identified as kelp-burning pits (R G Lamb 1980).

In conclusion, the topographical survey revealed several features within the survey area. The wall to the south of the excavation area and the large U-shaped bank with the oval mound to the south are clearly archaeological features. The rectangular platform and the small curving bank, as well as the linear bank to the west, are less clear and the possibility that they are artificial would have to be confirmed by excavation.

The geophysical survey

John Gater, Chris Gaffney & Dan Shiels

A geophysical survey of the area to the south-west of the boat burial was carried out to clarify the nature and extent of the stone wall and the mound close to the boat burial. The aims were: to locate any settlement features associated with the burial site; to provide further information about features recorded in the topographical survey; and to locate any other burials containing larger metal objects through the magnetic anomalies such buried objects would create.

An area of approximately 1.4 hectares (largely coinciding with the area surveyed topographically) was investigated using both magnetometry and resistivity techniques. The advantage of using two different techniques is that the methods complement each other and can produce a more complete picture of the buried archaeology.

Several factors adversely affected this survey. Spoil heaps and general excavation debris hindered geophysical work in the immediate vicinity of the grave. In addition, wire fences along the northern edge of the site, which would have affected readings, prevented magnetometry work from being carried out along the cliff edge. The resistivity survey was affected by the variable cover of wind-blown sand in the survey area. The ground had also

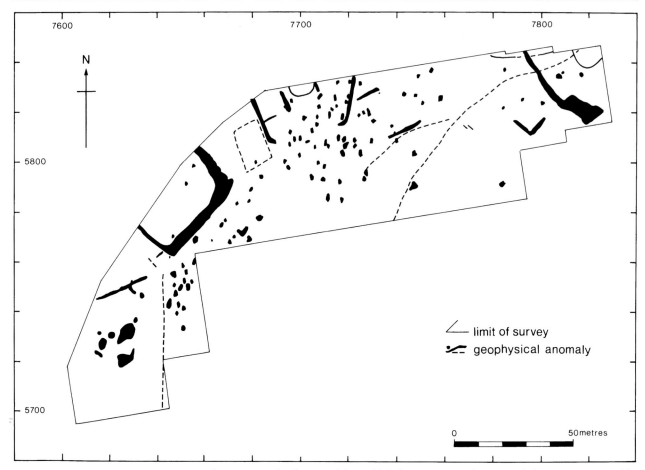

12. A summary of the results of the geophysical survey.

been severely damaged by rabbit burrows in places, and this creates variable background readings over which the anomalies caused by buried archaeological features are superimposed. As a result it was sometimes difficult to separate the variations caused by archaeological features from the variable background readings.

The magnetometry survey picked up a scatter of magnetic anomalies in the area to the south-west of the boat burial. Some of these were clearly associated with former kelp workings in the area, but this type of magnetic anomaly is also the sort of signal that might be expected from larger metal grave goods like a sword or axe, commonly found in Viking graves. Unfortunately, it was not possible to say which of these anomalies (if any) were archaeologically significant.

The elongated mound at the south-west end of the area produced strong magnetic signals within two discrete areas of the mound. The signals may indicate the position of a major burial, but it is much more likely that they are associated with a concentration of midden deposits presumably relating to occupation debris. Several anomalies on the west side of the mound might be related to kelp working, or possibly much older activities.

The resistivity survey recorded a high resistance anomaly confirming the line of the wall seen on the topographical survey. The survey shows the wall as a line of high resistance, 25m long, emerging from the north-west corner of a broader sub-rectangular area of high resistance.

The low linear feature seen on the topographical survey coincides with a linear high resistance feature. The resistivity data indicate a possible branch of the feature, not visible on the surface, running off from the middle towards the east. Immediately west of this feature is a sub-rectangular area of low resistivity which might be caused by clay-filled features cut into a more resistive matrix, possibly serving as foundations for a building.

To the east of this feature is a broad arc of high resistance surrounding an area of low resistance. The arc coincides exactly with the larger U-shaped bank, and is probably caused by the stone core of the bank seen in the beach section. East of the curving bank is a linear feature of high resistance leading down to the beach. It coincides with a groove in the terrain, probably created by an old track leading down to the beach.

In addition to the features mentioned above, the resistivity survey indicated half a dozen smaller linear features none of which was identified during the topographical survey. Two linear features of low resistivity were interpreted as some form of drainage gulleys.

The survey conclusions

Magnar Dalland & John Gater

The topographical and geophysical surveys indicated that there are several archaeological features in the area. The linear and large curving bank in the middle of the area, as well as the mound at the west end of the area, were identified independently by both surveys and are likely to be artificial features.

One of the aims of the geophysical survey was to identify further Viking graves in the vicinity and possibly define the extent of a Viking cemetery. Due to previous kelp-burning activity in the area and the presence of rabbit burrows, this was not possible. The pattern of the magnetic anomalies picked up by the magnetometry is fairly random and does not give any clues as to the presence or the extent of any Viking cemetery. The only way to address this question would be to investigate a sample of these anomalies by digging test pits.

Another aim of the surveys was to look for any settlement features associated with the burial site. The surveys have located a possible building with associated midden deposits about 200m south-west of the boat burial, but again only test excavations can confirm the nature of the feature and address the question of whether it is contemporary with the boat burial. The putative Viking long house, situated some 80m west of the boat burial, was not registered by the geophysical surveys and is therefore less likely to be an archaeological feature.

Given the likelihood that further graves are located in the vicinity of the boat burial, and the confirmed presence of a settlement site of unknown date some 200m south-west of the boat burial, this area is now protected by law and has been designated a Scheduled Ancient Monument.

THE EXCAVATION

Magnar Dalland

The excavation strategy

In the initial assessment of the site, human bones were noted in the exposed section, embedded in shell-rich sand derived from the beach. This calcium-rich environment was very favourable for the preservation of bone and bone objects. The bones seemed to be lying on a layer of small stone slabs, immediately below which were occasional fragments of corroded iron, presumably boat rivets similar to those found by Julie Gibson in the section a couple of metres east of the skeletal remains. Further to the east, clusters of stones visible in the section were interpreted as the remains of buildings, possibly boat noosts.

About 3m inland from the section was the north edge of the mound (12m by 18m and 1m high) recorded by Dr Lamb in 1980. Since then, the mound had been eroded on the north side, creating a sloping shelf 2–3m wide parallel to the beach. Across the middle of this mound, running north to south, the remains of a stone wall were exposed in its eroded north side.

At first, a trench 21m long and 2.5–4m wide was laid out along the eroded section, leaving a wide margin on either side of the remains visible in section. It was obvious that, as soon as the turf was removed and the excavation begun, the site would become even more vulnerable to sea erosion. In an attempt to protect the exposed remains, a wall of sandbags and stones was built in front of the section to provide some, albeit inadequate, measure of protection. It was also clear that, as excavation of the interior of the boat progressed, the deposits would become increasingly exposed to the sea and would be damaged by even the slightest wash of water. The sea wall erected during the first stages of the excavation could not provide adequate protection in the face of high tides and strong winds; it was consequently very important that the excavation should be completed before the next high tide.

This was easier said than done. The practicalities of the excavation were greatly influenced by the weather and the time of year (November/December). Both resources and time were limited. Working in Orkney in winter meant that there was daylight for only six to seven hours, depending on the weather. A generator and lights were brought on to the site to enable the team to work into the evenings, although these were used only occasionally because artificial light is not ideal for observing details and colour differences in soils.

Since the site was under immediate threat from the sea, the investigation concentrated on the features exposed in the sea-eroded section. From the section it was not possible to tell whether the rivets retrieved by Julie Gibson and Raymond Lamb originated from one or two boats, or to determine the orientation of the boat or boats. It was decided that the best way of excavating the site was first to establish the position of the boat(s) by excavating from above, in the normal archaeological way. By recording the position of the rivets three-dimensionally, it was hoped that the outline of

13a At high tide, waves washed over the site—luckily this was near the beginning of the excavation, before the boat burial had been uncovered.

13b. The team tried to protect the site with sand-bags, but it was obviously going to be a race against time to rescue the boat burial before the sea took it completely.

the boat(s) could be determined, as the pattern of the rivets revealed the lines of the planks. By excavating horizontally towards the level of the remains seen in section, it was anticipated that it would be possible to begin to see the outline of the boat at an early stage in the excavation, and also to determine the level from which the grave pit had been dug by the Vikings. In the event, because of the erosion of the site, these observations proved extremely difficult to make.

To ensure that all the finds were retrieved, including any that might not be in their original positions because of animal and sea disturbance, it was decided to sieve all the soil recovered, at least until the nature of the contexts and the outline of the boat(s) had been clarified. In addition, a 10–litre sample from each context was wet-sieved on site through a 1mm mesh, and the residue dried and kept for further examination. In order to avoid damaging any metal finds, a metal detector was used to locate the position of metal objects before they were revealed in excavation.

In the end, we were extremely lucky. In a roughly two-week 'window' of time before the next high tide, the team was blessed with a very cold, but mostly dry and bright, spell of weather, which made it possible to record the boat and its contents well, rather than just salvage them. A few days after the excavation had finished, a violent storm destroyed the site and finally removed all traces of the boat burial. This natural symmetry was matched by a very human one: metal detecting on the beach one last time as the team packed up, Magnar Dalland found a second lead weight—very like the one found and kept by John Deerness all those years earlier.

Archaeologists may dig backwards in time—from the present-day turf, through layers and layers of soil and ancient features, down to the undisturbed subsoil—but the results of excavations are normally recounted from the 'bottom up'. Here, the results of the Scar boat burial excavation are dealt with in the normal archaeological way, that is, the history of the site is divided into episodes, and the earliest features and deposits are described first.

Deposits earlier than the boat burial

At the base of the section, three superimposed layers were visible along the entire length of the sea-eroded section of the trench. These deposits were investigated only in a trial pit 0.3m wide at the west end of the trench, which was excavated down to the glacial boulder clay (Feature number: F18).

The boulder clay which overlies the bedrock has acted as a barrier to rainwater percolating through the porous overlying sandy deposits; the surface of the boulder clay is therefore waterlogged as the rainwater drains out towards the sea.

Overlying the clay was a greyish-white shell sand (F17), 5–15cm thick, probably formed from successive deposits of windblown sand. A brown layer of shell-sand (F16), some 25–30cm thick, overlay the windblown sand and probably represents a buried ground surface.

The possible boat noost

Towards the east end of the section was a low pile of densely packed, rounded flattish stones (F35), each on average 30–40cm across. Most of the stones were lying flat but a few were set on edge. This stone spread seemed to be artificial because it had a well-defined, straight eastern edge. It covered the entire width of the trench and continued under the south section, but its northern edge had been eroded by the sea. In section the pile seemed to comprise only two to four layers of stone. The pit dug to contain the boat burial had been cut into the western side of this feature and it is likely that stones were removed and used as packing stones for the boat burial itself.

Unfortunately, there was insufficient time to excavate this structure in 1991, but, on a visit to the site eighteen months after the excavations, by which time the upper stones in the pile had been displaced by the sea, the lower parts of two parallel stone walls were exposed, aligned north to south. The walls were 0.3m wide and continued under the baulk at the southern end of the trench. At the eroded northern end, the west wall comprised three layers of stones, and stood up to 0.2m high. However, the sea had cut back the section since the excavation, and the walls are more likely to have been over 3.5m long originally. These walls were probably once part of an elongated building, 2.2m wide and over 4m long externally, with an internal width of 1.6m. The building was aligned almost at right angles to the shore, and its shape, position and dimensions suggest that it might have been a boat noost. Although its exact length is unknown, the building would have been able to hold a boat roughly the size of the one used in the grave. It is most unlikely that the Scar boat itself had been kept in this building, however, because the structure was ruinous and covered with windblown sand by the time the boat was buried.

The sand layers covering the possible boat noost

The stone rubble from the noost, and indeed the whole trench, was covered by a layer of greyish-white sand (F7), probably windblown sand. A series of thin brown stripes and lenses within this layer probably represents short episodes during which the ground surface was more stable. A longer-surviving old ground surface, represented by a layer of light brown sand (F5), showed a marked colour difference with the sand layer below it (F7).

At the interface between these two layers, and partly embedded in the windblown sand (F7), were three stone spreads (F22, F23 & F54), all located in the same area as the stone rubble (F35), but stratigraphically later in date. These three stone accumulations were fairly indistinct and may not have been artificial features.

The sandy old ground surface (F5) underlay another windblown layer of mottled brown and white sand (F20), in places affected by rabbit burrowing. Although it was not visible at the time of excavation, it is likely that the original grave diggers dug the pit to contain the boat burial through this layer.

The stone wall

A substantial stone wall (F48) was erected on windblown sand (F20). As exposed in the southern extension of the trench, the wall was 0.9m wide, 0.7m high and extended 1.1m into the trench. It was aligned north to west, still stood at least seven courses high, and was built of rounded flagstones, mostly 20–30cm across. The lowest two courses of the wall had a slightly more north-westerly alignment which might indicate an earlier building phase. Against this wall was a heap of loosely tipped stones in a matrix of grey/white sand (F49), probably collapsed from the upper courses of the wall, which contained and was underlain by a significant number of animal bones. The rubble continued northwards into the trench (F6 & F19), where another layer of windblown sand (F9) had accumulated amongst it.

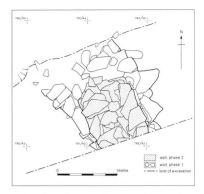

14. Plan showing the two phases of wall F48.

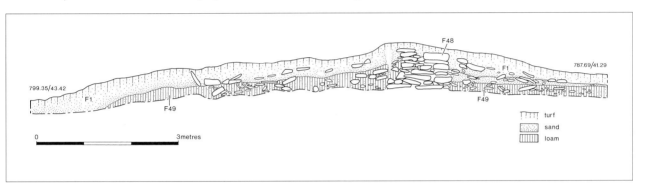

15. Section showing the stone wall (F48) and the rubble and sand spread (F49). The wall dates from c.450–650—some considerable time before the Viking period.

Between the mound and the shore edge was a narrow ledge, possibly caused by a track running past the mound on its north side. This track had cut into the side of the mound; and the eroded face of the stone wall was therefore some 2m back from the sea-eroded section. The erosion had left a disturbance layer which had later become covered by turf; this had effectively removed the ground surface from which the original cut for the grave had been dug. The stratigraphy of the site, therefore, could not help to determine conclusively the level from which the grave had been inserted into the ground.

At first it was assumed that the wall was later than the boat burial; but a radiocarbon date from the animal bones found amongst the rubble (GU-3825: 1510±50 BP [= 1,510 ± 50 years Before Present]; see Chapter 7) demonstrated that the wall was older than the boat burial; the grave was evidently cut into the sandy deposits accumulating around the ruinous wall. Due to the erosion, it was not possible to determine whether the north end of the wall had been damaged when the boat burial was inserted. This radiocarbon date indicates that the wall had been in ruins for at least a hundred years by the time the boat burial was inserted, and by then the wall might already have been partly buried by windblown sand. The low mound created by the ruinous wall and windblown sand accumulating around it could thus have provided a ready-made mound for the burial. By inserting the boat burial into the edge of this mound, the Viking grave diggers might have intended that there would be a visible monument on the site of the grave, without actually having to shift large amounts of soil to create a mound.

The boat burial

The Viking grave diggers first dug a large pit into the sand, with fairly steep edges along its south side and more gently sloping sides towards the east end. The flat base of the cut coincided with the surface of the glacial boulder clay, where ten tool marks were clearly visible, cut into the surface of the clay at the base of the pit. These tool marks were oval-shaped with a triangular long section, each up to 14cm long, 10cm wide and 7cm deep; most of them were aligned with the long axis of the cut. These were clearly the marks of the grave diggers' mattock-like tools. The pit would have been fairly easy to excavate: apart from the stone rubble encountered in the east end, the soil consisted of fairly stone-free windblown sand—at least until the compact boulder clay was reached at the base of the pit. It seems, from the shape of the pit, that the grave diggers originally intended it to be deeper in the centre, but stopped digging when they hit the boulder clay. As a consequence, when the boat was lowered into the pit, it would not have fitted quite as well as intended, with the pointed keel having to rest on the flat base of the pit. Large flagstones, 15–80cm across, were therefore packed around the outside of the boat to prop it into position, concentrated towards the two ends of the boat. The space between the pit and the boat would have gradually filled with sand.

As the wood in the boat gradually decomposed and became softer, the boat rivets would have settled into a position which partly reflected the shape of the pit. The curving outline of the boat was first detected during excavation marked by a line of rivets and the lining stones; a slight colour difference in the sand on either side of the outline was also discernible. No

16. *The Viking grave diggers used mattock-like tools to excavate the grave pit, and left about ten tool-marks at the base of the cut.*

17. *Stones were packed around the edge of the pit to prop the boat into position.*

18. *The empty boat was placed in the pit (here seen from above). Only the lines of boat rivets and a slight colour change in the sand on either side of the outline indicated the position of the boat to the archaeologists. Almost half of the boat had already been lost to the sea before it was discovered in 1991.*

wood survived apart from a few fragments of the keel and some fragments attached to the corrosion products of the rivets; but dark lines in the sand, coinciding with the lines of the rivets, represented the overlapping layers of the boat planks.

The boat was made up of six planks on either side (Chapter 3). The surviving outline of the boat was approximately 6.1m long, 0.8m wide from the keel to the south side, and 0.55–0.6m deep. The rivets had been hammered into the keel at 15–18cm intervals, and the width of the planks was 22–24cm. The west end of the boat, as well as most of the north half,

19. The boat and its precious cargo, photographed from above. The burial chamber at the west end of the boat was made by partitioning the boat with a large upright slab backed by a small wall. All of the skeletons were damaged and incomplete.

had been washed away by the sea, but most of the south-eastern quarter survived.

The space inside the boat had been divided in two by the insertion of a large stone slab (0.6m wide by 0.5m high). This was set on edge across the width of the boat and formed the eastern edge of a burial chamber which occupied two thirds of the interior of the vessel. A smaller triangular flagstone filled the curving gap between this stone and the south side of the boat. The two flagstones were supported on their eastern side (outside the burial chamber) by a small wall comprising seven courses of horizontally laid flagstones, on average 25–35cm across. This eastern end of the boat was filled with stones, some slumping as if they had been laid against a horizontal tie-beam set across the boat, and the rest lying along the curving sides of the boat. The western end of the boat was mainly filled with sand. At an early stage in the excavation, a small part of a human bone and a fragment of a bone comb were recovered in the upper levels of the sandy fill of the boat, indicating that the contents of the grave were probably disturbed in antiquity.

There was indirect evidence that the burial chamber had been 'roofed' or covered over with wooden planks. There were far more rivets and nails on the southern edge of the boat, along the side of the chamber, than further east. Identification of mineralised wood in the corrosion products of some rivets along this side of the chamber showed that two different species of wood were represented: oak and pine joined together (see Appendix 5). This suggests that the chamber was roofed with pine planks laid across the mainly oak-built boat and nailed to its edge. A row of flagstones, which lay along the south side of the chamber and overlay the contents of the grave, probably lay on top of the canopy originally, but fell into the chamber when the roof collapsed.

20. *The remains of the male skeleton in situ.*

The burials

The remains of three human bodies were found inside the burial chamber. At the west end of the boat lay the lower half of a male skeleton, which had been placed on a layer of small, sub-rounded flagstones, each up to 20cm across. Most of the upper part of the skeleton, including the skull, had been washed away by the sea, but the bones below the pelvis were almost intact, and showed that the body had been buried lying on its back with legs flexed. The surviving bones all lay in their articulated positions, with the exception of the lower right leg. The bones of this leg pose something of a mystery. They were articulated in relation to each other, but the bones of the foot and the toes were pointing backwards. From the relative positions of the tibia and fibula, it was clear that the entire lower right leg had been twisted 180 degrees at the knee joint. Moreover, from the position of the knee end of the two lower legs, the gap to be spanned by the right femur would have been 55–60cm long—almost twice as long as the left femur. This indicated that the right leg was not in its articulated position in relation to the rest of the body when found but, unfortunately, it is not possible to determine when this happened. The fact that all of the bones of the lower leg were still articulated suggests that the leg had been shifted into this deformed position when the bones were still attached to each other by body tissue. One possible explanation is that, if *rigor mortis* had set in before the body was placed in the grave, it might have been necessary to use force to get the body into the limited space available, thereby damaging the leg during burial. Alternatively, it is possible that the leg was broken as a result of some injury when the man was alive; such a severe injury could even have been fatal. The skeletal remains showed no indication of such an injury, although it should be noted that the lower part of the right femur—which might have been marked as a result of such an injury—was broken off and missing. This was one of the bones seen in section when the grave was first discovered, and it is highly likely that this break had been caused by sea erosion of the cliff face.

21. *The man's lower right leg had been twisted 180 degrees at the knee joint, and the foot and toes were pointing backwards. If* rigor mortis *had begun to set in before the man was buried, this might have happened during burial, when the body was forced into a crouched position at the west end of the boat. Copyright Richard Welsby.*

West of the male skeleton lay the skeletal remains of two further bodies, a woman and a child. The female body was lying in a supine position along the south side of the boat, facing east. Again, major parts of the skeleton were missing; only the right half of the pelvis and the right leg, and the lower half of the left leg, survived in their articulated positions. In addition, two large fragments of the top of the skull were found close to their anticipated articulated position. Just below the pelvis, three finger bones from the right hand were also found in an articulated position, probably indicating the position of the right arm. All of the bones of the torso and both arms were missing. Thick deposits of fish bones broken into tiny pieces, the tell-tale signs of otter activity, were found in this area; it seems that the female skeleton was damaged by otters invading the chamber some time after the burial took place (see Appendix 8).

The remains of the child's body were uncovered lying on the left side of the female body. Only the lower parts of the legs from the knees down survived *in situ,* the remaining parts of the body having been washed away. From the position of the leg bones it was possible to deduce that the child's body had also been placed on its back, lying next to and parallel with the woman. A displaced skull fragment belonging to the child's body had partly-erupted teeth, indicating that the bones were those of a child (we do not know if this was a boy or a girl) aged about ten (Chapter 4).

The way in which the bodies had been placed in separate areas of the burial chamber seems to indicate that they were buried at the same time, as does the fact that the chamber was built just large enough to accommodate the three bodies. There was no evidence of any rearrangement of the grave to make room for more bodies; nor was there any sign that the grave had been re-opened after burial.

Accelerator radiocarbon dates were retrieved for all three bodies. The child was dated to 940±75 BP (Before Present) (dating laboratory code: AA-1259/5); the male skeleton to 1040±60 BP (AA-1259/6); and the female to 1155±60 BP (AA-1259/7). The variation in these dates is somewhat puzzling in view of the fact that all the evidence suggests that the three bodies were buried at the same time. A full discussion of the dating evidence can be found in Chapter 7.

The finds

The bodies were accompanied by a rich collection of artefacts, most of which can be clearly attributed to the two adult individuals (see Chapters 5 and 6).

Although the male body was badly affected by erosion, several objects which had accompanied it were found in their original positions (*in situ*). Over the hip of the body lay a decorated bone comb. This had been placed across the palm of the left hand, with the right hand, palm down, placed over it, in simulation of the man holding the comb. A sword lay along the right side of the body with its grip lying next to the shoulder, close to the erosion face. The sword was complete except for the pommel, which had probably been washed away by the sea. On top of the sword blade lay an iron object,

22. The skeletal remains of the woman and the child in situ. *To the right of the woman's legs the whalebone plaque can be seen lying face-down. Originally it had been propped up against the chamber wall facing the woman. Copyright Richard Welsby.*

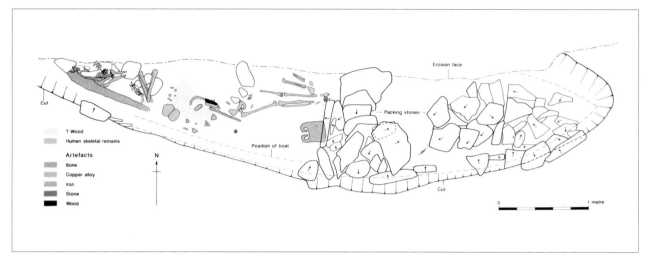

23. Plan showing the boat burial, the surviving human remains and the position of the artefacts as found.

24. Excavating the burial was difficult because the sides of the boat were very fragile. Luckily, the excavators were able to work from the beach and reach into the boat sideways.

identified in the laboratory as a bundle of eight leaf-shaped arrows, possibly in a quiver, which lay with their points towards the tip of the sword.

A pile of twenty-two bone gaming pieces was found immediately east of the flexed legs of the male skeleton, and to the left of the skull of the female body. On the basis of this position, it is not possible to be absolutely certain which body the gaming pieces accompanied, but it is more likely that they belonged to the man (see Chapter 6). They were found packed together in a pile, as if they had been buried in a bag. Also found between the male and female burials was a very fragmentary tinned bronze object, tentatively identified as a mount, perhaps from the rim of a wooden shield.

Most of the finds associated with the female body lay on her right side, between the skeleton and the side of the boat—probably because the left side had been more affected by animal disturbance and sea erosion. To the right of her feet was a magnificent carved whalebone plaque, lying with its decorated side face-down. It is likely that the plaque was originally put into the grave resting against the upright slab at the east end of the chamber, with its decorated side facing the woman, and that it fell over into its final position before the chamber became filled with soil.

To the right of the woman's hip was a sandstone spindle whorl; and, lying parallel with and very close to the body, there was a long iron object, later identified as a weaving batten. On the left side of the hip was a small fragment of a bone comb, not *in situ*, which belonged to the same comb as another fragment found higher up in the fill at the same end of the chamber. It is highly likely that this comb was placed in the grave with the woman.

Against the side of the boat, at approximately shoulder height, was a second spindle whorl, this time made of steatite, which had become corroded onto a pair of iron shears. Immediately around the whorl and shears were several other small iron objects. Laboratory examination showed that one was a needle tidy, and the others were fittings from a maplewood box, which was put into the grave probably with the needles, shears and spindle whorl inside it (see Chapter 5).

In the anticipated chest region of the body was an iron sickle, still with the remains of a wooden handle which partly overlay a gilded bronze equal-armed brooch. The brooch was found lying upside down, and the pin and the remains of textiles were preserved in its corrosion products. The sickle and brooch are likely to have been moved slightly from their original positions by animals since, apart from a few rib fragments surviving in the copper corrosion products of the brooch, the rest of the upper skeleton had been completely removed.

No finds were recovered which could be attributed to the child's body but, since this body was in that part of the boat which had been almost completely washed away by the sea, any objects buried next to the child would almost certainly have gone.

The quantity and quality of the objects recovered cannot disguise the fact that this was a badly disturbed grave. It is quite possible that many more items, perhaps as many again as were found, might have been buried in the grave originally. As well as objects lost to sea erosion or animal damage, the grave almost certainly contained items made of organic materials which would not have survived the conditions at Scar: items made of wood, textile and leather (for example, the cloth bag or leather pouch which probably contained the gaming pieces), would all have rotted away in the sandy soils. Mineralised remains found adhering to some metal objects, however, show that the bodies were buried fully dressed, in clothes made from several different types of textiles (see Chapter 6).

The collapsed soil and turf in front of the section (F47) was sampled separately to isolate it from the layers within the boat. A small blue glass bead was found when the wet-sieved residues from this context were examined in the laboratory, and it is very likely that this, too, originated from the boat burial. These sediments also contained the second lead bullion weight, discovered on the last day of the excavation and closely comparable to that found by the farmer at Scar several years earlier.

Collapse and fill inside the boat

The soil above the skeletons and the grave goods inside the chamber consisted of five different layers of shell-sand, each with different colours and contents. The lowest layer (F40) and the uppermost layer (F33) covered the entire extent of the chamber, while the middle three layers seemed mostly to reflect disturbance rather than variation between horizontally deposited layers. This was demonstrated by an irregular layer (F38) consisting entirely of small, broken-up fish bones, apparently deposited as faeces by otters living inside the grave (see Appendix 8). In addition, the fill inside the grave chamber contained sub-rounded flagstones, 15–35cm across, mostly lying along the side of the boat, and some tilting into the boat as if they had collapsed into the chamber from the south side. The layer of fish bones partly overlay these stones, showing that the otters entered the chamber after it had partly collapsed.

Over the stones in the east end of the boat were two layers of shell-sand, both confined within the outline of the boat; while over the east end of the boat itself were several other stone groups and spreads (F21, F24, F25 and F27), all likely to be associated with the boat burial. It was difficult to interpret these features, but they probably represent the disturbed upper parts of the stony backfill in the east end of the boat.

Over and at either side of the vertical slabs at the east end of the chamber was an area of densely packed flagstones, 10–40cm across, partly overlying the chamber. The south edge of this stone spread coincided with the outline of the boat, and must be part of the upper backfill of the grave. The sandy layer above this stone spread showed no indication of the outline of the boat. However, as the surface of this level sliced through the boat at an oblique angle, it must represent a disturbance horizon caused by later sea erosion, with subsequent stabilisation and turf formation.

Features later than the boat burial

The upper layers, especially those closest to the sea section, were badly affected by previous erosion. Only two contexts were recorded between the subturf and the old A-horizon (F5) in the eastern half of the trench, while the stratigraphy in the other half, closer to the boat and the wall, was more complicated.

Overlying the upper fill inside the boat was a layer of light brown shell sand (F32) which contained some small angular stones, possibly decomposed flagstones. Although most of this deposit lay within the boat, in places it also extended beyond the outline of the boat, and is therefore likely to reflect later disturbance.

Running roughly east to west were two shallow ditches (F13 & F52). Ditch F13, traced along the south section of the main trench, was about 4m long, up to 8cm deep, and 30–55cm wide. The ditch had an undulating base, and a well-marked south side, but a badly defined north side. It was filled with grey/brown shell sand with some stones.

Ditch F52 also ran east to west. The west end started in front of the eroded face of wall F48, and continued for about 3.5m eastward, for the first 2m running parallel with ditch F13. This ditch was 0.8m wide and 22–26cm deep. It was an irregular flat-bottomed trench, filled with brown/grey shell sand. The eastern half of F13 lay immediately north of the western half of F52.

It is clear from the present-day topography of the mound that it has been eroded on the north side. At present the track along the coast from the farmhouse at Scar passes the mound on the south side, where it has created a depression in the terrain. It is probable that the track previously passed the mound on its north side. As sea erosion gradually encroached inland, the track may have been moved, thereby eroding the side of the mound and creating a shelf on its northern side. The two irregular ditches might, therefore, be traces of different lines of this track. This interpretation is supported by analysis of the snail assemblages from the fill of the two gullies (see Appendix 9). The assemblages indicate open shell-sand habitats and appear to reflect small-scale and short-term patterns in snail abundance. A high proportion of the snails from the fills must have been alive within the last few decades, judging from the lack of re-crystallisation of their shells.

THE LIFTING AND ON-SITE CONSERVATION OF THE FINDS

Richard Welander

A conservator (the present author) was present on site throughout the critical period to lift artefacts and undertake any emergency conservation. The possibility of artefacts being damaged by ground frost while still *in situ* was a particular concern, especially when finds were exposed towards the end of a working day and it was not possible to record and lift them immediately. Sensitive areas were covered each night with layers of polythene packing material weighted down by sand and small stones. This provided effective protection both from frost and from the effects of strong winds and sea spray. The low ambient temperatures removed any concerns about biological activity during on-site storage (for example, mould growth on the organic objects or on dampened packing materials).

Both soil and burial conditions favoured good preservation of artefacts (except for the boat itself). The high proportion of calcareous sand contained in the soils (see page 36) had maintained a high pH burial environment around each of the artefacts and had effectively inhibited the rate of deterioration of both metalwork and organics.

One of three techniques was used to lift each artefact, depending on the general nature and condition of each object in the ground once it had been exposed. After recording *in situ,* the smaller, intact and well-preserved objects, notably the gaming pieces and spindle whorls, were lifted by hand without any additional support. To avoid accidentally marking the softened surfaces of the bone gaming pieces with metal tools, plastic spatulas or wooden 'lollipop' or cocktail sticks were used to loosen each of the pieces from the surrounding matrix. They were then lifted individually by hand and placed together in a polythene box, packed between layers of moistened tissue and well sealed with a lid. The spindle whorls were lifted and packed in a similar manner. The largest object to be lifted without support was the whalebone plaque. Face down *in situ,* it was possible to examine the porous bone surface on the back of the plaque in detail before deciding how to lift the piece. The bone appeared to be in a remarkably sound state of preservation; there were no signs of fracture or damage either to the exposed

25. Excavating the bone comb (left) was a delicate operation. The supported lift of the bone comb (right); the comb has been consolidated with Primal *prior to the lift, to protect the teeth. Note also the block containing the sword, which runs alongside.*

sides or back of the plaque. It was decided, therefore, to lift the plaque swiftly by hand in order to avoid further exposure to the worsening elements. Gripping the long sides of the plaque with fingertips and applying a gentle downward pressure with the knuckles, the surface tension adhering the face of the plaque to the wet sand was released and the plaque was lifted successfully. It was then packed in the same way as the other finds, in a sealed polythene container packed with damp paper tissue.

The more fragile, broken or damaged finds (for example, the antler comb associated with the male skeleton, and the iron sickle) needed strengthening and support prior to lifting. *Primal,* an acrylic emulsion commonly used in artefact conservation as a surface consolidant, was applied to damaged areas of the comb (notably the teeth) and to the remains of the sickle's wooden handle. Simple experimentation on site showed that, in spite of the high moisture content of the surrounding sand, when applied as small droplets from the end of a syringe onto the weakened, damaged or detached areas of the object *in situ, Primal* would dry sufficiently (within 2–3 hours' exposure to the strong prevailing wind but protected from direct rainfall) to ensure that these areas remained in their original positions while the complete artefact was being lifted with support. The equal-armed brooch was also lifted with support, but without any prior application of consolidant.

Usually, for a supported lift, the soil matrix around an *in situ* find was excavated to a depth of approximately 1cm beneath the object, leaving it on a small plinth of soil. A thin sheet of stainless steel (approximately 30cm x 45cm in area) was then slid carefully into the soil plinth in order to loosen it (and the find) from the matrix beneath. The steel sheet was then removed and substituted by an inverted lid of a suitable-sized polythene container, onto which the soil plinth and find were slid. The advantage of this substitution is that the amount of handling and consequent potential damage that might be done while packing finds following a supported lift is greatly reduced. Immediately after lifting the find, the containers were well-packed with dampened paper tissue, inverted and sealed onto the lid, thereby continuing to support the recovered find. The sealed container was then turned over onto its base and the lid removed to expose the underside of the object, resting on damp tissue. Following the minimal removal of loose soil debris and the addition of further padding, the box was resealed and ready for transportation.

The third lifting technique used, a form of 'block lifting', is intended to provide comprehensive support over the entire exposed surface of an object (typically large, long or heavy finds unlikely to be able to support their own weight when lifted). In effect, a rigid support mould is made on site to hold an object intact during lifting, transportation and initial post-excavation examination and treatment. Variations on this technique are commonly used to lift, for example, large, complete pottery vessels containing fills to be investigated in the laboratory rather than in the field. Because the technique normally involves some degree of stratigraphic disturbance (by cutting through undisturbed layers around and below the object to define its full extent), the value of an intact recovery by this technique has to be weighted against possible inadvertent damage to unexposed material beneath the find.

At Scar, two artefacts were block lifted: the sword and the weaving batten. Both were long, relatively thin, iron objects. An initial *in situ* examination revealed clear signs of preserved organic remains adhering to the surfaces of both artefacts. Moreover, it was suspected that, although complete, both finds were fractured in a number of places (see Chapter 6). The task of lifting the sword proved to be the more complex.

The full extent of the sword was determined using a metal detector, after which it was carefully excavated using small hand tools in order to reveal its full outline. Its general shape and context (immediately adjacent to a skeleton, the bones of the forearm of which had fused by iron corrosion onto the sword) strongly suggested that the find was a sword, although no attempt was made on site to expose it fully; instead a thin covering of compacted sand was left in place over the exposed areas. A large lump projected from its upper surface (later shown to be a quiver of arrows (see Chapter 6). It was decided to lift the entire assemblage in a single block for laboratory investigation.

In this case, very little stratigraphic disturbance of surrounding deposits occurred during the lifting. The ground around and underneath the longer edges of the sword was excavated to create an undercut of about 3–5cm, leaving the sword resting on a plinth of soil along its full length. The sword was then covered with a single large sheet of aluminium foil, which was pressed closely onto the exposed surface, tucked into the undercut and drawn out to form an upstanding lip above the level of the sword's upper surface. The foil sheet was carefully folded at both ends to create an elongated foil container (approximately 100cm by 30cm by 30cm) fully enveloping the sword. It was anticipated that, when lifted, this block would be of some considerable weight. Expanded polyurethane foam was selected as a suitable support medium, because of its properties of rigidity and lightness. The foam block was lightly covered and allowed to cure overnight. When fully set, the entire block was loosened from its plinth, rolled over onto its side and lifted in a single 'scooping' action. The block was then packed in a prepared cardboard box, strengthened with timber battens.

The amount of information obtained during laboratory and specialist study of the artefacts was due partly to the good preservation conditions on site, but much of this evidence, particularly for the materials and secondary finds associated with the recovered artefacts, would have been lost or compromised by traditional excavation and recovery methods. On-site consideration of artefact conservation needs ensured the maximum preservation of evidence.

THE FORMATION OF SEDIMENTS WITHIN THE BURIAL CHAMBER

Stephen Carter

This account draws together information from reports on other aspects of the site to provide a coherent account of the development of the sediments that accumulated within the burial chamber of the boat burial.

The decomposition of the corpses

The processes of decomposition would have started immediately after burial and are most graphically illustrated by the fly puparia, preserved as mineralised moulds, on the underside of the sword and arrows.

Analysis of the soil thin sections (Appendix 11) has shown that the layer of sand (F53) in the bottom of the boat lost its shell content through decalcification. This is consistent with the production of acidic fluids during the breakdown of the corpses. Since the fluid was contained by the boat, we can deduce that at that stage the boat was still watertight. The addition of rainwater by infiltration from the surface could have created a considerable volume of organic, acid fluid within the boat.

The condition of artefacts within the chamber provides some additional evidence for the nature of the chamber environment at this time. There is a great contrast between the condition of the man's comb, which survives in a fragmented but good condition, and the woman's, which was badly corroded before fragmentation. This difference probably results from the fact that the woman's comb lay in the bottom of the boat in acid conditions whilst the man's was held higher, in his hands, in alkaline conditions. Surfaces of the woman's comb that were exposed only after it was damaged by otters (see pages 87-8) are well preserved, indicating that the chamber sediments had re-calcified by this time.

The chamber therefore experienced a relatively short-lived period of exceptionally wet, acid conditions whilst the corpses decayed. Rapid iron replacement preserved casts of organic substances adjacent to iron objects, but most organic materials were decomposed at this time.

The infilling of the chamber

Decomposition in the burial chamber would not have ended suddenly, but a number of changes took place as the quantity of organic matter was reduced. Calcareous shell-sand gradually filtered into the chamber, covering the artefacts and de-fleshed skeletons, and re-calcifying the basal sand deposit. The boat timbers began to decay and therefore formed less of a barrier to the passage of water, so waterlogging would have been reduced within the boat.

At this point, there is evidence for the use of the burial chamber by otters. An extensive spread of pure fish bone (F38) is interpreted as the remains of otter faeces, and disturbance in the central area of the woman's body is also attributed to otters. The disappearance of the woman's head, upper limbs and torso indicates that the bones were no longer articulated and that the otters dug out this part of the chamber. What remained of the burials was protected from disturbance by a layer of sand which covered the skeletons.

The chamber roof must have been largely intact at this time as the area covered by the otter faeces is too large to suggest a sand-roofed burrow. It is not clear how the otters found the chamber, unless a partial collapse of the roof had revealed its presence. This would require the roof to have been close

26. The sickle, still with its wooden handle, overlay the woman's brooch which was found upside-down, covered in soft black organic material. Later analysis of this material showed that it mainly comprised decomposed plant and insect remains (see Appendix 10). Beetles had bred inside the chamber and doubtless fed on decaying timber and clothing. They may have crawled on to one of the bodies while they lay in a building awaiting burial, or been brought in with timber or cut plants.

27. This dense pile of comminuted fish bones was a tell-tale sign that otters had broken into and lived in the grave after it had been sealed (see Appendix 8).

to the contemporary ground surface. The roof was still largely intact when the chamber was abandoned by the otters: the sand that overlay the otter faeces and filled the boat contains high concentrations of land snail species indicative of an underground chamber (Appendix 9). It seems that sand filtered into the chamber through the disintegrating roof and filled the chamber before any major collapse of the roof occurred.

The later history of the burial site

Following the infilling of the burial chamber, the timbers of the boat decayed; the keel is the only element of the boat where significant quantities of wood have survived to the present day. Presumably the keel remained waterlogged where it was in contact with the boulder clay in the base of the grave cut. The fact that most clench nails were found in position indicates that there has been no large-scale disturbance of the sand surrounding the boat since the decay of the wood. The absence of rabbit bones (a frequent find in windblown sands, indicating the presence of burrows) supports this conclusion. Some small mammal bones were recovered from samples of the grave fill but their origin is uncertain (Appendix 7).

The sword blade may already have been broken when it was buried (see Chapter 6), but the sword also displays a number of breaks that occurred after the mineralisation of the scabbard. These are assumed to be the result of pressure from overlying sand on the long, brittle, corroded blade. This post-burial damage to the sword must have occurred at a late stage in the formation of the grave sediments; similar damage has been noted on the weaving batten and sickle.

The final episode in the development of the sediments was the partial destruction of the boat burial by progressive marine erosion. This appears to have been a rapid and recent process, and there has been insufficient time for the contents of the grave to be affected by exposure on the shore.

A chronology of events

The total timespan of the sequence of events outlined above is approximately 1100 years. Given the different types of processes and transformation involved, it is possible to suggest a rough chronology for the different stages. Initial decomposition and acidification of the contents of the burial chamber was probably achieved within a decade of burial. All the evidence suggests that the chamber was not re-opened by humans once it had been sealed the first time, and that, therefore, the three bodies must have been buried close together in time. Re-calcification and the use of the chamber by otters occurred before the roof timbers decayed, so a timespan of a few decades seems reasonable for this phase. The timber is unlikely to have supported the overlying sand for much longer and, therefore, infilling of the chamber by sand would have occurred soon afterwards and was probably complete within a century of burial.

28. The boat. The surviving remnants of the timber keel can clearly be seen towards the bottom-right of the photograph.

CHAPTER 3

THE BOAT

Anne Allen

EXCAVATION, RECORDING AND CONSERVATION

Scar is only the third Viking period boat burial to have been excavated in Orkney in modern times and is thus a significant addition to the corpus, even though virtually all of the wood had decomposed and the boat survived only as a ghost impression in the ground. The form of the boat was preserved in the pattern of iron nails and rivets which once fastened the planks together.

During excavation, each fastening was located three-dimensionally by theodolite, and given a unique number. In some cases the alignment of the nails and rivets was also recorded. Lack of time prevented detailed plans and profiles of the boat being made in the field; these would have been useful in determining which fastenings remained *in situ,* and as an initial interpretation of the boat structure. It was not possible to cut a section through the boat to determine the external form of the keel and stems, and their reconstruction is therefore conjectural. At the east end of the boat, part of the keel survived as a mass of organic material; this was sampled as a block and is now frozen. The possibility of taking a cast of the boat was considered, but was impractical given the wintry conditions and the immediate threat of the boat's destruction.

Back in the laboratory in Edinburgh, all of the boat fastenings were X-rayed and mechanically cleaned with hand tools under x10 microscopy. Measurements were taken of the head, plate and shank from both the object and the X-ray. The presence of organic remains, the grain direction of wood, the thickness of surviving planks and the presence and types of joint were noted where visible. The conservation report also detailed the orientation of the head, plate and shank to each other, and any additional metalwork found in association with the fastenings (Watson 1993). Mineralised wood remains attached to rivets and artefacts were analysed by Roderick McCullagh to determine species (see Appendix 5).

THE CONSTRUCTION OF THE BOAT

Over 300 iron fastenings were found, demonstrating that the craft was clinker-built with overlapping planks, in the Nordic fashion ubiquitous in northern Europe in the Viking period. In this tradition the boat was *shell-built,* that is, it was constructed from the outside in with the internal framing probably being added once the skin was complete. Construction began with laying the keel. The stems were then attached and planks were inserted from the keel up. It was the shaping of these planks which determined the form of the craft and provided its strength. Clinker-building in the shell-first technique on a keel is still practised today in Scandinavia and the British Isles.

Fig. 29 is a plan of the boat fastenings annotated to show the position of the keel, the strakes and the various types of fastening. The orientation of the fastenings was not recorded in all cases and it is not always possible therefore to determine which rivets were displaced and which remained *in situ*. It is clear from the figure that a significant portion of the western end of the boat and virtually all of the north side had been lost. In the ground the boat measured 6.3m long, had a beam of 1.6m and was 0.6m deep. There were evidently six strakes (rows of planks) on each side of the boat.

29. A plan of all the boat fastenings as excavated, annotated to show the position of the keel, strakes and various types of fastening.

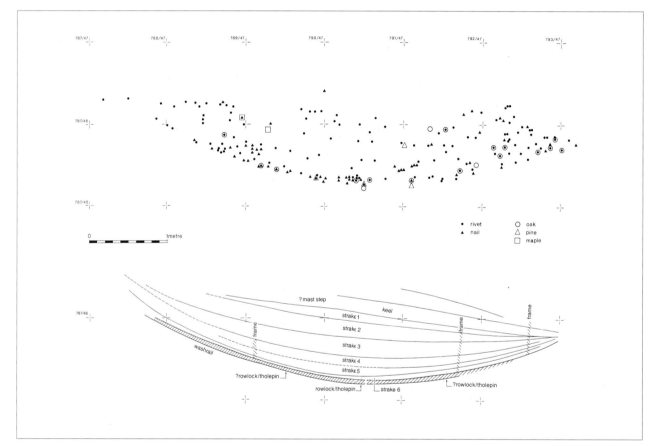

The fastenings

In studying a 'ghost' boat, careful recording of the fastenings is vital to understanding the original form. The detailed analysis of boat nails and rivets is a relatively new subject. Bill (1994) studied about 150 finds from northern and eastern Europe and established a typology of boat fastenings based on the shape of their head, the shank cross-section and the rove or nail ending. Of the 310 fastenings recovered from the Scar boat (see Table 1), almost 46% were rivets and just over 31% were nails. 33% could not be distinguished since the nail element of both was similar. A rivet could only be identified as such by the rove, or by the deformed end of the shank and a nail by the pointed end of the shank. The heads conformed to Bill's classes A, B and C;

the shanks to classes A, possibly B, and C; and the ends to his classes D, E, F and G. The fastenings were distinguished by the shape of their shank: 64% of all fastenings had square shanks and 31% had round shanks. This shank shape and the predominance of curved roves has important implications for the tradition in which the boat was built and possibly its origin.

Table 1. Fastenings from the Scar boat

Shank shape	Nail	Rivets	Nail/Rivet	Total
Square	73	86	39	198
Round	19	44	33	96
Indeterminate	7	9	–	16
Total	99	139	72	310

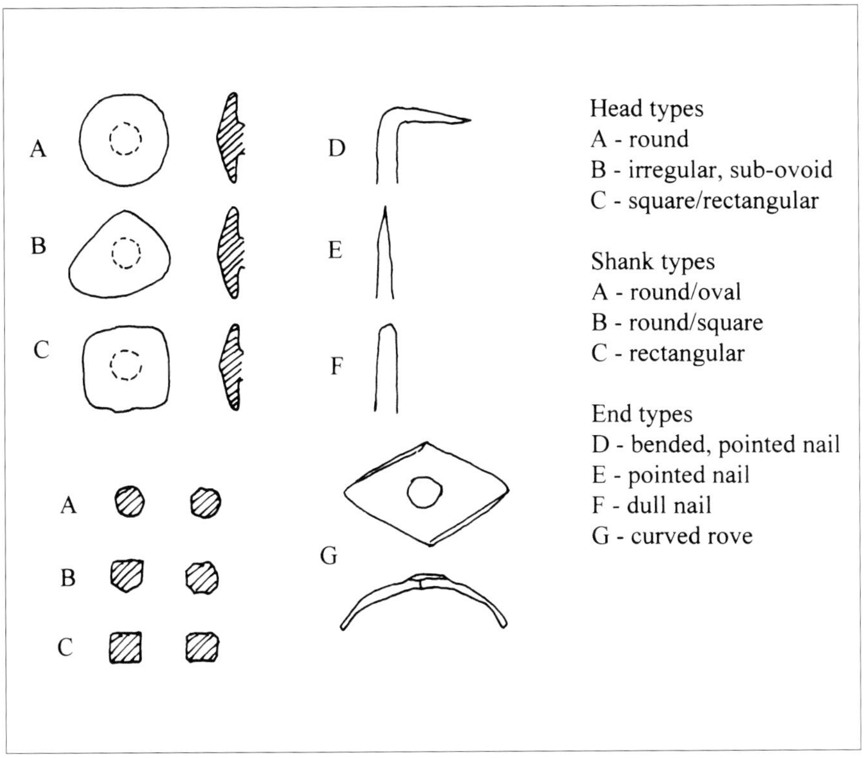

30. *Different types of boat fastenings.*

Head types
A - round
B - irregular, sub-ovoid
C - square/rectangular

Shank types
A - round/oval
B - round/square
C - rectangular

End types
D - bended, pointed nail
E - pointed nail
F - dull nail
G - curved rove

The assemblage comprised three classes of rivets: large, which were over 40mm long; standard, c. 28mm long; and small, c. 19mm long. The nails fell into two groups: large, with a shank length greater than 40mm and 5–7mm wide; and small nails with a shank length of less than 15mm and only 2–3mm wide (Watson 1993). This diversity is not unusual since different fastenings would be used in different parts of the boat. Strakes were fastened to each other through the plank overlap by standard rivets. The internal ribs were fastened to the strakes by both nails and rivets. Long iron nails fastened the tholepins or rowlocks to the washrail which was itself attached with similar nails to strake 6. The strakes were fastened to the stem with iron rivets.

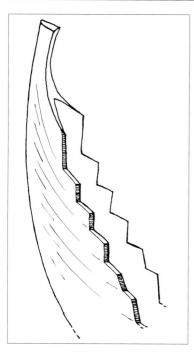

31. *Diagram to show McGrail's pre-formed stepped boat stem, type C (bevelled, hollow, stepped). The sides of this type of stem are extended inboard and shaped in steps, the ends of which are bevelled facing outwards to take the strakes. The stepped stem provides a greater area for fastening the strakes than a more continuous type of stem, and the end grain of the strakes is protected in the bevel. The hollow nature of the type C stem enabled through fastenings to be used.*

Hull structural elements

The keel and stems

The surviving part of the keel was T-shaped. The whole keel was about 5.4m long, had a maximum breadth of 17cm and was at least 6cm deep. The point at which the keel was scarfed to the stem at the east end of the boat is not clear. The small number of fastenings of the planks to the stem may indicate that the stem was a pre-formed stepped stem, like the one found in a bog on Eigg, Outer Hebrides (McGrail 1987, 124), McGrail's type C or possibly type D. In any case not all of the stem survived. It may have projected above the surface of the grave, acting as a grave marker, and was destroyed quite quickly.

Planking

The length of the rivets indicates that the individual planks were between 10mm and 13mm thick. Caulking, probably of animal hair and tar (although it proved impossible to identify), was inserted between the two planks in a specially cut groove to waterproof the seam. The number of planks per strake is less clear since it is difficult to locate the scarfs. At least two or three planks, each about 2–3m long, per strake seems likely. The breadths of three strakes were recorded in the field. The second strake was 22cm broad, the third strake 23cm and the fourth strake 24cm. The garboard strake was narrow, only 10cm broad, and was angled sharply to the keel. The fifth and sixth strakes, including the washrail, measured 17cm and 26cm respectively. Strakes usually overlapped by 17–20mm.

Framing timbers

The boat originally had six frames fastened to the hull to lend strength and to support thwarts for the rowers. The position of the frames is evidenced in the presence of certain nails and rivets which fastened the frames to the planks. Two frames in the east end of the boat and a third in the west are indicated in Fig. 29. The location of the easternmost frame was identified by a nail (Find 372) to which were attached the remains of a curved grown timber, possibly a tree branch with traces of a small knot (Watson 1993). The second frame was identified by two fastenings, a nail from the frame to the keel which contained mineralised oak or pine (Find 360; Appendix 5) and a second nail from the frame to the topstrake which incorporated the edge of a timber, cut at right angles through the grain (Find 412). The westernmost frame has been washed away with that end of the boat, and the midships frame was probably removed to make room for the burial chamber. In addition to these frames the boat may have had bulkheads like the ones found in the small boats at Gokstad (Fig. 36; Johannessen 1940).

Propulsion and steering

The location of three rowlocks or single tholepins was tentatively identified by iron rivets and nails which lay significantly higher than the surrounding ones. An antler tholepin was recovered from one of the two boat burials in the Viking cemetery at Westness, Rousay, Orkney (Kaland 1981). The Scar boat probably had similar tholepins of wood. Possible fittings for a mast were found just forward of amidships on the top of the keel (Find 452). There were no remains of a sail or oars, but these may have been removed to make room for the burial chamber. All three of the small boats from Gokstad had evidence for sails in the form of mast step fittings and holes in the washrail for shrouds (Christensen 1959).

Steering was probably by means of a side oar, usually attached to the starboard side of the boat. As there is no evidence for one on the south side of the boat, it is reasonable to deduce that it must have been attached to the north-east side. This would mean that the prow of the boat was orientated towards the west, as were the bodies of the man and woman. Alternatively, though perhaps less likely, it may have been removed before burial.

Identification of the wood

The planks and keel were identified by both soil thin-section analysis and analysis of mineralised remains as oak, *Quercus sp.* (see Appendix 11; Appendix 5). Four fastenings on the topstrake incorporated Scots pine, *Pinus silvestris,* probably a washrail which ran virtually the whole length of the boat and to which rowlocks were attached. The topstrake of all three small boats found in the Gokstad ship burial in Norway were of pine, although the rest of the wood was oak. The internal frames may also have been of pine, *Pinus silvestris.*

The analysed wood remains were all from mature, grown timbers which had probably been worked when green. This is also a characteristic of the *Nordic* building tradition.

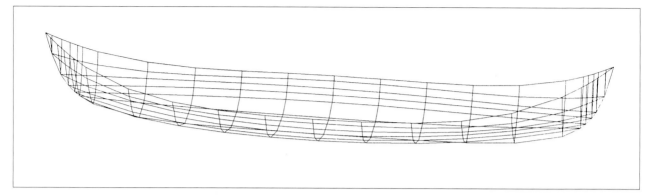

33. A reconstruction of the Scar boat, derived from sections plotted from the locations of the rivets and generated by the computer program Boatline 3D.

Reconstruction of the boat

Fig. 33 shows the shape of the boat derived from the sections and generated by the computer program *Boatline 3D,* part of the Boatcad software developed by Stan Goldman, University of Aberystwyth. Boat lines were initially drawn by hand and faired. The stem at the east end of the boat had been pushed in and upwards and the sides of the boat amidships have fallen outwards, giving the impression that the boat was much shallower, beamier and flatter than in reality. The westernmost surviving part of the boat had also slumped. It proved possible to reconstruct the west end by superimposing on it the east end. This reconstruction assumes that the boat was symmetrical about amidships. The boat was then created on computer by inputting its dimensions and recreating the elevation. Fig. 33 is a wire grid view of the boat generated from the elevation.

The boat has a reconstructed overall length of approximately 7.15m of which 0.8m had been lost to the west and 0.2m to the east, where the uppermost part of the stem had decayed. The reconstruction gives the boat a freeboard amidships of 0.6m with a sweeping sheer fore and aft. The details of the outside face of the stem and stern are hypothetical. This reconstruction gives an impression of the form of the boat but its accuracy is limited both by the limited data available and the design of the computer program.

WHERE WAS THE BOAT BUILT?

The identification of sand grains lodged in the caulking

Thin section analysis of sediments sampled at the floor of the burial chamber showed the residues of what were once the strakes of the boat (Appendix 11). The remains of caulking were identified in a 1mm-wide gap between the strake overlap, and this caulking material contained sand grains (Fig. 34). Detailed optical examination of the mineral grains identified a complex assemblage of both igneous and metamorphic minerals (Fig. 34; Table 2; Appendix 12). The minerals were subsequently analysed by electron-microprobe to determine their specific chemical composition. The sand grains were evidently trapped in the caulking during construction of the boat, and so their provenance should reveal where the boat was built. Dixon

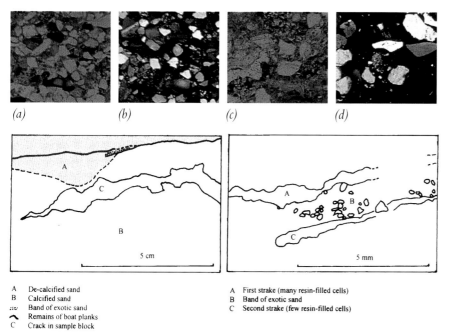

(a)   (b)   (c)   (d)

A   De-calcified sand
B   Calcified sand
::: Band of exotic sand
⌃   Remains of boat planks
C   Crack in sample block

A   First strake (many resin-filled cells)
B   Band of exotic sand
C   Second strake (few resin-filled cells)

34. The remains of boat caulking were found in a 1mm wide gap between the strake overlap. Thin-section analysis revealed that sand grains containing an exotic combination of minerals had become trapped in the caulking, presumably during construction of the boat.

a. 8mm wide photograph in plane-polarised light. Sample 17: general shot of possible plank overlap.

b. 8mm wide photograph in cross-polarised light. Sample 17: general shot of possible plank overlap.

c. 4mm wide photograph in plane-polarised light. Sample 17: close-up of possible plank overlap.

d. 4mm wide photograph in cross-polarised light. Sample 17: close-up of possible plank overlap.

Left: sketch of section through sample 17
Right: sketch of junction, sample 17.

(Appendix 12) considered there to be no suitable location on Orkney, Shetland or the northern Scottish mainland from which such a combination of minerals could be derived. There are no published comparable mineral analyses of beach sands, but it seems most likely that the boat was built in Scandinavia rather than Scotland, perhaps at one of the few known Viking Age boat-building yards, such as Foteviken, Skåne (Crumlin-Pedersen 1984). One *caveat* must be entered, however, in that the analysis was based upon a single sample, and it is just possible that this represents a repair to the boat, rather than the original hull.

Table 2. Minerals identified in sand trapped in the caulking

Basic Igneous association	Metamorphic association	Miscellaneous
Olivines	Amphiboles	Phosphate
Pyroxenes	Garnets	Unknown A
Feldspars	Epidote	
Spinel	Sphene	
Ilmenite	Haematite	

Unfortunately, analysis of the fastenings does not clarify the issue. While square-shanked rivets are a characteristic of the Baltic area in the Viking period (Bill, 1994), the curved roves on the rivets are characteristic of finds in the Western Isles and the Irish Sea. Bill identified these roves on the boat burials at Kiloran Bay, Colonsay and Knock y Doonee, Isle of Man. Where these roves are found elsewhere, they are used specifically to fasten the upper end of a rib to planking.

Oak (*Quercus sp.*) and Scots pine (*pinus silvestris*) are found both in western Scotland and in Scandinavia, and so it is not possible to distinguish the place of manufacture on the basis of available wood.

BOATS IN VIKING ORKNEY

Two boat burials, dated on the basis of grave goods to the ninth century, were excavated in the 1980s at Westness on Rousay, Orkney (Kaland 1981). Unfortunately neither has been published in detail and it has not been possible to analyse the rivets and plans of the site. A third boat survives in the National Museums of Scotland—as a collection of rivets from a nineteenth century excavation by James Farrer at the cemetery at Pierowall, Westray.

35. Small boats in the Nordic tradition are still made in places in Norway and Shetland. The Scandinavian tradition is clearly seen in the lines of this Shetland boat, known as a Ness yole. Copyright Shetland Museum.

A fourth boat burial may be represented among finds eroded out of the sand dunes at Pierowall; and there is also a tradition that a boat grave containing a sword, shield and spear was discovered in the 1790s on Sanday itself, at South Mire, near Pool (James Graham-Campbell, personal communication).

The two boats from Westness, found in a cemetery adjacent to a Viking period settlement, were probably færings. The boats are reported to measure 4.5m and 5.5m respectively, although this is probably not their reconstructed length, but merely the extent of the remains found in the ground. Up to 1m might be added to the length of each if the latter is the case. The larger boat contained the body of a man who was buried with his sword, shield, arrows, an axe and farming tools (see Chapters 7 & 8). The boat was constructed from four strakes of oak on each side and fitted with a rowlock and chafing piece made of deer antler, which show signs of wear. The smaller boat also comprised three or four strakes of oak on each side, and contained the body of a man with a sword, spear, axe, arrows, a shield, adze, hone stone, strike-a-light and flints.

The only contemporary account of the boat burial at Pierowall, a newspaper article (*Orkney Herald,* 4 August, 1863), reports merely the discovery of a 'Northman' and his horse; it was believed that the man and his horse had 'been left to decay where they fell'. The body was covered by a sandhill, probably a natural dune. The grave goods included two iron buckles, iron fragments, half a bone button and 21 boat rivets, the latter distinguishing this as a probable boat burial. There is no account of the size or shape of the boat.

Although other burials containing rivets have been found, the number of rivets is very small and so it is not possible to say with certainty that these were boat graves. Even the handful of rivets from Pierowall could represent re-used boat timbers, or the burial of only part of a boat, rather than the whole; although current re-analysis suggests that two boat burials may be represented here (James Graham-Campbell, personal communication). In the treeless islands of Orkney where timber was a precious commodity, it would not be unusual for only part of a boat to be buried as a symbol; there are precedents for this practice in Norway at Kaupang (Blindheim *et al* 1981).

BOAT BURIALS IN NORTHERN EUROPE

All four boats from Orkney were built in the Nordic tradition based on a keel with shell-built clinker sides. Over 250 such plank-built boat finds have now been discovered in northern Europe from the period AD 800–1100 (Müller-Wille 1970; 1974; 1995). Boat and ship finds might be classified into two groups on the basis of their size: small boats, that is, craft of less than 7–8m in length; and medium vessels and ships which are longer and generally beamier (Bowman 1992; McGrail 1993). Taking the Nordic tradition as an example, there are roughly six times more boats known than ships (some 180 boats as opposed to 30 ships). Despite this fact, work on medieval craft to date has concentrated on the larger vessels such as the Oseberg, Gokstad and Skuldelev ships. Little work has been done on the techniques of construction and types of craft represented amongst the small boat finds. In general they have been neither well preserved nor well recorded and, with the exception of the three small boats found inside the Gokstad ship and one or two other sites where the wood survived, the information which boat burials can yield has been largely overlooked.

The Scar boat is longer, beamier and deeper than the *færing* (four-oared rowing boat) from Gokstad which was just over 6.5m long, 138cm in beam and 49cm deep amidships and comprised only three broad strakes between 28cm and 38cm wide (Fig. 36).

Based on recent analogy, small craft are normally likely to be abandoned or buried close to their place of manufacture and it should therefore be possible to test ideas about local boatbuilding traditions. The results of this author's study of boat burials in two areas of Norway supports this theory. The rivet patterns showed evidence of repair, so this was certainly not a special ceremonial craft. On the other hand, the curved roves paralleled in boat burials from the Western Isles perhaps point to an independent insular building tradition in the Scandinavian colonies in the Northern and Western Isles in the ninth century. The building tradition in Viking Dublin is different again, although here the craft recovered were larger trading vessels of the eleventh to thirteenth centuries, usually fastened with round-shanked nails and rivets with diamond-shaped roves (McGrail 1993).

THE RITE OF BOAT BURIAL

Anne Allen & Olwyn Owen

The notion of boats and ships as symbols is well known in pre-Christian northern Europe, although their precise symbolic meaning remains elusive. Traditionally, the custom of boat burial has had three main interpretations: either the boat was there to serve a practical purpose (as a simple container in inhumations or as firewood for the pyre in cremations); or it had secular significance (as a symbol of secular power or maritime connections); or it had religious significance (as a ferry to the next world for the deceased, or as an attribute of a specific god or gods). Most recently, Crumlin-Pedersen (1995) has suggested that the religious significance of the ship or boat was paramount (see also pages 154-6).

36. (facing) The mound over a great ship burial at Gokstad, Norway, dating from around AD 900, also contained three smaller rowing boats, each between 6 and 10 metres long. Copyright Universitetets Oldsaksamling med Vikingskipshuset, Oslo.

In the past, studies have tended to focus on the great ship burials, where secular or religious explanations inevitably spring to the fore to account for the obviously elaborate burial rite. In the case of small boats, it is tempting to suggest that they had little significance other than that obsolete craft were being used as handy coffins, and that the status and symbolism which they are sometimes ascribed is perhaps exaggerated. In Orkney, however, the burial of a boat meant the disposal of a valuable resource, which suggests that a higher imperative was at work. In an area where wood was scarce, we

37. Boat-shaped stone settings in the Lindholm Høje cemetery, Jutland, Denmark. Copyright Olwyn Owen.

might expect that only an old, redundant boat would have been buried: such a boat could both retain its symbolic religious function and be a sign of prestige, since wood was normally too valuable to bury. The signs of repair on the Scar boat seem to support this theory, and may account for the burial of this particular boat rather than a more serviceable one. Analysis of the assemblage as a whole, however, strongly suggests that the small Scar boat was itself an important component of a symbolic and primarily religious burial, and that it was not merely a convenient coffin (Chapter 7). The same is probably true for the boat with the antler rowlock found at Westness (Kaland 1981), which indicates the special treatment of an otherwise everyday craft.

Boat burials are common in Norway, especially western and northern Norway (for example, the newly discovered boat grave from Føre, Bø i Vesterålen: see Chapter 7). Shetelig (1917–18, 251–78) listed 551 Norwegian examples of boat burials, although this was almost certainly an over-estimate, relying as it did on the occurrence of boat rivets in the graves (Sjøvold 1974, 190–4, 356). Nevertheless, Sjøvold agreed that there was a minimum of fifty Viking boat burials on record in northern Norway alone, and this figure has risen with a number of new discoveries over the last twenty-five years (summarised in Müller-Wille 1995).

The Scar burial is not an isolated occurrence of a boat burial in those parts of Britain colonised by Norwegian Vikings: examples occur in Orkney at the Westness (two boat burials) and probably Pierowall cemeteries; in the Western Isles at Kiloran Bay and Machrins, both in Colonsay; and on the Isle of Man at Balladoole and Knock y Doonee. Conversely, so far not a single boat burial is known from the cemetery at Birka, although there is a handful of boat-shaped stone settings (Gräslund 1980, 69–70). Boat-shaped stone settings are more common in Denmark: in the great cemetery at Lindholm Høje by the Limfjord, Jutland, for instance, 138 out of 589 excavated burials were boat-shaped stone settings (Ramskou 1954; 1976; Fig. 37); boat-shaped stone settings almost certainly had the same symbolic significance as the burial of real boats (Crumlin-Pedersen 1995, 97). Thus, actual boat burial in the Viking Age, especially small boat burial, is predominantly a Norwegian phenomenon—which, in itself, offers an important clue as to the origins of the people buried at Scar.

Glossary of boat terms

Beam:	The widest point across a boat's hull
Bulkhead:	A transverse partition in the fore or aft of a boat
Caulking:	Material inserted between two members to make the junction watertight
Clench:	To deform the end of a fastening so that it cannot be drawn out
Clinker:	Boat building in which the strakes are overlapped
Færing:	A four-oared rowing boat
Frame:	A transverse member made up of more than one timber, attached to the planking
Garboard:	The strake fitted into or next to the keel
Grommet:	Rope used to hold oars in place
Keel:	The main longitudinal strength member upon which the hull of a boat is constructed
Nordic:	Tradition of boat building based on a keel, with shell-built clinker planking
Rib:	A simple form of frame
Scarf:	A joint
Shell-first:	Technique of construction in which the hull is built first and then fitted with an internal framework
Shrouds:	Ropes leading from the mast to the sides of the boat to support the mast
Stem:	The timber which closes the hull
Strake:	A run of planks
Thwarts:	Planks which act as seats for rowers

CHAPTER 4

THE BODIES

Daphne Home Lorimer

The bones recovered from the Scar boat burial comprise the incomplete remains of three individuals: a male probably in his thirties at the time of death; a female possibly in her seventies; and a juvenile of about ten. Bass (1987) and Krogman and Iscan (1986) were used for ageing and sexing the bones and Gray (1977) for general anatomical reference. Non-metrical variations were seen neither on the few skull fragments, nor on any of the juvenile bones. The causes of death could not be determined from the bones recovered, but various possibilities are discussed below (Chapter 7). An inventory of the bones recovered is presented in Appendix 6.

THE MALE SKELETON

The skeleton recovered from the west end of the boat is that of a male of over twenty-five, probably in his thirties at the time of death, and about 5ft 11in in height (181cm). The bones were disturbed and the greater part of the skull, thorax and upper arms were missing. On the right side, the lower arm lay across the body with the radius rotated over the ulna (i.e. palm down) and adhering to a corroded surface. In addition, the lower right leg and foot were twisted out of position.

The male sex was deduced from the criteria given by Bass (1987) and a tentative age from epiphysial union and wear on the auricular surface of the ilium (Lovejoy *et al* 1985) and the symphysis pubis (McKern & Stewart 1957). These areas, however, are damaged, so this is only an estimate. The height was calculated using the formulae of Trotter and Gleser given by Brothwell (1981).

Bone is a plastic medium and responds to the pull and stress of active muscles, so that not only the pathological conditions, but pronounced non-metrical variations and enthesopathies seen in the skeleton indicated a very active lifestyle (Kennedy 1989). The same pull and the same stress, that is, the same occupational markers, can be produced by several activities. The changes in the male skeleton could have resulted from walking over hilly terrain, riding on horseback, and sailing and rowing.

Pathological changes include osteophytic lipping round the superior margin of the body of the first segment of the sacrum and an acetabular flange lesion of the left innominate. Non-metrical changes in the reaction area of the femoral neck are marked: Poirier's facets appeared on both sides, plaque on the right side and Allen's fossa on the left. There is a small exostosis on the inferior margin of the right femoral head in the region of the attachment of the capsular ligament and, in both femora, the gluteal ridge and the linea aspera and the point of insertion of the Gluteus medius on the greater trochanter are heavily marked, while the trochanteric fossae show

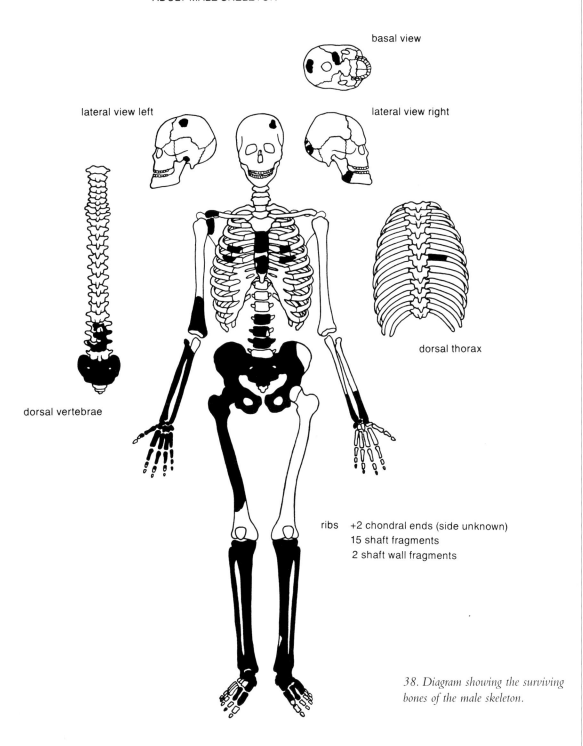

ADULT MALE SKELETON

basal view

lateral view left

lateral view right

dorsal thorax

dorsal vertebrae

ribs   +2 chondral ends (side unknown)
       15 shaft fragments
        2 shaft wall fragments

38. Diagram showing the surviving bones of the male skeleton.

39. Magnified details of the male skeleton:

a. Osteophytic growth round margin of body of first segment of the sacrum

b. Lesion on rim of broken left acetabulum

c. Plaque on neck of right femur

d. Allen's fossa on neck of left femur

e. Gluteal ridge and linea aspera of right femur

f. Lateral tibial squatting facets

g. Enlarged tibial tuberosities

h. Calcaneal spurs

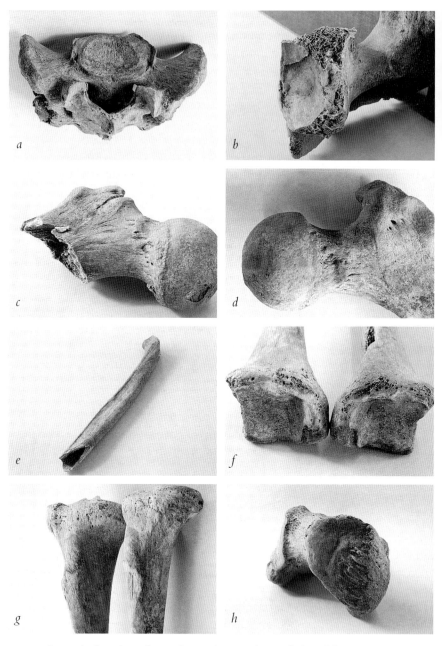

exposed cortical trabeculae where the tendon of the Obturator externus muscle was inserted.

Tight extension of the hip with slight abduction of the femur winds the circular zona orbicularis tightly round the femoral neck and tightens the two parts of the ilio-femoral ligament. This normal stress, applied intermittently, will produce the hypertrophy seen in Allen's fossa (Angel 1964). Angel suggested that the build-up of bone round the margin of Allen's fossa is a partial healing process which is seen completed in the crescentic border of typical plaque. If this is so, the activity causing this hypertrophy could have taken place in early adulthood, if this was followed by a reduction in strenuous activity, thus enabling healing to take place. If this was the case, the presence of plaque could indicate a maturer age group, while the acetabular flange lesion and the exostosis on the rim of the femoral head could suggest that the activity had been vigorous.

Angel considered the hyper-extension of the hip in running or even walking downhill sufficient to produce the changes seen in the reaction area, but, in this instance, the sacro-iliac joint is firm and, despite slight osteophytic lipping on the first segment of the sacrum, the available lumbar vertebrae are normal.

The well-developed linea asperae and gluteal ridges, however, suggest that the condition might have been produced by riding astride a horse, during which the adductor longus is liable to severe strain (it can even be ruptured by sudden gripping of the saddle (Gray 1977)). The lesion on the acetabular rim and the exostosis on the femoral head indicate that the activity could have resulted in trauma.

The proximal end of the left tibia is missing, but the rounded posterior margin of the right lateral tibial condyle (suggesting hyperflexion of the knee), and lateral squatting facets at the distal ends of the tibiae (the result of pronounced dorsi-flexion of the foot: Bacon 1990) indicate the possible habitual adoption of a squatting posture. This would not have accounted, however, for the marked enlargement of the lateral side of the tibial tubercle (extending onto the proximal end of the crest) which suggests a constant checking of inward rotation of the knee joint by the lateral patella ligament. The hyperflexion of the knee and foot together with this inward pressure of the knee were considered in relation to riding with a short stirrup. The short stirrup, however, was not introduced until the eighteenth century, when field enclosure forced hunters to be trained to jump and riders to develop a firm grip with the knee.

The Vikings and their contemporaries in northern mainland Scotland had a riding aristocracy and the 'Pictish' garron was similar to the modern Icelandic pony. The horses were trained to an extended walk for speed and comfort on long journeys and were ridden with high pommelled saddles and, if used, the stirrups long. The pelvis was tilted back (the rider sitting on his sacrum) and the legs extended forward with, possibly, an inward rotation of the knee—but the pressure would not have been great and might not have been sufficient to have produced the enthesopathy in normal circumstances. Although the larger Arab strain of horse had been introduced from the Caliphate into Sweden by the ninth century, there is no evidence of a change of riding style to balance rather than grip.

Changes in the femur and pelvis, similar to those seen on this individual, were found in skeletons from the *Mary Rose,* and were ascribed by Stirland (1991) to the heavy stresses placed on young bones by the activities necessary in handling a ship in rough waters. Low seats might account for hyperflexion of the knee and ankle and the action of rowing would produce a strong downward thrust on the braced foot with an inward rotation of the knee. This might account for the development of the protuberance at the insertion of the lateral patella ligament—as might the stress of maintaining balance in a boat. It could also account for the vertically orientated exostoses at the point of attachment of the tendo Achilles on the posterior surface of the calcaneus. A bony protuberance (21.8mm by 11.1mm) found on the anterior internal surface of the midpoint of the shaft of the left tibia is probably bony reaction to a superficial cut or lesion.

In addition, a small exostosis was found on the second phalanx of the right third digit. The bones of the hands are very large and marked by degenerative changes. These were slightly greater on the right side and consisted of slight osteoporotic changes on both triquetrals and both pisiforms, and the articular facet of the right pisiform was eburnated with osteophytes on the margin. (The pisiform receives the insertion of the abductor minimi digiti which abducts the little finger from the midline of the hand and also assists in flexing the proximal phalanx.) The distal end of the right first metacarpal is osteoporotic and the terminal phalanx has an osteophyte at the proximal end. These changes, which could have been produced by holding the reins of a horse, could also have been produced by rowing. Absence of bones of the thorax and shoulder girdle precluded confirmation and so it is possible that training in the use of the large sword found in the grave could have contributed to their development.

All the activities considered could have produced similar bone changes in the hips and lower limbs, but it is tentatively suggested that the combined evidence points towards shipboard activities as the most likely explanation. In particular, the stress necessary to produce the acetabular lesion and the exostosis of the femoral head was more likely to have been produced by the more strenuous activity of rowing than by the type of horse riding practised, where greater stress reaction should have been more apparent in the region of the linea aspera. It is also tentatively suggested that the activity took place in young adulthood and the activity was reduced with increasing age or status (i.e. rowing would have been an activity of youth).

THE FEMALE SKELETON

The skeleton recovered to the east of the male skeleton is that of a very elderly female, possibly in her seventies. Her height is unknown but the osteoporotic condition of her bones indicate an advanced age. This individual is represented by the parietal bones of the cranium, small fragments of ribs, the right os innominatum, three metacarpals, parts of both femora, tibiae, fibulae and hand and foot bones.

The sex was determined as female using the criteria given by Bass (1987) (which included a pre-auricular sulcus) and the age from the osteoporotic condition of the bones and the high degree of erosion of the symphysial region of the pelvis.

Pathological and non-metrical changes seen in the female skeleton suggest habitual sitting with legs crossed. Changes in the reaction area of the femoral neck, especially the formation of Allen's fossa, suggest continued hyperextension of the femur. A slight exostosis was noted in the trochanteric fossa, and a spur formation on the internal margin of pubic portion of the foramen magnum suggests stress on the points of origin and insertion of the Obturator externus muscle. This, in the sitting position, rotated the femur outwards. The point of origin of the rectus femoris muscle on the inferior

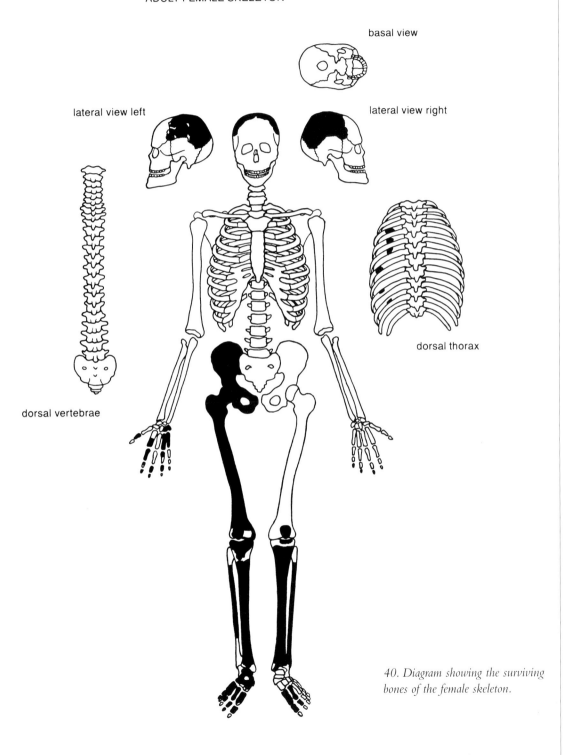

ADULT FEMALE SKELETON

basal view

lateral view left

lateral view right

dorsal thorax

dorsal vertebrae

40. *Diagram showing the surviving bones of the female skeleton.*

41. Magnified details of the female skeleton:

   a. Allen's fossa on anterior surface of right femoral neck
   b. Spur on obturator foramen
   c. Grooved rim of acetabulum
   d. Marked irregularity of symphys pubis
   e. Spurs on patellae
   f. Marked development of palmar and interosseous ligaments of fifth right metacarpal

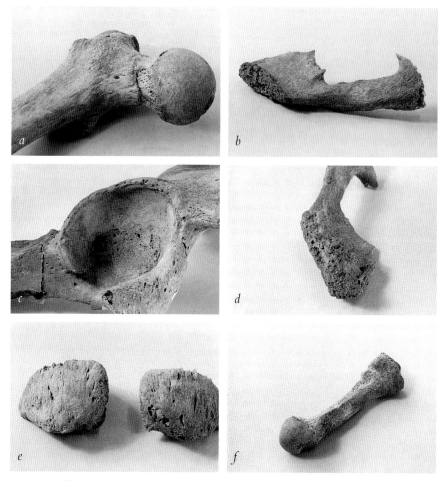

anterior iliac spine is roughened and the adjacent rim of the acetabulum grooved—all of which suggest hyper-extension and abduction of the femur. Marked irregularity of the symphysial area of the pubis (suggesting stress in the region of the origin of the gracilis and, more especially, the adductor muscles) is complemented by a pronounced and heavily marked upper portion of the linea aspera and the gluteal ridge. The adductor muscles not only adduct the thigh powerfully (as in horse-riding) but they rotate the thigh outward and, when the limb has been abducted, draw it inward (Gray 1977) as in sitting cross-legged. There is a slight spur formation at the point of insertion of the Quadriceps extensor tendon on the anterior surface of the right patella and slight osteophytic lipping on the inferior margin of its articular surface. Lateral tibial squatting facets, indicative of acute dorsi-flexion of the foot (Bacon 1990), are also present.

A small lytic lesion in the centre of the proximal articular surface of the first right metatarsal bone is probably *post mortem* erosion.

Examination of the extant metacarpal bones showed particular development of the points of attachment of the palmer and interosseous ligaments of the right fifth metacarpal. This might be expected in one engaged in spinning where the first two fingers and thumb are kept together and the fourth and fifth fingers spread (this spread is particularly important when spinning with flax). The bones of the left hand are missing.

THE CHILD'S SKELETON

The third skeleton recovered from the boat burial is that of a child aged about ten at the time of death. The child's sex could not be determined. Only a few cranial and facial bones were found with some loose teeth, a fragment of a right femur, the right tibia and fibula, eroded patella, talus and calcaneus and fragments of the left calcaneus and possibly talus and metatarsal shafts (side unknown).

Examination of the loose teeth indicated that the upper canine, second premolar and second molar were unerupted, the first premolar was erupting, the first molar had erupted and the second deciduous molar was still present. Altogether, this indicates an age of about ten (Brothwell 1981, 64). It should be noted that some juvenile teeth whose development was compatible with those of the juvenile skeleton, were found with the female skeleton.

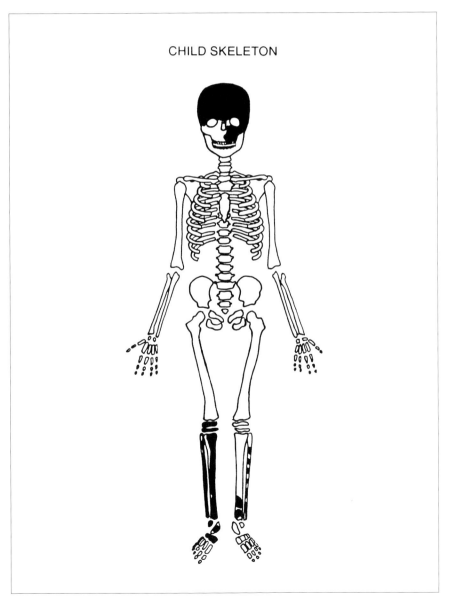

CHILD SKELETON

42. Diagram showing the surviving bones of the child skeleton.

CHAPTER 5

THE WOMAN'S EQUIPMENT

THE BROOCH

Olwyn Owen, with contributions by Amanda Clydesdale (conservation, manufacture and technology), Thea Gabra-Sanders (textiles) and Paul Wilthew (metallurgical analyses)

An equal-armed brooch was found lying upside down beneath the wooden handle of the sickle. Although these artefacts were found in the anticipated chest region of the woman's body, both had almost certainly been moved from their original positions by otter disturbance of the burial. As confirmation, a few human rib fragments survived in the copper corrosion products of the brooch while the rest of the upper skeleton had been more or less completely removed. Some two-thirds of the brooch survived intact with the hinge and pin still attached. In addition, a large fragment of one of the brooch arms and smaller fragments of the brooch and the bosses were recovered from the immediate vicinity.

The upper (decorated) surface of the most intact portion of the brooch had lain pressed against a compact mass of soft, brown-black organic material which lifted off the surface of the brooch in one piece. The same material also covered part of the edge of the brooch and extended over some of its underside, indicating that the brooch had become embedded in this organic material after burial. This was later confirmed by its analysis for macrofossils (see Appendix 10) which revealed that it comprised badly deteriorated plant remains and some insect remains, but had no association with the decay products of the woman's body. The soft organic material may have protected the surfaces of the brooch.

The brooch was lifted in a 'block' with the sand around it, which allowed sometimes minute brooch fragments to be retrieved later on in the laboratory. The sand around the brooch was also found to contain a fragmentary boat rivet and decayed wood remains, probably deriving from the boat timbers. The conservation and reconstruction of the brooch was a long and delicate process. During careful cleaning of the back of the brooch in the laboratory, it was noted that two parallel 'ridges' of sand, held in place by a tar-like organic substance, seemed to correlate in location, shape and size with a fold of cloth, such as that which might have formed in the garment through which the brooch pin was passed. This evidence suggests that the brooch was attached to a garment worn by the woman when she was buried.

Description

The equal-armed brooch is made of copper alloy, probably a quarternary copper-zinc-lead-tin alloy which would be closer to brass than to bronze (see Appendix 3). Its surface is mercury-gilded which gives it a glittering gold appearance. Originally, fourteen silver-capped bosses were positioned symmetrically over the highly decorated surface of the brooch, four in the central oval panel and five on each of the arms, each secured with small copper alloy pins. The contrast of the silver-capped bosses with the glittering gold body of the brooch was central to the craftsman's original design. Little now remains of the bosses themselves, but the circular platforms on which they were sited are clearly visible within the ornament. The brooch is 134mm long. It is relatively even in width but narrows slightly in the centre (34mm) and broadens towards the ends (51mm maximum width). Now, it weighs 55.4g. In profile, the central portion of the brooch is convex and the arms to either side are slightly concave. The remains of the pin, hinge and catchplate survive on the underside of the brooch. Mineralised textile remains and textile impressions of at least two distinct types are also preserved on the underside of the brooch, together with three non-mineralised threads of linen.

The ornament

The upper surface of the brooch is highly decorated with typical early Viking gripping beast ornament in relief, arranged into three main ornamental fields: the oval panel in the centre and the two brooch arms on either side. The (originally silver) bosses formed an integral part of the design. On each arm, four approximately equidistant bosses occur around the edge of the brooch and impinge on the plain, slightly moulded rim. The

43a. (above) The equal-armed brooch was in pieces when it came out of the ground

43b. below) After conservation

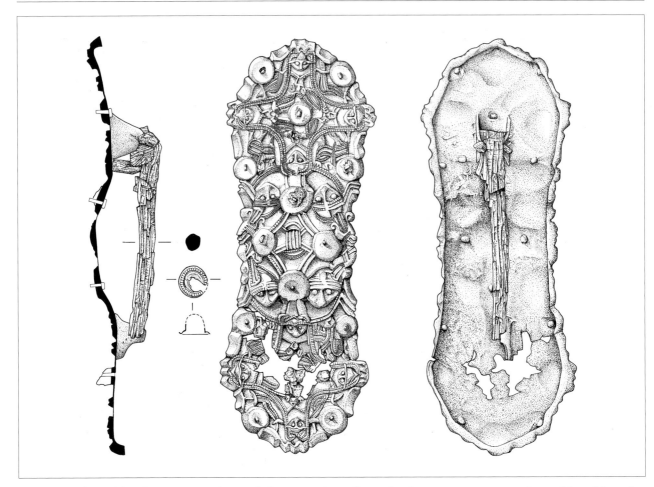

44. The equal-armed brooch. Notice the gripping beasts and the triangular animal masks; these are typical of early Viking period ornament.

45. Detail of triangular animal masks on brooch.

intervals between these four edge bosses are punctuated roughly midway by four inward-looking triangular animal masks, the ears of which also impinge on and form part of the rim. Their eyebrows, bulging eyes and snouts are all prominent features. Two narrow ribbons, transversely nicked to produce imitation filigree, emanate from each side of each animal mask and conjoin to form a dominant cruciform-shaped frame, at the centre of which is the fifth boss. Degenerate animal ornament occurs both within and outwith the cruciform-shaped frame. Beneath each animal mask, a small, sub-triangular body motif devolves into pairs of interlocked limbs, gripped by four pairs of small hands, which surround the central (fifth) boss and form a complex knot pattern. Outwith the cruciform-shaped frame, plain and nicked expanded ribbons occupy the outer fields; while expanded body quarters formed of plain and nicked ribbons occupy the inner fields, with double-contoured legs and feet which stand on the cruciform-shaped frame. The background is plain and slightly recessed. The ornament on the two arms is very similar but not identical.

The ornament of the oval panel in the centre of the brooch is less dense and the details are slightly larger in scale. A larger proportion of the available space is left plain. The oval panel itself is formed of two narrow, transversely nicked ribbons, interrupted at top and bottom and on either side where details of animal masks overlie them.

The four bosses, two of which are slightly larger than the bosses on the arms, are arranged in a lozenge shape around the centre of the brooch within the oval panel. Pairs of slightly curving ribbons with traces of transverse nicking conjoin the four bosses to form a lozenge-shaped field, at the centre of which is a segment of a 'ring-chain', an interlaced circular knot binding two further pairs of ribbons which cross the lozenge-shaped field between the smaller top and bottom bosses. Four triangular animal masks occupy the four ovoid fields formed between the edge of the oval panel and the lozenge-shaped centre field, and look out towards the arms of the brooch. These prominent animal masks are larger than, but otherwise similar to, the masks on the arms of the brooch, although they have triple eyebrow bands with transverse nicking. Other narrow, transversely nicked ribbons emanate from their heads and interlock, impinging on the top and bottom centre rim of the brooch.

The bosses

Although many Viking brooches of several different types still retain the platforms of bosses, it is unusual to find traces of the bosses themselves. The Scar brooch still has parts of its bosses intact, which has afforded a rare opportunity for their examination by X-Ray Fluorescence Analysis (see Appendix 3). The bosses were numbered 1–14 for the purposes of recording and analysis.

The shells of bosses 3, 10 and 12 were all silver. The silver may have contained copper, zinc, lead or tin, but it is also possible that these elements were detected as a result of contamination from corrosion products from the fill of the bosses or the copper alloy base metal of the brooch itself. The silver is very poorly preserved and has been completely converted to silver chloride.

Each of the samples of fill (from Bosses 4, 7 and 10–14 inclusive) was found to be rich in both lead and tin, suggesting that the bosses had been filled with a lead-tin alloy rather than with pure lead (Appendix 3). The analysis was qualitative and therefore only gives an indication of the relative proportions of the components. The slightly different results could simply reflect the fact that the samples were taken from different locations on the brooch. Alternatively, they could indicate either that a poorly mixed alloy was used; or that alloys of different composition were used to fill and solder the bosses to the body of the brooch. If the latter was the case, and if the solder and fills had differing compositions with consequently different melting points, the bosses would have had to be secured in at least a two-stage operation. Unfortunately, it was not possible to isolate samples of fill and/or solder as too little survives of the bosses.

None of the bosses was complete and all of them had lost their shells. Their original shape, or shapes, is uncertain but it is suggested from examination of the best preserved example (Boss 12: Fig. 44) that they may have been oviform rather than spherical. The indications are that two of the bosses in the central oval panel may have been slightly larger than those on the arms of the brooch; certainly, the boss platforms on either side of the oval panel are larger in diameter (9mm) than those on the arms (7mm). The silver boss caps appear to have been unornamented except for a narrow flange around the base of each boss. These flanges were each decorated with double circles filled with transverse nicks. The flanges may have served to ensure good contact with the body of the brooch, to fix the silver caps more securely to the lead-tin solder, and to conceal the means by which the bosses were attached to the brooch, as well as being decorative.

Through the centre of each boss platform are the remains of a small copper alloy pin (diameter c. 0.8mm). Each pin had been inserted from the underside of the brooch where their flattened heads are clearly visible. The other end of the pin served to anchor the boss itself to the brooch.

The pin

When being worn, the brooch was secured to clothing by an iron pin. The pin comprises a rod of circular section and, although its precise original diameter cannot be ascertained because of corrosion, at perhaps 2–3mm in diameter, it could probably have held fairly thick cloth. The tip of the pin (and most of the catchplate) is missing despite comprehensive and careful sieving of all the soil filling the boat, but may have been removed by the otter disturbance of this part of the grave. Alternatively, it is conceivable that the brooch was no longer capable of being properly secured for use at the time of its burial.

46. The pin, hinge and catchplate all survived on the underside of the brooch, although it was incomplete.

The hinge end of the pin appears to conform to Jansson's type b (Jansson 1985a, 115, fig. 104). The pin rod had been flattened and bent around an iron hinge pin. The flattened end runs parallel to the overlying pin rod for a short distance and is then bent at right angles to rest on the reverse of the brooch. By this device, the craftsman ensured that the pin would remain a fixed distance from the back of the brooch, allowing for a larger gather of cloth. Partly mineralised textile remains were found wound around the area adjacent to the stop (see Appendix 2).

The hinge

The hinge is made of copper alloy (not analysed) and was almost certainly cast in one piece with the brooch. It comprises two trapezoidal-shaped metal plates which project at right angles from the underside of the brooch. Holes had been drilled through the hinge plates to receive a fine iron pin, around which the flattened end of the main brooch pin moves.

The catchplate

The catchplate is incomplete. The recovered portion was found attached to a small fragment of the brooch. It consists of a single plate of copper alloy (not analysed), similar in shape to the hinge supports, but arched over to provide secure housing for the end of the pin when the brooch was in use. The catchplate had broken off at the point at which it arched.

Manufacture and technology

Amanda Clydesdale

The brooch was almost certainly cast in a two-piece clay mould. In this process, the lower part of the mould is lined with a slip-coated textile which both separates the two halves of the mould and establishes the thickness of the final casting. The textile itself would have been burnt out of the mould when it was fired (i.e. before it was used to produce a cast) (Maryon 1971, 225), but the impression of the textile has remained in the inner surface of the upper part of the mould. The additional thickness of the outer edge of the Scar brooch may have been due to puckering or deliberate gathering of the textile lining the mould. Any irregularities remaining on the edge of the cast would probably have been removed during the finishing process.

Although the brooch is relatively heavy, the metal is extremely thin in places. Producing smooth-based recesses on a positive master would have been extremely difficult. It seems more likely, therefore, that the master for the brooch was made in the negative, that is, as a mould (possibly of wax) which was used to produce a casting, which in turn produced the plain metal master for the mould from which the Scar brooch was made.

Even after casting, the brooch was still far from being a finished product. It would not yet have been gilded; only the platforms for the bosses would have been present and the bands of relief decoration would have had plain surfaces. Indeed, the cast brooch would probably have been as plain as possible, partly to facilitate removal of the brooch from the mould, and partly to allow for individual finishing touches to be added later.

It is not clear at what stage the hinge and catchplate were attached to the body, although they would have had to be attached before the bosses and boss caps were riveted into place because brazing is carried out at a much higher temperature than soldering—820–930°C—whereas a standard tin-lead solder melts at about 250°C (Maryon 1971). Thus, the bosses' solder would have melted if brazing took place after they had been attached. There is no indication that brazing occurred in the region of the hinge or catchplate and it is therefore possible that the hinge and catchplate were cast with the brooch. They may even have served as pours or risers for the molten metal during the casting process (a pour is formed where the molten metal is poured into the mould through a funnel-shaped cavity with a channel to the hollow part of the mould; and a riser is a rod of cast metal which forms in a deliberate cavity in the mould as it is filled with molten metal, so that the metalworker can tell when the mould is adequately filled by the height to which the molten metal has risen in the riser).

After the cast had been removed from the mould, it would have been trimmed and finished. All evidence of pours and risers would have been removed during the finishing process; all rough edges would have been sanded smooth; and additional details, such as the transverse nicking along the surfaces of the relief ornament, would have been added using a metal tool.

The next stage would probably have been the gilding. There is clear evidence that the Scar brooch was mercury-gilded using the mercury amalgam or 'fire gilding' technique (Dodwell 1961, 89–90); previous studies of Viking brooches have simply assumed that this was the case (e.g. Welander, Batey & Cowie 1987, 160). Holes would have had to be drilled through the boss platforms to accommodate the small pins which secured the bosses, but it is not possible to determine whether the gilding took place before or after the pin holes were drilled. The pins themselves seem to have been inserted after gilding since none of them has any traces of gold on it. Toolmarks are clearly visible on the gilded surface.

The bosses were added towards the end of the manufacturing process. The boss platforms were probably produced from silver sheet and shaped on a doming block (or equivalent) ready for infilling. Sufficient silver would have remained around the edge to allow for accurate trimming. The silver used for the shells appears to have been made in a single batch to judge from the homogeneity of the shell compositions; thus, the bosses, wherever located on the brooch, were all clearly intended to have the same surface appearance.

Analysis of the fills of seven of the bosses tentatively indicates that, although they are all lead-tin alloys, the fills of the bosses on the central oval panel may have had a different ratio of lead to tin (see Appendix 3). If this is correct, it may be possible to infer that solders of different melting points were employed and, therefore, that the bosses were secured in place in at least a two-stage operation with the higher melting point solder being applied first. Traditional lead-tin solders are of two main types: a soft solder (63% tin to 37% lead with a melting point of 183°C); or a plumber's solder (two parts of lead to one part of tin) which has prolonged malleability during cooling, allowing time for modelling and other manipulation. Analyses of the boss remains of one of the Kneep (Cnip), Lewis, brooches indicated that a plumber's solder had been used (*contra* Welander, Batey & Cowie 1987, 160). Analyses of seven of the Scar bosses tentatively indicates that five of the seven were attached with a soft solder (Appendix 3).

There are three different ways in which the bosses could have been secured to a brooch, and it is not possible to ascertain which method was used in this case. One method would have been to fill each boss with its lead-tin alloy and then, before it hardened, push or gently hammer the small copper alloy pins through the boss platforms from the underside of the brooch into the fills, which would then have become anchored into place as the fill/solder cooled. The silver cap could have been further secured by the pressure of immediately stamping/incising the ornament on the flanges.

Another option would have been to produce a former, bearing a negative impression of the brooch with bosses in place. The silver caps would have been set in place, each filled with lead-tin alloy, and the former then kept in the furnace at an appropriately maintained temperature (i.e. sufficient to melt the fill), while the body of the brooch was placed on top and the securing pins were inserted. It would then have been left to cool and the bosses finished as before.

The third option would have entailed pushing the securing pins through the boss platforms, brushing plumber's solder over their tips to form a suitable shape, and then fitting a soft silver sheet (the boss cap) over the top, perhaps already embossed with the ornament. Finally, sufficient heat would have been applied to melt the solder and secure the boss in place.

The textiles

Thea Gabra-Sanders

Around the pin fastener of the brooch were some red-brown textile remains which represent an item of the woman's clothing. The partly mineralised fragment in ? tabby weave is made from Z/? spun ? fibre with a ? thread-count. On the reverse of the main part of the brooch is a very faint textile impression embedded in the cast bronze. The broken-off part of the brooch (now re-attached) shows a better impression of a herringbone twill made of ? spin ? fibre with a count of 30–35 x ? threads/cm. This textile was used in the manufacturing process of the brooch, the clay mould being lined with textile (Almgren 1966, 209). If this brooch was an heirloom, the textile could date to earlier than the burial.

The only similar brooch with a herringbone twill impression from Scotland was found near Northton, Harris, Western Isles (Graham-Campbell 1975, 212). Impressions of a herringbone-patterned textile were noted on the reverse side of an oval brooch of Viking date which was found in the Kilmainham cemetery, near Dublin (Bøe 1940, 39). Woollen fabrics of herringbone twill are amongst the material from the ninth- to tenth-century graves at the Viking trading centre at Kaupang, Norway (Ingstad 1988, 136). Some finer herringbone twills have been found in Sweden (Margareta Nockert, personal communication).

This type of brooch was used to fasten an overgarment which could be worn differently; one could fasten it near the neck or lower down. In this case, where a textile fragment is still adhering to the pin, the pin was stuck directly through the material. Sometimes, to protect the material, the pin was put through an eyelet which was sewn onto the side of the garment. These brooches were mostly worn horizontally but could also be worn vertically (Hägg 1971, 144–5).

47. This impression of a herringbone twill textile was left on the underside of the brooch as a result of the manufacturing process; the clay mould would have been lined with this textile.

48a. (top) An equal-armed Troms type brooch actually from Troms in the far north of Norway, found at Austnes, Bjarkøy, in the probable double grave of a man and woman. Copyright Tromsø Museum.

48b. (bottom) ... An identical Troms type brooch, but this time from southern Sweden (from Norrgården, Hamneda, Småland). Copyright Statens Historiska Museet, Stockholm.

Discussion

The Scar brooch is one of the finest pieces of Scandinavian Viking metalwork to have been found in a grave in Scotland. It is of a type which the Norwegian scholar, Jan Petersen, named 'Troms type' (1928, 81–2), as most of the examples known at the time he was writing had been found in the far north of Norway, half of them in the Troms district (Fig.48a). It is a highly unusual type of Viking brooch to find in a British context and, indeed, one of the less common types in Scandinavia.

Petersen defined Troms-type equal-armed brooches as a richly ornate group, comprising only six Norwegian examples. He described them as normally about 15cm long and 'rather wide' (*temmelig brede*) at 5–6cm; they are of a relatively even width but narrow slightly in the centre. They have fourteen applied bosses and are completely decorated with animal ornament, masks or other motifs in a similar style, symmetrically arranged in a geometrical pattern.

The first Norwegian example to be published was a brooch from a grave at Hals, Tranøy, Troms (Rygh 1885, no. 659). Rygh's numbering of his illustrations has been used to label different types of object; thus, the Hals brooch is of type R659. Similarly, the group which Petersen first called Troms-type brooches (also illustrated by the Hals, Tranøy, Troms brooch: 1928, 80, fig. 64) is known as type P64 (Petersen 64). Thus, the Scar brooch belongs to type P64 (R659).

By far the most common type of Viking brooch is the oval brooch (sometimes called a tortoise brooch) of which an estimated 4,000 are known from all over the Viking world (Jansson 1985a, 221), including Scotland. Their function was to hold up the woman's dress, and for this reason they are usually found in pairs, one brooch for each shoulder strap. The sheer quantity of these brooches has invited detailed studies of their style, technology and chronology, as well as the identification of their production centres and trading movements, over more than a century (from Montelius 1877, 1892; through to Petersen 1919, 1928; and Paulsen 1933 onwards. The history of their research is summarised in Jansson 1972 & 1985a). Oval brooches are highly standardised and the total assemblage is dominated by very few types, which has led archaeologists to talk of a 'mass production' of cast bronze ornaments in the Viking period, a phenomenon which is often connected with the appearance of early settlements of urban character in Scandinavia—Kaupang (Norway), Hedeby (Haithabu, now in Sleswig, north Germany), Birka (Sweden), Ribe (Denmark) etc.—where large workshops may have developed and exported their standardised products (but see Jansson 1981 for a more cautious view).

It is unusual and somewhat surprising that no oval brooches were found in the Scar burial. Four Troms-type brooches have been found with oval brooches of type P37 (R647); while one was found with type P28 (R648) (Petersen 1928, 82). Another Norwegian equal-armed brooch very closely related in type to the Troms type (from Hundorp, Gudbrandsdal, Oppland: Petersen 1928, 82, fig. 65 (P65)) was also found with oval brooches of type P37. The P37 oval brooches are the most common type of oval brooch to have been found in the extensive cemetery and trading settlement at Birka,

Sweden, where they are predominantly dated to the Early Birka Period (EBP) (Jansson 1985a, 226–9), that is, between the eighth century and the latter half of the ninth century AD. This broad dating bracket therefore seems appropriate to the Troms-type equal-armed brooch and its variants as well.

Because of their predominantly north Norwegian distribution, Petersen inferred that the Troms-type brooches might have been made in this area (1928, 82). He noted that a variation on the type, very similar to the Hundorp, Gudbrandsdal, Oppland brooch, had been found at Birka, Sweden (*op. cit.*, P65; Bj 620), but concluded nonetheless that the Troms type of equal-armed brooch was 'developed independently in Norway' (*selvstændig norsk*). He suggested that the type dates to the first half of the ninth century.

Aagård, in her analysis of the sixty-one equal-armed brooches found in women's graves at Birka, Sweden, suggested a generally ninth-century date for the P65 type of brooch, on the evidence of its find associations with P37 oval brooches (1984, 109–10, fig. 11:1). The single P65 brooch from Birka falls into Aagård's Group V and is rather distinctive, again underlining the rarity of the P65 (and closely related P64) brooches.

Despite Petersen's confidence that the P64 brooches are a north Norwegian type, enquiries to the museums of Tromsø and Trondheim, though not exhaustive, have so far failed to locate any more recently discovered examples (Gerd Stamsø Munch (Tromsø) and Oddmun Farbregd (Trondheim), personal communication). Instead, three examples are now known from Sweden. An almost complete Troms-type brooch was found with two P37 oval brooches and other artefacts in a cremation grave from the Viking period cemetery at Norrgården, Hamneda, Småland (SHM no. 20522:I:5; Fig.48b). Part of the arm of a Troms-type brooch was found in a Viking grave at Trotteslöv, Berga, also in Småland (SHM 6638:17); and a fragment of the centre portion of a Troms-type brooch was recently found during excavations at Signhildsberg (Fornsigtuna), Håtuna, Uppland (Hedman 1991, 64, fig. 54), on a plateau on which a Viking longhouse had been built (*op. cit.*, fig. 16). No Troms-type brooches have so far been discovered in Denmark (Ann Pedersen & Ingmar Jansson, personal communication).

In the summer of 1993, towards the end of a five-year programme of research excavations in the 'Black Earth' at Birka, Sweden (Ambrosiani & Clarke 1992), a clay mould for a Troms-type equal-armed brooch was found (find no. 50402 in R004117). It was discovered in the later levels of a bronze-casting workshop from the beginning of the Viking Age. This level may be dated to the first half of the ninth century (Björn Ambrosiani, personal communication). Post-excavation is at an early stage and the large assemblage of clay mould fragments from the recent excavations is still being registered but, at present, 'there are parts of at least two copies and two underforms; or eight [P64] mould fragments out of c. 70 for large equal-armed brooches' (Björn Ambrosiani, personal communication). Again, the P64 moulds seem to derive from levels in which moulds for P37 (A–C) types of oval brooch are dominant. The recovery of mould fragments of this type from well-stratified, early workshop levels at Birka is highly significant. This is the only evidence to date of a production centre for these brooches.

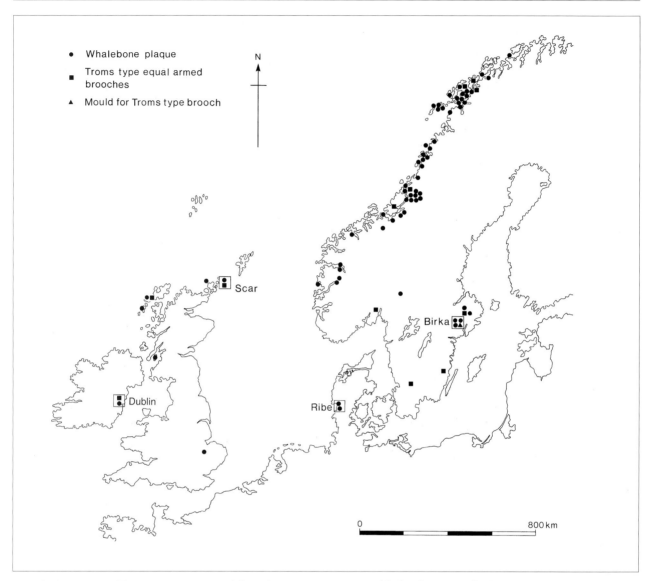

49. The distribution of known Troms-type brooches and carved whalebone plaques in Scandinavia and the British Isles.

Thus, it now seems very likely that so-called Troms-type equal-armed brooches were being manufactured at Birka, Sweden, at least in the first half of the ninth century. This does not of course mean that Birka was necessarily the only Scandinavian production centre; and, given the concentration of Troms-type brooches in northern Norway, it remains possible that a (north) Norwegian production centre(s) was also manufacturing Troms-type brooches. However, the term 'Troms type' is clearly misleading. This small group of opulent and extravagant brooches has a wide geographical distribution, with an apparent concentration in northern Norway and a scattering in central and southern Sweden, in other words, at almost diametrically opposed ends of mainland Scandinavia. This suggests that this unusual, possibly specialised type of brooch, perhaps valued for its very distinctiveness and opulence, was being traded over long distances. The Scar brooch is as likely to have been made in central Sweden as in northern Norway, and could even have been made elsewhere in Scandinavia.

Apart from the Scar brooch, two other fragmentary Troms-type brooches are known from the Viking colonies in the British Isles, one from Scotland and one from Ireland. A badly damaged fragment of a Troms-type brooch was found in Northton, Harris, in the Outer Hebrides (Graham-Campbell 1975, 212–15, Pl. 28a–c; NMAS IL 750). Unfortunately, this was a stray find from the sand dunes but it does have the impressions of a herringbone-patterned textile on its reverse, very similar to those noted on the Scar brooch; and it retains part of its catchplate. A large fragment, found in Ireland, probably Dublin, is now in the National Museum, Copenhagen (Shetelig 1954, VI, 241, fig. 83; NMK 10512). At first this was mistakenly reported as part of an oval brooch but it was correctly identified as a very worn fragment of a Troms-type equal-armed brooch by Bøe (1940, 95). Despite the poor condition of these two examples, they serve to show that the Scar brooch is a rare, but not an isolated, occurrence of the Troms-type equal-armed brooch in the British Isles.

The Scar brooch (and, indeed, all of the Troms-type equal-armed brooches) is decorated with characteristically early Viking art. The study of the art of this period is dominated by that unparallelled find, the Oseberg ship burial (its grave chamber dendrochronologically dated to the summer of AD 834: Bonde & Christensen 1993, 575–83), with its extraordinarily rich cargo of high-quality carved wooden objects and other items (Shetelig 1920; Christensen, Ingstad & Myhre 1992). Shetelig identified the work of two generations of artists in the Oseberg carvings; the younger generation created the new Viking-period style with its three-dimensional relief and baroque appearance ('the Baroque Master' etc.) The style is overcrowded, vigorous and extravagant, and often in three-dimensional relief. During this early period, motifs play an important role, especially the gripping beasts. However, the Oseberg burial is so exceptional, and the many objects it contained are decorated with such an eclectic collection of features, that the term 'Oseberg style' may not be particularly helpful when applied to more mundane objects from other locations.

The inadequacies of traditional nomenclature for Viking-style groupings have been well rehearsed and need no repetition here. The use of the gripping beast motif persists in the Borre style, for instance, but the animals tend to lose some of their vigour and become subordinated to the overall picture, the animal masks tending to turn inwards towards the centre or outwards towards the edge. In general, the Borre style is more formalised and there is less movement, the design often composed of shorter lines arranged in a symmetrical pattern. Interlacing elements and other joining features are common. The 'ring-chain' interlace motif, which is present to a very limited extent on the central oval panel of the Scar brooch, had a particular impact on Anglo-Scandinavian sculpture in the ninth to tenth centuries (especially on Manx sculpture: see e.g. Cubbon 1971).

Elements of both the Oseberg and Borre styles are well represented on early Viking brooches, with Oseberg style being predominant on the P37 oval brooches from Birka (Jansson 1985a, 229–30). Both styles were well suited to cast jewellery of the period with their established frameworks and elaborate ornamental fields. The styles appear to have co-existed over some time; some of the Birka graves contain Oseberg-style oval brooches worn together with Borre-style brooches (*op. cit.*). Nevertheless, the Oseberg style seems generally to be a little earlier while the Borre style seems to have continued in use for rather longer, especially in the Viking colonies. The Borre style is conventionally dated from around the middle of the ninth century to about the mid-tenth century.

The Scar and other Troms-type equal-armed brooches display elements of both the Oseberg and Borre styles in their use of the leitmotifs of the gripping beast and a formal framework. Stylistically, the ornament of the Troms-type brooches seems to belong to a phase which 'straddles' the Oseberg and Borre styles, and which is most commonly expressed on mass-produced items. This is early Viking art, then, but it is always wise to be cautious when using the ornament of an object to date its manufacture. Indeed, increasing scrutiny now attaches to AD 800 as the conventional date for the beginning of the Viking Age, since ongoing excavations, particularly at Ribe, Denmark, and Birka, Sweden, are now producing Viking cultural material from eighth-century levels (Hvass 1986; Bonde 1989; Jensen 1991; Christensen 1991; Bonde *et al* 1990; 1992).

It has already been mentioned that the absence of any oval brooches from the woman's burial at Scar is surprising. These were essential dress fasteners and are a common, indeed almost ubiquitous, feature of female Scandinavian graves, in Scotland as elsewhere (e.g. Islay, Argyll (Graham-Campbell 1980, 34, no. 118); Castletown, Caithness (*op. cit.* 35, no. 120); and many others). The Scar equal-armed brooch should have been the 'third' brooch, included with two oval brooches as part of the woman's attire (see Chapter 7). It would have been worn singly to fasten the shawl, cloak or jacket over the dress. Equal-armed brooches were widely fashionable for this purpose in the early Viking period, but alternative types of brooch were also used, including trefoil and large and small disc brooches (e.g. Graham-Campbell 1980, 37, no. 128; 30, no. 108; 39–42, nos. 137–42).

Although the Scar brooch is in generally good condition and was certainly intact when buried (with the possible exception of the tip of the fastening pin and part of the catch), it was evident from a detailed examination of the condition of the metals that some of the relatively thick gilding had been worn off in antiquity. Very little gilding survived on the edges of the brooch, apparently as a result of wear. The silver survived in very poor condition mainly as a result of post-depositional processes but, again, the silver caps on the bosses may have been partly eroded prior to burial. The iron, lead-tin alloy and copper alloy elements had all suffered corrosion but were probably in reasonable condition when the brooch was buried. Thus, it seems reasonable to assume that the brooch was a highly valued, well-cared-for personal possession, which was already of some antiquity when it was buried. It is tempting to deduce that the brooch may have been in the possession of the woman buried at Scar throughout much of her long life.

Summary

The Scar brooch is a so-called Troms-type (P64) equal-armed brooch, one of the less common types of Viking brooch, of which it is one of the finest and most complete examples known anywhere in the Viking world. This type of brooch was produced at Birka, Sweden, from at least the first half of the ninth century, and would doubtless also have been produced in other Scandinavian workshops. The Scar brooch was brought to Scotland, probably as part of the personal possessions of its Scandinavian woman owner rather than as a traded artefact. Its opulence and distinctiveness may have led to its being cherished over a long period of time, and it seems likely that, when it was buried, it was already of some antiquity.

THE CARVED WHALEBONE PLAQUE

Olwyn Owen (with conservation by Paul Watson)

The carved whalebone plaque was found lying with its decorated side face-down, immediately to the right of the woman's feet (Fig. 22). Originally, the plaque had been placed in the grave propped up against the upright slab marking the east end of the chamber, with its decorated side facing the woman. Probably quite soon after the burial chamber was sealed (before it became filled with sand), the whalebone plaque tipped over into its final position overlying the bottom of the boat and an iron boat rivet.

Condition and conservation

The plaque is in generally excellent condition and the whalebone remains hard, dense and heavy. Corrosion from the iron boat rivet has stained a small part of the surface of the plaque and there are slight traces of damage caused by fungal growth in the same area. The cancellous tissue on parts of the back of the plaque have decayed. The left side of the plaque (both front and back) has suffered a little more damage than the right. There are occasional minor losses from the decorated surface, particularly along the edges. The left animal head has become slightly distorted and is now bent marginally lower than the right head; this distortion has caused fragmentation of the bars adjoining the two heads and the cross-bar is completely missing.

The plaque was thoroughly waterlogged when received in the laboratory, and was stored in damp conditions at first to prevent it from drying out too quickly. It took two months to dry it out using natural air-drying methods (without the use of solvents). Throughout this period, the plaque was wrapped in blotting paper which was changed every day, and sealed in a box. In this way, water was very slowly drawn from the bone. Whenever a light 'bloom' of mould appeared, it was carefully removed by rinsing with Industrial Methylated Spirits (IMS). Eventually, the plaque was immersed in 100% IMS for four hours to remove the last of the water. After this it was allowed to air-dry over three days, while weighted and supported.

The completely dry plaque is lighter in colour than when it was excavated but it retains the 'golden' colour of natural bone and does not appear to have been bleached white. The drying process has also lightened the colour of the iron stain on its surface, making it less visible. Removing the water has enhanced the decorative and natural details, sharpening cut lines and clarifying other marks.

Description

The whalebone plaque was probably cut from a rib-bone. The whale was undoubtedly one of the larger species but, because no articular area is present, it is unfortunately not possible to identify the species (Finbar McCormick and Jerry Harman, personal communication).

The plaque is naturally slightly curved with a smooth upper convex surface. It is wider at the base (210mm) and narrows slightly towards the top where two (originally conjoined) inward-looking, stylised animal heads have been carved (185mm across at the eyes). Geometric ornament is carved around the edges of the plaque; the centre of the plaque is plain. The plaque stands 266mm high. It varies in thickness between 101mm minimum (on the outer edge adjacent to the left animal head) and 173mm maximum (at the top of the plaque, between the animal heads). The base is slightly curved outwards rather than straight, while the longer sides are very slightly curved inwards. The rougher cancellous tissue of the whalebone is exposed on the underside which is otherwise plain. Examination of the edges of the plaque indicated that the dense (non-cancellous) tissue is unevenly distributed across the plaque, the dense layer being 24mm thick on the right side and only 5mm thick on the left.

The ornament of the plaque is dominated by the two stylised, inward-looking animal heads at the top. The heads are identical, elongated, seen in profile and point downwards at the end of tightly curving necks. The confronted heads were originally conjoined in two places: at their forelocks and by a cross-bar (now missing) which would have connected their upper mouths. The heads have open jaws and five pairs of clearly defined, incised back teeth. Two large, pointed, interlocking front teeth connect the lower and upper jaw at the front of the mouth. A plain, square-ended tongue protrudes from each mouth, passes behind the large front teeth and curves down to impinge on the geometric ornament along the top of the main body of the plaque. The eyes are plain circular punches with a central dot. The shape of each head is emphasised by an incised line which follows the contours of the firmly drawn chin, mouth and forelock. The narrow, tapering forelock projections each have a central incised line which terminates in a small hollow just in front of the collar. The collar marks the distinction between the head and the neck and comprises two pairs of three incised parallel lines with a central break in which a short curved incision mirrors the curving lines of the neck.

The remainder of the ornament is geometrical and entirely symmetrical. Two incised narrow bands emerge from behind each of the collars and exactly follow the gently curving outlines of the plaque. The only sharp intersection occurs where the bands along the sides turn almost at right angles to follow the slightly curving line of the base. The bands are entirely filled with an incised geometric key-pattern. They are uninterrupted except where the tongues cross them at the top of the plaque. Each of the areas between the bands on the curving necks of the animals is filled with a series of nine, approximately equidistant, punched, double ring-and-dot ornaments. On each neck, eight of these double ring-and-dot ornaments are

50. (facing) The Scar whalebone plaque, after conservation. The cancellous tissue on the back (inset) was decayed in places.

0   5cms

placed in a curving line from behind the collar down to the top of the main body of the plaque; the ninth is placed horizontally adjacent to the last double ring-and-dot ornament in the line, thereby delimiting the animal ornament above the plain central area of the main plaque.

The Scar plaque was produced by a highly skilled craftsman entirely in control of both the design and the medium. The overall impression is of elegance and sophistication. The flowing and slightly curving outlines give fluidity and movement to the design, while the delicate balance of geometric patterns, animal ornament and plain areas gives it its bold and striking appearance. In the natural world, these heads might most closely resemble horses' heads, but naturalistic representation was not the craftsman's intention—they are part of an intrinsically artistic design which reflects the style and taste of the early Viking period.

Discussion

The function of whalebone plaques

Speculation about the function of whalebone plaques dates back to the 1870s when Rygh proposed that they were eating plates (*tallerkener*), and Lorange proposed that one example was a 'loom gate' (*vevgrind*)' (Petersen 1951, 336). By the turn of the century, it had become recognised that they were predominantly women's artefacts, perhaps associated with weaving. In 1905, Thomas Petersen reported two finds from Stor-Skomo, Overhalla, Nord-Trøndelag (Tromsø Museums Årshefte, vol 68). He questioned their interpretation as plates, suggesting that their beautiful ornament and simplicity implied that they must have been used for some 'clean' (*rene*) purpose, and pointed out that they did not normally display signs of knife marks or rigorous cleaning. Since they mostly occur in women's graves, he suggested that they must be specific to women's activities. Petersen referred to ethnographic parallels of smooth boards (*gnidefjæle*), used by women in Skåne, south Sweden, as late as the nineteenth century for ironing their linen caps or other linen garments with stone or glass linen smoothers. Anderson (1880, 63–4), writing about a glass linen smoother from a grave at Ballinaby, Islay, Scotland, reported that using this type of object for smoothing linen 'is still the custom in some districts of Norway … where the women still use similar implements for giving a gloss to their white caps'. Moreover, he had been shown a bun-shaped glass smoother found in the house of a woman from Caithness; the woman had told him that it had been used for smoothing or glazing linen 'long ago', but presumably within living memory (*op. cit.*, figs. 19–24).

Thus, although Grieg (1928) was later able to state unequivocally that these plaques were used for the preparation of leather (*skinnberedning*), the conventional interpretation, reinforced by Jan Petersen (1951, 336), is accepted here: that these plaques are smoothing boards, used for pressing small linen garments (such as caps), pleats or seams, normally with a bun-shaped glass linen smoother (Fig.52a). The heat-retentive glass linen smoother would have been heated over a fire or in boiling water, and then passed repeatedly over the material, like an iron.

51. The Scar plaque was exceptionally well preserved. Some of the details looked as if they might have been carved only yesterday.

a

b

c

d

Glass linen smoothers, presumably imported from the Continent along with other glass artefacts (Graham-Campbell 1980, 22, no. 89), have been found on a number of Viking sites in Scandinavia and elsewhere (Hævernick & Haberey 1963). Like the plaques, they frequently occur in wealthy female graves; and, also like the plaques, they are often found with other objects associated with weaving, such as spindle whorls or weaving battens. However, only one glass linen smoother has certainly been found in the same grave as a carved plaque (in Grave 854, Birka: Arbman 1943, 329, fig. 275,8,14), (Fig.52a), although even here the two items were not placed together; and a possible linen smoother was found with a plaque in a recently excavated grave at Føre, Bø i Vesterålen, Norway (Schanche 1991; Chapter 7). If the plaques functioned primarily as smoothing boards, then this apparent separation in death of the board from the smoother, two apparently complementary pieces of equipment, is difficult to explain.

Clearly, a larger and/or less ornate, wooden or whalebone board (or table) would have been more practical for the purpose of linen smoothing—and, indeed, was probably more commonly used for such a purpose. It is conceivable that some other object could have fulfilled the function of the glass linen smoother, such as a heated water-worn stone, but this seems a little unlikely given the likely quality of the garment being smoothed. This observation supports the contention that the highly carved plaques were valued as grave goods, and perhaps in life as well, primarily for their symbolism and perhaps as a statement of status, rather than as a functional implement.

The Scar plaque shows little sign of wear. The natural grain of the whalebone is clearly visible aligned with the long axis of the plaque; and a series of other lines, visible on the main body of the plaque running approximately at right angles to the grain, also appear to be part of the structure of the bone rather than wear marks. This suggests either that the plaque was relatively new when buried or—and perhaps more likely—that it was of some antiquity when buried, but had been little used. The Scar plaque was doubtless treasured for its intrinsic beauty and must have been a valuable item; but what was its significance in the grave?

Recent research by Britt-Mari Näsström on the Viking goddess, Freyja, may have supplied the answer. It seems likely that carved plaques like that from Scar had a religious significance and were used primarily on ceremonial occasions. Näsström's work has highlighted the symbolic value of flax—a connection which may also link the carved plaques to Freyja. Indeed, one of the names given to Freyja derives from the Old Norse word for flax. Näsström (1995, 85–6) says that flax was 'surrounded by many magical perceptions'. It protected against evil and gave fertility to humankind. Flax was connected with women; it was even called the 'seed of woman' and it had to be sown on a Friday (Freyja's day) by women dressed in their best clothes. The spinning of flax was also connected with Freyja, and the product, linen, was an important part of bridal dress. It is a reasonable supposition, then, that the finest carved whalebone plaques were used for pressing precious linens for ceremonial occasions, perhaps especially the linen elements of the 'best clothes' worn to sow the flax seed or get married

52 facing (a). The carved whalebone plaque from Grave 854, Birka, Sweden, with a glass linen smoother found in the same grave. Copyright Statens Historiska Museet, Stockholm. (b). Whalebone plaque fragment from Sigtuna, Uppland, Sweden. Copyright Sigtuna Museum. (c). The plaque from a rich female grave at Loppasanden, Finnmark, in the far north of Norway. Copyright Tromsø Museum. (d). An unusual (?unfinished) whalebone plaque reportedly from Ely, Cambridgeshire, England. Copyright Cambridge University Museum of Archaeology and Anthropology.

in. Little wonder, then, that the symbolic Scar plaque was placed in the grave in such a prominent position, upright and facing the elderly woman.

The Scandinavian distribution of whalebone plaques (Fig. 49)

Carved whalebone plaques are a relatively rare Viking artefact and only about sixty are known altogether from the Viking world (Petersen 1951, 329–37; Sjøvold 1974, 253–6; see Appendix 4 for a handlist). The vast majority have been found in Norway, many from the northern part of Norway (especially Nord-Trøndelag, Nordland, and Troms) and mostly from along the coast. They are very often found in rich female graves when they are recovered from archaeological contexts, often with imported objects. At Loppasanden, Loppa, Finnmark, Norway, for example, a richly furnished female inhumation contained a whalebone plaque (Fig. 52c), a Finno-Ugrian chain and other objects (Graham-Campbell 1980, 23, 30, nos. 91 & 108). However, three are thought to have been found in men's graves (Petersen 1951, 336; but questioned by Sjøvold 1974, 253); and several examples have also been found on early settlement sites, such as Birka, Sweden (Arwidsson 1984, 202) and, very recently, at Ribe, Denmark (Claus Fevejle, personal communication; below). A number of plaques are of unknown provenance; for example, since 1981, at least three plaques of unknown or uncertain provenance, but probably from Norway, have passed through the hands of London auction houses and been sold for between £1000 and £5000 each (Lesley Webster, personal communication).

Carved plaques were noted by Rygh (1885; R449:Vikestad, Nærø, Nord-Trøndelag) and other early authors, but it was not until 1951, when the Norwegian scholar Jan Petersen produced his comprehensive work on Viking tools (*Vikingetidens Redskaper*), that their probable function and primarily northern Norwegian distribution became widely recognised. Petersen listed thirty-four Norwegian examples, twenty-five from northern Norway (1951, 330; see Appendix 4). The remainder come from western Norway (Hordaland, Sogn og Fjordane and Sør-Trøndelag), with one from Hedmark. Since 1951, a number of new discoveries have been made (Sjøvold 1971; 1974, 253–6), including some from western Norway (Sigrid Kaland, personal communication), but they do not significantly alter this markedly northern, and to a lesser extent western, Norwegian distribution pattern. Whalebone was more easily available in these areas, as demonstrated by a preference for manufacturing weaving battens in whalebone in Norway, as opposed to the use of iron more commonly elsewhere (FVTC 1992, 241, no. 50).

Whalebone plaques have been found elsewhere in Scandinavia in small numbers. In Sweden, the plaque found in Grave 854, Birka, with a glass linen smoother, has already been mentioned (*op. cit.;* Fig. 52a). A further two fragmentary plaques were found in the 'Black Earth' at Birka in Hjalmar Stolpe's pioneering excavations at the end of the nineteenth century (summarised in Ambrosiani & Clarke 1992, 27–51). Part of a plaque was found many years ago in or near Sigtuna, Uppland (Sigtuna Museum no. 522; Nordahl 1982, 18 and plate; Fig. 52b), decorated with the same double ring-and-dot punched ornament as found on the Scar plaque, but in this case around the edges as well as on the animal neck. A badly damaged and fragmentary plaque, also decorated with a double ring-and-dot punched ornament, was found in Grave A 48 at Hjulsta, Norra Spånga, Uppland (Biuw 1992, 153–5), an exceptionally rich cremation grave which also contained an oriental silver belt mount of the eighth to ninth centuries, which had later been converted into a pendant (Jansson 1985b, 185, no. 4).

No whalebone plaques or fragments were known from Denmark until 1993 when, during excavations in Ribe, fragments of at least two plaques were recovered, one of which has an unintelligible runic inscription on the reverse (Claus Fevejle, personal communication). The finest piece comprises part of one inward-looking animal head terminal from a blackened (partly burnt) plaque. It is clear that, originally, this must have been comparable in quality to the Scar plaque. It was found in a rubbish deposit beneath the clay surface of the market place, tentatively dated to the first half of the ninth century (Claus Fevejle, personal communication). The second fragment comprises the lower corner of a simpler plaque, decorated only with an incised line around the edge and also heavily burnt. This derives from levels tentatively ascribed to the third quarter of the eighth century by the excavators. More precise dates should become available for both contexts in due course.

It must be remembered that whalebone is a relatively robust medium and will often survive better than wood. Moreover, it is notable that artefacts of whalebone survive particularly well in the soil conditions of northern Norway (cf. Graham-Campbell 1980, 12–13, no. 15; 21, no. 76). It is highly likely that other plaques or boards, which served similar functions but were made of wood (or even whalebone deposited in less favourable conditions), may not have survived. Thus, although the carved whalebone plaques seem indisputably to be Norwegian products, it is possible that this general artefact type may also have occurred in wood and been manufactured elsewhere.

There is little doubt that carved whalebone plaques are primarily a Norwegian artefact. It is highly likely that the sophisticated Scar plaque was also made in Norway, probably northern Norway, and brought to Orkney as one of the personal possessions of its owner.

Whalebone plaques from Britain and Ireland

Several plaques have been found in Britain and Ireland. In England, a complete but primitive and unfinished plaque is known from Ely, Cambridgeshire (Shetelig 1940, IV, 67, fig. 39; Fig. 52d). However, it was part of the Cole Ambrose collection acquired by the Cambridge University Museum of Archaeology and Anthropology in 1922 (Christopher Chippindale, personal communication); and since it is known that Ambrose purchased artefacts as well as collecting them locally, it must be a possibility that the plaque, albeit unfinished, derives from Scandinavia rather than Cambridgeshire. One of the plaques recently sold in a London auction house was reported to have been dug up in Devon in the eighteenth century (Lesley Webster, personal communication), but this is unlikely to be true.

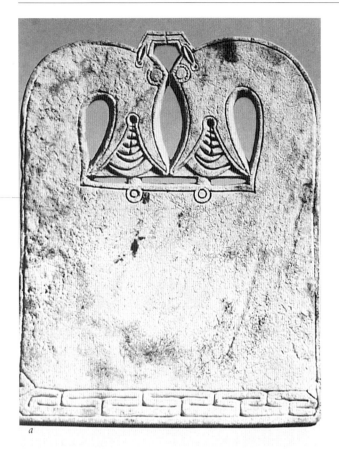

a

b

c

d

The five known Scottish examples are generally much better provenanced and are here described in a little more detail. Firstly, a fragmentary, heavily burnt and badly damaged plaque was found in a grave mound at King's Cross Point, Arran, early this century, together with an iron casket hasp, iron? boat rivets, a bronze coin of Wigmund, Archbishop of York (AD 837–854), and other objects (Balfour 1908–9, 371; Grieg 1940, II, 27, fig. 10). Four separate fragments have been glued together to produce a small portion of the top right corner of the main part of the plaque with part of the animal neck attached. Other small plain fragments also survive. The animal neck is decorated with double ring-and-dot punched ornaments but these are poorly executed and several overlap each other. A double line is incised along the top edge of the plaque separating the animal ornament from the main body of the plaque.

The other Scottish examples are all more recent discoveries. A small piece of whalebone is known from the settlement mound at Saevar Howe, Birsay, Orkney. Described as a 'superficial' find (from Trench B in Hedges' 1977 excavations), it was tentatively identified as a plaque fragment by Batey and Morris (in Hedges 1983, 93, fig. 13:148), and comprises part of the edge of the main body of the plaque. An incised line follows the edge contours of the board. The fragment has small score marks on it which Rackham has suggested may indicate the use of sand for smoothing the surface or cleaning (*ibid*.). The tentative interpretation of this small fragment highlights the possibility that some other fragments of whalebone, not an uncommon find on Viking settlement sites, may not have been recognised as deriving from plaques.

The Scar whalebone plaque was only the third example to be discovered in Scotland, and is by far the finest; but a further two fragmentary plaques have been found since then. In 1992, on a beach at Berneray, North Uist, in the Western Isles, a young girl found a badly worn piece of carved whalebone identified as part of the animal head terminal from a plaque of indifferent quality (Batey 1994–5, 109–11, fig. 1). The terminal fragment seems to have been broken off and then re-worked in antiquity. In 1995, several small fragments of whalebone, probably from a further plaque, decorated with parallel incised lines around the edge, were recovered from excavations of a Viking Age settlement at Bornish, South Uist (Sharples, Webster & Parker Pearson 1995).

A fragment of whalebone discovered in 1963 in a rich female inhumation grave at Westness, Rousay, Orkney (Crawford 1987, 120, fig. 33; Chapter 7), always used to be described as a plaque fragment, but has recently been re-identified as part of a rubbing bone—also a textile implement, used in weaving to smooth down the web as it is woven (Caroline Paterson, personal communication; Anderson 1870–2, 560–1).

It should also be noted here that some eleven glass linen smoothers have been found in Scotland, some as stray finds (e.g. one from Perth: NMS IL 364); some from archaeological sites (e.g. Howe, Stromness, Orkney: Marwick 1927–8, 121–2; probably incorrectly reported as from a grave by Grieg (1940, 80–1)); and at least one from a grave (Ballinaby, Islay: Anderson 1880, 63–4). Not all such finds must be Viking: as mentioned above, there is

53 facing (a). This very fine whalebone plaque from Grytøy, Trondenes, Norway, is as well preserved as that from Scar. Until the Scar plaque was discovered, this was considered to be the finest Viking plaque anywhere in the Viking world. Copyright Historisk Museum, Bergen Universitetet.
(b). A carved whalebone plaque from Kvæfjord, Troms, Norway, provides perhaps the closest parallel for the ornament of the Scar plaque. Copyright Tromsø Museum.
(c). A recently discovered whalebone plaque from Slägstad, Bjarkøy, Troms, decorated with Style E ornament, is likely to be a very early example of this type of artefact. Copyright Tromsø Museum. (d). The animal head bed-posts on this reconstructed bed from the Oseberg ship burial bear similarities with the decoration on some of the whalebone plaques. Copyright Universitetets Oldsaksamling med Vikingskipshuset, Oslo.

some evidence that these implements remained in use for glazing white linen caps in parts of Scotland, Norway and Sweden into the nineteenth century.

Finally, a fragment of a very fine plaque, which closely resembles the famous example from Grytøy, Trondenes, Troms (Fig. 53a) and the newly discovered animal head terminal from Ribe (above), is recorded 'from Ireland' (Bøe 1940, 98, fig. 67). Graham-Campbell (1980, 23) notes that this is more precisely provenanced by an unpublished drawing in the National Library of Ireland (Petrie ms.795) to the Kilmainham/Islandbridge cemetery, near Dublin (see Chapter 8).

Ornament and dating

Perhaps the finest known example of a carved whalebone plaque, prior to the discovery of the Scar plaque, comes from Grytøy, Trondenes, Troms (Fig. 53a). This plaque is so well preserved that the Norwegian archaeologist, Gabriel Gustafson, in a letter to Karl Rygh at the turn of the century, expressed some doubt as to whether it had actually been found in the ground (Petersen 1951, 334–5). Its similarities of ornament with the Scar plaque are obvious. The upper part of the plaque is cut in openwork in the form of a pair of inward-looking animal heads in profile, linked at the ears by means of a double-contoured band. The jaws are open with three large, pointed, interlocking front teeth and four pairs of back teeth. A bar links each head to the main part of the board; below each head is incised a pair of concentric circles which break the contour line, just as the tongues of the Scar animals break the contour line on the Scar plaque.

The Grytøy plaque is a typical example of the ornament of whalebone plaques. It is notable that several other plaques are extremely similar (the fragment from Ireland: Bøe 1940, fig. 67; one recently sold in London; and one of the new Ribe fragments, amongst others), suggesting that there may have been a common prototype, or that the design was transmitted by copying from plaque to plaque. Certainly, very few of these similarly ornamented plaques were executed to such a high standard as the Grytøy plaque, indicating that more than one craftsman was active in their production. One of the two Norwegian plaques in the British Museum (not in Petersen's 1951 list), from a barrow excavated in 1886 by Alfred Cocks at Lilleberge, Namdalen, Nord-Trøndelag (British Museum no. 91,10–21,67), is a good example of a much less accomplished plaque; nonetheless, its maker clearly had the same design intentions as the makers of the Grytøy (and Scar) plaques. Even this example is relatively sophisticated compared with many others (e.g. Vikestad, Nærø, Nord-Trøndelag: Rygh 1885, R449; and Ommestad, Hof, Vestfold: Oslo Museum no. C22536p) which are clearly the products of much less skilled craftsmen.

Although inward-looking animal heads are most common, outward-looking animal heads also occur, as on the well-known Birka plaque (Fig. 52a) and on a plaque from Sommarøy, Lenvik, Troms (Sjøvold 1974, 256). The plaque from Loppasanden, Loppa, Finnmark (Fig. 52c) is an unusual example in having backward-looking quadrupeds rather than a pair of animal heads, although it is paralleled by an unfinished example from Enge, Somna, Helgeland (Sjøvold 1974, 5–6, 256). The unfinished plaque from Ely, Cambridgeshire (Fig. 52d) is another unusual variant with a projection at the top for a handle, and a design comprising almost no openwork, lightly incised, 'sketched' ?animal ornament, and irregularly positioned, double ring-and-dot motifs.

Perhaps the closest parallel for the ornament of the Scar plaque itself occurs on an elegant plaque (Fig. 53b) acquired by Tromsø Museum in 1970 (Gerd Stamsø Munch, personal communication), which was found in a farm mound in Kvæfjord, near Harstad, Troms, an area with a particular concentration of finds of this type. This plaque is smaller than usual (188mm maximum length; 133mm maximum width). Like the Scar plaque, it has the double ring-and-dot motif over the necks of the animals; collars separate the animal heads from the necks; and a band of geometric key-pattern occurs along the edges of the board (although only at top and bottom in this case). However, despite its elegance, the style, proportions and execution of the Kvæfjord plaque are all somewhat less accomplished than those of the Scar plaque. The two plaques are most unlikely to be by the same hand; but given their similarities, the possibility of a common prototype again suggests itself.

The double ring-and-dot motif is a common feature of the plaques. However, on the Scar plaque, the motif is used with restraint and to great effect; on other plaques, more often than not its use is more profuse and less disciplined (e.g. Meløy, Nordland: Petersen 1951, 331, fig. 179; Gåre, Kvæfjord, Troms: *ibid.,* fig. 182; Hjulsta, Norra Spånga, Uppland: Biuw 1992, 155, fig. 114; Vik, Buksnes, Lofoten-Vesterålen: Sjøvold 1974, Pl. 74; and King's Cross Point, Arran). Double and single ring-and-dot motifs are also found on other types of whalebone artefact, such as line winders (e.g. Graham-Campbell 1980, 12, no. 15). Other small circular ornaments sometimes occur on plaques, as at Grytøy, Trondenes, Troms (Fig. 53a). The concept of a geometric pattern along one or more edges of the plaque is also common, varying in complexity from a single incised line as on the Saevar Howe, Birsay plaque, through to use of the double ring-and-dot ornament along the edges of the Sigtuna, Uppland plaque (Fig. 52b), to the controlled key-pattern along the edges of the Scar plaque, or the rounded fret-pattern in a band along the base of the Grytøy plaque (Fig. 53a).

The animal ornament is pre-eminent on almost every plaque. It is distinguished in the repertoire of early Viking art by being relatively simple and two-dimensional, an aspect at least partly dictated by the functional shape and flatness of the object. The closest parallels on other types of artefact occur on similarly 'flat' objects, such as the wooden bed-posts and tent-posts from the Oseberg and Gokstad ship burials (Fig. 53d). Both of these crucially important burials, each containing individuals of high social class, are now dated by dendrochronology: Oseberg to the summer of AD 834 and Gokstad to AD 900–905 (Bonde & Christensen 1993, 575–83). The usual *caveat* must be entered even in the face of such precise datings, since many of the Oseberg and Gokstad artefacts were clearly of some antiquity when buried. The animals on the Gokstad bed-posts (Fig.53d) are similar in concept to the Scar plaque animal heads, but are more elaborate and ornate;

the differences may at least partly be accounted for by the different media, wood being an easier and more familiar medium to carve than whalebone.

Gjessing (1939, 43) proposed that the animal heads on carved whalebone plaques are a variation developed from pre-Viking art of Salin's Style II, a primarily seventh-century Germanic style in which the motif of a stylised horse was not uncommon. Petersen (1951, 337) suggested that three 'defective' Norwegian plaques (all from Overhalla, Nord-Trøndelag) could date from the pre-Viking period on stylistic grounds, but concluded (as did Sjøvold 1974, 254) that this artefact type dates from the beginning of the Viking period, then thought to be around AD 800. Arwidsson (1984, 202) accepted a ninth century date for the two Birka plaques in line with Petersen's general dating for the Norwegian examples. Recently, however, an earlier, very fine, almost complete plaque was discovered in a grave at Slägstad, Bjarkøy, Troms, in the far north of Norway (Fig. 53c). Its ornament is different from most plaques; this type of decoration, known as Style E, is normally dated to the period immediately before the Vikings, or to the very beginning of the Viking Age, in the second half of the eighth century.

Carved whalebone plaques, therefore, generally date to the early Viking period, and most date from the late eighth to the second half of the ninth century (Graham-Campbell 1980, 22–3; FVTC 1992, 242, no. 53). The two newly discovered fragmentary plaques from Ribe, Denmark, recovered from excavated levels tentatively ascribed to the third quarter of the eighth century and the first half of the ninth century respectively (Claus Fevejle, personal communication; and above), corroborate this view. However, with Viking culture now attested in Ribe from around AD 750 (Jensen 1987, 180–2), and in Birka, Sweden, from at least the second half of the eighth century (Björn Ambrosiani, personal communication), and with the recent discovery of a Style E plaque in Troms, it is possible that further earlier examples may be recovered in due course.

Summary

Of the approximately sixty carved whalebone plaques known from the Viking world (Appendix 4), the Scar plaque is one of the finest. Only the Grytøy and Slägstad, both Troms, plaques come close to its craftsmanship in terms of both the style and the medium. The plaque was probably valued more as a symbolic and decorative object than as a functional piece of equipment. The Scar plaque was almost certainly made in Norway, probably northern Norway, sometime between the second half of the eighth century and the second half of the ninth century. It was brought to Orkney, probably not as a traded artefact but as one of the personal possessions of its Scandinavian woman owner.

THE COMB

Michél Carlsson (incorporating comments by Andrea Smith; with conservation by Amanda Clydesdale)

The comb associated with the woman was found as over a dozen fragments

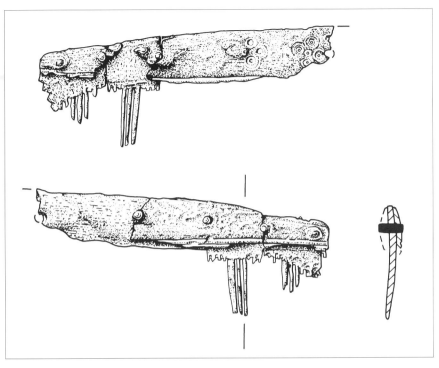

54. The woman's comb was very poorly preserved, even after conservation.

(together forming around 50% of the comb) scattered over the central area of her body, with one of the larger fragments recovered from just above hip level. It was in much worse condition that the man's comb: the outer surfaces of the side-plates were severely pitted and abraded; only one fragment (of one end of the comb) survived with all three sections still riveted together; and hardly any of the teeth had remained attached to the tooth-plates. It is likely that it became badly damaged in the few years after burial, when it lay in the bottom of the boat in acidic conditions as the bodies decomposed. The upper parts of the tooth-plates, which would have been protected while the

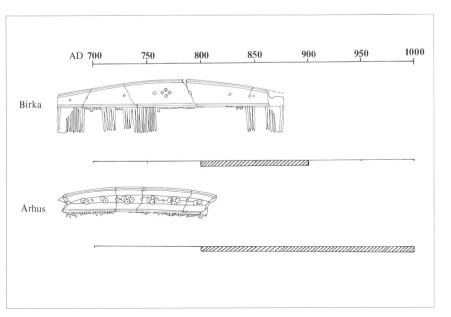

55. Comparative combs from Århus and Birka showing approximate date ranges.

comb was still intact, are generally in very good condition. This suggests that the damage to the surface of the side-plates occurred while the comb was intact, and that by the time it became broken up into fragments, conditions in the grave had 'improved' (i.e. the sediments had re-calcified), so that the tooth-plates did not become damaged in the same way. One advantage of the fragmentary nature of the comb is that it makes identification of the material easier; the pattern of cancellous tissue on the back of the side-plates is almost certainly that of antler.

The comb appears originally to have been some 20–24cm long, and ornamented with a double line border along the lower side-plate edge, and probably also along the upper edge. In the centre of the side-plate is an ornament consisting of one dot surrounded by four ring-and-dots; there are the vestiges of a similar group of ring-and-dots immediately to the left of this. The poor condition of the surfaces of the side-plates mean that there may well have been additional ornament on this comb which is now lost.

This comb, like the man's (see Chapter 6), falls into Ambrosiani's Type A2 (1981, 62f), and the ring-and-dot decoration has a number of parallels. From Århus in Denmark, a Type A2 comb found in layers dated to AD 800–1000 was recovered (Andersen *et al* 1971, 144f). This comb has double lines following the edges of the side-plate and the middle of the side-plate is marked by a plano-convex field. Within the field, on either outer edge, is a group of paired ring-and-dots. The centre of the field is ornamented with three groups of four ring-and-dots which are applied in the same way as on the comb from Scar, though without the central dot. Similarly decorated combs have also been found in Birka; as mentioned above, Type A2 combs from Birka are commonly dated to the ninth century (Ambrosiani 1981, 27, fig. 10).

Two graves excavated in Uppland, central Sweden, contained combs with similar decoration, except that they have only a single line along the edges of the plate. These can be dated to the second half of the eighth century (Petré 1984, 347f; Elfstrand & Fernholm 1986, 16, fig. 8). Double-line borders along the plate edges, as seen on both the man's and the woman's combs from Scar, do not occur on this type of comb before the end of the eighth century (Petré 1984, 70). There are three finds of combs with similar ornamentation and double line borders which could be dated to c.AD 775–850: from Skåne in southern Sweden, Ribe in Denmark and Dorestad in the Netherlands (Stjernqvist 1951, 96, fig. 449; Roes 1965, fig. 208; the Ribe comb is not published). This type of decoration occasionally also occurs on tenth century combs, such as two examples from Staraja Ladoga (Davidan 1992, 37, 39, Abb. 14:63, 15:64).

Clearly, this style of comb decoration is found from the second half of the eighth until well into the ninth century, although the type of comb itself seems to be most frequent in the first half of the ninth century. This type of decoration is fairly uncommon in Scotland, and in Britain as a whole, and may indicate either that these combs are significantly earlier than many others from burials and settlements in Scotland, or that the people from Scar had contacts with parts of eastern Sweden and the Baltic which many of their contemporaries in Scotland did not.

THE SICKLE

Andrea Smith (with conservation by Kim Nissan)

The sickle was found in what was presumed to have been the chest region of the woman's body, with the handle partially overlying the equal-armed brooch. During conservation it was noted that the iron of the sickle was in slightly better condition than much of the other ironwork from the site,

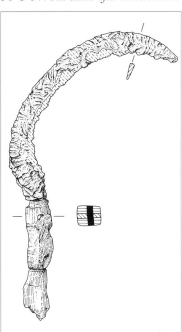

56 & 57. The sickle after conservation.

which, together with the survival of the wooden handle, indicated that it had lain in a wet or waterlogged area of the boat.

The sickle is relatively small, measuring 130mm across the chord, with the surviving part of the handle measuring 75mm in length and 20mm wide by 20mm thick. Even although it is relatively well preserved for Scar, the blade is still thin and fragile, with a width of 14mm on the bow and 25mm near the tang, and is only 4mm thick. A band of mineralised textile remains was found to run along the inner edge of the blade for almost the whole length; this tabby weave textile was probably part of the woman's clothing with which the sickle blade was in contact (see Appendix 2). X-ray showed that it had a tapering blunt-ended tang, with a single rivet-hole holding it in the wooden handle.

The Scar find is rather smaller than other sickles recovered from Viking graves in Scotland, which range from 190–220mm across the bow. It was suggested that the Kneep (Cnip) sickle (at 220mm one of the largest found) would have been too small and fragile to have been effective in larger scale crop-gathering (Welander, Batey & Cowie 1987, 163), although it did appear to have had a case-hardened cutting edge. However, a discussion of the use of sickles for cereal harvesting in an agricultural manual makes it clear that size is not important; what is important is that the sickle is kept sharp, that the curvature is right, and that the size and weight of the sickle are matched to the size and strength of the person using it, so that they would not tire quickly (Stephens 1850, 330–1). At harvest-time everyone would be expected to help, even the smallest children and the elders of the household, male and female.

Sickles have been recovered from the graves of Viking men and women in Scotland, and although it is difficult to assess true numbers from existing records, there appear to be a greater number from female graves than from male. Sickles were recovered from female graves at Gurness, Orkney (Robertson 1969, 290), at Kneep (Cnip), Lewis (Welander, Batey & Cowie 1987, 151–2, 158–9), at Cruach Mhor, Islay (Gordon 1990, 155–6), and at Pierowall, Westray (Grieg 1940, 96) and Westness, Rousay (Crawford 1987, 120), both in Orkney. In the first two graves the sickle is also recorded as having lain on the body, in the area of the torso: a similar placing to the Scar sickle. Two sickles are recorded from male graves, at Reay, Caithness (Edwards 1927, 203), and from Eigg (Grave 2) (Grieg 1940, 68).

This preponderance of sickles in women's graves in Scotland may be significant in the light of Petersen's observations on the distribution of sickles in Norwegian graves (1951, 515–6). He noted that, taking the country as a whole, sickles were found in three to four times as many male as female graves, but, in the western part of Norway, more women had sickles than in the east. In Norway, sickles are the most numerous group among the agricultural implements found in graves (c. 900 in all), with the largest number found in the west, in Oppland and Vestfold (*ibid.*), and with the overall numbers decreasing towards the north of the country, where the cooler climate renders cereal growing impossible (Sjøvold 1974, 297). Petersen (1951, 516) identified a typological progression from curved broad-bladed sickles with an unperforated tang (the tang was bent around the handle to secure it), some of which may date back to the Migration Period, to a type with a tapering tang and single nail-hole, still with a fairly broad, curved blade. Later sickles are straighter, with a shorter tang, sometimes pinched in on one inner edge. Saw teeth become much more common in the later, straighter sickles; curving sickles rarely having teeth. Petersen again noted an east/west divide; the saw-toothed sickles are an eastern type, the curved ones being a western type and older. The Scar sickle most closely resembles the older, western type, with curved blade and perforated tapering tang; this type is most common in Oppland and Buskerud.

THE WEAVING BATTEN

Andrea Smith (with conservation by Kim Nissan)

The weaving batten was found close to the right side of the woman's body, with one end level with the equal-armed brooch, and the other end level with the top of the right femur. Weaving battens, sometimes called weaving 'swords', are an implement used to beat the weft upwards into the warp on an upright warp-weighted loom.

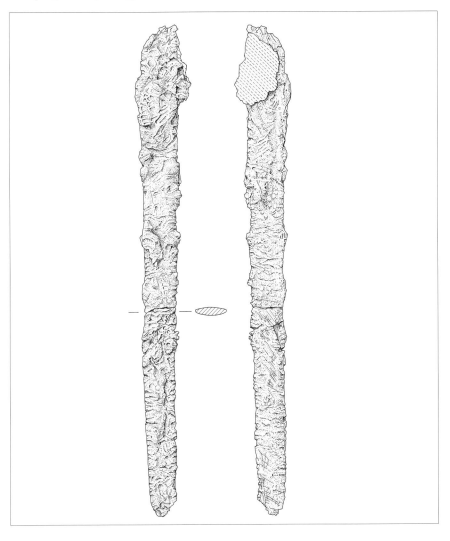

58. The weaving batten after conservation.

The batten consists of a tapering bar of iron 365mm in length, with a maximum width of 30mm, and maximum thickness of 13mm. The cross-section is irregular due to corrosion, but appears to be thicker in the centre than at the edges. During conservation it was noted that there was a line down the centre of the object which suggests that it may have been made from a folded-over length of metal. The wider end appeared to have been broken across a single central hole, possibly the remains of a riveted tang, or the remains of a repair or shortening of a damaged object.

The distribution of weaving battens in Scottish graves has recently been discussed by Gordon (1990, 153), who notes that while they are a common find in Viking Age women's graves in Scandinavia, particularly Norway, they appear until now to have been relatively rare in Scotland. She argues that this apparent rarity is, however, probably due to lack of recognition, as many of these items have been wrongly identified as weapons, the socketed handle and attached blade fragment having been mistaken for a socketed spear head. Four socketed iron weaving battens have been found in Viking graves in Scotland: two from Westness, Rousay, Orkney; one from Cruach Mhor, Islay; and one from Ardvonrig, Barra. These are all considerably longer than the Scar example (365mm); the Barra batten has a blade 84cm in length, and one of the Westness examples has a blade 60cm long, plus a handle 17cm long. The other examples are too fragmentary for any measurement. There is also a reference to 'swords made of the bone of a large fish' from the Westray graves which are presumably weaving battens (Barry 1805, 206).

The batten was one of the more common textile implements found in Norwegian graves, with over 280 examples (Petersen 1951, 522), with an average length of 70–80cm. While all the Scottish examples identified so far have socketed handles, Petersen noted that a very small proportion (fifteen) of the Norwegian battens had a pinned handle, similar to the Scar find. Weaving battens made of whalebone are also found in Norway (a total of 72), usually from the northern areas; in southern areas of the country, iron is the predominant material (Sjøvold 1974, 249).

At 35cm the Scar blade is considerably shorter than the norm; there are a number of possible explanations for this. The narrower end appears to be a shaped end, and not a break, while the wider end is broken across a rivet hole. If it is presumed that the rivet had been used to attach the handle, it is odd that the wooden handle has not survived in the same way as the sickle handle has. The batten may therefore have been broken, and lost its handle before it was deposited in the grave. This would also imply that the batten had been in use at the shorter length. Alternatively, the rivet hole could be interpreted not as a handle attachment, but as a repair to the blade after it had been broken during use, although this means that part of it is still missing, if a section of blade (and handle) had been riveted back on. There has been significant post-depositional disturbance in this part of the boat, but the remaining part of the weaving batten appears relatively undisturbed in its relationship to the line of the woman's body. It seems more probable that the weaving batten had been placed in the grave incomplete, than that either a handle or replacement blade fragment has been subsequently lost.

The textiles

Thea Gabra-Sanders

There were a number of areas of mineralised textile on the weaving batten, which represent several different pieces of textile with which the batten had been in contact, possibly a combination of the woman's clothing and grave furnishings such as covers or hangings (see Appendix 2).

On side A of the weaving batten is a red-brown mineralised textile fragment in tabby weave. Most of this side is covered with various fragments of yarn. Attached to the top on side B is a textile fragment with a self-patterned tabby weave. It is a combination of five-span floats with tabby weave interlacing forming a diagonal pattern. It is not possible to establish if it is a warp- or a weft-float patterned textile. Warp-floated patterned fabrics have been found in a number of north European graves of the Merovingian Period (Bender Jørgensen 1992, 145). Also on this side are three areas of mineralised reddish-dark-brown Z-spun yarn which are lying diagonally and are probably part of a different textile.

59. The weaving batten had a number of areas of mineralised textile remains on it, representing several different textiles, probably a combination of the woman's clothing and grave furnishings. Here we see a self-patterned tabby weave on side B.

THE SHEARS

Andrea Smith (with conservation by Kim Nissan)

The shears were found lying up against the side of the boat to the right of the woman's body, on about the same relative line as the sickle. Attached to the shears by corrosion products were a spindle whorl and various mineralised textile and wood fragments, and around the area of the shears were spread a number of iron band fragments and nails, also with mineralised wood attached, which are believed to represent the remains of a maplewood box (see below) in which the shears and whorl had been placed.

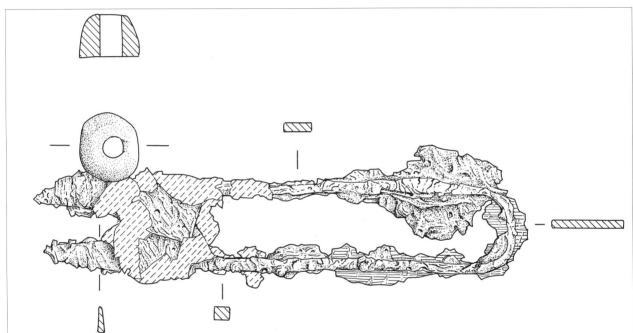

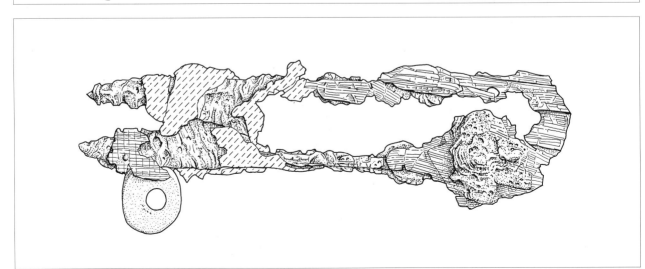

The shears are 210mm in length, of plain design with gradually tapering arms and short blades (70mm), with a pronounced angular heel. They appear to have been wholly or partly wrapped in cloth, with most of the mineralised textile remains around the blades and lower handles (see Appendix 2).

Shears are the second most common textile implement (after spindle whorls) found in Viking period women's graves (Sjøvold 1974, 314). At Birka shears were present in the majority of graves identified as female, usually placed below and to the right of the pair of oval brooches, and often accompanied by a knife and needle case. These objects sometimes appeared to have been suspended either from the right hand oval brooch or from a belt on the right side. The small number of shears placed on the left may correspond to a small number of left-handers. Shears in a box are not unknown; at Fyrkat Grave 4 (Roesdahl 1977, 97) a pair of tinned iron shears nestled inside a fitted case of poplar or willow wood within a chest of oak with a complex locking mechanism. At Birka, where small chests and caskets accompanied a number of female burials, one box contained a pair of shears and a needle case (Arwidsson 1989, 117, Bj 585).

It is likely that most of the relatively small examples which have come from women's graves were used as scissors, possibly primarily in garment making, but with many other domestic uses. Shears used in sheep clipping or in trimming the nap on woollen cloth generally have blades with a much longer cutting edge. Typologically, the Scar shears belong to the simplest, most basic type, and also the oldest: U-shaped with flattened arms. Later types have expanded, rounded heads with added loops and knops, and the arms have a rounded cross-section (Petersen 1951, 523).

The textiles

Thea Gabra-Sanders

Various folded and crumpled mineralised brown textile fragments are found around the blades and handles of the shears, but there appears to be a discrepancy in the thread-count which may be due to the fact that the spring of the blades had pulled the fabric and stretched it.

THE NEEDLE TIDY

Andrea Smith (with conservation by Amanda Clydesdale)

The needle tidy was found with several other objects immediately to the north-east of the blade end of the shears, and consists of wood and other organic remains preserved within iron corrosion products. The object appears to be a wooden cylinder or tube wound around with an S-plied yarn/string made of ? fibre (see Appendix 2). The thread is either wool or a plant fibre. One end is wider and appears to have originally been rounded, and in cross-section the object is triangular. An X-ray of the object shows that the bottom, wider part (8mm long) is solid, but that the remainder is hollow, with at least one denser thin region within the hollow, probably an iron needle. At the upper, narrower end, which appears to be broken, two

60 & 61. (facing) The shears after conservation, with the talc spindle whorl attached to them by corrosion products. The drawings below the photo show both sides.

| | 20mm |

62. The needle tidy was only identified in the laboratory after an X-ray and conservation. X-rays are routinely taken of metal artefacts and are a valuable guide for conservators and specialists.

thin broken-off iron stumps can be seen, both with thread wrapped around the top, the fibres of which are very similar to that wound around the outside. The interpretation is that this is a wooden needle case or needle tidy, containing at least two iron needles, each with thread wrapped around, either from the last use or to secure them more firmly within the case. Examples of tubular bone needle cases (often of goose bone) have been found at several sites: five from the ninth- and tenth-century middens at Jarlshof, Shetland (Hamilton 1956, 123, 146); three from the Brough of Birsay in Orkney (Curle 1982, 61); three from Pool, Sanday, also in Orkney, including one with iron needles inside (Smith in Hunter *et al*, forthcoming); and examples in both bone and metal are known from Kneep (Cnip), Western Isles (Welander, Batey and Cowie 1987); and Birka (Arbman 1940, Taf 167–169). Iron needle cases are also known; but no close parallels have yet been found for the wooden needle tidy from Scar.

THE BOX FITTINGS

Andrea Smith (with conservation by Amanda Clydesdale)

During excavation it became apparent that there had been some kind of wooden and iron construction in the area of the shears, as this object was surrounded by a scatter of iron nails and fragments of iron bands all of which had mineralised wood attached (Fig. 63). Most of the components appeared to have become concentrated on the downhill side (the box was lying in the

63. The box fittings after conservation.

50 mm

steeply angled side of the boat), and some appeared to have been scattered some distance away, possibly due to animal disturbance. In the conservation laboratory it was also noted that the type of nail from this area was completely unlike the boat-rivets, and had different mineralised wood attached. A total of thirty-one fragments which probably formed components of the box were eventually brought together, comprising sections of iron bands, all with mineralised wood on one side, some with mineralised textile remains on the other side, and small round-headed nails with mineralised wood attached. An object which may have formed part of a sliding bar closing mechanism was also found.

The putative components of the box consist of the following:

13 iron band fragments
15 iron nails, round-headed, and a small staple
1 possible lock component

A complete catalogue of these fragments is included in Appendix 1.

Iron bands

The iron band fragments were, with one exception (Find 120), fairly uniform in width, between 20 and 25mm. The condition of the iron makes it difficult to tell whether the edges represent the original length. The maximum length, represented by fragments 153/155, and by 144, appears to be 70–100mm. In those fragments whose long axis can be identified with certainty, the wood grain runs at right angles to it, and the corrosion drips on 153 indicate that after deposition the piece had been positioned with its long axis oriented horizontally. Most of the pieces have nail stumps or scars on the underside, with a spacing of 40–50mm between nails. There are two fragments of angled bands (Finds 102 & 146B), probably representing corner or edge bindings.

Fragment 120 is different from the others: larger at 28 by 57mm, and with wood grain running parallel to the long axis. The piece had probably originally been larger, as the edges are uneven and appear broken. There is also a break in the wood grain which may represent a crack or break in the wood. It is possible that, if this did belong to the box, it may have formed part of a lock plate or similar fitting larger than the binding straps. This fragment, along with some others, had mineralised textile fragments on the outer surface. These have been studied by Gabra-Sanders (below; Appendix 2) and appear to represent several different fabrics: a brocaded textile on 120, a ribbed effect repp weave on Find 153, and 2/1 twill on 161 and 204.

The nails

There were a total of fifteen individual nails complete with heads. The heads were generally round and 10mm in diameter. The shanks, as is often the case with hand-made nails, were not uniform in section, and varied from square-sectioned to rounded. The shanks were generally incomplete, with an average length of 20mm, and a maximum length of 35mm. Most of the nails had mineralised wood preserved under the head and on the shank in a distinctive pattern, a 4–5mm thickness of wood under the head with the grain running parallel to the plane of the head, and with wood preserved on the shank with the grain running parallel to the long axis of the shank, that is, at right angles to that under the head. It was suggested in the conservation report that this pattern was the result of a technique using a small wooden dowel inserted into the wood, into which the nail was hammered, but it is

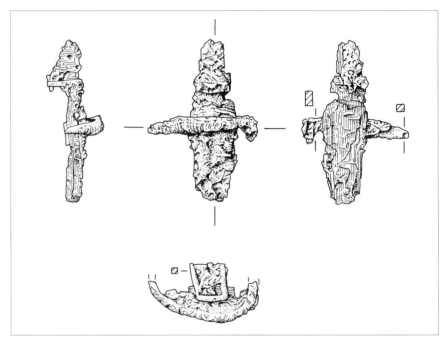

64. The possible lock component after conservation.

hard to see how this would produce the distinctive pattern. It is more likely that these nails were used at the joined edges of the box, and that the nail has penetrated through one thin layer of wood and into a thicker layer, as happens at a lapped joint.

Possible lock component

Amongst the group of six objects numbered as Find 146 was a tapering or shouldered iron bar, crossed at right angles by two staple-like objects, one large and one small. The underside of the bar bore the customary mineralised wood remains, unusually for the bands, with the grain running along the long axis of the object. This may have formed the end of a fastening mechanism similar to that illustrated in (Fig. 105). This is the part which would have fitted inside the box; there would have been two slots cut through the box wall, one through which the hasp would fit, and one through which a handle, or handle and key, would be placed. The mechanism may simply have been slid back and forth using a permanently fixed handle without a key, or may have been similar to that illustrated, with a leaf spring lock operated with a key. This interpretation assumes that the remains of the hasp and the handle are missing.

65. Detail of an iron band (fragment 120) from the box, after conservation. On its outer surface is a mineralised brocaded textile fragment, perhaps from a pillow or cover.

The textiles

Thea Gabra-Sanders

Among the textiles on the surviving remains of the box is a brocaded textile (Find 120) which suggests that it could have been from a pillow or cover. Brocaded textiles in wool and ? linen were found among the textiles from Birka, Sweden (Geijer 1938, 56) and from seventh- to tenth-century graves at the Viking trading centre at Hedeby in Sleswig (Hägg 1991, 218–220). Another fragment (Find 153) has a textile with a ribbed effect. Ribbed textiles are known from Lagore crannog in Ireland (Hencken 1950, 211–12); a boat burial at Balladoole, Isle of Man (Bersu & Wilson 1966, 44); Birka, Sweden (Geijer 1938, 14, 19); a tenth-century female Viking burial from Kneep (Cnip), Isle of Lewis (Welander, Batey & Cowie 1987, 166); and from the tenth-century male boat burial at Gokstad in Norway (Ingstad 1988, 134). An iron band fragment with nail stump (Find 204) is covered with two layers of mineralised textile. At one corner, where the top layer is broken away, a second fine textile—a 2/1 twill weave—is exposed. Both layers may be from the same textile (a folded textile) but could also be two different textiles.

Discussion

Reconstruction

Reconstruction of the box was difficult: the components have been disturbed and scattered by animal activity, and some appear to be missing. There are no traces of anything that might represent hinges, or of any external fastening such as a hasp, and the only fragment of a possible locking or fastening device is incomplete. The surviving remains indicate that the box was made of maple (*Acer sp*), with finely smoothed and finished surfaces, that it was lap-jointed and fixed with iron nails, and that it had iron bands nailed onto the outside. The orientation and positioning of the bands can only be determined in relation to that of the wood grain. The position of some objects which may still have been *in situ* around the shears suggests that the box was probably between 25 and 30cm long, and possibly as little as 10–15cm wide. The height is impossible to estimate. The box contained a pair of iron shears, a steatite spindle whorl and possibly a sandstone spindle whorl, and a needle tidy or small tool handle. The shears had been wrapped in cloth, and there were traces of at least three different types of fabric on iron bands and nails from the outside of the box. These may have been in contact with parts of the woman's clothing or with grave furnishings.

Maplewood

In the Viking Age, maple was principally restricted to the mountains of central Europe, where it was widespread along the Alps, Carpathians and associated ranges (Huntly & Birks 1983, 90–92, 103, fig. 5.26). It occurred only sparsely in northern Europe, apart from one area in northern Germany, just south of the Jutland peninsula, close to the Viking Age entrepôt at Hedeby. The maple used to make the Scar box most probably came from this north German source. Indeed, it is a reasonable guess that this box, made of a relatively exotic wood rarely found in Scandinavia, might have passed through Hedeby as a traded artefact.

Parallels

Finds of metal fittings from chests and caskets are not uncommon in women's graves of this period in Scandinavia, but have not yet been widely recognised in Scotland, possibly because the fragile and rather unprepossessing remains are particularly vulnerable to poor-quality excavation. An iron casket hasp and possible iron casket fittings (with textile casts) are recorded from a woman's grave at King's Cross Point, on Arran (Grieg 1940, 26). More recently, during excavation of a woman's grave at Peel, on the Isle of Man, an area of organic remains over the upper right chest area was noted and tentatively identified as the remains of a work-box, with two needles (Crawford 1987, 122). Petersen records Norwegian grave finds of iron box fittings, mostly dating to the later part of the pagan Viking period (1951, 531), but also including the finding of the back and lock of a casket, and three nearly complete chests from the Oseberg ship. The cemetery at Birka produced many graves with chests, boxes and caskets of a variety of shapes and sizes, many sufficiently complete to allow reconstructions (Arwidsson & Thorberg 1989). Their Groups A and B (most similar to the Scar find) consisted of plain rectangular boxes (*schachteln* defined as less than 25cm long) fitted with iron bands and nails, differentiated by the presence of a simple hasp and staple closure in Group A, possibly with padlock, and by the presence of a key-operated locking mechanism in Group B. In one of the Group B boxes (*ibid.* 117, Bj 585) were iron shears, a knife and sheath, and an iron needle case, although it seems that here most of the boxes were used to hold more delicate and precious things such as glass vessels and jewellery. A richly furnished woman's grave at one of the Danish Viking Age 'fortresses' (Roesdahl 1977, 97) produced a pair of tinned iron shears nestled inside a fitted case of poplar/willow and a spindle whorl, within an oaken chest with a lock. These, however, are quite late in date, thought to be from the latter part of the tenth century, but nevertheless the author notes that grave goods in tenth-century Denmark conformed to a well-recognised norm in well-to-do circles, and that 'a box with various small objects (such as sewing materials) was almost standard equipment as far as women were concerned...' (*ibid.* 190).

THE SPINDLE WHORLS

Andrea Smith

Two stone spindle whorls were recovered from the Scar boat burial: one attached to the shears by iron corrosion products, and a second, red sandstone whorl found 30cm east of the box remains, close to one end of the weaving batten.

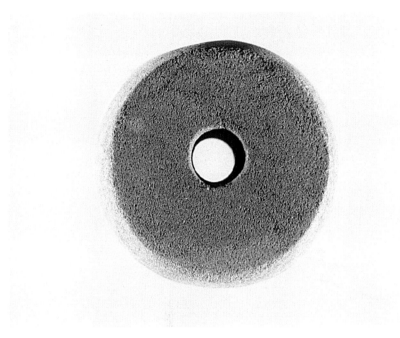

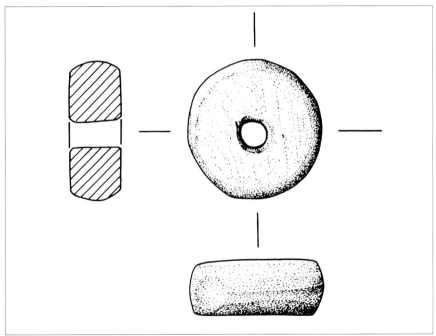

The whorl attached to the shears is slightly domed with a flattened top, a diameter of 24mm, height of 18mm, and a perforation 8mm in diameter. It was not possible to weigh the whorl because of its attachment to the shears. Petrological examination of the whorl by Dianne Dixon revealed it to have been made from a type of talc rock composed entirely of talc and chlorite, with unusually well-formed talc crystals, which are formed and preserved only under very rare conditions at the end of the metamorphic phase. Such rocks are not known in Shetland, the nearest source of talc rocks, or elsewhere in Scotland, and it is therefore probable that the whorl was made from Scandinavian rock, and brought over from Norway.

The second whorl is of flattened cross-section, and considerably larger, with a diameter of 41mm, a thickness of 14–16mm, and a perforation 7mm in diameter. The whorl weighs 39.2g, which is at the heavier end of the weight range for spindle whorls. The whorl is of a red sandstone common on Sanday, and may have been made locally. Indeed, this whorl is the only artefact from the Scar grave which is likely to have been manufactured in Orkney rather than in Scandinavia.

Spindle whorls form the largest group of textile implements to be found in graves, and in Norway the custom of placing whorls in graves dates back to the earlier Iron Age (Sjøvold 1974, 313–4). In the Norwegian Viking period soapstone was the favoured material, but the greatest variation in materials was found in the southern regions (*ibid.*). It has yet to be demonstrated that there is any chronological or distributional significance in the various profile types.

The method of spinning, using a distaff, spindle and whorl, is an ancient one. The distaff was a simple cleft stick which held a mass of combed wool and may not have been used in all cases. A length of yarn was teased out from the bundle and twisted around the spindle, another simple stick somewhat smaller than the distaff, up to c. 25cm long. The spindle was then twisted and dropped, with the whorl acting as a flywheel to maintain the momentum of the spinning. This action simultaneously drew out the yarn and put a twist in it, which helped to bind the yarn and strengthen it by keying together the individual fibres. Instead of dropping the spindle, which may cause fine wool to break, it may have been rested on the ground or a convenient surface, thus exploiting the twisting action without placing undue strain on the wool. Spinning is an activity which has been associated with women for many thousands of years, and from the skeletal remains of the woman from Scar it is evident that spinning was a frequent activity. Daphne Lorimer has identified particular changes in the right hand which would be expected in someone engaged in spinning, who habitually kept the fourth and fifth fingers spread, while the first two fingers and thumb were held together. The spread of the fourth and fifth fingers is particularly important when spinning with flax (Lorimer, below).

CHAPTER 6

THE MAN'S EQUIPMENT

THE SWORD AND ITS SCABBARD

Kim Nissan

An iron sword and mineralised organics representing the substantial remains of a scabbard were recovered from the right side of the male skeleton. The sword was identified as of Petersen's type H (see below). The blade is double-sided; the lower guard is plated with alternating bands of silver and brass, and there are remains of a binding strip and a tang. A total length of 980mm of the sword has survived: the upper half of the hilt (pommel, upper guard and

67 & 68. The sword and scabbard after conservation. The drawing (left) shows the location of the different identified materials on both sides of the sword.

Legend:
- iron
- horn
- wood
- silver wire
- fleece
- textile

0
10
20 cms

some of the tang) had been lost to the sea. The scabbard was made of two laths of wood, bound together by textile and lined with a layer of fleece.

The sword was block lifted on site (by Richard Welander), using expanding polyurethane foam. Micro-excavation began shortly after its arrival in the laboratory. Careful removal of the soil and corrosion products under the light microscope allowed the mineralised organic remains to be revealed. Cleaning was mechanical, using a variety of hand tools and the air-abrasive. X-rays were used throughout as a guide to micro-excavation. An initial set of X-rays was taken by Paul Wilthew at the National Museum of Scotland, using an industrial X-ray unit to allow for the large size of the sword. Once micro-excavation commenced, X-rays were taken using the Faxitron machine at Historic Scotland/AOC (Scotland) Ltd.

The iron is very corroded; the blade has completely converted to corrosion products. Before conservation, metal inlay on the lower guard was seated within iron corrosion, and was initially apparent only from the X-rays. One side, and a third of the other side, have now been exposed. The metal inlay is mostly intact, although rather worn in places. There are sheets of plating on the upper and lower faces of the lower guard which are particularly worn. The scabbard remains have totally mineralised. Almost all the wood is intact, with substantial areas of textile and lining.

The sword

The blade

The blade is double-sided and lenticular in cross-section. It measures 840mm in length and is 69mm wide at the hilt end, tapering gently to a pointed tip.

The X-rays were studied for signs of pattern welding, a fuller and any inscriptions, but none were detected. It was thought that some metal core may have remained in the middle section of the blade, where the X-rays showed a slightly denser area of metal. However, a cut through the blade revealed that the iron has completely converted to corrosion products. Therefore, metallographic analysis of the blade (attempted by Dr J McDonnell of Bradford University) was not possible.

Previous metallographic analyses of similar swords suggest that four types of iron were in use between the fifth and eleventh centuries: ferritic iron, phosphoric iron, steel and piled and banded structures (McDonnell 1989, 375). As analysis of the X-rays of the blade showed that the Scar sword was not pattern welded, it can be supposed that the iron was ferritic, phosphoric or steel. The lack of pattern welding is in accordance with a trend observed by Lang and Ager (1989) in their radiographic survey of 142 swords from Anglo-Saxon and Viking periods at the British Museum. Their results show that half of the swords sampled were pattern welded and that the proportion of pattern welded swords rose dramatically after about AD 500 and fell again during the ninth to tenth centuries (1989, 107).

A significant break was noted in the blade; it is only apparent from the X-rays, as the area of the break is covered with scabbard remains. The X-rays show that the broken section has moved within the scabbard (Fig. 69). Mineralisation of the scabbard above and below the area has proceeded and

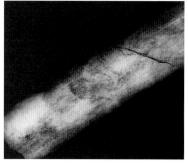

69. The break in the sword blade can only be seen on the X-ray.

does not show any signs of the break in the iron beneath it. Therefore, it can be concluded that the fracture occurred before mineralisation was complete. Rob Janaway's experimental work has shown that mineralisation can be a very rapid process in a burial site (1987, 142). This may indicate that the blade was broken at the time of burial or, less likely, shortly afterwards. A number of bent or broken Viking Age swords have been found, and it seems that blades may have been broken intentionally prior to burial. Coffey and Armstrong (1902, 110) reported that many of the Scandinavian swords found in Kilmainham, Ireland, were broken and concluded that this must have been done at the time of interment. A more recent find is the Viking Age sword from Upper Borough Wall, Bath (Watkins 1991), where the sword blade's corroded edges indicate that it may have been broken before burial. Further examples are quoted by Bersu and Wilson (1966, 88). If the Scar sword was broken before burial, the evidence suggests that the blade was replaced in its scabbard after being broken.

The lower guard

The lower guard consists of a straight bar 88mm long and 22mm high in the middle, tapering slightly to each end. Its surface is slightly keeled and it is elliptical in horizontal section, measuring 25mm at its widest point. There is an oval hole in the middle of the guard where it fits over the tang.

The surface of the guard has been plated with alternating vertical strips of silver and brass. The metals were identified by Phil Clogg (Durham University) using X-Ray Fluorescence Spectroscopy (XRF). The strips are divided in half horizontally by a ridge of iron.

Each strip of brass is slightly wider than the silver; there are five grooves beneath the brass strips and four beneath the silver. The average width of the brass stripes is 2.7mm and the silver, 2.1mm. There is a total of twenty brass and nineteen silver strips across each side of the guard. Vertical hairline cracks can be seen within each strip, and in some areas the raised sections of plating are worn, leaving behind only the metal in the grooves.

The technique used to plate the guard with bands of silver and brass is apparent from the X-rays. The X-rays show fine vertical lines in the iron. These are thin strips of denser metals which fill fine grooves cut into the iron. Initially, the grooves were incised into the iron, probably using a fine chisel. Silver and brass wires have been placed in the grooves and hammered flat onto the iron so that the wire metal spread sideways until it touched to form a seemingly homogenous band. In this way, the softer metal of the plate was forced into the cuts and was attached securely to the iron. It is apparent from the vertical hairline cracks within each band of plating that it is made up of fine wires rather than one sheet of metal. This method of plating is a very common feature of sword hilts of the ninth century. In his extensive survey of Viking Age swords, Petersen (1919, 93) found only three examples of this type of sword without 'stripes'. It is most usual for the whole guard (and pommel) to be covered by the grooves, groups of lines being less typical. In these cases it is likely that just one type of metal was used to plate the guard. It has often been stated that the grooves are decorative; this belief probably stems from examination of swords where the plating has worn away

70. *The lower guard and tang after conservation.*

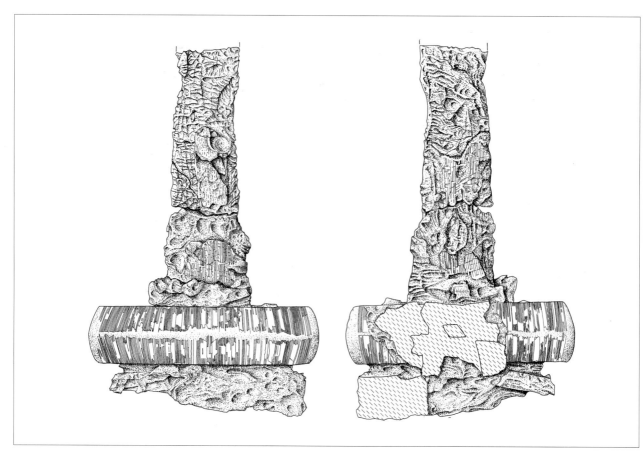

or has not survived burial. The evidence here suggests, however, that the grooves are part of the metal plating process, as described, and not meant to be visible or decorative in themselves.

On contemporaneous parallels, either a single metal, or alternating bands of a white and a yellow metal have been used as plating. The former has been catalogued as tin (Oakeshott 1960, 140) or silver (Petersen 1919, 91; Graham-Campbell 1980, 69) and the latter as copper (Graham-Campbell *op. cit.*), brass (Dunning & Evison 1961, 125) or bronze (Petersen *op. cit.*). None of these descriptions is backed by any form of analysis. The XRF results for the Scar sword confirm that silver and brass were used as plating on Viking Age hilts.

An oval, 1mm-thick sheet of brass (or more precisely, a zinc rich copper with small amounts of tin (see Appendix 3) has been plated onto the upper and lower faces of the lower guard (the sides from which the tang and blade protrude). The sheet is less than 1mm thick. The sheets were fixed using a different method: the guard seems to be pierced by two circular holes which run vertically through it at approximately 10mm from each end. Owing to the corrosion in this area, the diameters of these holes are not known. It can be postulated from these holes that the brass plates were attached by means of two rivets, one inserted through each end of the plate, piercing the hilt vertically. The rivets are not visible; it is very possible that they have corroded away.

Petersen (1919, 92) has noted a few swords with similar plates on the upper and lower sides of the lower guard and states that the metal used is usually bronze, with only one case where silver has been used. Other references to these plates have not been found, although it has been noted that cross-section drawings of hilts often include the two circular holes, possibly indicating the presence of such plating.

Binding strip

Directly above the lower guard is a metal binding strip, generally used on sword hilts to hold the organic grip in place. The strip is made of tin (see Appendix 3) and is approximately 1mm thick and 10mm wide. It is oval, measuring about 50mm by 25mm (measurements estimated from the X-rays).

A small number of binding strips, similar in shape to the one on the Scar sword have been found. Petersen (1919, 93) lists three examples of contemporary swords with a binding strip. All are bronze; one from Vig (Norway) has been decorated with a row of upward- and downward-pointing animal heads.

Wilson (1965, 47–8) presents three ninth-century swords with silver binding strips. The first, a late Anglo-Saxon sword from Fiskerton in Lincolnshire, has three strips, one at each end of the grip and the third in the middle. The second, from Hegge in Nord-Trøndelag (Norway), has two, one at each end of the grip, and the third is a sword with no provenance with one remaining strip at the lower guard end. Whereas all these strips have an incised decoration, the X-rays of the Scar sword do not show any signs of a decoration.

The use of tin for the Scar binding strip is so far unique. Tin is an attractive, malleable metal, although not very durable.

The tang

The tang measures 85mm in length, 60mm of which comprise two fragments broken off from the rest of the hilt. It is 30mm wide and 8mm thick and in cross-section it is oval, with parallel sides. The top end has broken off and was lost along with the pommel. The X-rays did not show any sign of an inscription on the tang.

The grip

It is almost certain from a very small area of mineralised remains on the tang that the Scar sword had a wooden grip. The wood grain runs parallel to the length of the tang. On one side of the grip are the remains of a thin, translucent material thought to be mineralised horn. The shape of the binding strip indicates that the grip was oval in shape.

The missing upper guard and pommel

From the typology of the sword (see below), and from contemporary parallels, it can be assumed that the sword would have had a triangular pommel, fixed by nails or rivets to a narrow, straight upper guard. The upper bar would be fixed over the tang, the top of the tang being clinched over it to hold it in place (Davidson 1962, 53). The pommel and upper guard are likely to have had the same silver and brass plated decoration.

The upper guard and pommel of the Scar sword were lost due to marine erosion of the cliff face at which they were lying. It is interesting to note, however, that several other swords have been found with the pommel and upper guard missing. Examples include a sword found in the River Lark (quoted by Davidson 1962, 53) and two Viking swords catalogued by Bøe (1940, 68). This may suggest that the construction of the hilt was not too secure, easily allowing the pommel to come away from the sword.

Typology

Viking sword hilts developed greatly between the sixth and tenth centuries and have been used to form the basis of a typological distinction between various swords.

Dr Jan Petersen compiled a comprehensive typology of Viking Age swords based on hilts and pommels in 1919. Virtually all Viking sword descriptions since have been based on this typology or on one of its several simplified versions (for examples see Wheeler 1927, 31; Oakeshott 1960).

The keeled surface of the lower guard of the Scar sword, combined with the wide elliptical horizontal section and vertical strips of metal plating, are characteristics of Petersen's Type H (1919, 90), the most common type of Viking sword. It is dated to the period between AD 800 and 950.

The scabbard

Extensive mineralisation of the organic remains on the sword has allowed a good reconstruction of the composition of its scabbard. The scabbard consisted of two thin laths of wood, one on each side of the blade. These were bound together by textile wrapped around the object. The wood was lined with a layer of sheepskin or a similar animal skin.

Mineralisation

Organic material is often preserved from non-waterlogged sites in the form of mineralised remains in the corrosion products of metals. This occurs if the salts produced by corroding metalwork cover the organic material before it is consumed by micro-organisms (Watson 1988, 65). Mineralisation is dependent on two decay rates: the rate of degradation of the organic material, and the rate of corrosion of the metal. The latter must occur before the former in order that the evidence be preserved (Janaway 1987, 134). Inhumation graves create an environment favouring very rapid corrosion of metals (Janaway 1985). Although the Scar burial environment was shell sand and totally alkaline, the soil would have become very acidic during the decomposition of the body, creating an environment aggressive to the metals. Furthermore, decay of the metals would have been encouraged by the well-drained, and therefore well-oxygenated, environment created by the sand. These factors have contributed to the extensive mineralisation of the sword.

Organic materials are preserved by metal salts in one of three ways: coating, replacement, or impregnation (Janaway 1983, 48–49; Keepax 1975; Watson 1988, 65–67). In the first of these processes, metal salts coat the organic material, inhibiting micro-organism activity. This is mainly applicable to copper-alloy corrosion, and therefore not relevant here.

Where replacement occurs, the corrosion products cover the organic material. The original structure then decays, leaving a negative cast of the organic material in the mineral. The interstices often become filled with soil to form a solid matrix. The process of impregnation involves the replacement of the organic material by corrosion products, forming a positive replica. Scanning Electron Microscopy (SEM) of the Scar scabbard remains, carried out by Dr R Janaway at Bradford University, revealed that both replacement and impregnation have occurred in the preservation of the organic material of the scabbard. In some cases, a combination of both processes was observed, a negative cast having been formed and some of the fibre or wood still remaining inside.

The textile remains

Kim Nissan

There are eleven areas of textile on the sword. All the textile remains on the blade are aligned and are convincingly part of the scabbard. An exception is the fragment on the reverse side of the lower guard, which is very similar to

71. Mineralised organic and textile remains on the scabbard show that it was made of two thin laths of ash wood, bound together with linen.

the other textile, but was found to be slightly misaligned and much further up in the corrosion layers. The proximity of the man's arm implies that the textile may be a piece of clothing rather than remains of the scabbard.

In two places, three layers of textile can be seen. In most areas the textile lies directly above the wood, confirming that the wooden layer lies beneath the textile, with the notable exclusion of any leather between.

Sample identification, conducted by Dr R Janaway (Bradford University), was by Scanning Electron Microscopy (SEM). Two samples of textile were removed, one from the reverse side of section B and the other from the reverse side of the guard. The locations of the samples were recorded on a plan and photographed. Both samples were identified as bast fibres.

The most common bast fibre from Scandinavian antiquity is flax, the bast of the linseed plant (Hald 1980, 129), used for the manufacture of linen; it is likely that the scabbard textile is linen. The linen would have served the function of binding the scabbard wood together. It is envisaged that this was achieved in one of two ways: either a continuous piece of textile was bandaged all the way up the scabbard, or smaller bands of textile were tied around certain points of the scabbard. If the latter was the case, the position of the textile remains on the sword suggests that at least two bands were present. The fact that three layers of textile can be seen in two places could imply that it was wrapped around the wood at least three times.

A predecessor of these bands can be seen on seventh-century Anglo-Saxon swords. There are three examples displayed at the British Museum; these swords, from Broomfield, Sutton Hoo and Caplaw, have remains of a wooden scabbard, with the wooden laths bound at the hilt end with a fine woollen tape.

A number of textile remains have been found in Scandinavian Viking Age graves. The majority are tabby woven linen (Welander, Batey & Cowie 1987, 166). A small number of other textile remains from Viking Age scabbards have been published to date. The fibres from three small areas of textile on a sword recovered on the Isle of Man were identified as bast (Cubbon 1982, 455). As with the Scar remains, the fibres on this scabbard were single ply and Z,Z spun. The textile was slightly coarser, however, with a thread count of 12 and 14 threads per cm. The Viking sword from the Upper Borough Walls, Bath (Watkins 1991) has a layer of tabby woven textile covering its wooden laths. Similarly, the Ballateare and Cronk Moar Viking swords (Bersu & Wilson 1966, 52 & 71) have a layer (or two) of textile covering the wood. In the latter three cases, the textile was then covered by leather.

The wood

The scabbard wood from both sides of the sword was identified as *Fraxinus excelsior* (ash) (see Appendix 5). Radially split laths have been used. No obvious joins were visible, so it must be presumed that on each side of the scabbard a single lath was used.

The use of ash for the scabbard offered a lightweight, flexible and durable wooden support for the sword. Ash is a tough deciduous timber, generally used for its strength, attractive grain and its ability to be bent to curved outlines (Edlin 1985, 37).

The actual method of producing two thin, long strips of wood is not apparent from the specimen; the task is achievable with an axe or a froe and requires little more than basic woodworking skills (McCullagh, below).

Scabbard wood identified from a number of Viking and Anglo-Saxon swords demonstrates the variety of species used for this purpose. Scabbard remains from the Viking Age sword found at the Palace of Westminster were identified as oak (Dunning & Evison 1961, 126). The wood from the Skerne Viking sword is willow or poplar (Watson 1993). The following examples are from Anglo-Saxon swords of about the same date: two Saxon swords recovered at a cemetery at Charlton Plantation, near Salisbury, both retained traces of their scabbards in the form of mineralised wood. These were identified by Anne-Maria Bojko (1982, 11); one was found to be alder and the other, poplar. Bojko also examined mineralised wood from the scabbards of three further swords, and all were found to have been constructed from different species. Two samples were from Anglo-Saxon swords from Black Patch cemetery; these were identified as maple (sword SK 22) and either willow or poplar (SK 47). The third sample was from the hilt of a sword from Collingbourne Ducis which was identified as hazel. Scabbard wood from the Anglo-Saxon site of Ozengell in Kent proved to be willow or poplar (Cronyn *et al* 1985, 26).

All the species above are deciduous, or hardwood trees. All are easily split and are reasonably flexible, which are the main essential characteristics for wood for a scabbard. The great variety of species suggests that, as long as the general requirements were met, the actual species used was not particularly important.

The lining

Two samples of the scabbard lining were taken from the reverse of sections B and E for identification by SEM. They were identified as leather with wool fibres: that is to say, an animal skin, possibly sheepskin.

Scabbard linings would provide a secure hold for the sword in its scabbard, while allowing easy withdrawal. The use of an animal skin, with the fleece side facing the blade, would provide lanolin which may have offered the blade some protection against corrosion.

A small number of contemporary parallels of animal skins used as a scabbard lining for Viking swords are known: the sword scabbard from Upper Borough Walls, Bath, has a layer of animal skin next to the blade (Watkins 1991). The Skerne Viking sword scabbard from Hull was also fleece-lined, possibly with goatskin (Watson 1993). Fibres in random association were detected on the Viking Age sword from the Isle of Man, although a definite identification was not possible (Cubbon 1982, 446).

Scabbard fittings

It was established from X-rays and from micro-excavation that the scabbard remains did not include any metal fittings, such as a mount or chape. The position of the sword, high up in relation to the corpse, suggests that the sword was not 'worn' in the grave. Therefore it was not expected that a baldric would be found, nor were traces of one detected.

As metal bindings (a chape in particular) were not found with the sword, it is not certain whether or not the textile alone held the scabbard together. According to Bone (1989, 68), metal fittings are commonly found with swords of the sixth and seventh centuries and are rare from later periods.

Discussion

The wooden laths of the scabbard were held together only with textile binding; no leather cover or scabbard mounts were found. This would have resulted in a poorly bound scabbard which is unlikely to have provided a full, permanent support for the sword.

Leather is the most common covering found on scabbards (see Davidson 1962, 88 for a number of contemporary examples; also Bersu & Wilson 1966, 53 & 71). Leather provides a strong, durable cover for a scabbard as well as an aesthetically pleasing surface which easily lends itself to decoration. Experimental work has shown that wooden scabbards without a leather cover rarely survive for very long when in use (Russell Scott, personal communication). The possibility remains that the Scar scabbard did have a leather cover which has not survived. However, the excellent mineralisation of the textile, and its cleanly preserved surface, makes this option very unlikely. It is especially unlikely, as owing to differential preservation there is a bias for proteinic remains on iron objects (Janaway 1989, 21), so although the leather layer would have been further away from the iron than the textile, some trace would have been expected. There are three published examples of contemporary Viking scabbards composed of a textile layer over the wood, covered by leather: the Ballateare and Cronk Moar Viking scabbards, as described by Bersu and Wilson (1966, 52 & 71), and the Upper Borough Wall scabbard (Watkins 1991).

This evidence may suggests that the Scar 'scabbard' was for storage and/or a support for the sword rather than being a functional scabbard.

THE ARROWHEADS

Kim Nissan, Rod McCullagh & Andrea Smith

As excavated, the sword had an amorphous mass corroded onto it. Once the lump was X-rayed and cleaned in the conservation laboratory, it became clear that the mass consisted of a tightly packed bundle of arrows, with leaf-shaped iron heads and mineralised wooden shafts. The flight ends and most of the shafts of the arrows had not been preserved. Fragments of thin mineralised wood attached to the outer surface of the lump probably represent the remains of a quiver. There was a void down the centre of the bundle, indicating that some organic object had originally lain there.

Description

The whole bundle is approximately 19cm in length, and consists of nine mineralised wooden arrow shafts, with eight iron arrowheads, arranged in a tight bundle around the central object. The shafts are approximately 1cm in

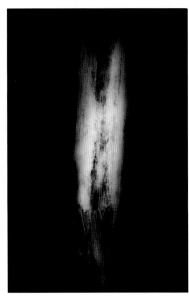

72. In the laboratory, X-rays revealed that this was actually a tightly packed bundle of arrows, with leaf-shaped heads and mineralised wooden shafts, all in the remains of a quiver.

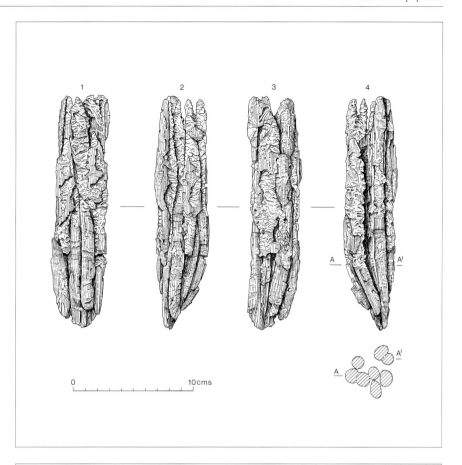

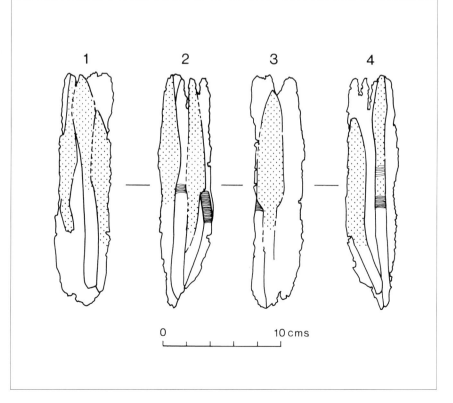

73 & 74. The bundle of arrows after conservation. The drawings show the bundle from different angles (above right) and with the iron arrowheads identified (below right).

diameter, and the iron heads 10–12cm long and 2–3cm wide. The shape of some of the arrows is obscured by corrosion products and by overlying quiver material, so that it is difficult to tell the exact shape of each, but there appears to be some variation within the basic leaf shape. Some have more elongated points, and others appear to be slightly shorter and broader. The arrowheads have tangs which appear on the X-ray to extend into the wooden shaft for at least 2cm, and on three of the arrows mineralised twine can be clearly seen binding the top of the shaft at the junction with the head. The overall diameter of the bundle indicates a diameter for the quiver of 4–5cm.

Mineralised wood identifications

Two fragments from the arrows were examined, both of which could be unambiguously identified as Scots pine (*Pinus sylvestris*). The alignment of the annual growth rings, seen in section to be travelling across the width of the arrow shafts, showed that the shafts had been converted from a larger block of wood. An alternative method of arrow shaft production is the selection of fast-growing, small twiggy branches from trees such as ash (*Fraxinus excelsior*).

Fragments of the putative quiver were unfortunately too thin and too heavily mineralised to permit assignment to a particular species. However, certain characteristics could be observed (the wood was clearly dicotyledonous, and possibly also ring-porous) which indicated that the wood had been a hardwood, and definitely not a conifer, unlike the arrow shafts.

The cylindrical void in the centre of the bundle was also examined, and in some places thin concave sheets of mineralised wood formed a vestigial wall to the void, indicating that there had been an organic object present around which the arrows had been arranged. Samples of the mineralised wood were difficult to obtain because of the fragility of the arrow bundle, and because of the poor preservation of the wood. The mineralised wood also had a very abraded or weathered appearance. The identification was therefore unsuccessful; the wood was certainly different from that of the arrow shafts, and being ring-porous was not from a conifer, but beyond that no greater refinement was possible. The identification to this most general of classes must argue against the lost object having been a bow; European bows are almost invariably made from Yew (*Taxus baccata L*), sometimes with bone or antler splints at the ends. An alternative explanation is that there had been a wooden rod within the quiver which had acted as a spacer.

Discussion

At the time of burial, the quiver, complete with arrows, appears to have been placed alongside the sword, on the man's right hand side, with the end containing the arrowheads pointing towards the man's feet, as it would have been carried in life. The tips of the arrowheads were sited 25cm from the point of the sword, so that, if the arrows had been of average length (60–70cm), the top of the quiver would have been in alignment with the top of the sword. A bow and arrows formed one element of the suite of 'folk-weapons' which a Viking man of any standing would be expected to have, and Norwegian male graves of the Viking period very often contained a bunch of up to a dozen arrows (Sjøvold 1974, 291). This has not been found to be the case so far in Scotland, where the only published occurrence of arrows in a grave is from the lavishly equipped male burial at Kiloran Bay, Colonsay (Grieg 1940, 51). It is, however, rare to have not only the mineralised remains of the arrow shafts preserved, but also traces of a wooden quiver. The void in the centre of the quiver appears not to have been occupied by a bow, but probably by an internal spacing rod; this may have had additional radial spacers attached at the top of the quiver to prevent the flights becoming entangled and damaged. The quiver seems to have been a slender object, less than 5cm in diameter, which held at least nine arrows. The leaf-shaped arrowheads have no barb or additional swelling above the junction with the shaft. A study of Viking-period arrowheads in Sweden (Wegraeus 1973) concluded that this type (A1), with a long symmetrical blade, and no barb or elongated neck between the blade and the tang, belonged to the early Viking period (ninth century), and was a general-purpose arrowhead which was used both in hunting and in warfare. However, as Sjøvold (1974, 291) observed, 'the value of the arrow as a long range weapon was fully realised in the Viking period, not least in fighting at sea'.

THE COMB

Michél Carlsson (incorporating comments by Andrea Smith; with conservation by Kim Nissan)

The comb found with the skeleton of the male individual was lying between his hands and over the centre of his pelvis, with its long axis oriented parallel to the line of the body, and with the teeth to the left of the body. It was lifted on site in a block of soil, as it was apparent that, although the comb was virtually complete, it had broken in several places, and had suffered some distortion in the ground. Once the comb had been cleaned in the laboratory, however, it was seen to be in very good condition, much of it, including a large percentage of the teeth, retaining its original polished appearance. The teeth were found to have some traces of wear on their inside edges. Ten iron rivets had been used to hold the comb together, sited, as is usually the case, at the joins of the side-plates, with one through each end-plate. Fragments of mineralised textile remains were detected on the iron rivets on both sides of the comb; these have been examined by Gabra-Sanders (Appendix 2) and identified as tabby weave, using a Z-spun plant fibre, probably flax. The textile may represent the man's sleeve and shirt.

Identification of the raw material was made more difficult as the comb is intact; it was not possible to examine sufficient of the reverse of the side-plates to make a positive identification, although it is most likely that they are of antler.

The comb has an overall length of 225mm, and is ornamented with double lines following the upper and lower edges of the side-plates, and two centrally placed pairs of double lines angled towards each other, each pair

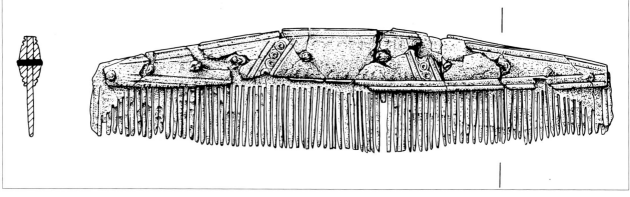

75. The man's comb after conservation.

framing four ring–and–dot motifs. The low plano-convex profile of the side-plates, in combination with the double incised border and ring-and-dot decoration, places the comb in Ambrosiani's Type A2 (1981, 62–3, 70–82, fig. 26). Type A2 is the oldest of the A combs, with its origin in the eighth century (*ibid.*, 27). In the Viking period, combs were a personal artefact; all individuals probably had their own comb, which was usually buried with them when they died. Combs are therefore one of the most commonly occurring artefacts from Viking graves, both male and female. Because they were such a personal possession, and probably not as valuable as some weapons and jewellery, they seem always to have accompanied their owner to the grave, and do not appear to have been handed down from one generation to another, which makes them useful for artefactual dating.

A close parallel for the Scar man's comb is a Type A2 comb from Gotland, in Sweden, which is 220mm in length and ornamented in the same way. The only difference between the two combs is that the central ring-and-dot fields are vertical on the Gotland comb, not angled. The Gotland example is dated to AD 700–750, that is, immediately prior to the Viking period (Nerman 1969, table 292, fig. 2316). A comb from Staraja Ladoga has similar ornament to the Gotland comb, and has been dated to AD 750–900 (Davidan 1982, 173, fig. 2; Ambrosiani 1981, 182). The same type of vertical ornament can also be found in the Frisian area (Roes 1963, plate XVIII). There are several examples of similar combs from eastern central Sweden, including one from a boat grave cemetery at Tuna, in Alsike. The comb from Tuna has, like the comb from Scar, two lines following the edges of the side-plate and double vertical lines along the outer edges of the tooth-plates; also, in the middle of the side-plate is a field with a line of three vertically placed ring-and-dots framed by two vertical lines on each side (Arne 1934: taf.VIII, fig. 4). It is dated to AD 850–875 (*ibid.*, 71). There are identical combs from Hedeby (Ulbricht 1978, taf. 31, fig. 3; Tempel 1969, taf. 18) which can be dated to c. AD 875–925 (Tempel 1969, 78).

A number of combs with this same ornamentation have been recovered from Birka's 'Black Earth'—seven examples from the recent (1990–1995) excavations alone. Four combs of this type from earlier excavations in the 'Black Earth' were radiocarbon dated to between the late ninth and early tenth centuries (Thunmark-Nylén 1995, 602); but the more recent excavations have shown that combs with this style of ornamentation were circulating from the early ninth century, even if they are most frequent from the second half of the ninth century (Carlsson forthcoming). Six combs, all from a relatively well-defined area in eastern central Sweden, all have their decoration angled in the same way as on the Scar comb. Two of the six were found in the same gravefield and are dated to the ninth century (Drotz & Ekman 1995, 162ff.). The Birka excavations have demonstrated that this type

76. *Fragments of mineralised textile remains detected on the iron rivets of the comb seem to have been linen, perhaps from the man's sleeve and shirt.*

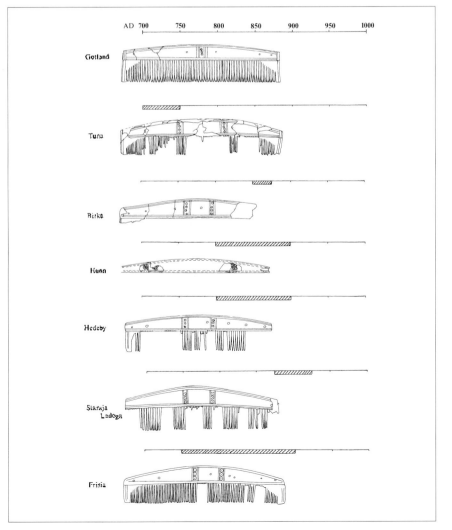

77. *Types of comparative combs from the Viking world with an indication of their dates*

of comb was in circulation as early as the early ninth century, but it is clear that a majority of these combs dates from the middle of the ninth century. The man's comb from Scar can probably be dated to c. AD 850–925.

Finally, mention should be made of a Norwegian comb, found in a cremation grave dated to the ninth century (Resi 1986, 80). This comb has elements of ornamentation which correspond well to the decorative elements on the comb from the male burial at Scar. The side-plates are ornamented with double lines along the edges, and the ends are ornamented with a group of three ring-and-dots. In the middle of the side-plate are two rows of double ring-and-dots which are angled towards each other in the same way as the Scar comb, though without the framing double lines of that comb (*ibid.* 1986, plate 24, 2).

The type of ornament found on the man's comb is relatively rare in Scotland, and in the rest of the British Isles. Absence of evidence is never conclusive, but the absence of this type of comb from large assemblages from settlement sites in Orkney and Shetland (Pool, Sanday; Skaill, Orkney; Brough of Birsay, Orkney; Jarlshof, Shetland), as well as further afield, such as at York, appears to have some significance. This significance could be chronological; the comb is an early type, and some of the settlement sites may have been established after it went out of fashion. The parallels indicate a southern and eastern distribution. This would suggest that the Scar man had at one time had access to goods from this part of the Viking world, to which many of his contemporaries in Scotland, and even the rest of Britain, had not.

THE LEAD BULLION WEIGHTS

Olwyn Owen (with conservation by Amanda Clydesdale)

Several years before the boat burial was discovered, a Viking lead bullion weight (Weight 1) was found in its immediate vicinity by the late Mr John Deerness of Scar. Several years later, on the last day of the excavation, Magnar Dalland combed the beach with a metal detector for the last time and found a second lead bullion weight (Weight 2) of a similar type to Weight 1. Although neither of the lead weights was found *in situ* within the burial, their association with it is not in doubt.

Description and technology

Weight 1 weighs 26.65g and is cylindrical in shape. It is 24mm in diameter and stands 6mm high. Both upper and lower surfaces have been hammered and are slightly concave with raised rims. The upper surface is decorated with a circle of seven, irregularly spaced, punched holes. Three of the holes are slightly larger (c. 2mm diameter) than the other four (c. 1.8mm). These punched holes all have angular edges and are straight-sided and flat-bottomed. They vary in depth from 1.5 to 2.5mm. The underside has six small, irregular indentations, all flat-bottomed and with a depth of c. 0.8mm, which cluster around the centre of the weight; these are probably casting flaws. The rim on the underside is cracked and deformed.

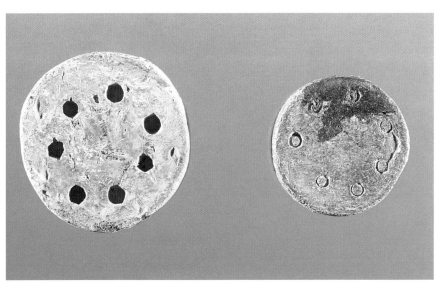

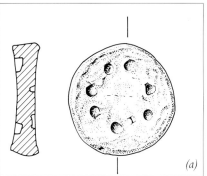
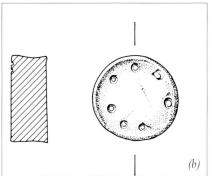

(a)   (b)

Weight 1 is in good condition and little damaged (except for a scratched and burnished area on part of one side) with minimal corrosion. There was some lead carbonate in the holes and a mixture of lead carbonate and oxides on the surfaces. Both surfaces have slight cracks and are brittle. An area of light green colouration on part of the upper surface and on one side may have resulted either from proximity to a copper alloy object in the burial, or to algal staining. A small iron stain on one side may indicate that it had lain close to an iron object. The weight needed almost no cleaning apart from the removal of a little sand from within the punched holes. It was degreased, rinsed in distilled water and then thoroughly dried.

Weight 2 also weighs 26.65g and is cylindrical in shape, but it is smaller in diameter (19mm) than Weight 1 and stands a little higher (8mm). Again, both upper and lower surfaces have raised rims. The upper surface is decorated with seven, irregularly spaced circles (each with a diameter of 1.9mm). These were made with a hollow punch, the wall thickness of which was c. 0.15–0.2mm. The underside has an irregular indentation just off-centre and a small scratch near the edge, both apparently the result of accidental damage.

When found, the object was sand-covered. It had some iron corrosion adhering to its upper surface and lead corrosion products elsewhere. The sand and loose corrosion products were removed with scalpels and a glass

80. A Viking trader weighing out hacksilver and ring-money on his portable scales. Drawing copyright David Simon.

bristle brush. The iron stain was secondary to the object; traces of it are still visible overlying two of the seven punched circles.

Both weights were roughly cast from lead which had already been measured out to the required amount (c. 26.65g in today's metric system). The weights were then rotated and their surfaces hammered to form the raised rims. The hammering also caused slight 'puckering' of the surfaces. The holes were probably produced after the metal had cooled. They were punched with different tools: a solid punch for Weight 1 and a hollow punch for Weight 2. These ornaments probably functioned as weight markings (below). The angular edges and interiors of the holes of Weight 1 display toolmarks from the extraction of the punch.

Minute examination of both weights revealed no trace of any organic materials or any other container.

Discussion

The context of Viking Age weights

Throughout the Viking Age most of Scandinavia was without a coin-using economy; instead, silver and gold were treated as bullion. In the early Viking period, silver was obtained in vast quantities from the east in the form of arabic silver coins which were normally melted down in Scandinavia and cast into ingots for compact storage or made into jewellery which could be worn for a conspicuous display of wealth. Both ingots and jewellery could be cut up later if small change was required (known as hacksilver). Silver hoards, some of immense value, containing a variety of coins, objects and hacksilver, were buried in the ground for safe-keeping and often not retrieved. Payments for goods or services were made in weight of silver; any silver, whether coin, ornament, hacksilver or ingot, was valid in this metal-weight economy. The silver was weighed out on a small pair of scales (Fig. 80), which was designed to fold up and fit into a small box for portability. Weights, made of lead, iron or other metals, were used by merchants, chieftains and others to weigh out the silver as required. Viking Age weights are normally found either in male graves, or at trading centres such as Birka, Hedeby and Dublin (below), but it is relatively rare to find a whole set of weights and the scales to go with them.

81. *Part of the great Skaill hoard, Orkney, which weighed over 8kg in total. Like most Scottish hoards, the Skaill hoard contains ring-money as well as magnificent artefacts and pieces of hack silver, cut up for exchange. Copyright National Museums of Scotland.*

The context of the Scar lead weights

Although the Scar weights were found on the beach immediately adjacent to the boat burial, their association with this boat burial is not seriously in doubt. A more relevant question is which burial they originally accompanied: the man, woman or child? Weights have been found in female and child graves; for instance, weights were found in at least six children's graves in the massive cemetery at Birka, Sweden (Gräslund 1973, 174; Chapter 7). Nevertheless, when found in graves, weights normally accompany male burials, in Scandinavia and elsewhere, and it is at least a reasonable assumption that they accompanied the man in this case too. It cannot be ascertained whether a set of weights, and perhaps even the balance scales to go with them, had originally been deposited in the grave. However, this is perhaps unlikely given that, although many weights do form part of sets, in a large number of cases weights occur alone or in pairs, even within graves (Blindheim, Heyerdahl-Larsen & Tollnes 1981, 146). Moreover, it is odd that the Scar weights both weigh exactly the same; since the owner of a set should not have needed two identical weights, this might rather suggest that they were not in fact part of a set at all, but derived instead from two similar sets. This must cast some doubt on how useful they were. Normally, lead weights might be used as evidence that their owner was a merchant, chieftain or leader—someone who needed to weigh out bullion for commercial transactions or to make payments to followers. However, given the circumstances at Scar, it seems best not to comment on their significance for the burial.

Viking weight systems

In later medieval Scandinavia, the standard unit of weight was the mark, divided into eight øre, each of which consisted of three ørtugar. There is little doubt that variations of this system were in use in the Viking Age. However, the actual system underlying exchanges of Viking silver is not at all clear; the more research is carried out, the more it seems likely that weight systems varied across the Viking world. The important early metrological studies of Brøgger (1921) and Arne (1911–12; 1914) focused on Norwegian and Swedish weights respectively, most of which were deposited in graves, sometimes in sets, sometimes singly or in pairs. More recent studies have focused on weights found in the trading centres of Hedeby, Germany (Steuer 1973) and Birka, Sweden (Kylhberg 1980). However, many of the weights are severely corroded, which hampers metrological analysis.

Brøgger (1921, 102) identified two units, both considered øre, an early Viking Age unit of c. 26.65g and a later unit of c. 24g, but did not cite an absolute target weight. Kyhlberg (1980, 265) and, independently, Steuer (1973, 15, 18–19) felt that the Birka and Hedeby weights provided some evidence of a 4.26g and probably a 4g unit. More recent (unpublished) studies by Nielsen have indicated a weight unit of 24.4g +/- 0.8g, and a unit of 8.1g +/- 0.4g for flattened spherical weights (Kruse 1988, 287), which is close to Brøgger's postulated later unit. Kruse's (1988) analysis of ingots from the hoards found in England revealed a clustering of weights in the mid-20g zone, 'a fuzzy unit of 26g' (*op. cit.*, 295) with basic units of one-third, two-thirds, one, three, five and ten, but without any great precision. Kruse concludes that the imprecision was due to lack of a tradition of science of weights and measures and the fragmented political situation: 'standardisation of weights over large areas would have been impossible, and some imprecision inevitable' (*op. cit.*, 297); and suggests it may have been tolerated in a weight-money economy when hacksilver would usually have been on hand to top up the scale pan (Kruse 1993, 196).

This conclusion finds some support in the work of Wallace (1987, 212–14) on more than 200 lead weights recovered from excavations in Dublin (this total excludes 'blobs' and offcuts of lead for which weight evidence alone suggests their original purpose). The Dublin basic unit of weight was 26.6g, and the surviving specimens were multiples or fractions of this standard weight, no matter what their shape. This is slightly heavier than the Scandinavian norm, an observation which, together with the absence of Scandinavian-type polyhedral weights (below), of stamped weight markings and the apparent infrequency of the one-third (ørtugar) unit in Dublin, strengthens the argument that the weight systems of Viking Age Scandinavia and Dublin were slightly different. Preliminary analysis of the weights from York suggested that they might be 'more easily grouped with the Dublin series both in terms of weight and shape than with Scandinavian specimens' (Wallace 1987, 213). However, most of the York weights are in poor condition, which hampers metrological analysis; recent work (Kruse 1992) has suggested that although some of them as recovered relate to the Dublin standard weight, and one or two to the later Scandinavian øre, most of the surviving York weights do not relate closely to either system.

Analysis of the weight system current in Viking Age Scotland and the Isle of Man is further complicated by the inclusion of 'ring-money' in the silver hoards, a distinctive type of plain penannular arm-ring which seems also to have functioned as a means of exchange (Graham-Campbell 1980, 64, no. 235; Fig. 81). Warner (1976) postulated a target weight for them of 24g ± 0.8g. However, he also found a (disconcertingly high) standard deviation of 5g which suggests that craftsmen 'were not too careful about their accuracy' (1976, 141).

The Scar weights are identical in weight, both 26.65g, which is close to Brøgger's postulated older øre (26.65g); to Kruse's 'fuzzy' 26g unit; and to Wallace's postulated basic unit of weight in tenth- to eleventh-century Dublin (26.6g). As there is little evidence of corrosion, it seems likely that the present weight of the Scar weights more or less accurately reflects their original weight. On this basis, they conform generally to a Viking Age metrological system, albeit imprecise, and were almost certainly each intended to weigh one øre.

Recent efforts to establish the weight systems of Bronze Age Scandinavia (Malmer 1992; Sperber 1993), based on the weights of bronze figurines, 'Goddesses of Wealth', and on gold arm rings, also discovered a unit of weight of 26.6g ± 1.0g, with more than a 99% level of confidence. This striking correspondence suggests that the Scandinavian metrological system, with slight variations, has an ancestry which stretches back over several millennia. This system can also be seen to conform at least in general terms with other areas: unit weights of around 26.6g persisted for thousands of years in Europe and the Near East (see Sperber 1993, 616–9 for summary). The expansion of the Roman Empire made their preferred system universal for a time; but after the end of the empire, weight systems were bound to vary once no international authorities were there to control them.

Weight markings

There are some close parallels for the simple Scar lead weights in the Scandinavian Viking Age material. For example, two of three similar cylindrical weights from a poor grave at Ytre Arne, Haus, Hordaland, Norway (Brøgger 1921, 74–5, figs. 17–18) also have markings on their upper surfaces. The largest (weighing 20.84g) is stamped with seven small triangular ornaments arranged irregularly around the edge; another weight (17.38g) has six, small, irregularly spaced circles around its perimeter. Brøgger used these weights (among others) to demonstrate (not surprisingly) that there was a relationship between the Roman weight system and the old Scandinavian system of N.*ertog og øre,* under which one øre = seven drachma = 28 scripula. By analysis of a number of pre-Viking and early Viking Scandinavian weights, he was able to identify a middle value for the smallest unit (the ?scripulum) of 0.952g, which is only 0.021g different from the known Roman scripulum unit of 0.973g. From this, he deduced that one drachma = 3.808g and, therefore, one øre ¯ 26.656g.

He further suggested that, by the Viking period, the drachma unit had been reduced from four to three scripula which gives an unnamed unit weighing around 2.92g (0.973 multiplied by three = 2.92g; he proposed a general 2.9–3.1g weight bracket for this unit). These weight values may be indicated by the markings on the upper surfaces of some weights. For instance, the seven stamped triangles on the largest Ytre Arne weight are each worth 2.977g (20.84g divided by seven drachma = 2.977g per triangle); each triangle contains three dots (2.977g divided by the three dots gives an (increased 'scripulum') unit of 0.992g). The second marked Ytre Arne weight (17.38g) has six circles (17.38g divided by six drachma = 2.896g).

It should be emphasised at once that Brøgger's thesis, undertaken more than seventy years ago, clearly requires modern testing. For instance, it is not clear how large a dataset he examined; nor is the condition of the weights on which he based his conclusions known. In some other cases weight markings have been shown to indicate a weight's place in a series or set of weights, although there are so few complete weight sets of comparable types that it is hard to argue this with any certainty (Susan Kruse, personal communication). In other cases, no sense can be made of the weight markings at all, which might suggest that their function and/or the intended weight system was not understood by the manufacturer.

Nevertheless, taken at face value, the Scar weights fit with Brøgger's thesis. Each of them weighs 26.65g. Each is ornamented with seven circles (weight markings). The weight of 26.65g divided by seven drachma gives a unit of 3.807g (as opposed to the 'target' drachma weight of 3.808g). If the drachma are divided by four supposed scripula, the scripula unit for the Scar weights is 0.952g, precisely as would be expected for weights of the pre- and early Viking Age according to Brøgger's thesis. The fact that the Scar weight markings seem to indicate use of the four-scripula system might therefore imply that they are relatively early in the sequence (i.e. made before the introduction of Brøgger's proposed three-scripula system).

This must remain speculation for the time being, and it should be repeated here that there are many variables and variations in any analysis of larger assemblages of weights. However, it does seem indisputable that the 'ornaments' on the Ytre Arne weights, the Scar weights and many others (though not all) are actually weight markings, intended to indicate at a glance—at least to those who were used to using them—the weight of the piece.

Typology, distribution and dating

Weights are well attested throughout the Viking world and come in a wide variety of shapes and forms (as well as weights). In Scandinavia, flattened spherical weights (normally made of iron coated with bronze) and smaller polyhedral weights (usually exclusively bronze) are particularly common and probably had oriental prototypes (e.g. five weights from Hemlingby, Valbo, Gästrikland, Sweden: FVTC 1992, 266, no. 151). The flat areas on all but the lightest of the Hemlingby weights carry weight markings in the form of one, three, four and five circles. A ninth-century set of eight plain lead weights from Jåtten, Hetland, Rogaland, Norway (Graham-Campbell 1980, 88, no. 306), which range in weight from 2 to 43g and were contained in a linen bag, have differing shapes, including cylindrical, sub-conical and rectangular. In general, then, the shapes and forms of individual weights appear to be of little significance.

A 'large number' of mostly simple, cylindrical weights have been recovered from recent excavations of the early Viking market place in Ribe, Denmark (Jensen 1991, 18), and twenty-one were recovered from the vicinity of a bronze-making workshop (Stig Jensen, personal communication). Some appear to be superficially similar to those from Scar, including bearing weight markings of punched or incised circles. However, some are very small indeed, weighing around 1g, and none are much heavier than the equivalent of about one øre (Claus Feveile, personal communication). Post-excavation analysis is continuing but the excavators have suggested that these small and simple weights might have been used by bronzesmiths for weighing out base metals (personal communication). For

Dublin, too, Wallace has suggested that not only might precious metals have been weighed out in tiny quantities, but also base metals 'which were probably sold to bronzesmiths in pre-weighted ingots or their fractions' (1987, 213).

However, the vast majority of the Dublin weights, as elsewhere, were probably used to weigh silver by being placed on the pans of balance-scales, the latter also well attested in the Dublin assemblages. The common shapes of the weights from Dublin include discs, bowls, hemispheres and cones of both plain and perforated varieties, as well as rings, hammer-finished lumps and lead-filled copper alloy containers; but the less common Scandinavian-type polyhedral weights are absent (Wallace 1987, 212). The simple, cylindrical form of the Scar weights is closely paralleled in the tenth- to eleventh-century Dublin assemblages (Pat Wallace, personal communication).

The Scar weights are without exact parallel in Scotland where weights are in any case rare. Surprisingly, only two other weights have been discovered in Orkney, the wealthy centre of the Norse Earldom: one from Buckquoy, Birsay (Ritchie 1977, cat. no. 96); and a new find from middens at Cleat, Westray (James Barrett, personal communication). No weights are so far known from Shetland or Caithness. The remains of pairs of scales are also scarce in this area, although part of a balance was found at Gurness (James Graham-Campbell, personal communication), and half of a bronze box probably once used for containing scales was found on Unst, Shetland (NMS cat. no. IL 314). Given the plentiful evidence for the use of 'ring-money' and hacksilver, and of 'nicking' (repeated testing of the quality of silver objects in the northern hoards, signifying repeated silver exchanges), it is interesting to speculate on the reasons for this general lack of weights and scales from the north of Scotland. If general absence does not simply reflect the accident of survival and genuinely implies that little use was made of weights and scales in this area, then there must be some doubt as to how useful the Scar weights would have been in the Orkney Earldom—although they would still have been useful to traders, itinerants, men in the earl's retinue, or others who travelled further afield in the Viking world.

From elsewhere in Scotland, a well-known and very fine set of seven weights was found in a grave at Kiloran Bay, Colonsay (Grieg 1940, 56–7; Graham-Campbell 1980, no. 307; Fig. 82); and another set was found on Gigha (Grieg 1940, 29–30). Single weights were found in the Talnotrie, Kirkcudbrightshire hoard (Maxwell 1913, 13), deposited around AD 875; and in excavations at Little Dunagoil, Bute (Marshall 1964, 52); and, more recently, at Whithorn (Hill 1997, 392–3).

The Colonsay weights all have lead bases and all but one of them (the weight with unusual 'knobs' on top) are capped with gilt-bronze decorated mounts of Insular manufacture. Despite the Irish and Anglo-Saxon origins of the mounts (Graham-Campbell 1980, 88–9), the Colonsay weights were part of the rich assemblage of a mid ninth-century Viking boat burial and clearly had a Scandinavian or colonial Scandinavian owner. They are a variety of shapes (octagonal, irregular, two truncated pyramids, sub-rectangular, curved and a truncated cone). They weigh between 12.94g and 129.6g; one of them approximately equates to an øre at 25.81g. Although the

82. A fine set of seven weights was found in the wealthy male grave at Kiloran Bay, Colonsay, capped with gilt-bronze mounts of Insular manufacture. They weigh between 12.94 and 129.6 g; one of them approximately equates to an øre at 25.81 g. Copyright National Museums of Scotland.

condition of the weights precludes fine metrological interpretation, some correspondence with the 'ring-money' may be present (Kruse 1993, 195).

Nine similar weights were found in the later ninth-century Kilmainham /Islandbridge cemetery outside Dublin, together with the remains of four pairs of scales (Graham-Campbell 1980, 89, no. 308). Again, they are capped or inset with gilt-bronze mounts of Insular manufacture. Four of them are cylindrical, recalling the Scar weights at least in shape; the others are sub-conical, sub-circular, rectangular and two are sub-rectangular. Wallace (1987, 212–13) argues that there are weights of both Scandinavian and Dublin standards present in the Kilmainham/Islandbridge material. Kruse (1993, 195) points out that the Scottish weights can be correlated with both standards, with neither proving more convincing; indeed, Kruse questions just how much bullion exchange actually took place in Scotland. The Kilmainham and the Colonsay weights may be typical of weights of the Irish Sea area (Susan Kruse, personal communication), since there are no complete sets from Scandinavia and more and more of this type are being found in Britain and Ireland (e.g. very recently from the River Blackwater, Ulster: Bourke 1994). If so, this begs the question of the interrelationship of this type with the plain lead weights with markings such as those from Scar.

Even this brief overview has shown that the shapes and forms of Viking lead weights are extremely varied and of limited significance. Individual weights and sets of weights are more reliably to be dated by their find associations than typologically. Lead weights were primarily functional; what was important was their weight and weight markings. Further regional and international, metrological and comparative analyses of Scandinavian weights and hoard assemblages, and of the British assemblages, especially from Dublin, should in time enable a better assessment to be made of the variations in metrological systems in use during the Viking Age. In the meantime, it must be at least a possibility, following Brøgger (his thesis apparently finding support in the Scar weights) and given the results of more comprehensive analyses of recent assemblages, such as those from Dublin, Birka and Hedeby, that in time some indication of the origins and relative chronology of lead weights may be ascertainable from their actual weights.

Summary

The Scar lead weights were probably originally part of a set (or two sets) of weights but they may already only have been a pair when they were deposited in the grave, probably to accompany the male burial. They were almost certainly made in Scandinavia and may have been of only limited use in the Orkney Earldom. They conform to a recognised if imprecise Viking weight system and are each approximately equivalent to one øre in weight; they are close to Brøgger's postulated early Viking øre (26.656g). The seven punched circles on their upper surfaces are weight markings. Although this artefact type is of limited use for dating, the Scar weights seem more likely to date to the early Viking period (eighth to ninth century AD) on the available published evidence and, tentatively, on the evidence of their weight and weight markings.

THE GAMING PIECES

Olwyn Owen (with conservation by Paul Watson)

Twenty-two whalebone gaming pieces were discovered *in situ,* immediately to the east of the man's flexed legs. They were found in a well-defined pile indicating that, when placed in the grave, they had been contained in a pouch or purse of textile or leather which has completely rotted away.

83. *The gaming pieces were found in a well-defined pile, suggesting that they had been placed in the grave in a leather or textile purse or pouch which had completely rotted away.*

All of the pieces were wet-cleaned in the laboratory using a fine water spray. Because many of the pieces were in a fragile condition, they were de-watered by repeated bathing in solvents with an increasing concentration of Acetone; the final bath was 100% Acetone. The pieces were then air-dried, after which an acrylic consolidant was applied.

Description

84. *The gaming pieces after conservation.*

The twenty-two gaming pieces are all made of lathe-turned whalebone. The condition of the pieces ranges from poor to good, with areas of differential preservation sometimes exhibited on the same piece. Although differing in size, the pieces are all of similar form, hemispherical but with flat bases. Most have convex sides but some are slightly straighter. The single, large 'king' piece has a poorly preserved, iron pin with a rounded head inserted into its top. Slight grooves on the upper surface may be turning marks. The surfaces of the better preserved pieces are smooth and were evidently highly polished.

The bases are rough with the cancellous tissue exposed (Fig. 87). Each of the bases has an approximately central peg-hole, some of which contain traces of iron inserts, usually iron corrosion products. These peg-holes would originally have accommodated metal pegs used to affix the pieces to holes

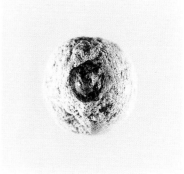

85. *King piece (profile and from above.)*

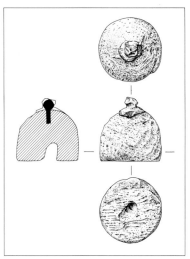

86. Details of the gaming pieces: the iron pin in the 'king' piece.

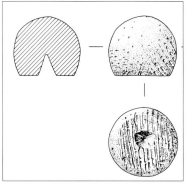

87. A typical gaming piece. Note the cancellous tissue and central peg-hole in the base.

in the gaming board. Cut-marks and other toolmarks are visible in and around the peg-holes. The holes are normally conical in shape and taper to a point internally. They vary in shape from circular to almost square; in diameter from 2.9 to 8.5mm (5.4mm on average, excluding the 'king' piece); and in depth from 4 to 12mm (7.5mm on average). The peg-hole in the underside of the 'king' piece is 6.8mm in diameter and 12.5mm deep, but otherwise of similar form to the others. These variations are partly, though not wholly, accounted for by the variable state of preservation of the pieces.

The original dimensions of the three least well preserved pieces cannot be ascertained, which inhibits analysis of the size range. The 'king' piece was clearly the largest piece, standing to a height of 33mm and with a base diameter of 34mm. The heights of the remaining measurable, eighteen pieces range from 18 to 27mm; their base diameters range from 21 to 34mm. It seems likely that three sizes were intended: the large 'king' piece, medium pieces (although one of these is not much smaller than the bone element of the 'king' piece), and smaller pieces. Size clusterings are visible on the basis of both height and base diameter but these do not exactly correlate; in at least two cases, pieces which are relatively small in height have relatively wide base diameters (Fig. 00). This imprecision of size means that the relative proportions of medium to smaller pieces cannot be determined with certainty. However, there were fewer medium pieces than smaller pieces, by a probable factor of approximately 8:10 on the basis of both height and diameter, plus the single 'king' piece. The three pieces of indeterminable size are likely originally to have been smaller pieces by analogy with comparable sets (below). If so, the original proportion of the pieces would have been 1 (king): 8 (king's men/defenders): 13 (attackers), which suggests that the set was perhaps incomplete when it was deposited in the grave (below).

Discussion

Gaming pieces of glass, amber, bone or walrus ivory are relatively common finds in Scandinavian Viking male graves and on settlement sites (e.g. FVTC 1992, 143, cat. nos. 71, 123, 321, 342, 360, 572; Graham-Campbell 1980, 24–5, cat. nos. 94–101; the Norwegian sets are listed in Grieg 1947, 57–9), testifying to the popularity of board games in the Viking period (Fig. 88). Chess (and its variants) was only introduced into England in the eleventh century, and into Scandinavia in the twelfth century (Murray 1952, 56). Our knowledge of games before then is patchy but the game of *hnefatafl*, which means literally 'king's table', is occasionally referred to in medieval Icelandic literature. In Fms. VI 29, for example, it says of King Magnus the Good: 'the king sat and played *hnefatafl*' (ON. *konunger sat ok tefdi hneftafl*) (Grieg 1947, 62–3). The game seems to have been popular over a long period (Murray 1952, 55–7); it developed over the centuries, and different versions of the board have been found on sites from Ireland to the Ukraine (below).

Hnefatafl is a simple but subtle game of attack and defence for two people. The 'king' piece and a small force of defenders occupy the centre of the board; and a larger force of attackers is placed around the edges. The object of the game is for the attacking player to capture the opponent's king in which case he wins, or for the king to escape to one of the corners of the board in which case the defending player wins. Another game, known as *tablut* and encountered by Linnæus being played amongst the Lapps (Murray 1952, 63–4, fig. 26), was directly descended from *hnefatafl*. In this version, one 'king' and eight 'Swedes' were attacked by sixteen 'Muscovites'.

The pieces in a single set are always of the same form, apart from one which diverges in colour, size or shape, the so-called 'king' piece. The number of gaming pieces in each archaeological find varies from one to forty-seven (below). The sets are more often than not incomplete; even so, the Norwegian examples often contain more than twenty pieces (Grieg 1947, 56). A set in imported glass, dating to around AD 800 and found at Gunnarshaug, Karmøy, Rogaland, Norway (FVTC 1992, 258, no. 123), is thought to be complete but contains only sixteen pieces. The maximum number found together is forty-seven from a male grave (or graves) at Nes, Hammerø, Nordland, Norway (Sjøvold 1974, 78, L.324). However, the unknown circumstances of this discovery and the unusual presence of three walrus tusk dice prompted Sjøvold to suggest that the burial had originally contained three sets of sixteen gaming pieces each.

The Scar gaming pieces are of the very common and simple R474 (Rygh 1885) type, which has a wide distribution across the Viking world. The fact that they are of lathe-turned bone suggests that they were not home-made, but manufactured in a specialist workshop, probably in Scandinavia. Lathe turning was not a common technique in bone working in Scotland in the late Iron Age/Viking period, and is not normally found on objects from domestic sites (Andrea Smith, personal communication).

A close parallel for the Scar gaming pieces is a set of twenty-seven, plain, spherical gaming pieces of lathe-turned bone, found in a rich male chamber grave at Birka (Grave 624: Arbman 1943, 13, fig. 163, Pls. 149,3 & 150,6; Graham-Campbell 1980, 24, cat. no. 94; Fig. 89). An iron-mounted wooden gaming board was also discovered in this grave, with twenty-five of the gaming pieces actually on it. The grave dates to the early or middle Viking period, sometime between the late eighth and tenth centuries. If this set is complete, the proportion of the pieces is 1:6:20. A particularly well-preserved, complete set, also containing this simple type of gaming piece, was found in Grave 74 at Oldenburg, Germany (Gabriel 1988, 229–30, Pl. 49), comprising thirty-seven pieces: twenty-two of walrus ivory, fourteen of whalebone and a bronze 'king' piece. Some of their undersides are decorated with ring-and-dot motifs and incised crosses, perhaps to distinguish them from each other. A set of twelve spherical gaming pieces, similar to those from Scar but made of antler and (probably) walrus tusk (FVTC 1992, 322, no. 360), was found with a die in the only known male Viking grave in France, at Île de Groix, Morbihan (Price 1989, 64–74, 95–7). This exceptionally rich cremation grave, which contained two bodies in a ship, is dated to the first half of the tenth century.

Other more exotic gaming pieces include two spherical examples in amber from Hedeby, Germany (Graham-Campbell 1980, 24, no. 97); and an oblong playing piece of jet decorated with early Viking Borre style ornament from Bawdsey, Suffolk, England (*op. cit.*, no. 98; Wilson 1970, 38–42). Several

88. *Vikings playing* hnefatafl. *From a Swedish runestone.*

89. *A comparable set of gaming pieces from a rich male grave at Birka (Grave 624). Most of these were found actually on a wooden gaming board where they had been placed in the grave. Copyright Statens Historiska Museet, Stockholm.*

three-dimensional pieces, carved in openwork in the form of a seated figure with arms resting on knees, and hands clutching a twisted beard which falls to the ground, are also known: for example, one in ivory from Lund, Skåne, Sweden; one in whalebone from Baldursheimur, Skútustaðahreppur, Iceland; one in bronze from Eyrarland, Akureyri, Iceland (Graham-Campbell 1980, nos. 99–101 respectively); and one in amber from Roholte, Sjælland, Denmark (FVTC 1992, 247, no. 77).

The Baldursheimur, Iceland, figure (and therefore perhaps the other figures) is the 'king' piece of a set of twenty-five gaming pieces, found with a bone die. The remaining twenty-four pieces are all plain and spherical, like those from Scar but made of walrus ivory. If complete, the proportion of the Baldursheimur pieces seems to be 1:8:16. It is more than possible that the original proportions of the set from Scar might also have been 1:8:16, with three smaller pieces (attackers) now missing. If this hypothesis is correct, since the gaming pieces were placed in the grave in a cloth or leather container and were found in an apparently undisturbed pile, the Scar set may not have been complete when it was buried. The Baldursheimur set also recalls the Scar set in having rather imprecise size differences between the medium and smaller pieces. This suggests that perhaps some other form of distinction was originally present, such as different colouring or other markings (Grieg 1947, 55), as noted on the Oldenburg pieces (above).

Until very recently, no sets as complete as that from Scar had been recovered in Scotland, only single examples. At least two examples have been found on the Brough of Birsay in unrelated contexts, although only one is a close parallel to the Scar pieces (Curle 1982, 75, no. 271, illus. 38); the other is a conical gaming piece of antler with an acorn shaped terminal found in the church (*ibid.* 89, no. 275, illus. 50). A single bone gaming piece with a pointed top was found on a rare excavation of a Viking settlement in the Western Isles, at Drimore, South Uist (MacLaren 1974, 17, no. 37). More recently, at least one male grave in the Westness, Rousay, Orkney, cemetery has produced gaming pieces and a die in an assemblage which quite closely parallels the male assemblage from Scar (Kaland 1993, 313, fig. 17.6; Chapter 7). The burial of a 12 to 14–year-old boy at Balnakeil, Durness, Sutherland (Gourlay, Low & Batey forthcoming; Chapter 7), found in 1991, was also accompanied by a set of bone gaming pieces very similar to those from Scar.

Most of these examples, like the set from Scar, have holes in their bases which once housed pegs to affix them to a gaming board. They may have been designed like this specifically for play on board ship, so that the pieces did not slide off the board (Anna Ritchie, personal communication). However, gaming pieces are frequently found in male Viking graves without an accompanying gaming board or die, as at Scar. Indeed, gaming boards, which were usually of wood, are generally much rarer finds than gaming pieces (although, interestingly, several fragmentary boards made of more durable materials (stone, slate or whalebone) are known from Viking settlement sites in Scotland (see below)). On balance, although it is conceivable that a wooden gaming board in the Scar grave had completely rotted away in the ground, this seems unlikely (see Chapter 6).

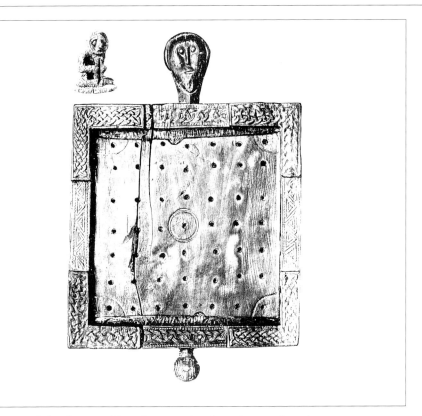

90. This very fine wooden gaming board was found on a crannog at Ballinderry, Co Westmeath, Ireland, but was probably made in Viking Dublin. Copyright National Museum of Ireland, Dublin.

One of the finest Viking Age gaming boards was found on a crannog at Ballinderry, Co. Westmeath, Ireland (Hencken 1936; Fig. 90) but was probably made in Dublin (Graham-Campbell 1980, 23, no. 92). The forty-nine (seven by seven) peg-holes suggest that it was used with playing pieces similar to those from Scar, probably for playing *hnefatafl* (Murray 1952, 59–60). Iron pegs in the bases of the gaming pieces would have slotted into the peg-holes on the board; hence, the game was played from intersection to intersection rather than from cell to cell. Murray (1952, 55) argues that *tafl* could be played on the points of a lattice of 18 by 18 cells, or on the cells of boards of 13 by 13, 11 by 11, 9 by 9, or 7 by 7 cells. However, as well as Ballinderry, an unstratified fragment of a peg-hole gaming board of whalebone recovered from the Brough of Birsay, Orkney (Curle 1982, 89, no. 274, Illus. 50), is probably from a board smaller than 18 by 18 cells. Interestingly, even the very informal stone gaming boards from sites along the Brough Road, Birsay (Ritchie 1977, 187, 198–9, figs 9–10, pl. 3c; and Morris 1989, 220–21, no. 280, Illus. 171–2), with their indentations at the cell intersections, seem to suggest that the game was traditionally played from intersection to intersection. Other gaming boards have been recovered from Viking and later Norse settlements on Shetland: a slate board from Jarlshof (Hamilton 1956, 145, pl. XXXI) and fragments of simple boards and counters from Underhoull, Unst (Small 1968, 67–8, pl. 2).

From Scandinavia and elsewhere, other types of Viking gaming board are also known (Grieg 1947, 57–64), including a fine double-sided example from the Gokstad ship burial (the burial dated by dendrochronology to AD 900–905: Bonde & Christensen 1993, 582). A late (c. 1100–1150) *hnefatafl*

91. The very fragile and fragmentary tinned bronze object after conservation. This is interpreted as a mount, perhaps from around the rim of a wooden bowl or, more likely, from the rim of a shield or shield boss.

board (eleven by eleven squares), from Trondheim, Norway, is also double-sided with another game (tric-trac, a form of backgammon) incised on the back (FVTC 1992, 378, no. 572). One of the earliest known examples, a double-sided oak board found on a tenth-century farm at Toftanes, Eysturoy, Faroes (Stumann-Hansen 1988, 72, fig. 11), has a wheel game on the upper side and a *hnefatafl* chequerboard on the underside.

Summary

Gaming pieces are a common feature of male graves from across the Viking world and were in use throughout the Viking period. The set from Scar was almost certainly part of the man's grave goods and, in this and all other respects, it is a fairly typical example. It has no diagnostic features which might allow it to be dated more closely; and, given the wide distribution and frequent occurrence of this type of object, neither is it possible to ascertain where the Scar gaming pieces might have been made. The pieces were almost certainly for playing a version of the Viking board game *hnefatafl* and may originally have comprised eight medium pieces and up to sixteen smaller pieces, as well as the obvious 'king' piece. The set of gaming pieces was placed in the grave in a leather or textile pouch or purse, which had completely rotted away. It is unlikely that they were accompanied in the grave by a gaming board.

THE TINNED BRONZE OBJECT

Andrea Smith (with conservation by Amanda Clydesdale)

This object was found close to the erosion face, between the male and female burials, and was in a very fragile and fragmentary state. It was lifted in a block of sand for excavation in the conservation laboratory; most of the description of the object here is taken from the first-hand observations recorded in the conservation report. The object was in a large number of small fragments, some cemented together by a black tarry organic material and in very poor condition, from which a composite picture has been built up. The object appeared to consist of a wooden core with one edge rounded off, covered over with a thin sheet of copper alloy which had tinning over much of its upper surface, which may have measured approximately 20mm by 30mm, with a thickness of 5mm. There were small iron pins or rivets along the longer sides at right angles to the rounded edge; but also traces of tiny wooden pins within the wooden core. The wood was identified as a non-coniferous species. A small fragment, possibly of leather, was found close to the broken end of one long side.

This composite object is perhaps some kind of mount, possibly a strap-end. However, a number of similar objects have been recovered from the cemetery at Birka which suggest other possible uses, for example as mounts around the rims of wooden bowls (Arbman 1940, Taf. 214–16), and also around shield rims and shield boss edges (*ibid.*, Taf. 15–18). The male burial at Scar might have been expected to have a shield; this fragment may represent all that is left.

THE LARGE IRON HANDLE

Andrea Smith (with conservation by Amanda Clydesdale)

A relatively large iron handle, 133mm in length, with expanded rounded terminals, each with a single rivet 6–8mm in diameter, was found some 2m to the east of the other finds. The handle has a flattened profile, and one end appears to have been bent upwards. Attached to the underside of the handle terminals are fragments of mineralised wood, with the grain running at right angles to the long axis of the handle. The conservation report noted that at the end which had been bent up there were layers of white material within the corrosion products, indicating that a gap existed between the iron and the wood at the time of burial.

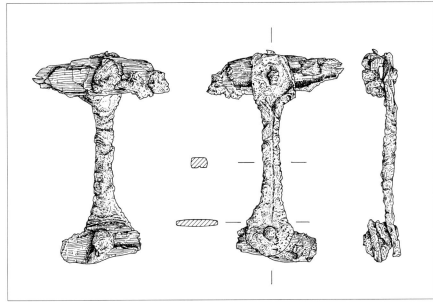

92. The large iron handle after conservation. This was found outside the burial chamber and we do not know what it was originally attached to.

It was thought at one stage that the handle might have belonged to the maplewood box found next to the woman, but the identification of the wood remains on the handle as Scots Pine (*Pinus sylvestris*) makes this unlikely. The flattened profile of the handle means that in order to get any kind of grip on it there must have been a void below; this is not easy to visualise in the context of box construction, and is more commonly seen on articles such as shield bosses. However, given the position of the object well away from the burial chamber, it could equally have belonged to part of the boat or to some fitting added at the time of burial.

THE TEXTILES FROM SCAR: A SUMMARY

Thea Gabra-Sanders

The textiles from Scar represent a significant addition to the textiles so far recovered from Viking graves in Scotland (Gabra-Sanders 1998). The fragments probably derive from five or more different weaves: a tabby weave, a repp-like tabby, more balanced tabbies, a self-patterned tabby, a textile with a 'brocaded' effect; and a 2/1 twill weave. The majority of fragments are in

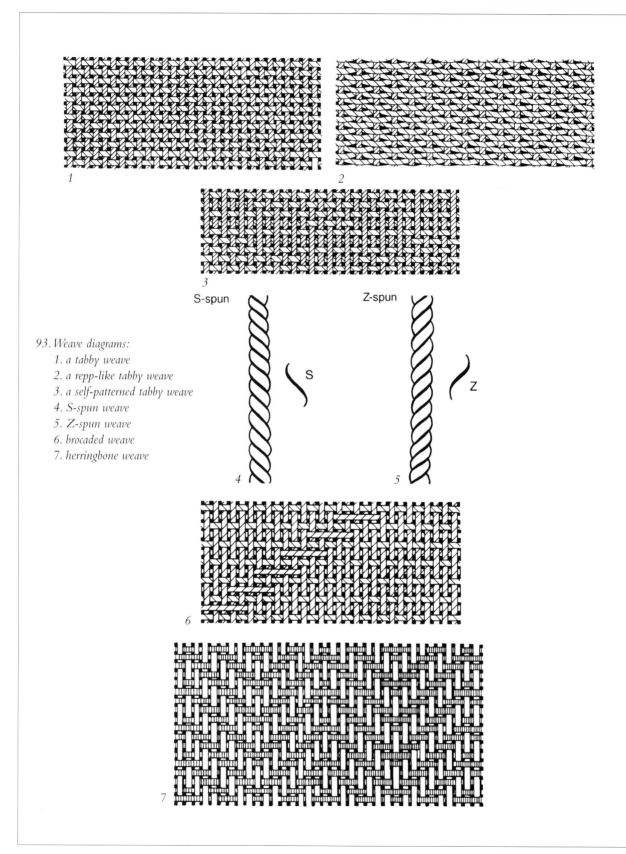

93. *Weave diagrams:*
    1. *a tabby weave*
    2. *a repp-like tabby weave*
    3. *a self-patterned tabby weave*
    4. *S-spun weave*
    5. *Z-spun weave*
    6. *brocaded weave*
    7. *herringbone weave*

tabby weave (also known as plain weave). The fragments are of different qualities and are worked from Z-spun single yarn in both warp and weft with an average thread-count of 10–25 x 6–15/cm.

The Scar textiles are mineralised, preserved only by their contact with metal. In only two cases (the textiles adhering to the comb and sword) was it possible to determine the fibre. Both samples were identified as plant fibre, probably flax (Rob Janaway and Kim Nissan, personal communication). Similar linen tabbies have been found in various ninth- and tenth-century Viking graves of north-west Britain, for example Kildonan on Eigg (Crowfoot 1949, 26) and Balladoole, Isle of Man (Bersu & Wilson 1966, 44). Similar fine and coarser fragments are also known from Kneep (Cnip), Lewis (Welander, Batey & Cowie 1987, 165–6), Oronsay (Henshall 1952, 16–17), Pierowall, Westray (Hedges 1980, 357) and Westness, Rousay (Kaland 1973, 77–102). Viking Age textiles from Scottish and Irish graves comprise a distinct group in the British Isles: the urban Viking sites of Great Britain and Ireland have yielded textiles clearly different from those of the graves (Bender Jørgensen 1992, 38–41). The textile remains in tabby weave from Scar belong to the same general cloth type, one which is common in Viking Age graves in Scandinavia (Bender Jørgensen 1984, 131).

A reconstruction of how the dead man and woman were robed for burial is very difficult, given the fragmentary nature of the textiles. The tabby weave cloth covering the rivets on both sides of the single-sided comb could be remains of the man's sleeve and shirt, and the tabby weave cloth on the sickle is possibly the remains of the woman's shirt. However, the fragment of self-patterned tabby weave which is attached to the weaving batten does not necessarily have to be a part of the woman's garment but could be a type of cover, cushion, or perhaps a wall hanging, which was deposited with the burial. Among the textiles on the surviving remains of the box is another interesting fabric in the form of a brocaded cloth. The other fragments represent a repp weave and a 2/1 twill weave. These textiles could be part of the woman's clothing and/or grave furnishings such as a blanket and/or a pillow.

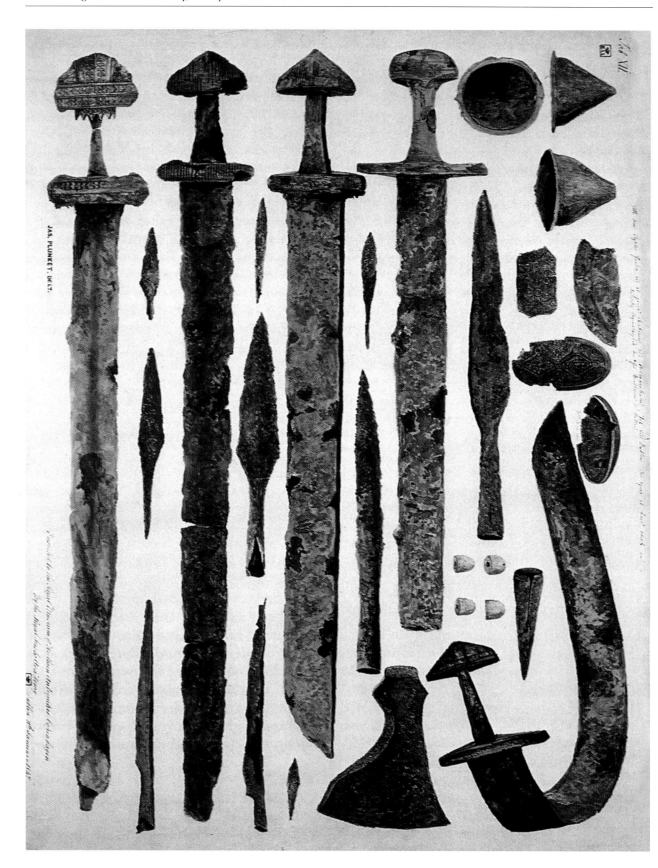

CHAPTER 7

DISCUSSION

94. (facing) A nineteenth-century water-colour painting of Viking weapons recovered from the cemeteries at Kilmainham/Islandbridge, Dublin. Copyright Nationalmuseet, Copenhagen.

THE ASSEMBLAGE AS A WHOLE: AN OVERVIEW

Olwyn Owen

The quantity and quality of the objects recovered from the Scar boat burial are impressive, and yet this is only part of the picture: an unknown number of the grave goods which originally accompanied the three bodies has almost certainly not survived. As Allen notes (Chapter 3), about half of the boat itself had been eroded away before excavation; perhaps as many as half of the grave goods had also been lost. To some extent, this hinders comparisons between the assemblage from Scar and elsewhere. It is particularly difficult to compare the Scar male assemblage with others as, because of its incompleteness, it is a rather unusual collection of grave goods. Nor is it possible to comment much further on the child burial, whose lack of accompanying grave goods may be entirely a product of erosion of the grave—or not.

The surviving assemblage comprises two distinct, gender-specific assemblages: one male and one female. These are first considered here as individual grave groups.

The male grave goods

The male burial was accompanied at least by a sword in its scabbard; a quiver of eight arrows; twenty-two gaming pieces (originally in some kind of container); a comb; possibly two lead weights; and, tentatively, a shield. Despite the caveat about how many items may have been lost to the sea, it is striking that no common domestic or agricultural tools have survived. On the basis of the surviving group alone, the man buried at Scar seems to have been equipped primarily as a warrior who enjoyed some leisure time.

The weapons

Any items placed along the man's left side, on or near the upper part of his body and head, or in the east end of the boat, had already been washed away, together with the handle and pommel of the sword. These are precisely those areas where other weapons might have been expected to be found. Enough male Viking graves have been discovered intact elsewhere in the Viking world to allow speculation as to what might be missing from the Scar man's assemblage of weapons.

After the sword, the commonest weapon found in pagan Viking graves is the spear, the symbol of a warrior's death (Ellis Davidson 1982, 35). The weapon most associated with the Vikings in popular imagination, and also very common in male graves, is the battleaxe (the most commonly occurring combination of weapons in north Norway is the sword and axe, rather than the sword and spear: Sjøvold 1974, 266). The principal defensive weapon was the shield, typically a circular wooden board with a central iron boss. Shield bosses are common finds in pagan male graves, often located under or over the head (e.g. at Westness, Rousay, Orkney: Kaland 1993, 315–16, fig. 17.7). It is possible that a shield may be represented in the male assemblage from Scar, in the form of the fragmentary tinned bronze object which perhaps derived from a shield rim or boss edge (Chapter 6). Arrows are fairly common finds in male graves, in Britain and elsewhere (e.g. Sjøvold 1974, 263, Table 2; Chapter 6), though less common than swords, spears and axes. Much less common Viking Age weaponry includes combat knives (the Germanic sax), javelins, lances, maces, helmets (of leather or metal—but never horned) and, at least by the tenth century, chain mail and riding equipment.

Only sometimes does a 'complete' set of common weapons—sword, spear, axe, shield and arrow(s)—occur in a single grave. Sjøvold records only one 'complete' set of weapons out of roughly a hundred Viking period male graves in north Norway (1974, 56, L.228). A Scottish example of a 'complete' set of weapons (amongst much else) is provided by the very rich male grave from Kiloran Bay, Colonsay (Grieg 1940, 48–61; Chapter 8), with its well-preserved shield boss and two arrows, as well as the sword, spear and axe. On the other hand, single male graves frequently contain more than one example of a weapon type. A boat chamber-grave from Hedeby, Germany, dated to around AD 900, contained three swords and four shield bosses, and is thought to be an exceptional triple male burial (Müller-Wille 1976; Wamers 1994; 1995). In Scotland, Grave 1 at Ballinaby, Islay, contained two axe-heads and one adze (Grieg 1940, 34, fig. 15; Chapter 8).

Although we cannot know for certain what weaponry is now 'missing' from the Scar boat burial, therefore, we can be reasonably confident that the man was equipped in the grave not only with the sword in its scabbard and the quiver of eight arrows, but also with a shield and probably at least one spear and/or battleaxe.

It is tempting to deduce that the man might have been a warrior or soldier in life. However, the inclusion of weapons in graves must have been at least partly symbolic. Viking weapons were often bent or broken, apparently deliberately, before being put in the ground (e.g. Hesket in the Forest, Cumbria; Ingleby, Derbyshire: see Chapter 8). The Scar sword also had at least one break in the blade when it was deposited in the grave (Chapter 6). A more clearly symbolic reference is seen in the deliberate embedding of spears in grave walls or platforms in the chamber-graves at Birka (Gräslund 1980, 30–1); and in the 'thrusting' of weapons—swords, spears and axes—into cremation deposits from a range of sites in eastern Sweden (*ibid.*, 76). Weapons occur most often in men's graves, but not exclusively; they are occasionally also included in women's graves.

Objects other than weapons

Only three items other than weapons were recovered from the male burial: a comb, a set of gaming pieces and, possibly, the two lead weights (excluding

95. One of the two Westness boat burials containing a man in his burial chamber. What looks like a hat set at a jaunty angle on the skeleton's head is actually an iron shield boss; the rest of the wooden shield had rotted away in the ground. Copyright Olwyn Owen.

the tinned bronze object; see above). There were no personal objects other than the comb (e.g. strap-ends, belt buckle, tweezers); no objects of adornment (e.g. brooch,? beads); no everyday tools or utensils (e.g. knives, strike-a-lights, flints, locks, vessels of steatite, pottery or metal); no fishing equipment (e.g. fish hooks, line or net sinkers); no agricultural implements (e.g. sickles, scythes, socketed axes); and no smithing equipment (e.g. hammers, tongs, metal shears, anvils, files, chisels). One, several or many of these 'workaday' items, in whatever combination, normally occur in male Viking graves and might have been expected at Scar.

Perhaps the closest comparisons to the male assemblage at Scar in terms both of grave type and geography are the two boat burials from Westness, Rousay, Orkney, each of which contained a single male. Each burial was accompanied by a sword and shield, arrows and axes, and one also had a spear. Both graves contained farming tools, such as a sickle and an adze. One grave also contained flints, a strike-a-light and a whetstone; while the other had a fishing weight and a bone comb (Kaland 1993, 316). Both men had been fighting, though probably not with each other: one shield boss was badly slashed; and the other man had been hit by four arrows, the tips of which remained in his body. The body of another young man at Westness, in a stone-lined grave symbolically shaped like a boat, was accompanied by a shield boss, arrowheads, sickle, ringed pin, comb, gaming pieces and die (Kaland 1993, 313, fig. 17.6). This latter assemblage more closely parallels that from Scar but again includes at least one agricultural tool and an object of personal adornment. These examples of intact, wealthy, male Viking assemblages from Westness, Orkney, are fairly typical and indicate the types and quantity of equipment which might originally also have been deposited in the male grave at Scar.

Although the association of the lead weights with the Scar boat burial is not seriously in doubt, it is not certain that the weights originally accompanied the man. In general, there is a high correlation between the gender of the deceased and the types of goods contained in graves, but some types of artefacts are common to both sexes (Jesch 1991, 13–14). Additionally, apparently gender-specific items sometimes occur in graves of the opposite gender; hence, the possibility that the lead weights might have accompanied the Scar woman or even the child, rather than the man (Chapter 6). Nevertheless, when found in graves, lead weights normally accompany male burials, in Scandinavia and elsewhere, and it is at least a reasonable assumption that they accompanied the man in this case too. Since both weights were discovered on the beach, and since the male and child burials had suffered a much greater degree of disturbance than the woman's, it is much less likely that they were buried with the woman.

These circumstances of discovery also confirm the evidence for only partial survival of the assemblage. It is now impossible to ascertain whether a whole set of weights, and perhaps even the balance scales to go with them, had originally been deposited in the grave, although this may be unlikely. Although many weights form part of sets, in a large number of cases weights occur alone or in pairs, even within graves (Blindheim, Heyerdahl-Larsen & Tollnes 1981, 146). Moreover, it is strange that the Scar weights both weigh exactly the same; since the owner of a set should not have needed two identical weights, this might suggest that they were not in fact part of a set at all, but derived from two similar sets. These considerations, added to the doubt as to whether the weights would have served any useful purpose in Viking Orkney, make their appearance in this grave all the more anomalous. Normally, lead weights might be used as evidence that their owner was a merchant, chieftain or other leader—someone who needed to weigh out bullion for commercial transactions or to make payments to followers. However, given the circumstances, it seems safest at best to return an open verdict on their significance for the male burial at Scar.

Gaming pieces are frequently found in male Viking graves without an accompanying gaming board or die (Chapter 6) and, given the lack of any trace of a board, it is perhaps reasonable to assume that none was deposited in the Scar grave. However, this cannot now be finally determined; nor can the nature of the container in which the gaming pieces had been kept, although comparisons with Norwegian examples (e.g. Jåtten, Rogaland) suggest that a linen pouch is perhaps the most likely. Even without a gaming board, graves containing gaming pieces are often those of individuals from the higher strata of society which are richly furnished in general; they include several so-called 'chieftains' graves, including Gokstad (Petersen 1914, 84). This view is echoed by Sjøvold (1974, 324) who used the inclusion of gaming pieces in three richly furnished north Norwegian male graves, which also contained blacksmith's tools, to point to the high prestige enjoyed by the blacksmith's craft: 'it is well known that the board game was an entertainment for people high up on the social ladder'.

Apart from the weapons, the comb in the Scar male assemblage is the only common type of artefact to have survived and is less indicative of the man's status or occupations. Ambrosiani (1981, 49) postulates that most adults, male and female, possessed a comb; next to pottery, combs are the most common objects found in Viking Age graves of both sexes. Despite the fact that combs were made in many places, the finished products show a remarkable consistency throughout a very large area, stretching from Staraja Ladoga in the east to Dublin in the west. Thus, the inclusion of a fine comb in the male (and female) Scar assemblage adds little to the interpretation of the assemblage as a whole.

Summary

The male assemblage recovered from Scar would be an unusual group of male grave goods in any circumstances and is almost certainly the result of only partial survival. However, although the curious absence of a single common item of male equipment (other than weapons) may be more apparent than real, the element of uncertainty seriously inhibits any attempt to determine the status and occupation of the man buried at Scar. The gaming pieces indicate that the man may have been of at least higher than average status, while the weapons indicate that he was equipped in the grave as a warrior. It is unwise to draw any conclusions from the lead weights. Thus, despite the wealth of this grave as a whole, we are left with only conjecture as to the role and rank of the man buried at Scar—his position

96. A selection of the Scar man's grave goods.

97. A selection of the Scar woman's grave goods.

in society, his relationship to the woman and child, and the skills or trades he practised in his everyday life.

The female grave goods

The female burial was accompanied by at least: a carved whalebone plaque; a gilded bronze equal-armed brooch; a comb; two spindle whorls, one of steatite and one of sandstone; a pair of shears; a needle tidy containing two iron needles; an iron weaving batten; a small sickle; and a box made of maple. Two objects among the woman's assemblage stand out as exceptional finds: the brooch and the carved whalebone plaque. Both items suggest that the woman was comparatively wealthy and that she belonged to the upper strata of Viking Age society. This impression is reinforced by the concentration of items associated with weaving and sewing (below).

The woman's assemblage should have survived more completely than that of the man because her body lay in the best preserved section of the burial chamber. However, due to otter disturbance, the goods which accompanied her in the grave have probably also only survived in part. There had been gross post-burial disturbance of the woman's body from the upper pelvis to the head, precisely the area where many if not most of the grave goods would have been deposited. Even those items which were recovered had been displaced, which hampers analysis of the original disposition of the goods (Smith, below). The survival of a few fragments of bone comb within this area of the grave, when the man's undisturbed comb was relatively well preserved, serves to underline the fact that other items of her grave goods may now be 'missing' altogether. For instance, the question of the apparent lack of oval brooches cannot be resolved under these circumstances.

Nevertheless, many more of the woman's grave goods have survived, with a greater number of everyday objects as well as 'special' objects represented. Unlike the male assemblage, there are no obviously 'missing' categories of artefact—with the important exception of the lack of oval brooches and, to a lesser extent, the lack of a necklace. Despite this, it is highly likely that the female assemblage as recovered in excavation is also incomplete. A study of the female graves in western Norway showed that more than a quarter of them contained cooking utensils (Jesch 1991, 19), but none were recovered at Scar. Moreover, Viking women often carried small implements, such as knives, scissors, small hones or keys, by hanging them from their strings of beads or from their brooches on straps or rings. If any were deposited with the woman at Scar, they would have been located in the chest area—that area of the burial which had been badly damaged by otter disturbance. Given that they would not have been protected within a container, this disturbance might have fragmented them and ultimately caused all traces of them to be removed.

Nonetheless, it must be admitted that the absence of any trace whatsoever of such common items raises the real possibility that none of these items were buried with the woman at Scar. Given the quantity and quality of the surviving artefacts, the possible absence of these common items from the original burial would again be somewhat unusual.

Textiles, implements and the question of status

The inclusion of a selection of items associated with weaving and spinning is one of several common denominators among wealthy female graves in Scandinavia and Britain. Textile-working implements could include weaving battens, loom weights, spindle whorls, shears, wool combs, needles and needle cases, linen smoothers, whalebone plaques etc. At Scar, of the nine categories of artefact recovered from the woman's grave, five are associated with textile working: the weaving batten, the shears, the two spindle whorls, the two needles in a needle tidy, and the carved whalebone plaque. In Norway, weaving battens, spindle whorls, shears and loom weights are especially common finds in women's graves (Petersen 1951, 522–5). In Sogn, west Norway, textile implements are the category of tools most regularly found in women's graves; and often the whole process of textile preparation is represented among the artefacts from a single grave (Dommasnes 1979, 107; 1982, 76).

In her analysis of female roles and ranks in Sogn on the basis of the grave goods and burial customs, Dommasnes (1982) argued that accompanied pagan Viking graves represent only a minority of the population and that, therefore, *any* pagan burial is indicative of relatively high rank. Since only about one-quarter of the Sogn (and, indeed, of the Norwegian Viking period) graves are of women, and since these tend to contain a more restricted range of artefact type than those of men, it seems likely that fewer women achieved high rank than men. However, on average, their graves were more richly furnished than those of men and the burials themselves were often lavish. For example, women were often buried in large mounds; and, interestingly, 'every second scientifically excavated woman's grave in Sogn can be interpreted as a boat-grave, as compared to every third man's grave' (*ibid.*, 80). It is noteworthy that the wealthy female graves in Sogn, which resemble that from Scar in terms of the types and quantities of their grave goods, the lavishness of the burial customs exhibited, and the rarity of one or more of their inclusions, tend to occur in the best and longest-settled agricultural areas, usually in coastal areas. Dommasnes tentatively concludes that more women achieved high rank in Sogn in the ninth century than previously because of a shift of economic and political power towards women in the Viking period, especially in fertile coastal areas, presumably because of the absence of large numbers of men on military service.

Clearly, on the evidence of the female graves in Norway, textile production was a common activity of well-placed Viking women. Agricultural tools, normally sickles, are also frequently found in female graves and, at least in Sogn, are more commonly found in women's graves than men's. This may indicate that women played an important part in harvesting. It is notable that the sickle in the woman's assemblage was the only agricultural tool found at Scar. However, this equation of tool to individual task may be over-simplistic since pagan burial was primarily a symbolic act. It seems reasonable to assume that the grave goods selected for burial symbolised both the tasks *and* responsibilities of the deceased, in which case the emphasis on textile production and agricultural tools may

98. A plan of the very rich Grave 854 from Birka (after Almgren 1966).

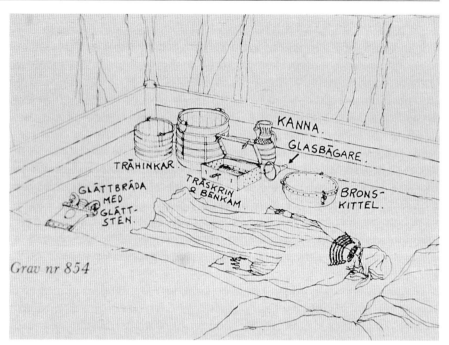

99. Equal-armed brooches from Birka. The larger one was found in Grave 854 which, like Scar, also produced a fine whalebone plaque. Copyright Statens Historiska Museet, Stockholm.

100. The cemetery at Birka, Sweden, contained some 1100 grave mounds. Copyright Olwyn Owen.

have symbolised the woman's wider *responsibilities* for providing clothing and food. Clearly, typical female grave assemblages do not embrace all of women's activities and responsibilities; any evidence of child rearing, for example, is notably absent from the grave assemblages.

It seems reasonable to assume that the wealth and energy invested in both grave goods and memorial type must have reflected to some degree the deceased person's rank; and that a rare element in a grave assemblage symbolises a higher rank than a more common element. The woman at Scar was richly accompanied by textile tools and an agricultural tool; with her companions, she had an elaborate burial within a chamber on a boat; and she was buried with a carved whalebone plaque of exceptional quality. On all these criteria, therefore, the Scar woman seems likely to have been of high rank and probably held a position of some responsibility within her family or community.

Two factors above all others may have enhanced both her rank in later life and the respect accorded to her in death. One is the great age to which she lived, at least by the standards of her time; the other, perhaps even more important, is her possession of a highly symbolic whalebone plaque, with its apparent association with the Viking goddess Freyja (page 79). In the plaque, we may have another clue as to the Scar woman's unusually elevated place in society. In a recent re-analysis of the Scandinavian boat grave custom, Crumlin-Pedersen (1995, 94; following Müller-Wille 1970), has argued persuasively not only that a boat was a religious symbol, but that it was present in a grave as an attribute of one of the heathen gods. He points out that only a fraction of the population received a boat burial and suggests that: 'the best explanation for this fact is to consider those buried with boats as persons involved directly in the fertility cult as priests or their helpers and therefore so closely connected to the god—or even to be looked on as part of the family of the gods—that they are 'authorised' to be marked out with the attribute as an offering in their graves'. If so, might not this be the real significance of the plaque, displayed so prominently within the boat grave? Could it be that the plaque marked out the Scar woman not only as a worshipper of Freyja, but as one of Freyja's servants in the Viking world? This is highly speculative of course, and casts no light on the roles of the man and child, but it might help to explain some of the stranger aspects of this burial.

Comparable female graves

Because of the greater completeness of the woman's assemblage than the man's, it is easier and more valid to propose parallels for the Scar female burial. In one of the richest graves excavated at Birka, for instance, Grave 854 (Arbman 1943; Fig. 98), a wealthy woman was buried in a wooden chamber along one side of which lay a bronze bowl, a wooden casket containing a comb and a glass linen smoother (recalling the maplewood box at Scar which contained the shears, at least one of the spindle whorls, and the needle tidy), a wine jug and drinking glass from the Rhineland, and two buckets. In the opposite corner was a whalebone plaque (Fig. 52a). The woman was buried fully clothed with her brooches and beads in place, including a large equal-armed brooch (Fig. 99). An iron ring with Thor's hammer pendants was found under the skull and had presumably been placed around the neck of the dead woman. This is the only grave found so far which certainly contained both a carved plaque and a linen smoother (Chapter 5; but see also the Føre, Bø i Vesterålen, north Norway grave, below), although the two objects were not found together within the grave. Unlike the Scar grave, Birka Grave 854 contained imported European objects, indicative of a more cosmopolitan environment as might be expected at Birka; otherwise, the similarities are obvious. The cemetery at Birka produced many graves with chests, boxes and caskets (Chapter 5), including Grave 854, but until the maplewood box was recognised at Scar, none had previously been confirmed in the Scottish corpus (although an iron hasp and possible iron casket fittings in the woman's grave at King's Cross Point, Arran, suggests that a wooden box was also among the grave goods here (Balfour 1908–9, 371; Greig 1940, II, 27, fig. 10)).

Within Scotland, rather few female graves have proved as rich in grave goods as that from Scar. A ninth-century female grave dug into the ruins of Gurness broch, Orkney, provides a typical example: the woman wore a pair of oval brooches and an iron necklet, and beside her were an iron knife and sickle (Ritchie 1993, 59, figs 43–4; Fig. 102). In those rich women's graves which have been discovered (and, indeed, in the less wealthy female graves), textile implements, agricultural tools and items of personal adornment remain the common themes. For example, the first grave discovered at Westness, Rousay, Orkney, in 1963, contained a very wealthy, rather fat woman, who sadly must have died in childbirth as she was buried with her newborn twins (Daphne Lorimer, personal communication; Fig. 110). The objects buried with her included a pair of oval brooches (Type P37, generally dated to between the eighth century and the latter half of the ninth century: Jansson 1985a, 229), a necklace of forty variegated beads, a comb, two bronze

101. The grave of the 'Pagan Lady of Peel', Isle of Man (after Freke 1986).

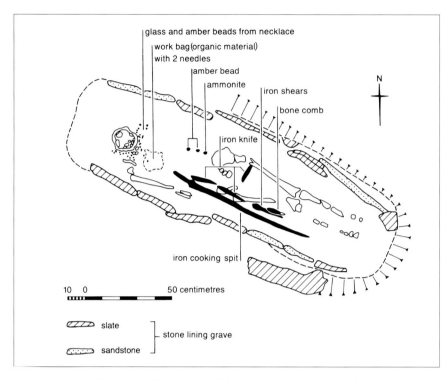

glass and amber beads from necklace

work bag (organic material) with 2 needles

amber bead

ammonite

iron shears

bone comb

iron knife

iron cooking spit

N

10   0   50 centimetres

slate ⎤
      ⎬ stone lining grave
sandstone ⎦

102. Sickle found in a female grave at Gurness, Orkney Mainland, with an iron knife. This woman was wearing a pair of oval brooches and an iron necklet. Copyright National Museums of Scotland.

strap ends, two iron heckles, a pair of shears, an iron weaving batten, a sickle, a small bone tool, a whalebone rubbing bone, a fragment of Celtic metalwork (Stevenson 1989, 239) and, most important of all, a very fine Celtic brooch which was perhaps more than a century old when it was buried (Stevenson 1968, 25–31). This grave has not yet been published in full but probably dates to the ninth century (Kaland 1993, 314). Unfortunately, nothing is known about the form of the grave but its assemblage is similar to the female assemblage from Scar, and possibly even richer. Subsequent excavations at Westness have produced other similar female graves, though none as wealthy as the first.

In 1979, at Kneep (Cnip), Lewis, in the Western Isles, a wealthy, tenth-century female grave was found containing two oval brooches, forty-four glass beads, a comb, an iron knife, a pendant whetstone, a bone needle case with two iron needles, a sickle, a ringed pin, a matching bronze belt buckle and strap-end, and an iron rivet (Welander, Batey & Cowie 1987). A woman's grave at Ballinaby in Islay included a pair of oval brooches, portions of three decorated double discs of bronze or copper, a fine silver dress-pin and safety-chain, twelve beads, a bronze ladle, a needle case, a glass linen smoother and an iron heckle for the preparation of flax fibres (Anderson 1880).

Many Viking graves were found a long time ago and are poorly recorded. However, when circumstances permit the scientific excavation of newly discovered Viking graves, as at Scar, much more information can be recovered. Two recently excavated female burials, one in Norway and one in the Isle of Man, serve to highlight that the female assemblage from Scar (and those from comparable Scottish graves) bears similarities to wealthy female graves in Norway and elsewhere in Britain.

A grave found at Føre, Bø i Vesterålen, north Norway, excavated in 1989–90, contained the richly accompanied body of a petite but adult Viking woman, buried in a c. 10m-long boat together with a small dog (Schanche 1991). The grave goods include: an iron weaving batten, a whalebone plaque, an iron bowl, an axe for domestic use, a knife, a polished stone (possibly a linen smoother), four glass beads, two spindle whorls, and flints (for use with a strike-a-light). This female boat burial, with its iron weaving batten, well-preserved whalebone plaque and two spindle whorls, provides a strikingly close comparison for the Scar female burial. The grave had been plundered some time before its excavation—which may account for the lack of jewellery.

Recent excavation of the long cist burial of a wealthy Viking woman at Peel, Isle of Man, euphemistically known as the 'Pagan Lady of Peel' (Freke 1986, 102; 1987, 41; 1995, 17–20; Fig. 101), produced a comb, a pair of shears, two sheathed knives with silver wire decorated handles, a cooking spit, two needles in a work box or pouch, a charm pendant of two amber beads, a pierced ammonite and a most spectacular necklace of seventy-one glass, amber and jet beads.

The jewellery question

Like the Scar woman, the 'Pagan Lady of Peel' had no oval brooches. Oval brooches were by far the most popular type of personal ornament for Viking women, precisely because they functioned in pairs as essential dress fasteners, one for each shoulder. They are found in female graves across the whole Viking world, but do not occur in every female grave. Approximately two out of every three Swedish female graves contained oval brooches. If the Scar woman was buried without oval brooches, then it is conceivable that this reflects a regional pattern and that the woman might have come from one of the few parts of Scandinavia where oval brooches are rarely found in female graves. In Sweden, for instance, female graves in south-east Uppland and Södermanland do not normally contain oval brooches (Björn Ambrosiani, personal communication); but then, graves in this area are mostly cremation burials with very simple grave goods, which demonstrates a more general diversity in the burial customs of this region (Gräslund 1980, 72). By the middle of the tenth century, oval brooches were going out of fashion. This may be the explanation for their absence from the grave of the 'Pagan Lady of Peel' who was buried about then, and it is just possible that the Scar grave is as late as this in date (pages 162-5).

It is thought that beads were used as a connecting string between oval brooches. However, as at Peel, necklaces of beads can also occur alone. Among the female graves of northern Norway, beads often occur in too small numbers to have functioned as a connecting string—which led Sjøvold (1974, 207) to question whether they were normally worn in conjunction with oval brooches in northern Norway. The same may be true for the Scottish female graves. Despite these caveats, the fact that no oval brooches or definite Viking beads were discovered with the female burial at Scar remains somewhat incongruous.

The Scar woman's equal-armed brooch is an opulent and relatively rare brooch which is doubtless another indication of her high rank. Such a brooch would usually be the 'third' brooch, after a pair of oval brooches. However, there are more than twice as many finds from Norway which contain only a pair of oval brooches as there are finds which contain both oval brooches and a third brooch (Petersen 1928, 205). Thus, the association of a pair of oval brooches with a single brooch of another type is not as incontrovertible as is often portrayed. The ratio is in fact rather higher in northern Norway, which led Sjøvold to suggest that the standard of personal ornaments was somewhat higher in northern Norway than in the rest of the country (1974, 207). Equal-armed brooches seem to be more popular in northern Norway than elsewhere in the country, where trefoil-shaped brooches are the prevalent type of 'third' brooch overall.

The numbers of equal-armed brooches which have been discovered so far are relatively small compared with oval brooches, even allowing that the latter are invariably found in pairs. In northern Norway, six equal-armed brooches were discovered in female graves as 'third' brooches (that is, together with oval brooches); while another three equal-armed brooches have been discovered in graves without oval brooches (two others are not certainly from graves) (Sjøvold 1974, 207). Petersen (1928, 92) recorded only some sixty examples from the whole of Norway, although he believed them to be a Norwegian type. Even in the great cemeteries at Birka, Sweden, only sixty-one equal-armed brooches have been recovered prior to the recent excavations (Aagård 1984, 96), although they are the most popular brooch there after oval brooches. To put these numbers in perspective, approximately 4000 oval brooches are known from across the Viking world (Jansson 1985a, 221). The particular rarity and opulence of the Troms type of equal-armed brooch, as found in the Scar burial, has already been described (Chapter 5); no other brooches of this type have been found *in situ* within Viking graves in Britain.

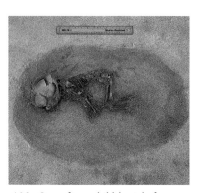

103. One of two child burials from Kneep, Lewis, in the Western Isles. One infant wore a necklace of amber beads and its clothing had been secured by a fine bone pin, while the other child had an amber bead and pendant, both presumably worn round the neck.

Summary

Thus, it is the quality and rarity of the equal-armed brooch, the presence of the very fine carved whalebone plaque and the elaborate burial of this woman—in a chamber within a boat and with male and child companions—which distinguish the Scar woman's grave as exceptional, rather than the quantity or types of items it contained. There can be little doubt that the woman buried at Scar was of high rank, and it is very likely that she held a position of responsibility within her family or community. It is even possible that she was directly involved with the cult of Freyja, perhaps as a religious leader. In short, the respect accorded to her in death is likely to reflect the esteem in which she was held in life. During her later years, respect was probably magnified into awe, given the great age to which she lived, though what she herself made of her biological rarity we can only imagine.

The child's burial

It is not certain whether the child's burial was originally accompanied by grave goods. Children (and servants or slaves) are sometimes accompanied by grave goods, including quality items. For instance, the burial of a 12– to 14–year-old boy recently excavated at Balnakeil, Durness, Sutherland (Gourlay, Low & Batey forthcoming), contained full-sized adult weapons: a sword which was too big for the boy to use easily; a spear and shield which seem to have been set up as a sort of canopy over the boy's head (*John O'Groats Journal* 10.12.93); two ringed pins; three beads (one of glass and two of amber); two hair combs; a set of bone gaming pieces; several flat pieces of wood (possibly from a gaming board or wooden coffin); flints and other objects (Colleen Batey, personal communication). However, it could be argued that someone aged 12 to 14 was viewed as a young adult rather than a child: hence the full-sized weapons.

At Westness, Orkney, a number of unaccompanied child graves were excavated, but most were of infants and very small children and some of them probably date to the pre-Viking period (Kaland 1993, 312–17). Westness is a very important site for many reasons—not least because the skeletons have survived in the sandy soils and the whole community is represented there. In more acidic soils, or where Viking graves were excavated many years ago, the skeletons do not normally survive or were not recorded. In such cases, graves are identified as to sex on the basis of the grave goods: typically, weapons for men and jewellery for women. Using these criteria, and the results of modern excavations, several recent large-scale studies of Viking graves within an area or country have revealed that roughly equal numbers of women and men were buried. However, the smaller bones of children are particularly susceptible to poor preservation or to being overlooked in older excavations; therefore, in cemeteries with poorly preserved or absent skeletons, the number of children's graves can be difficult to determine. At Birka, Gräslund (1980, 82) has suggested that some 17% of the inhumation graves were children's but, in other cemeteries, she suggests that children's graves normally number c. 25–30% of the total.

Children's graves tend to be gender-specific rather than age-specific; in other words, they normally contain fairly typical male or female grave goods, appropriate to the sex of the child. Diagnostic children's artefacts, such as toys in the form of model boats, weapons and animals, are known, but are not usually found in graves (e.g. Graham-Campbell 1980, nos. 104–7). It is conceivable that the Scar weights had been passed down to the child, perhaps as toys. At Birka, for instance, weights occur in 129 graves, of which six are certainly those of children (Gräslund 1973, 174). This is most unlikely to mean that the children engaged in trade (Kyhlberg 1971, 36), but it could signify instead that they were the children of merchants or traders.

Gräslund (1973) argues that some types of artefact occur most frequently in, and can therefore be used as indicators of, children's graves. These include small bronze bells, pendant lockets and, perhaps, mirrors. Interestingly, one of the two accompanied child burials excavated in the cemetery at Peel, Isle of Man, contained a bronze bell, as well as a necklace of glass and amber beads;

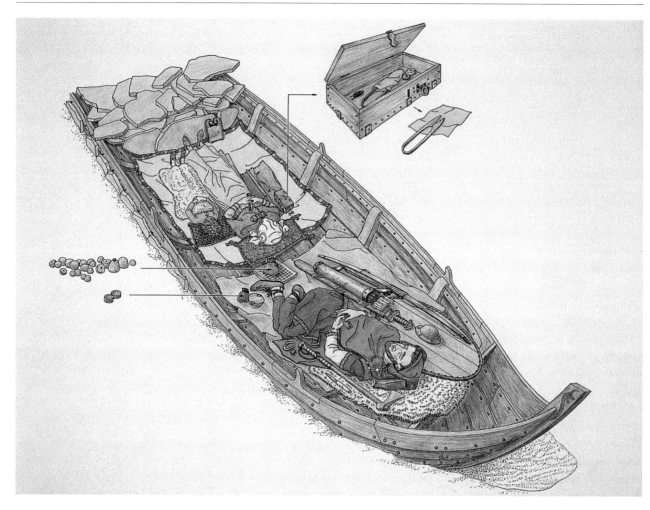

105. A reconstruction drawing of the Scar burial. Drawing by Christina Unwin.

104. The blue glass bead from Scar.

the other had a single glass bead. One also had an Eadred halfpenny of AD 946–55 placed in his mouth, 'apparently respecting the custom of "paying the ferryman"' (Richards 1991, 103).

In short, it is quite possible that the child at Scar was originally accompanied by as rich a collection of grave goods as the man and woman undoubtedly were. Alternatively, and perhaps just possible, in contrast to the man and woman, the child may have been buried without accompanying grave goods.

Uncontexted finds

Three finds were uncontexted, that is, not found with any of the burials: the two lead weights and a single bead. The two lead weights are considered most likely to have come from the male burial. However, the single uncontexted bead may or may not have been deposited with the boat burial. It has not been possible to ascertain whether this is even a Viking artefact; still less whether it was once part of a necklace and, if so, whether it was buried with the man, woman or child. In addition, five small flints and one piece of quartzite were recovered from sieved samples, but these were probably not associated with the grave.

The arrangement of the grave goods

Andrea Smith

In Viking Age pagan graves, a few general principles seem to have governed how and where objects were positioned on and around the body. In the main, these reflect the manner in which the objects had been worn, carried and used by their owners during their lives.

Male burials

The Scar man had his sword, with the quiver of arrows on top, laid along his right-hand side close to his body, and his comb between his hands, over the centre of his pelvis. A similar pattern can be seen in many other cases. The Balnakeil boy (Gourlay, Low & Batey forthcoming), for instance, had his sword under his right side, his comb at his hip, and a spearhead and shield boss near his head. The shield may have been propped up on the upturned spearhead, to form a kind of canopy over the boy's head. Male graves in the cemetery at Birka were usually laid out along similar lines: the sword along the right side of the body, the shield above or over the head, and the axe on the left side of the body. Spearheads were mostly found in the head area, to the left or right, and occasionally there were two shield bosses, one at either end of the body. As the upper half and the left side of the man's body at Scar had been lost to the sea, it is not surprising that the shield, spear and axe are absent from this assemblage. Combs were generally found in the waist and hip area, suggesting that they were kept in pockets or bags hung from the waist. At Birka, antler comb cases were more common in male graves than in female graves (Ambrosiani 1981, 14).

The position of the sword to the right of the body is interesting in that right-handers would normally wear their sword to the left. This indicates that it had been deliberately placed there and was not worn on the body in a sling or belt. There seems to be some significance in the consistent placing of the sword by the right hand and closest to the body. The sword was probably the most significant weapon for the Viking, both in terms of monetary, military and perhaps symbolic value. The Scar sword had at least one break in the blade when it was placed in the grave, and a lightweight scabbard which seems to have been intended only to hold the sword in one piece until it was buried (Chapter 6). Much has been made of the supposed deliberate 'killing' of weapons deposited in Viking graves (e.g. Bersu & Wilson 1966, 81; Richards *et al* 1995, 61), but at Scar the presence of the scabbard holding the sword together seems to imply that the break in the sword was not publicly displayed, and may indeed have been hidden. The sword could have been broken accidentally, perhaps even in combat; but it certainly seems to have been old and well-worn at the time of burial, and may even have been a family heirloom.

Female burials

At Scar the equal-armed brooch and sickle were found lying in what would have been the woman's chest area. Other objects might have been sited on her upper body but not survived the otter disturbance, such as a pair of oval brooches, perhaps with a string of beads suspended between them. The positioning of the sickle over the woman's torso can be paralleled in two other Scottish graves, although in none of them was it possible to tell whether it had been held in their hands, or simply laid on top of the body. Shears are almost always found at waist level on the woman's right-hand side, and appear to have been most often suspended from one of the oval brooches or from a belt at the waist, thus forming part of her dress. The woman's comb was found scattered in fragments, but centred on the woman's pelvic area, suggesting that this may also originally have been suspended from a belt. Further to her right were the remains of a maplewood box, which had contained a pair of shears and a spindle whorl, and possibly also a needle tidy and a second spindle whorl. The collection of sewing equipment in a box appears to have been less common in Scotland and Norway, although there are problems of retrieval of this type of evidence. In those graves at Birka where boxes were present, they were generally placed either to the person's right, or at the foot of the grave. There is very little evidence available relating to the placement of weaving battens, but the position of the Scar batten, along the woman's right side, mirrors that of the man's sword. Another strange similarity is that the weaving batten also seems to have been broken; here the evidence is not quite so clear, but part of it seems to have been missing, either through deliberate breakage, or simply due to the fact that it was old and damaged.

Some distance from the woman's body, beyond her feet to the right, was the whalebone plaque, which was originally set upright and facing her. Whalebone plaques have rarely been excavated from burials under controlled conditions, but in one example from Birka, the positioning is very similar to that at Scar, at the foot of the grave away from the woman's body, although in this case it was slightly to her left, and had fallen over sideways rather than face down. This distance placed between the plaque and the body can be contrasted with the closer proximity of perhaps the more everyday tools and more personal ornaments, such as the sickle, shears and equal-armed brooch. This in itself, quite apart from the aesthetic qualities of the plaque, seems to indicate that the plaque was not an item of everyday use or personal ornament, but an object of particular significance and symbolism; and had been placed so that the woman could see and admire it in death as she had in life.

Other furnishings of the grave

Small clues have survived in the form of mineralised textile fragments to indicate that, not only were the people buried in the grave dressed in probably their best clothes, but other textiles had been present too (pages 133–5). Grander burials, such as the Oseberg ship (see below), give some idea of the tapestries, hangings, cushions and other textiles used to decorate Viking homes. Casts of feathers and straw on the sword of the Balnakeil boy suggest that he may have been laid down on straw or straw matting, with a feather pillow under his head; and at Birka some of the dead appear to have been laid on furs and animal skins.

In apparent contrast with this care to dress the deceased and make them comfortable can be set the frequent practice of placing large stones in the grave, which at Birka was interpreted as having binding or warding-off significance, in an attempt to prevent the dead revisiting the living (Gräslund 1980).

Summary

There is no way of knowing who was actually responsible for the laying out of the grave, whether it was simply the immediate family, or whether there were particular individuals in a community who carried out such tasks. It is common in many societies for women in particular to preside over death, as they do over birth. An eyewitness account of a Viking funeral among the Rus tells of an ugly old woman called the 'angel of death', who was the ritual specialist in charge of the whole ceremony (Warmind 1995). Aided by her daughters, this woman played a central role in the killing of a slave girl to accompany a wealthy dead man to the afterlife.

Whoever was responsible for overseeing the funeral rites for the Scar people was fully aware of customs and traditions which were widespread throughout the Viking world. The dead would be fully dressed, complete with the jewellery and other small objects (comb, knife) which they would have worn every day on their persons. Around them, in pre-ordained places, would then be set those items which further defined their occupation and status. For most Viking males (and possibly some females) the tools of their trade also included weapons, and pride of place, closest to the right hand, was given to the sword. Women of middle and higher rank, such as the woman buried at Scar, were generally provided with various items of equipment relating to textile production. Spinning and weaving have become so strongly identified with women that these occupations, and allegory and metaphor derived from them, have entered into myth and legend throughout much of the history of western Europe. In the pagan Viking period, spinning, weaving and sewing seem to have held a particular significance, and, among the few references to women in *Orkneyinga Saga,* is the story of how the sisters Helga and Frakkok wove a poisoned shirt which was accidentally put on by Earl Harald (Helga's son). The addition of a sickle to the Scar woman's grave goods, given her evident wealth and status, is a reference to the role of women in agricultural activities and the bringing in of the harvest. This, on a prosaic level, may be an indication that she was a matriarch who took care of the family farm while the men were away, whilst also invoking the theme of fertility and fruitfulness.

The Scar grave as a multiple burial

So far, we have examined the Scar assemblage as if it were in fact two (or three) distinct assemblages: that of a man and woman (and child). However, the Scar grave is an elaborate multiple burial within a single boat. This fact above all others distinguishes it from the vast majority of pagan Viking graves in Britain and Scandinavia which contain single burials. At Birka, for instance, of the 1100 or so graves examined: 'the great majority … were single burials, regardless of burial method and type' (Gräslund 1980, 75); only ten graves contained definite double burials and no graves at all appear to have contained triple burials, a picture repeated across the Viking world. Triple Viking Age burials are extremely rare indeed: only the Scar burial and a triple male burial from Hedeby are known to this author (see above); while a mass Viking grave excavated at Repton, Derbyshire, England (Biddle, Kjølby-Biddle *et al* 1986) relates to an isolated and very particular incident (see Chapter 8).

This observation inevitably raises the question of the cause or causes of death of the three individuals buried at Scar. Unfortunately, in no instance could a direct cause of death be ascertained from the surviving skeletal remains (Chapter 4). This is not surprising: even had the three skeletons been complete, many of the most likely causes of death would not have left any trace. This is particularly true of acute infections which must have been one of the principal causes of death in the pre-antibiotic era. It is suggested that by far the most common cause of death of the 210 children's skeletons (out of a total of only 364 individuals) analysed from an early medieval gravefield at Västerhus, Jämtland, Sweden, was acute lung infection (Gräslund 1973, 164). There is generally no time for changes in bone to develop during the short course of fatal diseases, and inflammatory bone change would normally only occur in chronic infections of long duration (e.g. leprosy, tuberculosis).

Similarly, accidental death by drowning could not be determined from the surviving remains. Skeletal analysis indicates that the man probably rowed frequently, at least as a young man (Chapter 4). In his case at least, therefore, it might even be that boat burial symbolised one of his main or favourite occupations and/or the manner of his death; in which case a symbolic boat journey to the afterlife may have been entirely appropriate.

The woman was unusually old when she died, possibly in her seventies (Chapter 4), and it is therefore not at all unreasonable to assume that she died of natural causes in old age. The oldest individual out of some 40 graves in the Westness, Orkney cemetery was only around 50 years old (Kaland 1993, 317); and the average lifespan in medieval times has been estimated by Brothwell (1972) to be 35 years for males and 31 years for females. There has been some recent discussion about how accurately ages at death can be calculated from skeletal remains and, on those few occasions when it is possible to compare archaeological data with historical evidence, it seems that the ages of older individuals in archaeological assemblages have tended to be underestimated (Aykroyd *et al* 1999). It may be that more people in antiquity survived into their sixties and seventies than used to be thought, but there is nonetheless no doubt that the Scar woman reached a very great age by the standards of her time. The people who buried her may never have known anyone else who lived this long and, for perhaps the last 20 or even 30 years of her life, she must have been a figure of increasing awe and reverence.

This observation must raise the unpalatable possibility that, when this exceptionally old woman finally died, two companions were sacrificed to accompany her to the grave. There is no archaeological evidence that the three bodies buried at Scar were interred at different times—which suggests that all three people died within a few hours or, at most, days of each other (although see radiocarbon dates, pages 162-5). Elementary analysis of the arrangement of the bodies within the grave suggests that the woman had been allotted pride of place, laid out flat on her back in the central part of the chamber with the child next to her; and that the man had been rather 'squashed' into the stern of the boat, presumably after the bodies of the woman and child were already in place. Indeed, the unlikely angle of the man's right leg and the odd disarticulation of his foot and ankle suggest that it may have been an effort for the gravediggers to 'fit' him into the available space, perhaps because *rigor mortis* had already begun to set in. This might imply that he died slightly before the other two; alternatively, all three bodies may not have been buried immediately after death, but *rigor mortis* might not have been discerned in the woman's and child's skeletal remains because they were laid out straight on their backs.

We have already seen how the use of a boat in the grave was undoubtedly symbolic and had religious significance, and it has even been suggested that the woman might have fulfilled a religious role in life (pages 144-5). The use of a chamber was clearly also important to the gravediggers for, obviously, without the insertion of the drystone walling across the boat, there would have been ample space to lay out all three individuals and their possessions with plenty of room. On these grounds, it is just conceivable that the man was placed in the grave some time after the woman and child—but it must be emphasised that there is little archaeological evidence to support this hypothesis; indeed, at face value the radiocarbon dates contradict it. The boat burial seems to have been covered once and not disturbed until much later when otters broke through its side and the sea encroached. Had the woman and child been buried first and the man some time later, some sign of ancient human disturbance of the female and child skeletons would have been expected. It should also be remarked that subsequent Viking Age disturbance of the boat burial in order to bury another individual would be highly unusual. Secondary Viking Age burials, in mounds for instance, would not normally involve the opening up of the primary burial. Even at Birka, very few graves showed signs of having been re-opened to accommodate a second body (Gräslund 1982, 36–7, 74); most double burials had been buried simultaneously.

It therefore seems that the construction of the chamber, albeit a fairly primitive one in this case, was an integral part of the burial rite. The boat itself was in no sense considered by the gravediggers to be a 'quasi-coffin' or suitable container for a corpse or corpses: its symbolic importance was paramount and a burial chamber had to be built on the boat especially to contain the bodies. The frequent occurrence of chambers at Birka has already been noted, although these normally wooden structures were not placed within boats. In Orkney, each of the two boat burials from Westness contained a central stone-built burial chamber to accommodate the body of a single man (Kaland 1993, 316, fig. 17.17), which is reminiscent of the Scar boat burial chamber. Also excavated at Westness was a fairly massive, boat-shaped stone setting (Kaland 1993, 316–17, fig. 17.9), or 'empty' chamber, which may have been a form of cenotaph since no burial was found within it.

Perhaps the most famous chamber on a boat, however, is that on the great ship burial from Oseberg, Norway (Brøgger, Falk & Shetelig 1917–18; Christensen, Ingstad & Myhre 1992), which is dated to AD 843 on dendrochronological evidence and is traditionally thought to contain the body of Queen Åsa and her servant. Here, a wooden burial chamber, located behind the mast, contained the bodies of two women: one young, in her twenties, and the other about fifty, with very bad arthritis. These two women were accompanied in the ship by everything they could need on their journey, but we do not know for certain the relationship between them. Even if we assume that one was a queen (to judge from the splendour of the grave goods) and the other her servant, we do not know which was which, nor can we be sure if they died at the same time, or if one was sacrificed to accompany the other.

Evidence of the sacrifice of animals to accompany their owner is not uncommon; the possibility of human sacrifice, however, is much harder to establish, and certainly rarer. Only where there is at least a double burial, and clear evidence of maltreatment of one of the skeletons, can human sacrifice be deemed a possibility. Perhaps the clearest examples come from Denmark (Ramskou 1965); at the old royal centre of Lejre, for instance, in a grave containing two male skeletons, one was well-equipped while the other had been decapitated and buried with his hands and feet tied. At Dråby, also in Denmark, a woman was accompanied by a decapitated male skeleton; while a woman buried at Gerdrup was buried together with a man whose feet had been tied and his neck broken (Jesch 1991, 25). These cases demonstrate that males could also be sacrificed to accompany females to the other world.

In Britain, the clearest evidence for human sacrifice comes from the Isle of Man, from a grave at Ballateare, Jurby (Bersu & Wilson 1966, 45–62). In a layer overlying the body of a well-equipped male was part of another disturbed human burial—that of a young woman in her twenties, with her arms raised upwards and a large hole in her skull created by the slashing blow of a heavy implement (Fig. 106). Whether she was killed at the site or not could not be determined. She could not have survived such a blow but whether the blow itself was the cause of death or delivered soon after death is also uncertain. Nevertheless, that the woman had been sacrificed to the dead man seems a logical conclusion. The Balladoole, Isle of Man, ship grave contained a richly accompanied male; a female was probably also buried in the ship though without any goods, which might suggest that she too had been sacrificed to accompany the man (Bersu & Wilson 1966, 7).

Shetelig (1910) identified the need to look for a 'special explanation' for the burial of two individuals within the Norwegian Viking Age graves, given that single burial was the standard rite. He looked for examples of simultaneous double burials of a man and a woman, where both bodies were equally richly accompanied by grave goods, to identify the possible custom of 'suttee' (where a widow would kill herself or agree to be killed to accompany her dead husband to the grave). Despite the difficulties of interpreting the evidence, he concluded that this practice was known in Norway, as well as in those parts of the Viking world where the evidence is less equivocal. The evidence for Viking Age human sacrifice is augmented by contemporary accounts. The Arab chronicler, Ibn Fadlan, described the burning of a Swedish chief in his ship at a Viking settlement on the Volga (Warmind 1995). One of his slave women consented to accompany the chief to the afterlife: after being feasted and feted for some time, she was ritually killed in a tent on the ship by strangling and stabbing, while the men beat on their shields to drown her screams. Adam of Bremen, writing in the eleventh century about Swedish paganism, also gives a detailed account of human sacrifices at the temple at Uppsala, although he had not seen these himself (Tschan 1959).

At Scar, given the age difference, it seems most unlikely that the man and woman were married and we can probably discount the possibility of 'suttee' in this case. It seems equally unlikely that both the man and the woman would be so richly accompanied if one of them was sacrificed to accompany the other, in some form of master-servant relationship. Given that human sacrifice was itself a relatively rare phenomenon in the Viking Age, it is perhaps also unlikely that the child was sacrificed to accompany the two adults. Nonetheless, all the evidence suggests that all three bodies were interred within the crude stone-built chamber in the boat burial at the same time and, therefore, that they all died at around the same time. Although the possibility of a human sacrifice at Scar cannot be entirely discounted, it is much more likely that these three people either drowned together or perished from some disease at around the same time.

THE DATE OF THE SCAR BOAT BURIAL

Olwyn Owen & Magnar Dalland

The dating of the Scar burial is fraught with difficulties which, unfortunately, not even scientific (radiocarbon) dating has resolved (see below). The burial includes some diagnostic objects, but art-historical and typological dating is notoriously unreliable: art styles and types of artefact could have evolved differently in different parts of the Viking world at different times, and there is 'inevitable haziness of the chronological distinctions' (Morris 1985, 211). These problems are compounded in the case of Viking graves because it is often not known how old the objects already were when they were buried. Grave assemblages can only provide a *terminus post quem* for the date of the burial itself, i.e. the artefacts must have been made before the likely date of the burial. In the Viking colonies, attempting to date graves is even more difficult when based, as is usual, on artefacts found in contexts distant from their source. At Scar, the situation is worse than usual because the scientific and artefactual datings do not agree. Here we examine the artefactual dating first, and then present the scientific dating evidence, with all their contradictions—and, finally, give our 'best guess' as to the date of the Scar boat burial.

106. *A female skull from the grave at Ballateare, Jurby, Isle of Man. This poor young girl may have been a slave, killed to accompany her master into death. Copyright Manx Museum and National Trust.*

How do we date artefacts?

Wilson (1978, 135) defined the criteria by which artefacts might be dated in order of their reliability. Firstly, they can be dated if they have a meaningful inscription; secondly, they can be dated by association with a known historical personage; thirdly, by association with a known historical event (that is, by political probability); fourthly, by inclusion in a coin hoard; fifthly, by inclusion in a stratified archaeological context; and lastly, on stylistic or typological grounds.

In the case of Scar, there are no inscriptions and the assemblage cannot be dated by association with any known historical person or event, except in the broadest terms (i.e. by 'political probability') in that it must have been deposited after pagan Vikings began to visit Orkney and before the islands were finally re-converted to Christianity. Even these broad dating parameters are imprecise. The Viking presence in Orkney is traditionally thought to date from around AD 800 but, in the total absence of documentary sources for Scotland in this early period, the only evidence for the earliest stages of settlement is inferential. For instance, we know from English and Irish sources that Viking raids were having an impact around the coasts of Britain and Ireland in the last two decades of the eighth century, most likely in the form of direct seasonal raiding from Scandinavia (Graham-Campbell *et al*, 1995, 61–2); and it is possible that pirate bases (and perhaps settlements) may have been established in the Northern and Western Isles by then (e.g. Wainwright 1962, 129–30; Crawford 1987, 118).

Similarly, the rate of progress towards conversion to Christianity 'is a very difficult thing indeed to monitor' (Crawford 1987, 163). The Kiloran Bay, Colonsay, boat burial is a classic ninth-century pagan Scandinavian grave in every respect, except that two of the stone slabs surrounding the grave enclosure carry crude representations of a Christian cross (Grieg 1940, 59, fig. 33). This indicates clear Christian influence on incomers to Colonsay from an early period. A decline in the numbers of tenth-century pagan burials in Scotland probably correlates with a decline in adherence to pagan beliefs, but cannot demonstrate how and when Christianity was adopted. It is highly likely that conversion was gradual and perhaps sporadic in different parts of the Viking colonies. In Orkney, the Norse leaders were a powerful dynasty of jarls who maintained stronger and closer cultural links with pagan Norway and the Norwegian kings during the tenth century than with Christian Ireland or England. It is probably not true (as used to be thought, e.g. Wainwright 1962, 160), that paganism was dying out in Orkney by about AD 900. It was not until AD 995 that Earl Sigurd of Orkney was forcibly baptised by the Norwegian king Olav Tryggvesson (who had himself been baptised only a year previously), probably for political expediency as much as from religious fervour (Crawford 1987, 68–71). Although Christianity was probably tolerated in Orkney long before 995, the earl's conversion must have marked a turning point and, thereafter, tolerance and encouragement of Christianity would have become the norm. Thus, dating by political probability would strongly suggest that the Scar grave dates from sometime between about AD 800 and 1000.

Wilson's fourth most reliable type of dating evidence for artefacts, dating by inclusion in a coin hoard, is irrelevant to Scar in the absence of any coins. Coins are relatively rare in Viking Orkney and Shetland, even in silver hoards, and so far only three graves in Scotland have been found to contain coins, including one at Buckquoy in Orkney (Ritchie 1977, 190). Even the hoard from Skaill, Orkney, which contained a total weight in silver of over 8kg, only included twenty-one coins (Graham-Campbell *et al* 1995, 34).

Wilson's fifth method is dating by inclusion in a stratified archaeological deposit. The grave as a whole is a well stratified archaeological deposit but it probably marks a single event—the burial of three bodies in a boat—which cannot be stratigraphically related to any other event. Nevertheless, three radiocarbon dates for this single event have been obtained, one from each of the three skeletons buried at Scar (see below).

That leaves typological and stylistic dating of the artefacts and their ornament—the least reliable dating method of all. Even then, a significant proportion of the Scar assemblage is not susceptible to dating any closer than to the Viking Age. This is true of almost all the undecorated, functional objects recovered, the forms of which changed little throughout the Viking period, or from place to place. At Scar, this applies to the spindle whorls, the sickle, the weaving batten, the shears, the needle tidy, the maplewood box, the gaming pieces—and even the boat itself. The tinned bronze object is too fragmentary to permit consideration of its date; and the bead cannot even be shown to be Viking Age.

Looking at this more positively, dendrochronological dating of well-stratified Viking Age deposits and some important artefacts has so far indicated that the traditional stylistic and typologically deduced dating brackets are, in broad terms at least, not wildly inaccurate (Else Roesdahl, personal communication). The relevant benchmarks here are the dates of the Oseberg and Gokstad ship burials, dated to the summer of AD 843 and to AD 900–905 respectively; and the burial of King Harald Bluetooth at Jelling in AD 986. With this in mind, the diagnostic artefacts from Scar can be considered.

The diagnostic artefacts

We would expect the brooch and the carved whalebone plaque, the most highly decorated artefacts, to provide the closest dating evidence and, indeed, arguments have been made for dating their manufacture to sometime between the late eighth and late ninth centuries, on the grounds of decoration and typology (Chapter 5). However, even this assessment allows for their production at any time within a period of more than 100 years; the actual date of manufacture of either object cannot be defined with precision. Moreover, as we have seen, there is a good case for arguing that both the brooch and the plaque were already of some antiquity when they were buried in the ground. In the case of the brooch, there is evidence of wear; conversely, in the case of the plaque, it is argued that the object was rarely used but had been a cherished possession for some time before being deposited in the ground with its elderly owner.

Nevertheless, the discovery of a mould for the Scar type of equal-armed brooch in deposits at Birka dated on stratigraphic grounds to no later than the first half of the ninth century is highly significant (Chapter 5). For this and other reasons, it is tentatively proposed here that both the brooch and the plaque found at Scar are most likely to have been manufactured sometime between the late eighth and the first half of the ninth century AD.

A ninth-century date has also been proposed for the Type A1 arrows on typological grounds (Chapter 6); while the classic Type H sword is also dated broadly to sometime between AD 800 and 950 (Chapter 6). The lead weights are less diagnostic in terms of their form; but it has been argued here (Chapter 6) that they conform to an early Viking metrological system and, again, a late eighth to ninth-century date of manufacture seems likely.

Perhaps the most reliable artefactual dating evidence is provided by the two combs since Viking combs were normally personal items of relatively short durability, and tended to be buried with their owner. K Ambrosiani (1981, 15) suggested that 'they ought to mirror that person's generation …'. Carlsson (Chapters 5 & 6) ascribes the male comb to the period c. 850–925. Stig Jensen (personal communication) has suggested a probable ninth-century date for the combs, perhaps the first half of the ninth century, on the basis of comparative material from Ribe. On the basis of all the diagnostic artefacts, then, the assemblage as a whole appears to date from sometime during the ninth century.

In the case of Scar, however, another important factor has to be considered: there must have been some time lag between the manufacture of these objects in Scandinavia, their acquisition and transfer from Scandinavia to Orkney by whatever means, and their placing in the ground with the man and woman buried at Scar. This is true of the entire Scar assemblage, diagnostic and undiagnostic artefacts, all of which are demonstrably Scandinavian—with the exception of the sandstone spindle whorl which might be made of local Orkney stone. The length of time that these three people had been in Orkney before their death cannot be ascertained; but, given the overwhelmingly Scandinavian character of the surviving assemblage, a relatively short period of stay might be indicated. Thus, although the time lag between comb manufacture and burial in the ground at Scar could have lasted anything from a year or two to half a century or more, perhaps something very roughly in the order of ten to twenty years might not be an unreasonable estimate.

There is another complicating factor at Scar, however, one which is of particular importance for this burial and which might pose still further dating problems: the age of the three people buried in the boat. The woman buried at Scar may have been in her seventies when she died (Chapter 4), and it seems a little unlikely that a woman of this great age would have newly arrived on Orkney from Scandinavia to start a new life. Perhaps she was compelled to leave her own country through some personal danger or strife; or had she chosen or been forced to follow her son, kinsman or master to Orkney rather than remain behind in Scandinavia; or had she chosen, even at that age, to make the long and hazardous journey overseas for a very particular reason, with every intention of returning home afterwards? Alternatively, had she lived in Orkney for twenty, thirty, fifty or even more years, without any obvious signs of assimilation of any native culture?

These possibilities all have a bearing on the relationships between the grave group, and their relative status and origins. However, the fact of the woman's great age and evident wealth further confounds any attempt to date the grave on the basis of the likely date of manufacture of the brooch and the plaque. For as well as accepting that there must have been some interval of time between their manufacture, acquisition and transfer to Orkney, in their case we also have to admit the real possibility that they might have been in the possession of the woman for most of her long life, perhaps for fifty or sixty years. Not only that, but given their 'special' nature and probable high value, it is conceivable that they were already heirlooms when they came into her possession. On this basis, the grave could conceivably be as late as the tenth century.

Given the possibility that at least some of the items may have been quite old when they were buried, it is interesting also to note a general impression that some of them may no longer have been very useful by the time they were buried. The plaque was rarely used and possibly out of fashion; the lead weights may have had no place in the economy of Viking Age Orkney; the sickle was small; the weaving batten was short and broken; the sword was broken and not in a usable scabbard; the gaming pieces were probably an incomplete set; the tip of the brooch pin may have been absent etc. There are caveats to all these observations, of course, and it might be misleading to take this argument much further. However, there is an impression that the assemblage overall may reflect a period when paganism was flourishing in Viking Age Orkney, whilst not being actually contemporary with it. It is almost as if the Scar burial reflects the type of accompanied burial the woman might have wished for, had she died when she might have been expected to by the standards of the Viking Age—twenty, thirty, forty or more years earlier. If this burial can be interpreted as a late gesture to the old gods and old customs of the homelands, this might go some way to explaining why aspects of the assemblage seem 'odd', and why some common items appear to be missing. The scale and wealth of this burial quite probably reflect the respect accorded to this old woman, who clearly adhered to the old faith, perhaps especially the cult of Freyja. It is also worth recalling here Lamb's (1993, 269) interesting suggestion that extravagant Norse funerals in Orkney might represent 'a self-conscious pagan revival at the time of the establishment of the earldom' in the later ninth century. Another possibility could be that they represent a self-conscious flourishing of pagan belief and ritual in the face of an encroaching acceptance of Christianity after about 900—and what better way to symbolise the vitality of pagan beliefs than by an elaborate boat burial?

Whatever the age of the brooch, plaque and the undiagnostic items when they were buried, there is one parallel and ameliorating consideration: the man was probably only in his thirties when he died and a very fine comb was buried with him. If we accept the triple premise that the comb was his and his alone, that it was new when he acquired it, and that he came to Orkney from Scandinavia—then the comb cannot have been much more than twenty years old when it was buried with him. On these grounds alone, the grave seems most likely to date to the second half of the ninth or first few decades of the tenth century. The radiocarbon evidence, however, suggests it might be later still.

The radiocarbon dates

Magnar Dalland

Four samples were submitted for radiocarbon dating: a bone sample from each of the three skeletons; and a fourth sample from animal bones found amongst the rubble (F49) next to the stone wall (F48). This sample was dated at Scottish Universities Research and Reactor Centre in East Kilbride using the conventional method, while the three skeleton samples, which contained small amounts of collagen, were sent to Arizona for accelerator dating.

The radiocarbon concentrations in the four samples, measured in years BP, are presented in Table 3.

Table 3. Uncalibrated radiocarbon dates from Scar

Lab. no	Sample	Years BP	^{13}C measurement
GU–3825	F 49, Cattle	1510 ± 50	–21.5 ppm
AA-1259/5	Find no 135, Juvenile	940 ± 75	–21.1 ppm
AA-1259/6	Find no 134, Male	1040 ± 60	–21.1 ppm
AA-1259/7	Find no 133, Female	1155 ± 60	–21.6 ppm

Table 4. Calibrated radiocarbon dates from Scar

Lab. no	Sample	1 sigma range	2 sigma range
GU–3825	F 49, Cattle	AD 520 – 625	AD 435 – 650
AA-1259/5	Find no 135, Juvenile	AD 995 – 1150	AD 970 – 1260
AA-1259/6	Find no 134, Male	AD 960 – 1040	AD 880 – 1130
AA-1259/7	Find no 133, Female	AD 825 – 965	AD 730 – 1020
Combined date of the skeletons		AD 965 – 1025	AD 895 – 1030

The dates were calibrated using the radiocarbon dating curve produced by the University of Belfast (Pearson *et al* 1986). The earliest date, from bones found amongst rubble at the foot of the stone wall F48, is significantly older than the dates from the boat burial, and demonstrates that the stone wall pre-dates the boat burial by several hundred years. Although there was no direct stratigraphical link between the wall and the boat burial, the foot of the wall is at a level which is likely to have been cut by the pit made for the boat. In this instance the dates helped to clarify the field interpretation. The date of the wall is most likely to fall within the period AD 450 to 650 (93%). It is 74% probable that the wall is older than AD 600. Comparing this result with the combined skeleton dates shows that the age difference between the wall and the boat burial is 420 ± 70 years.

The dates of the three skeletons show a surprisingly large variation given that the field evidence strongly suggests that all three people were buried at around the same time. At its most extreme, the difference between the uncalibrated dates for the woman and the child is 215 ± 96 years.

Turning to the individual calibrated dates, the date of the female skeleton is most likely to lie within the ninth (49%) or tenth (36%) century; the probability of the date being earlier than AD 900 is 60%. According to the calibrated probability distributions, the age difference between the female and the male skeletons is 100 ± 90 years (one standard deviation). The date of the male skeleton is most likely to lie within the period AD 950 to AD 1050 (74%); the probability of the date being earlier than AD 1000 is 52%. The difference between the calibrated dates of the female and the juvenile skeletons is 185 ± 110 years. The date of the juvenile skeleton is most likely to lie within the period AD 1000 to AD 1050 (34%); the probability of the date being earlier than AD 1100 is 60%, while the probability that the date is earlier than AD 1000 is only 11%.

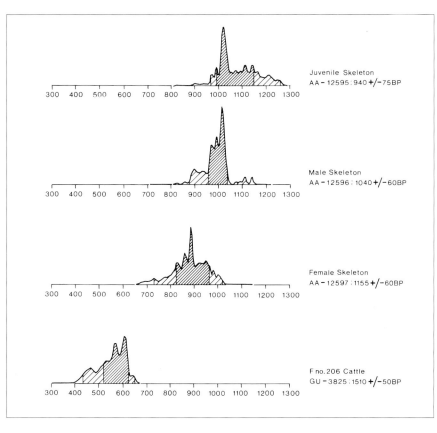

107. The calibrated radiocarbon dates from Scar.

At first sight, this apparent discrepancy in the dates seems to contradict the assumption that the three bodies were buried at the same time. Although the boat burial was badly disturbed by the sea and otters, which would make it difficult to identify any disturbances caused by possible re-opening of the grave, it is most unlikely that the burial of the three bodies was spread out over a period of 185 ± 110 years (or 9 ± 5 generations); and yet this, at face value, is what is indicated by the difference between the oldest and youngest skeleton dates.

However, statistical analysis of all three dates does not demand rejection of the field evidence. Given that it is highly likely that the people all died at least in the same season of the same year—based on both the field evidence and what we know of burial practices of the period—the dates can be combined to provide a weighted mean of 1059 ± 37 BP. The calibrated ranges of this date lie between AD 965 and AD 1025 (at the 1 sigma range), and AD 895 and AD 1030 (at the 2 sigma range) (Table 4). The probability distribution of the combined date is made up of two almost rectangular areas of equal duration (width) but different probabilities (heights). The lower area covers the period AD 895 to AD 960; the probability of the date lying within this period is about 22%. The higher probability area (75%) falls within the period AD 960 to AD 1030; the probability that the date falls within the tenth century is 65%. It is only 3% probable that the date is earlier than AD 900, and 32% probable that the date is later than AD 1000.

Why should there be this apparent discrepancy between the dates? One possibility is that the radiocarbon age of the collagen in the bones of the bodies at the time of death may have differed slightly between the individuals according to their age. This factor, however, should only contribute in a minor way to the differences between the dates. Although the $d^{13}C$ values include a contribution from diffraction during the measurement process (see Table 3), neither is there any reason to suspect that the dating results reflect a marine effect caused by the three individuals eating fish. It is possible that the samples were contaminated by non-contemporary material, although every care was taken in the field and subsequently to avoid contamination. Without dating control samples, this can be neither proved nor disproved as the cause of the large difference between the dates.

Radiocarbon dating is not always a precise science, nor an infallible one; but there is no obvious reason to reject the three dates as unreliable. Within the 95% confidence limit, it could not be claimed that the three dates come from different populations. In other words, if three sub-samples from the same bone had been submitted, we could see similar variations between the radiocarbon dates in at least five out of one hundred cases. Given the overwhelming probability that all three individuals died at around the same time, it is most likely that the apparent difference between the dates is the result of statistical variations in the measurements of the dates.

Conclusion

Olwyn Owen & Magnar Dalland

The radiocarbon dating evidence alone would seem to suggest that the most likely date for the grave is sometime between about AD 895 and 1030, and more probably after 960; while the most likely date for the grave on the basis of the artefactual assemblage is somewhat earlier, from the second half of the ninth or first few decades of the tenth century. At first glance, the results of the two approaches seem almost mutually exclusive. The contradictory dating evidence invites two extreme models of interpretation, which will both be rejected here. At one extreme, the conventional dating of the artefacts may be seriously wrong; at the other, the radiocarbon dates may be seriously wrong for unknown reasons.

A more constructive way forward is to view the results as complementary rather than contradictory. In other words, taking the artefactual and radiocarbon dating evidence together, perhaps the true date of the boat burial lies somewhere in the potential overlap between the two date ranges, that is, towards the later end of the date range suggested by the artefactual evidence, and towards the earlier end of the date range suggested by the radiocarbon dating evidence.

We have opted for this approach here and propose—on the basis of all strands of evidence from the excavated assemblage, backed up by analysis of comparable graves in the British Isles—that the grave most probably dates to sometime between the last quarter of the ninth century and the middle of the tenth century (*c* AD 875 to 950), while acknowledging that a still later date cannot be entirely discounted.

As we have seen, the dating of Viking graves on the basis of the artefacts they contain is almost always precarious, especially when they are found far removed from their source. At Scar, the age at death of the woman poses additional problems for dating the burial and raises the possibility that the type of burial as a whole, and its inclusions, may not in fact accurately reflect the date of the grave at all, but an earlier era of Viking paganism. Overall, the dating evidence leaves little doubt but that the most diagnostic female artefacts—the plaque and the brooch—were already of some considerable antiquity when they were buried at Scar. In human terms, all that the suggested dating bracket (AD 875 to 950) implies is that the Scar woman was buried with heirlooms handed down from her mother or grandmother (or from someone of their generation), rather than from her great or great great grandmother.

CHAPTER 8

SCAR AND VIKING GRAVES IN BRITAIN AND IRELAND

Olwyn Owen

MAINLAND ENGLAND

Despite several centuries of Viking settlement in Britain, relatively few graves have been identified. This is particularly true of England: whereas the Anglo-Saxon invasions have bequeathed to archaeology several thousand cremation and inhumation graves of the fifth to seventh centuries AD, less than thirty ninth- and tenth-century individual Scandinavian graves are known from the Danelaw area of eastern England, while a further cluster of tenth-century Viking graves occurs in Cumbria (Richards 1991, 112, fig. 71). There must have been more settlers than would be implied by this small number of graves—so why are they are almost 'invisible' in the archaeological record? One important clue is the number of Viking Age finds recovered in Christian churchyards and from cemeteries around the great Saxon cathedral churches. It seems likely that many first- and second-generation Viking settlers were more rapidly assimilated into the native population in England than elsewhere, were 'converted' to Christianity and given a Christian burial. Clearly, pagan believers, faced in England with a thoroughly Christianised country, were sufficiently flexible and pragmatic to accommodate Christianity within their pantheistic belief systems, either genuinely or expediently, within a relatively short space of time.

Several clearly Christian graves may have been those of people of Scandinavian origin since they include Scandinavian features. For instance, several of the burials beneath York Minster were marked by recumbent graveslabs sculpted in an Anglo-Scandinavian style (Richards 1991, 110, fig. 70); and a bier from one of the York Minster graves was partly constructed (perhaps symbolically) from re-used boat timbers. Conversely, a number of clearly Viking burials and isolated finds of Viking weapons and other objects have been recorded from English churchyards, and sometimes even from within churches, but it cannot be assumed that their owners were Christian. A sword found in the churchyard at West Seaton, Workington, Cumbria, for instance, had been bent and broken as if ritually 'killed' in the pagan fashion (Cowen 1948, 75).

A typical example of a Cumbrian Viking grave was found in 1822 beneath a burial cairn at Hesket in the Forest (Cowen 1934; Edwards 1992, 45–6, fig. 5.2). It contained spurs, a shield boss, axe, sword, two spearheads and other items, but apparently no human skeleton. Instead, the burnt bones of a number of animals, which had presumably been cremated on the funeral pyre, were recovered. The weapons had all been deliberately damaged: the sword and spears were bent and the shield had been broken in two. A second burial mound was cut through by accident at Claughton Hall, Garstang,

Lancashire, also in 1822 (Edwards 1992, 46). Viking Age finds including two oval brooches and weapons were recovered, perhaps from within a wooden chamber. Outside Cumbria, Viking burial mounds and cairns arc rare indeed.

The site of Repton, Derbyshire is of particular note amongst the English assemblage for, here, a mass grave in the vicarage garden contained the disarticulated remains of at least 249 individuals whose bones had been stacked charnel-wise against the walls of a massive, two-roomed stone structure beneath a mound (Biddle & Kjölby-Biddle 1986; FVTC 1992, 319, no. 353). This mass interment dates to sometime after AD 871 on coin evidence. Despite their burial in a probably Mercian mausoleum (Richards 1991, 19), some 80% of the deceased were non-local, robust men aged between 15 and 45. This unique burial of kingly status may contain some of the 'Great Army' of Viking warriors which wintered at Repton in AD 873–4 (Logan 1983, 146–7). Biddle postulates that most had died from an epidemic or been gathered from graves elsewhere as there is little evidence of battle wounds. Individual pagan Viking warriors' graves are also known from Repton. The earliest, found in a marked grave near the east end of the church, is that of a man who had died violently from a massive cut to the top of his left leg. He was buried with a sword, a knife and a key, and wore a silver Thor's hammer amulet and necklace. A jackdaw bone and a wild boar's tusk had been carefully placed between his legs in a clearly symbolic reference to expectations of an afterlife (FVTC 1992, 318, no. 352).

Not far away, at Ingleby, several of about sixty mounds on a commanding ridge overlooking the River Trent have been excavated (Clarke & Fraser 1946; Clarke & Munslow 1949); and some proved to be Viking cremation burial mounds dating from the late ninth to tenth century. This is the only known Scandinavian cremation cemetery in England. Some graves contained the bodies of women, suggesting the local presence of a Viking community, but there is no evidence as yet of any settlement nearby where the community might have lived. Recent field survey (Richards *et al* 1995, 58–60) has shown that the barrows are in distinct clusters, and that some have encircling ditches. Re-analysis of the 1940s work, moreover, suggests that the deceased in many of the Ingleby graves were cremated possibly upon sections of planking derived from boats, as a token form of boat burial (*ibid.*, 62–5).

However, these Cumbrian and Derbyshire graves are the exception. Elsewhere, it is the very scarcity of evidence for pagan graves in mainland England that is intriguing. For example, in York, despite many years of systematic excavation including that at the famous Viking site of Coppergate (Hall 1984), only a handful of pagan Viking burials have been discovered. Moreover, there is no conclusive evidence of any Viking boat burials in England, despite the presence at Sutton Hoo, Suffolk, of a Scandinavian-style royal ship burial from the pre-Viking period (Bruce-Mitford 1972; 1975; Carver 1992).

IRELAND

Any study of the Irish corpus of Viking graves is bound to be frustrated by the handful of earlier, inadequately recorded excavations, notably that at the famous cemeteries of Kilmainham/Islandbridge, near Dublin, which completely dominate the picture (Wilde 1866, 13–22; Coffey & Armstrong 1910, 107–22; Bøe 1940, 11–65). Most of the Kilmainham/Islandbridge cemeteries were destroyed around the middle of the nineteenth century by workmen digging the foundations for a hospital and railway line. It is safe to assume that many of the grave goods went unobserved by the workmen; while others were probably purloined and failed to make their way into the possession of the Royal Irish Academy. No records were made and it is not clear which objects (now in the National Museum of Ireland) came from which grave. Hence, scholars have tended to analyse the recovered material by artefact type: e.g. the forty or so swords etc.

Despite these problems, it is clear that the Kilmainham/Islandbridge cemeteries were probably the largest in western Europe outside the Viking homelands, and that they represent a semi-permanent community of ninth-century Scandinavian men and women nearby: a minimum of thirty male and seven female graves has been postulated (FVTC 1992, 320, nos. 354–8). Graham-Campbell (1976, 40) observed that the material displays 'a remarkable homogeneity and includes nothing which has to be dated as late as the tenth century'; indeed, the particular importance of this cemetery is that it may be historically dated to the period c. AD 841 to 902. According to Irish annalists, the Scandinavians established a *longphort* or raiding-cum-trading base around AD 841 at Dublin, although no ninth-century settlement has yet been identified. The Kilmainham cemetery may bear archaeological witness to its existence, and perhaps to its abandonment when the Vikings were driven out by the Irish in AD 902. When they returned to Dublin a dozen or so years later, they may have established a new trading settlement on a virgin site further downstream (although see Smyth 1979, 238–9 for a different view). Whatever the truth, there is no disputing that Dublin grew into a very wealthy town in the tenth and eleventh centuries (Wallace 1992). Burials associated with this later settlement include a small group (a possible cemetery) from College Green, as well as single burials (Bøe 1940, 65–7; Graham-Campbell 1976, 59).

Outside Dublin, only a dozen or so graves in Ireland may be those of pagan Scandinavians (Graham-Campbell 1976, 40–1, 59–61: Map 1 and Appendix A). These have an essentially eastern distribution and the total corpus is not spectacular. The widespread chance finds of Viking weapons and other objects, several from native sites, seem to corroborate the records of the Irish annalists for wide-ranging Viking raiding activities within and around Ireland, but tell us little else. Similarly, the inclusion of items of Irish manufacture in the Kilmainham/Islandbridge cemeteries is difficult to interpret: these may support the evidence for widespread raiding, but they could also indicate limited ninth-century trading resulting in the interchange of artefacts.

By later in the tenth century, trading had clearly begun to play a major part with the establishment of centres in Limerick, Cork, Wexford and Waterford. However, the Scandinavian settlers in Ireland seem to have remained concentrated in the tenth-century settlements they founded and to have been resistant to integration with native populations. Indeed, Smyth

(1979, 192–3) would see the essential character of Dublin as 'a Norse fortress under permanent siege from its Irish enemies', and suggests that its politically astute positioning, in the no-man's-land between two ancient Irish tribal enemies, offered the opportunity to play one side off against the other. He uses the evidence of female Scandinavian graves at Kilmainham/Islandbridge to argue for the migration of entire households from Scandinavia, thereby obviating any early need or desire for integration: 'the Scandinavian colony [of Dublin] could draw on a population not only from the Scandinavian homelands but from Norse communities in the Hebrides and the Northern Isles' (*ibid.* 194).

THE ISLE OF MAN

The relative dearth of pagan Viking graves in England is put fully into perspective by the contrasting picture on the Isle of Man. Here, on an island only some 600 km² in area, over twenty-four definite Viking grave sites are known (Graham-Campbell 1995, 75–8), of which several are exceptionally rich, both in terms of grave goods and the variety of burial rites represented. Interestingly, the Isle of Man lives up to its name in that, until the discovery of the 'Pagan Lady of Peel' (below), there were no certainly female, accompanied graves. However, the Isle of Man provides some of the best parallels for the Scar boat burial as there are several exceptionally wealthy Manx graves.

108. *The Balladoole boat burial, Isle of Man. Copyright Manx Museum and National Trust.*

To the Vikings the Isle of Man occupied a nodal position on the main sea route south from Norway, via the north and west coasts and islands of Scotland, to Ireland. Moreover, it has good natural harbours and was an ideal base for raiding in the Irish Sea. It formed part of no known kingdom at the start of the Viking Age, which must have facilitated the intensive Viking occupation suggested by linguistic, place-name and archaeological evidence. Eventually it became part of a Norse kingdom which also included the Western Isles of Scotland, and continued under Scandinavian authority until 1266. To this day, many of its distinctive cultural affinities can be traced back directly to the Viking period.

At St Patrick's Isle, Peel, the incoming Norse used the site of an extensive earlier Christian cemetery to bury their own dead. At least seven pagan burials of the tenth century are here, including the famous and richly accompanied 'Pagan Lady of Peel' (Freke 1995, 17–20; Chapter 7). There were also four other, less richly accompanied adult graves, one in a wooden chest like some of the Christian burials; and two accompanied child burials, one with an Eadred halfpenny of AD 946–55 placed in its mouth. Peel provides ample evidence that the Vikings sometimes continued to use Christian cemeteries. However, as in mainland England, their relationship to Christianity is ambiguous. Norse-period unaccompanied burials in wooden coffins at Peel may or may not have been those of Christianised Scandinavians; conversely, it has even been suggested that the 'Pagan Lady of Peel' might not have been Viking at all but a Celt who had married a Viking settler (Richards 1991, 103).

The discoveries of a number of Viking weapons in Christian graveyards on Man are as difficult to interpret as they were in England. Cubbon (1983, 18) suggests that, in the tenth century, there might have been tacit acceptance by the Church of the Viking custom of burying weapons with the dead, in order to establish acceptance of and respect for Manx burial grounds. However, the recent discovery at Claghbane near Ramsey of a sword, shield boss, spear and glass bead which were not part of a Viking burial suggests here some form of cenotaph or ritual deposit dating to between AD 850 and 950 (Cubbon 1982, 439–57).

Deliberate damage to an earlier Christian cemetery of cist graves seems to be indicated at Balladoole, one of several important excavations carried out by Professor Gerhard Bersu (originally a German prisoner-of-war on the island) between 1944 and 1946 (Bersu & Wilson 1966, 1–44). Balladoole is the site of a famous Viking boat burial on a low hilltop overlooking the sea. Here, the Vikings can hardly fail to have been aware of the earlier cemetery; their preparation of the site involved removing a number of cist cover slabs and disturbing the bodies. The earlier burials were redeposited with elements of the skeletons still articulated—which means that some of them were probably still held together by soft tissue when disturbed by Viking gravediggers, and therefore cannot have been very old. Wilson suggests that the Vikings wished to demonstrate their dominance of the islanders by placing a high-ranking pagan burial here (Bersu & Wilson 1966, 13).

At Balladoole, the wooden boat or ship of oak, some 11m long and 3m wide, was buried within a stone-built boat-shaped cairn (Fig. 108). Like the Scar grave, this grave may have contained more than one body. A richly accompanied male was laid out on his back on the bottom of the boat; and a female may also have been buried in the ship though without any goods, indicating a possible human sacrifice (Bersu & Wilson 1966, 7; Chapter 7). Two further skulls may have been disturbed from the earlier graves. The male equipment included an ornate set of horse harness mounts and a bit, as well as iron stirrups and spurs; a typical bronze ringed cloak-pin; a silver-gilt belt buckle of Carolingian workmanship; and a range of other equipment, such as an iron cauldron, a flint strike-a-light, a small hone, a shield (placed over the knees in this case) and two knives. Most unusually, there were no offensive weapons at all: no sword, spear or axe. The burial cairn was overlain by the bones of cremated livestock including horse, ox, pig, sheep or goat, dog and cat. The grave had been marked on the ground surface by a substantial wooden post beyond the end of the boat, which must have ensured its prominence in the landscape and recalls the hypothesis that the prow of the Scar boat had stood proud of the grave as a marker.

At Ballateare, Jurby, Bersu excavated a particularly fascinating grave (Bersu & Wilson 1966, 45–62), which seems to offer conclusive evidence of female sacrifice. Here, a man in his twenties had been buried in a wooden coffin (or timber burial chamber) beneath a substantial burial mound formed entirely of top sods imported from elsewhere. Bersu estimated that an area some 500m² would have had to be cleared to provide this quantity of sods. A wooden post had been inserted in the top of the mound to mark the grave. The man was buried dressed in his cloak secured by a bronze ringed pin; and was accompanied by his knife, throwing spear and silver-decorated sword in its scabbard. The sword had been deliberately broken into three pieces before being placed in the coffin. The bronze strap distributor and strap ends of a leather baldric or shoulder-sling also survived. Two thrusting spears and the remains of a battle-damaged shield had been placed beside the coffin—apparently too big to go inside it. As at Balladoole, a layer of cremated animal bones including ox, horse, sheep and dog had been spread over the mound. But this layer also included part of another disturbed human burial—that of a young woman in her twenties, with her arms raised upwards and a large hole in her skull created by the slashing blow of a heavy implement (Fig. 106). That this woman had been sacrificed to the dead man seems an almost inescapable conclusion, in which case the possibility of human sacrifice at Scar would not be an isolated phenomenon in Britain (pages 154-6).

The burial mound at Cronk Mooar (Bersu & Wilson 1966, 63–83), of a similar size and character to Ballateare and again positioned with a commanding view, was built over plough marks on a previously undisturbed ground surface—which tempted Wilson to speculate that this land had been taken into arable cultivation for the first time by a Viking colonist, perhaps by the man buried in the mound (*ibid.* 70). The body had been placed in a planked rectangular chamber within a central grave pit. Again, the man had been buried wrapped in a cloak and with a knife at his belt. A sword in its scabbard was in three pieces but, in this case, it is not clear whether it was broken before burial. Interestingly, the remains of his shaggy woollen cloak contained many fly pupae which indicated that the body had been 'lying in state' for some time before burial (perhaps about three weeks) and had in fact begun to rot (Bersu & Wilson 1966, 70, 87). Whether excarnation was an element of the burial ritual here, or whether it is simply a reflection of how long it took to prepare for the burial (preparation of the ground, construction of the grave pit and chamber, accumulation of mound material, cremation of animals etc), all apparently in high summer, is not known.

A rich ship burial, from Knock y Doonee, Andreas, again beneath a substantial mound, was excavated in 1927 but was not so well recorded as those examined by Bersu (Kermode 1928, 91–3; 1930, 126–33). The boat may have been roughly the same size as that from Balladoole, both perhaps powered by four pairs of oars and capable of use as small coastal fishing vessels. The grave goods of this 'plain farmer' (according to Kermode 1930, 129) included a sword, battle axe, spear, knife, shield boss, smith's hammer and tongs, an iron cauldron covered with a cloth (possibly a food offering), a silver-inlaid bronze cloak pin, a set of horse harness and a lead fishing-line weight. Again, he was buried wrapped in his cloak, and a horse and possibly a dog were buried with him.

Several other Viking burial mounds are recorded, including Ballachrink, Ballaugh and St John's, and there is a notable concentration of thirteen in the parish of Jurby (Richards 1991, fig. 65), but none have been excavated recently. A number of other graves or sites of gravefields are also known (Wilson 1974, 19, fig. 8), as well as single discoveries of Viking weapons and other items, but many of these were casual finds made long ago and are poorly recorded.

Bersu & Wilson (1966, 85, 87) date all four of the great Isle of Man pagan burial mounds—Balladoole, Ballateare, Cronk Mooar and Knock y Doonee—to 'the same chronological horizon', probably to between AD 850 and 950 and perhaps to between AD 850 and 900, that is, roughly contemporary with the suggested date of the Scar burial (c. AD 875–950: Chapter 7). He suggests that they are the graves of fairly wealthy landowners, buried in accordance with Scandinavian burial custom, probably on their own land within a generation or so of Viking settlement on the island. The physical prominence of the mounds, their choice locations and their rich contents, including women and animals, all seem to signify the invaders' power over the land, its livestock and people. The lack of female accompanied graves on Man, except for the 'Pagan Lady of Peel', suggests that few Scandinavian women got as far south as Man. As corroboration, the majority of the female names recorded in the Manx runic inscriptions are Celtic rather than Scandinavian (Olsen 1954; Page 1983). It seems likely that, after an initial assertive phase, second- and third-generation Norse settlers in Man intermarried with local women, became secure in their adopted land and were gradually assimilated: 'it is therefore not surprising that Christian beliefs were being re-established in the island by the second quarter of the tenth century' (Cubbon 1983, 19), by which time the heyday of pagan Viking burials in Man may already have been over.

SCOTLAND

Scotland is much better endowed with pagan Viking burials than England and Ireland but, even so, the quantity does not seem adequately to reflect the longevity, intensity and full extent of Viking settlement in the country. What is clear is that, as elsewhere, the picture is incomplete: many graves were discovered by accident during agricultural or building works; and many of them were excavated many years ago and are poorly recorded. Nevertheless, the distribution of pagan Viking graves in Scotland in general complements and accords with the evidence of Scandinavian place-names, silver hoards and known settlement sites (Crawford 1987, 117, fig. 31). All these strands of evidence point to a distinct western and northern bent to the Viking presence in Scotland, with concentrations in the Western Isles and Orkney. The Scottish evidence is described here in a little more detail.

Only five Viking cemeteries have been definitely identified in Scotland: at Pierowall, Westray, Orkney; Westness, Rousay, Orkney; Reay, Caithness; and, in the Hebrides, at Kneep (Cnip) headland, Valtos, Lewis; and Ballinaby, Islay. A further cemetery is suspected at Cornaigbeg, Tiree, on the basis of documentary evidence (Grieg 1940, 63); it may be possible to infer another on Eigg (below). Of all of these, only the Westness cemetery has been systematically excavated using modern archaeological techniques—and that has not yet been fully published. At Kneep (Cnip), graves continue to erode out of the sand dunes and several have been scientifically excavated over the last few years (Welander, Batey & Cowie 1987; Cowie *et al* 1993, 165–72; Dunwell *et al* 1995), but the full extent of the cemetery and its wider significance awaits exposure by future storms and winds.

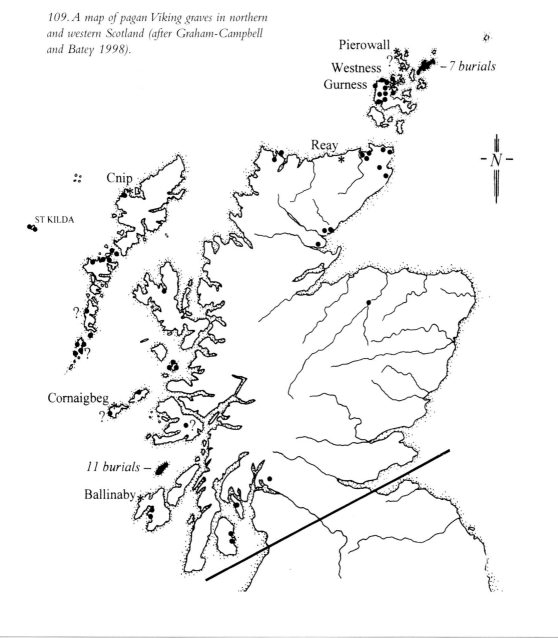

109. A map of pagan Viking graves in northern and western Scotland (after Graham-Campbell and Batey 1998).

Pierowall
Westness
Gurness
— 7 burials

Reay

Cnip

ST KILDA

Cornaigbeg

11 burials —
Ballinaby

−N−

The distribution of the total number of graves known from Scotland is 'skewed' by these cemetery sites. Although the corpus as a whole lacks modern systematic study and enumeration, somewhat over one hundred individual graves are known in Scotland of which about two-thirds have been found within cemeteries (a minimum of 17 from Pierowall (Thorsteinsson 1968, 164–71); around forty from Westness although some of these are probably pre-Viking Age (Kaland 1993, 312–17); at least three from Reay (Batey 1993, 152–4); at least three from Ballinaby (Grieg 1940, 32–42); possibly three from Eigg (Grieg 1940, 63–70); and a minimum of seven from Kneep (Cnip) (Welander, Batey & Cowie 1987; Dunwell *et al* 1995)). The remaining, approximately one-third of the graves are known only as single graves; however, the inadequacy of recording in some cases, or their location in badly eroded or actively eroding areas in others, may have so far concealed the fact that some apparently single graves may originally have been part of other cemetery sites. Scar is just one example where the presence of a Viking cemetery as more than just an isolated grave seems a distinct possibility.

The Northern Isles

The 'benchmark' for Viking burials in the Northern Isles, and indeed Scotland, is the Westness, Rousay, Orkney cemetery where approximately forty graves have so far been examined (Kaland 1993, 312–17), although only eight actually contained Norse grave goods. This cemetery was discovered in 1963 when a farm worker, Mr Ronald Stevenson, buried a dead cow and chanced upon the grave of a Viking woman and her new-born twins. The three had been buried in a pit apparently lined with horizontal slabs, and the woman was richly accompanied by grave goods (Stevenson 1989, 239; Chapter 7). A wide range of Viking grave types is represented at Westness: rectangular cists, stone-lined oval pits, boat-shaped graves and boat burials, shallow rectangular pits, child burials, graves with and without grave goods etc. Nearby, a Viking settlement of three buildings, a house and two byres, as well as a boat noost, has also been excavated (Kaland 1993, 308–12), but it is not yet clear whether, in the Viking period, the cemetery served this settlement and/or a wider population. Preliminary analysis of the human skeletal assemblage has revealed that the whole community is represented in the cemetery: men, women and children, from infants (including the new-born twin babies discovered in the 1963 grave) to relatively elderly people aged about 50 at death. It should be noted that, even in this relatively large sample, none of the graves contains the body of anyone even remotely close to the age at death of the woman found at Scar.

Two of the graves were boat burials, each of which contained the body of a single man. The boats themselves were similar to the Scar boat (though possibly smaller: Chapter 3), that is, clinker-built rowing boats built of oak strakes; and each of them contained a central stone-built burial chamber to accommodate the body, which is also reminiscent of the Scar boat burial chamber. In both cases, the bodies were richly accompanied by grave goods of weapons and tools (Fig. 95). Also excavated at Westness was a fairly massive, boat-shaped stone setting (Kaland 1993, 316–17, fig. 17.9), which

110. The Westness woman. Drawing copyright David Simon.

111. One of the Westness boat burials, emptied of its contents. Copyright Olwyn Owen.

may have been a cenotaph since no burial was found within it. The only other possible boat burial known from the Northern Isles is from the cemetery at Pierowall, Westray (below), but the evidence is inconclusive.

Despite the variety of grave types, all the Westness burials were inhumations (Viking period cremations are rare in Scotland) and they are all 'flat graves', that is, like the Scar boat burial, apparently not marked on the ground surface by mounds or cairns. Nonetheless, there are indications that, when the cemetery was in use, some or all of the graves were marked in some way. Most importantly, burials of whatever type never cut through or impinged on earlier pre-Viking or Viking graves, which implies that the gravediggers must have been aware of the locations of earlier graves. In one or two cases, the types of grave markers can be deduced. For instance, in an oval stone-lined pit containing the body of a young man accompanied by grave goods, the stone setting, whose shape perhaps symbolised a boat, had a higher 'prow' stone which may have stood proud of the ground surface. In the case of the two actual boat burials at Westness, as at Scar, the sterns of the boats may have stood proud of the graves. Other graves may have had wooden markers which have since rotted away. It is also possible that any low cairns or mounds may have been removed over succeeding centuries.

Interestingly, of the forty or so excavated burials, as few as eight were accompanied by grave goods. It appears on the evidence of the radiocarbon dates obtained so far that at least some of the unaccompanied graves pre-date the Viking period, which would imply that the Norse settlers continued to use or re-used an earlier Christian, probably Pictish, burial ground. Whether there was a religious or political motive for this is not known. The Vikings were almost certainly aware of the presence of the earlier cemetery, given that the later burials all respect the locations of earlier graves. It is also possible that some of the unaccompanied burials are Viking Age Christian ones. Others may have been unaccompanied by goods for other reasons, ranging from poverty or lack of status (below), through to motives which would not be recoverable through the archaeological record, such as a lack of regard for the dead person or even simple meanness.

The evidence for the date of conversion of Orkney to Christianity is briefly reviewed elsewhere (Chapter 7). It is increasingly accepted that the traditional date of AD 995 for conversion of the islands is probably too late. As well as such clues as the early presence of cross-inscribed stones in the Northern Isles (Crawford 1987, 169–71) and the discovery of a pagan axe in a Shetland churchyard (Shetelig 1954, 69), the continued use of Celtic religious sites in the islands, such as is inferred at Westness, points to an earlier and less disruptive process of conversion of the Viking settlers in the Northern Isles. Eldjárn (1984, 7) asserts, less cautiously, that the pagan Viking graves in Scotland are primarily those of first-generation, heathen emigrants from Norway—people who were actually born and bred in Norway and came over as adults: 'already the second generation might very probably have adopted the Christian faith'. The surprisingly early radiocarbon dates from Westness, which seem to indicate that the cemetery was in use from as early as the seventh to *only* the ninth century AD, may support this view (Kaland 1993, 312), although the full radiocarbon dating evidence awaits publication. The nature of the Scar boat burial and the overwhelmingly Scandinavian character of the Scar artefacts might indicate, very tentatively, that it too was a 'first generation' grave. However, it has been suggested here (Chapter 7) that the grave may actually be later than it seems on the evidence of the grave type and artefacts; and that, perhaps because of the woman's great age, it 'harks back' in some way to the *floruit* of paganism in Viking Orkney. In truth, such conjectures are never clear-cut: for instance, it is perfectly possible that a first wave of settlers was followed by others later on who, also born and bred in Norway, might still have arrived as pagans in the Northern Isles during the later ninth century—some time after the first generation of settlers.

The possibility of Christian Viking burials at Westness, and of Viking burials unaccompanied for other reasons, raises a familiar conundrum for scholars of the Viking period: the difficulties of identifying the graves of ethnic Vikings which are unaccompanied by grave goods. The traditional argument would be that, since pagan Viking graves are accompanied by grave goods, then unaccompanied graves cannot be Viking. The fallibility of this premise is apparent from the brief overview of the graves in England, many of which must have been buried in Christian contexts with scant or no indications of their ethnic origins. It is highly probable that some or many unaccompanied graves in Scotland, either at known Viking burial locations or elsewhere in known areas of Viking settlement, are actually the graves of Viking settlers. This conundrum is amply demonstrated in the cemetery at Kneep (Cnip), Valtos, Lewis in the Western Isles where, of the seven graves so far examined (excluding an early discovery of a wealthy female burial 'from Valtos': MacLeod *et al* 1916), only four are demonstrably Viking (accompanied by Viking-type grave goods). The others are similar in type and were found within the immediate vicinity (in fact, five of the Kneep (Cnip) graves form a discrete cluster); but there are no clear indications as to whether the unaccompanied graves are those of Vikings, or not. Even Viking-period radiocarbon dates have not solved the problem at Kneep (Cnip) for, as the excavators point out (Cowie *et al* 1993, 170; Dunwell *et al* 1995), it is possible that some of the burials are those of members of a native Celtic population—which certainly survived in the Western Isles.

Viking finds and graves have been discovered on the Links at Pierowall, Westray, Orkney, as a result of sand-blowing and piecemeal excavations between 1839 and 1863 (Thorsteinsson 1968, 151–63). Other chance finds and amateur excavations have almost certainly gone unreported. The records are poor and, in many cases, the finds have been dispersed. It is not always possible to be confident which finds came from which of the reported graves, and there may have been mixing of grave groups. Nevertheless, thanks to the sterling efforts of Thorsteinsson (1968), some sense has been made of the relics and records which have survived. On the basis of this evidence, Thorsteinsson proposes a minimum of seventeen graves, although it is likely that there were many more: Wainwright (1962, 148) reports that 'at least a score were found between 1830 and 1870'; and recent re-analysis also suggests a minimum of twenty graves, including possibly two boat burials (James Graham-Campbell, personal communication). Only two of Thorsteinsson's seventeen are recorded as without grave goods, but it is highly likely that other unaccompanied graves have gone unrecorded, given the antiquarian preference for objects rather than skeletons. For the same reasons, the apparent lack of child burials is probably illusory. Of the remaining fifteen adult burials, six contained oval brooches on which basis they can be assumed to have been the graves of women, indicating that the cemetery is representative of a community in the area. Indeed, Pierowall is thought likely to have been a Viking trading station (Brøgger 1929, 121; Lewis 1958, 339; Fig.117). There are some scant references to burial mounds in the records but it is probable that these were natural sandy hillocks and that, again, most or all of the burials were actually flat graves. One of the graves (Grave 17) may have been a boat burial containing the body of a man and a horse but the evidence is inconclusive (pages 46-7).

Other Viking graves in the Northern Isles appear relatively few and far between, with the slim evidence from Shetland being particularly surprising. Again, slight indications of a Christian Norse presence have been inferred from the discovery of two east-to-west aligned wooden coffins found at the east end of a putative wooden chapel at Kebister, Shetland, radiocarbon dated to around the tenth century (Owen & Smith 1988, 2; Owen & Lowe 1999). Two pagan Viking graves are known from Unst (Grieg 1940, 103–5), one of which (a female burial from Clibberswick) included a 'full' assemblage of

112. The eroding dunes at Kneep (Cnip), Valtos, Lewis, continue to yield Viking graves.

jewellery: a pair of oval brooches and a Borre-style trefoil brooch, two glass beads and, unusually, a silver arm-ring of plain Hiberno-Viking type (Graham-Campbell *et al* 1995, 154, pl. 71, b).

Wainwright (1962, 149) expresses a common frustration when he refers to the 'inextricably muddled' reports, and the 'chaos' between reports and surviving finds, which bedevil attempts to classify and quantify the graves in the Northern Isles. Other than the Pierowall cemetery (Westness had not yet been discovered), Grieg (1940, 80–102) lists only a dozen or so Viking graves known from Orkney, but this must be a serious underestimate. Nor are the Westness cemetery and the Scar burial the only Orcadian Viking graves to have been discovered more recently. There has been a particular concentration of excavation efforts in the Birsay area over the last twenty years or so, with a concomitant rise in the known number of Viking Age burials, for example: a pagan Viking grave from Buckquoy, Birsay, dated to the tenth century on coin evidence (Ritchie 1977, 190); and probably Viking Age cist burials found overlying Pictish burial cairns along the Brough Road, Birsay (Morris 1989, 109–27). The Westness, Rousay, cemetery also lies close to a recently excavated Viking settlement, although the first grave was discovered here independently of the excavation. In short, it is highly likely that modern excavations in prime areas of Viking settlement in Orkney (and probably Shetland) will continue routinely to reveal a few or many associated Viking Age graves, pagan and/or Christian. Conversely, the discovery of a Viking grave or graves is quite likely to indicate the presence of Viking settlement(s) in the vicinity—as must be likely at Scar. For this reason, and because of physical indications of the presence nearby of other archaeological features (Chapter 2), the immediate vicinity of the rich Scar boat burial has now been designated a Scheduled Ancient Monument.

Mainland Scotland

Turning to the north Scottish Mainland, the evidence for a Viking cemetery at Reay, Caithness, like that for the Pierowall cemetery (above), was recovered in a haphazard way earlier this century. However, its identification as a cemetery site seems indisputable (Batey 1993, 152–4). The minimum number of graves is three but this is highly likely to be an underestimate. After the consecutive discoveries of three definite Viking graves in 1912, 1913 and 1926, it is not clear whether a 1927 reference to 'several graves' (Edwards 1927, 203) actually refers to the same graves or additional ones; while other unaccompanied graves, found in long cists in the immediate vicinity, may or may not date to the Christian Norse period (Edwards 1929, 139; Batey 1993, 154). Thus, Reay encapsulates many of the problems touched on already, including those of early excavations and inadequate records, and the difficulty of ascertaining whether unaccompanied graves might in fact date to the Norse period.

One of the definitely pagan Viking graves at Reay seems to have contained the body of a woman accompanied by two oval brooches and other objects; but, as the brooches are not an identical pair, it is possible that even this assemblage actually represents a mix of goods from more than one grave (Batey 1993, 161). The other two confirmed Reay graves were both apparently male and one of them, discovered in 1926 and somewhat better recorded, comprises a fully extended inhumation laid on a paved surface, accompanied by an axe, a shield boss, a knife, a sickle, an iron buckle, a ringed pin and a whetstone (Edwards 1927). Altogether in Caithness and Sutherland, pagan Viking graves are known from at least seven sites; probable Norse Christian graves from a further three sites; and isolated Viking artefacts from a further five sites (Batey 1993, 150, fig. 6.2). Of these, the 1991 discovery of a richly accompanied child burial from the sand dunes at Balnakeil, Durness, Sutherland, is of particular note (Gourlay, Low & Batey forthcoming).

Elsewhere on mainland Scotland, only a handful of Viking graves are known, stretching from Moray in the north-east down to Dumfries and Galloway in the south-west. A pair of oval brooches reportedly found near Perth is a tantalising indication of possible Scandinavian settlement in the Tay area (Shetelig 1954, 72), although it is also possible that they do not represent a grave but were acquired directly from Scandinavia (James Graham-Campbell, personal communication); while, in south-west Scotland, an accompanied male grave from St Cuthbert's, Kirkcudbright, is especially notable for having been found actually in the churchyard (Grieg 1940, 13).

Western Scotland and the Western Isles

Before the recent identification of a cemetery at Kneep (Cnip), Valtos, Lewis, Viking graves in the west of Scotland seemed primarily to comprise a number of individual, often especially wealthy sites, amongst which the Kiloran Bay, Colonsay, boat burial is of particular note (Anderson 1907, 443–9; Grieg 1940, 48–61). Excavated in 1882–3, this is clearly one of the most important male Viking graves from Scotland (currently being re-

113. The assemblage found in a wealthy female grave at Kneep, Lewis.

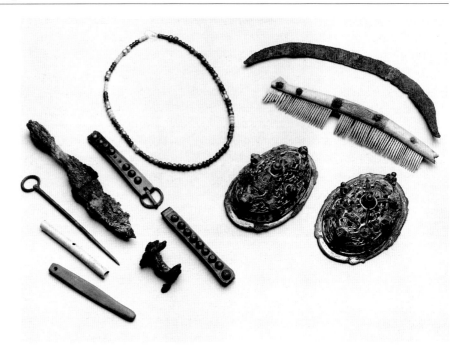

analysed: Graham-Campbell & Paterson forthcoming). A powerfully built, middle-aged man had been buried in a crouched position within a stone-built, rectangular enclosure. It appears that a boat had been inverted over the whole burial deposit and a mound of sand erected over the top. Buried with him was a horse (just outside the stone enclosure but still under the boat), and an exceptionally rich assemblage of Scandinavian and Insular grave goods. These included balance scales and a set of weights (Fig. 82); a 'complete' set of weapons—sword, spearhead, axe, shield boss and arrowheads; a fragmentary iron-handled pot, sickle, knife and whetstone; bronze pins and bronze mountings for a harness; and three Anglo-Saxon stycas which indicate that the grave cannot date to any earlier than the mid-ninth century. The Kiloran Bay grave is reminiscent of, and similar in date to, the great Isle of Man graves. Like them, it is thought to be that of a wealthy 'aristocratic' pagan Scandinavian settler—and yet, two of the slabs from the enclosure are crudely carved with Christian crosses, clear evidence of a Christian influence and perhaps of someone who was hedging his bets in death.

Records of a number of other relics 'found in Viking graves in Colonsay' (Grieg 1940, 46–8) are supplemented by two definite further graves from the sand dunes at Machrins—in an area whose name, Cnoc nan Gall, means, perhaps significantly, 'Hillock of the Foreigners' (Crawford 1987, 121). The first, a rich male boat burial found in a mound in 1891, was accompanied by weapons, objects of personal adornment, horse harness and the horse itself. The second, a recently excavated, possibly female burial (Ritchie 1981) was accompanied by a small dog with its head on the woman's knees, perhaps a lap dog, recalling the newly excavated burial of a woman with a small dog at Føre, Bø i Vesterålen, north Norway (Schanche 1991; page 147). The woman's upper body had been badly disturbed by rabbits which may have removed her oval brooches and other demonstrably Scandinavian items, but a ringed pin did survive—which is also highly suggestive of a Scandinavian presence (Fanning 1983, 330).

From Oronsay, very close to Colonsay, there are confused accounts of another presumed boat burial. A large mound at Càrn a'Bharraich on the east side of the island, excavated in 1891, proved to contain the double burial of probably an elderly man and woman, and a third skeleton was discovered in 1913. The first excavation produced male and female objects of Scandinavian and Insular type, and a 'great number of rivets', presumably boat rivets; and the second, a typical female assemblage: including a pair of oval brooches, bronze pin, iron shears and a fragmentary bone needle case and bone needle (McNeill 1891, 432–5; Anderson 1907, 437–41; Grieve

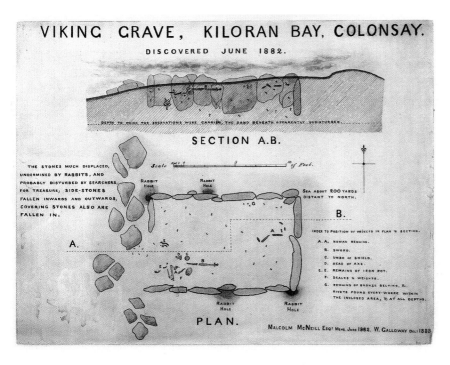

114. The original excavation plan of the Kiloran Bay burial, excavated in 1882. Copyright Royal Commission on the Ancient and Historical Monuments of Scotland.

1914, 272 ff.; Grieg 1940, 42–6). A bone pin-head turned up as a stray find in the area in 1921. Unfortunately, both episodes of work at the site are so poorly recorded that it is difficult to interpret what went on here.

The records are somewhat better for the Ballinaby, Islay, cemetery where at least three wealthy graves are known to have been found between 1878 and 1932 (Edwards 1934; Grieg 1940, 32–42). Two male burials were lavishly accompanied by weapons, and the grave goods of the burial found in 1878 also included blacksmithing tools (a hammer and forge tongs), an iron cauldron and a probable bronze terminal from a drinking horn. The woman, whose grave is comparable to that of the Scar woman in terms of its textile implements—glass linen smoother, iron heckle, bronze needle case and needle—also had oval brooches, repoussé-worked bronze mountings, a silver dress pin and safety chain, twelve beads and a bronze ladle. Nearby, another pair of oval brooches was found, probably marking the site of a fourth grave, and complementing eighteenth-century accounts of many other human bones and weapons from this vicinity (all now lost).

The grave from King's Cross Point, Arran (Grieg 1940, 26–7) is notable for having been a cremation grave. Coin-dated to after the middle of the ninth century, like the Kiloran Bay, Colonsay, inhumation (above), it was contained within a stone enclosure beneath a mound. More notable are probably three graves discovered in substantial mounds in the nineteenth century on Eigg: amongst the finds is a magnificent late eighth- or ninth-century Norwegian sword hilt (Fig. 115) but its find circumstances are imprecise. Two other graves, both apparently wealthy male burials, contained penannular brooches as well as other artefacts (Grieg 1940, 67–70). Several other poorly recorded graves have been found in the Western Isles: a female burial from Ardvonrig, Barra (Edge & Williams 1863), and nearby stray finds are suggestive of a male burial close by; a male grave from Eriskay accompanied by sword, spear and whetstone; a grave with a bone comb from South Uist; and an early discovery of a female grave from what is now clearly recognised as the area of a Viking Age cemetery at Valtos, Lewis (Grieg 1940, 72–9).

CONCLUDING REMARKS

The picture of Viking graves in the British Isles is disparate in terms of distribution: from the surprising scarcity of the English evidence; through to the sporadic, poorly recorded concentrations in Ireland; through to the extraordinary wealth of graves on the Isle of Man; and, finally, to the wide geographical spread of a relatively small number of known Norse burial sites in Scotland, concentrated in the north and west. The reasons for this are manifold but must include the differing origins of the Viking settlers. All the evidence suggests that the eastern English settlers came mainly from Denmark; the northern Scottish settlers mainly from Norway; the western Scottish, Isle of Man and Irish settlers mainly from Norway or via northern Scotland; and the north-west English settlers mainly from Norway, perhaps via Ireland or Scotland.

Perhaps the predominant reason for this disparate picture, however, is the speed or otherwise with which the Viking settlers became assimilated into— or themselves assimilated—native culture in different parts of the country. Inevitably, the very nature of Viking colonisation and settlement in different areas was a reaction to prevailing local circumstances and was partly dictated by the varying degrees of vigour and persistence of native cultures and the sheer numbers of existing inhabitants. Similarly, the obviously variable rates at which Viking settlers in different areas were converted to Christianity, although hard to gauge accurately, must account in a significant way for the apparent discrepancies in the surviving evidence for Britain and Ireland as a whole.

The burial rite in Scotland was predominantly inhumation; cremation graves are extremely rare. A wide variety of grave types is represented, most of which are exemplified in the cemetery at Westness, Rousay, Orkney: rectangular cist graves, pit graves, stone-lined oval graves, proper boat burials, stone-built boat-shaped graves, and so on. The majority of the Scottish graves seem to have been flat graves, which have left no trace on the ground surface today but which may have been marked on the ground originally, as inferred at Westness and Scar. Substantial burial mounds have so far only been securely identified in the west, as at Kiloran Bay, Colonsay, and King's Cross, Arran; and on the Isle of Man—itself part of the 'Scottish' Norse kingdom.

The evidence for pagan Viking burials in Scotland was first gathered together by Grieg (1940) in that invaluable series, *Viking Antiquities in Britain,* edited by Haakon Shetelig (although much of this evidence was first published by Brøgger in 1929). The confused nature of much of the original record must be clear from this brief overview. Unfortunately, Grieg's survey is also deeply flawed: his account of the Pierowall graves is 'terribly confused' (Thorsteinsson 1968, 154) and, in general, 'his documentation left something to be desired' (Eldjárn 1984, 6). The modern, systematic and scientific study of all the evidence for Viking graves in Scotland which has long been needed is at last underway (by James Graham-Campbell and Caroline Paterson on behalf of the National Museums of Scotland), including a re-assessment of all the antiquarian notes, accounts and early publications, including contemporary newspaper accounts and museum records, in an effort to disentangle them.

This would also be an opportune moment at which to re-examine the hypothesis that there is a general distinction between Viking graves in the west and the north of Scotland. The impression that the Isle of Man and Hebridean graves, typified by those from Balladoole, Isle of Man and Kiloran Bay, Colonsay, are those of 'an aristocratic class of Norsemen' (Crawford 1987, 125, following Brøgger 1929, 66, 126–7 and others), uninfluenced or unfettered by contacts with local populations or local circumstances—may be more apparent than real, and has been questioned by Eldjárn (1984). The apparent high status of the Viking graves in the west is inferred primarily from the evidence of monumental burial and elaboration of the burial rite, e.g. the cremation or burial of sometimes several animals; the inclusion of that most precious of commodities, especially in wood-sparse islands, the boat or ship; and, especially, the amount of labour and support which must have been involved in erecting a mound or in carrying out an elaborate burial. The quantity and quality of the finds only serve to support this hypothesis. However, if it is true that these graves generally seem to contain fewer of the routine domestic and agricultural tools and implements than do their counterparts in Norway, then this is also true of the Scottish graves as a whole. In fact, with the Westness cemetery, the Scar boat burial and the Balnakeil boy as new 'benchmarks' in northern Scotland, the difference between the Isle of Man and Western Isles graves, and those in northern Scotland, begins to look primarily like one of grave type and, perhaps, taste for elaboration of burial rite, rather than one of actual status or wealth.

Indeed, the perceived difference between western and northern graves cannot be said to be based on the types of artefacts they contain, or even necessarily on the quantity and quality of those artefacts. Therefore, despite the combined wealth and complexity of the richest graves from the Isle of Man and the Western Isles, and the usually less elaborate burial rite and the sometimes less conspicuous wealth of the Orcadian graves, it is perhaps unlikely that the early Viking settlers in Orkney were any less wealthy, generally speaking, than those in the Western Isles and Isle of Man. The reasons for the differences in grave type and burial ritual are likely to be cultural and/or political rather than purely economic; they may reflect the differing nature and development of Viking colonisation and settlement in west and north Scotland—which must have been, at least in part, a response to prevailing local circumstances.

The question of status is a dangerously fraught issue for students of the Viking period (and indeed of other periods), and it is worth recalling here Dommasnes' (1982, 73) proposition for Sogn, Norway, that *any* accompanied pagan Viking grave is indicative of relatively high rank. The sample represents only that part of the population which controlled an economic surplus, albeit sometimes only a small one. In Britain, this proposition may (inadvertently) have found some support in the frequency with which contemporary excavators have argued that newly investigated Viking period graves may be high status: Peel, Balnakeil and Scar, to name but three. Perhaps it is time to accept that most pagan Viking graves in Britain (and perhaps most settlements too) are, by their very nature, those of the mobile upper strata of Viking Age society: people who, for whatever reason, elected and could afford to travel to, trade with and colonise other lands. Whatever the truth, the more 'ordinary' graves now being excavated at Kneep (Cnip), Valtos, Lewis, in the Western Isles, and the wealthy and elaborate boat burial from Scar, Orkney, serve to highlight how rash it may be to draw cultural, political and economic conclusions on the basis of such a small, and often poorly recorded, sample.

What is clear is that the continuing discoveries of pagan Viking graves, their excavation by modern archaeological techniques, and the careful re-examination of some of the records and artefacts from earlier discoveries, all hold promise that answers to some of these vexed questions will be found in time. In the meantime, we can only marvel at the wealth and variety of the Viking graves, and the strength and strangeness—at least to us—of the pagan beliefs which underpinned them.

116. This rather romantic version of A Viking's Funeral *was painted by the much respected late Victorian artist, Frank Dicksee, in 1893. The idea of setting fire to a richly furnished funerary ship and pushing it out to sea is encountered in the tenth-century Anglo-Saxon poem,* Beowulf, *and in Old Norse poetry; but Dicksee may have been inspired by the then recently completed excavation of the Gokstad ship burial, Norway. Copyright Manchester City Art Galleries.*

CHAPTER NINE

SOME COMMON QUESTIONS AND ANSWERS

Olwyn Owen & Magnar Dalland

Who was buried at Scar?

Very unusually, three people were buried at Scar—most Viking graves contain only one person. These three were:

- a woman probably in her seventies, laid out flat on her back;

- a man probably in his thirties, placed in a crouched position in the stern of the boat;

- and a child aged about ten or eleven (we don't know the child's sex), laid out on his or her back alongside the woman.

What was the relationship between them?

We don't know. At first we thought this might be a family group—husband, wife and child—but once the human bone specialist had determined that the woman was very old, while the man was only in his late twenties or thirties at the time of death, this was obviously unlikely.

Other possibilities suggest themselves: perhaps this was a grandmother, son and grandson; or a matriarch, warrior kinsman and child slave? We may never know for sure. The woman must have been highly respected because she lived to such a ripe old age and was buried with a very rich collection of grave goods. The man probably also held a high rank within society, because he, too, was richly accompanied by grave goods. We do not know if the child was buried with any possessions because the part of the grave where he or she was buried had been mostly washed away by the sea before it was excavated by archaeologists. This makes it very hard to tell the status of the child.

Did they all die at the same time?

Yes, we think so—or at least within a few days or, at most, weeks of each other. They were almost certainly all buried at the same time. There is no evidence that the grave was re-opened to take the body of another person after it had been sealed the first time. Because of the way the bodies were positioned in the grave, we think that the woman and child were placed in the boat first and then the man was squeezed into the stern of the boat afterwards. In fact, the man may already have had *rigor mortis* when he was buried, as his foot had been broken off with the force necessary to fit him into the available space; and it is quite possible that all three people lay unburied for a while after they died.

What did they die of?

It is not often possible to tell what ancient people died of by studying their bones, and it is even harder in this case because of the incompleteness of the skeletons. Nonetheless, there are no signs of massive injury or trauma on the surviving bones, which suggests that the three may not have died a violent death. If the woman had been buried in a grave on her own, we would probably have assumed that she died of old age. This simple answer is confounded in this case, though, by the fact that three people were buried together. This raises the unpalatable possibility that one or even two of them were killed to accompany the other into the afterlife. Human sacrifice is not common in the Viking Age, however, and the fact that both the man and woman were buried with a rich panoply of belongings suggests that neither of them was a slave. On balance, we think that they probably died together as a result of an accident, such as drowning, or within a few days of each other from disease.

Why were they buried in a boat?

In the ninth and tenth centuries, the Vikings were pagans who worshipped many gods—and a dead person was equipped in the grave with everything that he or she might need in the afterlife, including sometimes a boat or ship. But only a few Viking men and women were buried in boats, and they were not always the wealthiest members of society. Some scholars have argued that the boat was simply a handy coffin for a burial, or a source of firewood in

117. Artist's impression of a beach market in Orkney where settlers and traders might exchange or barter goods. Copyright David Simon.

the case of a cremation, but this seems unlikely. Others suggest that the boat was a symbol of secular power or of maritime connections. This may be partly the case at Scar, where the man and woman were clearly both wealthy and of high rank, and the man had done much rowing in his life. But the burial of boats was primarily a symbolic act and had a religious significance. The boat could symbolise that the deceased was going on a journey to the next world. Equally plausibly, the boat might have been included in the burial as a mark of the deceased person's close connection to the gods. The presence of the whalebone plaque suggests that the Scar woman worshipped the Viking fertility goddess, Freyja (see below).

What is the date of the boat burial?

Our best guess, on the basis of the style of the artefacts and the radiocarbon dates, is that the grave dates to sometime between AD 875 and 950.

The almost entirely Scandinavian nature of the find seemed at first to indicate that the grave was that of early settlers, perhaps dating from around AD 850—but the picture is not so clear-cut. Radiocarbon dates, obtained for each of the skeletons, proved to be imprecise and contradictory but, nevertheless, suggest that the grave is not as early as we thought at first. The most closely dateable objects are the woman's whalebone plaque and equal-armed brooch and the man's comb. The plaque and brooch were both made in Scandinavia, probably sometime between the late 700s and late 800s, but may already have been quite old when buried. The man's comb can probably be dated to c. AD 850–925 and, because it was probably not in use for so long, may be a better indicator of the date of the grave. If we accept that the comb was his and his alone, that it was new when he acquired it and that he brought it to Orkney from Scandinavia, then the comb cannot have been much more than twenty years old when it was buried with him.

On close inspection, several aspects of the grave assemblage seem 'odd': many of the objects are incomplete and some common items appear to be missing. There is an impression that the assemblage overall may reflect the high point of paganism in Viking Orkney, whilst not being actually contemporary with it. It is almost as if the Scar burial reflects the type of burial the woman might have wished for, had she died when she might have been expected to by the standards of the time—twenty, thirty, forty or more years earlier. For all these reasons, we have suggested that the Scar burial can be interpreted as a late gesture to the old gods and old customs of the homelands—and that this is why it is later than it looks at first glance.

Where did the people come from?

Almost certainly, this group of people came from the western seaboard of Norway, and possibly from the far north of Norway—perhaps even from north of the Arctic Circle. Small boat burial is frequently a west Norwegian Viking burial rite. The whalebone plaque was almost certainly made in western or northern Norway; and, although the Scar equal-armed brooch is a rare type, several identical examples have been found in the far north of Norway.

On the other hand most of the objects, including the boat itself, could have come from elsewhere in Scandinavia (we believe that the boat is Scandinavian because, on geological evidence, sand grains trapped in the caulking could not have derived from any source in northern Scotland). The Vikings were great traders, and it is perfectly possible that objects made or traded in southern Sweden or Denmark eventually ended up in Norway. Moreover, most Viking settlers in Scotland came from western Norway originally, for simple reasons of geography. Of course these three people might have been in Orkney for some time before they died (we have no way of knowing for how long), but, interestingly, the only probably non-Scandinavian object in the grave was a spindle whorl made of Orkney sandstone.

Did they live in Orkney, and if so where?

It seems most likely that these people were living in Orkney before their death. We think this partly because of the strange composition of the group (a very old woman, a man in early middle age and a child), and partly because the boat was not an ocean-going vessel: this sort of boat would have been used for local transport and inshore fishing. In addition, there must have been other members of a Viking community in Sanday to give them this elaborate pagan burial.

We do not know precisely where they lived, but they probably lived in Sanday, perhaps not that far away from the site of the boat burial. A survey of the area immediately around the burial revealed a nearby settlement mound of unknown date and other archaeological features, some of them perhaps graves; but none of these have been excavated. The presence of Vikings in Sanday is well documented, the most direct evidence coming from recent excavations of a long-lived settlement at Pool on the west coast of the island. Results from Pool have confirmed that Viking settlements were established on the island at the time these people were buried in a boat at Scar.

What exactly was found in the grave?

The grave pit contained a clinker-built wooden rowing boat, some 7.15 metres long, made of oak with a washrail of Scots pine; some 310 boat fastenings (rivets and nails) were also recovered. A burial chamber had been constructed within the boat, by the insertion of a stone-built partition wall. Within the chamber were the skeletal remains of three people.

The woman was buried with:
- a gilded bronze equal-armed brooch
- a carved whalebone plaque
- an antler comb
- an iron sickle with wooden handle
- an iron weaving batten
- a pair of iron shears
- a wooden needle tidy with at least two iron needles, wound round with thread

- a maplewood box with iron bands around the outside and a possible lock
- and two spindle whorls, one made of talc rock and the other of Orkney sandstone

The man was buried with:
- an iron sword, its guard inlaid with silver and brass, all in a scabbard made of two laths of ash wood, lined with sheepskin and bound round with linen
- nine iron arrows with leaf-shaped arrowheads in a wooden quiver and, possibly, a bow
- an antler comb
- a set of twenty-two whalebone gaming pieces, probably originally in a pouch or purse
- a fragmentary tinned bronze object, possibly part of a shield rim
- and two lead bullion weights (we are not certain that these were buried with the man)

Two other objects could have been associated with the boat burial:
- a blue glass bead
- and a large iron handle, perhaps a boat fitting

In addition, there was a wide variety of textile remains (see below). The grave was covered over with pine planks laid across the boat and nailed to its edge. A mass of tiny fishbones was deposited in the grave, probably by nesting otters after it had been sealed.

What were the people wearing when they were buried?

The people would have been buried completely clothed and the grave may also have been furnished with pillows, hangings or covers. Textiles rarely survive on archaeological sites in the Northern Isles but, at Scar, we were lucky enough to find traces of a wide variety of textiles, representing five or more different weaves: a tabby weave, a repp-like tabby, more balanced tabbies, a self-patterned tabby, a textile with a 'brocaded' effect and a twill weave. Most of these were attached to objects, however, and rather little evidence survives of the outfits worn by the grave's occupants. Both the man and the woman may have worn shirts of a tabby weave cloth, and the woman at least probably wore a red-brown cloth cloak, pinned together at the front by her brooch. Linen tabbies were found attached to the comb and the sword. The weaving batten had been in contact with several different textiles, possibly a combination of the woman's clothing and grave furnishings such as covers or hangings. Attached to the maplewood box was a brocaded textile, perhaps from a pillow or cover. The needle tidy was wound round with thread—all ready for repairs.

What was the whalebone plaque used for?

Whalebone plaques were essentially smoothing boards, used for pressing small linen garments such as caps, pleats or seams, normally with a bun-shaped glass linen smoother. The smoother would have been heated over a fire or in boiling water, and then passed repeatedly over the material, like an iron.

We believe, though, that the highly carved plaques were valued in death (and perhaps in life as well) primarily for their symbolism and religious significance, and perhaps as a statement of status, rather than as a functional implement. The carved plaques may be linked to the Viking goddess, Freyja. One of Freyja's names derives from the Old Norse word for flax, which was thought to protect against evil and give fertility to humankind. Flax was connected with women; it was called the 'seed of woman' and had to be sown on a Friday (Freyja's day) by women dressed in their best clothes. The spinning of flax was also connected with Freyja, and the product, linen, was an important part of bridal dress. The carved whalebone plaques may have been used for pressing precious linens for ceremonial occasions, especially the linen elements of the 'best clothes' worn to sow the flax seed or get married in.

Little wonder, then, that the symbolic Scar plaque was placed in the grave in such a prominent position, upright and facing the elderly woman. She might even have been directly involved in the cult of Freyja—possibly even a 'priestess'.

What game was played with the gaming pieces?

Almost certainly the Viking game of *hnefatafl,* a simple but subtle game of attack and defence for two people. The 'king' piece and a small force of defenders occupy the centre of the board; and a larger force of attackers is placed around the edges. The object of the game is for the attacking player to capture the opponent's king, in which case they win, or for the king to escape to one of the corners of the board, in which case the defending player wins.

How much of the grave survived?

The sea erosion which exposed the site and brought it to our attention had removed about half of the boat grave before the excavation started, and of the remaining part a large fraction was badly affected by animal disturbance. Although it was possible to reconstruct the shape of the boat, and the arrangement of the burials, the objects recovered from the grave—rich as they are—may only be a fraction of what was originally put into the boat burial.

What is so special about the Scar boat burial?

This enigmatic burial is one of the richest Viking graves known from the British Isles, and some of the objects it contained are as yet unparalleled both in their quality and state of preservation. The whalebone plaque survived in excellent condition thanks to a fortunate combination of being both waterlogged and embedded in calcareous sand. The rare and highly ornate gilded equal-armed brooch also survived virtually intact. The fact that the boat's precious cargo accompanied not one, but three people, one of them an exceptionally old woman, makes it unique in the Viking world. Boat burials are also very rare in Britain, though more common in western Norway.

Most Viking graves in the British Isles were discovered many years ago and are poorly recorded; the Scar grave gave us a rare opportunity to excavate a wealthy Viking burial using modern scientific techniques. Careful retrieval of the finds in the field allowed further micro-excavation and investigation in the controlled environment of the laboratory, which revealed much new information. For example, it was possible to identify several different types of textiles of which no organic remains had survived; the types of wood used in the boat; the nature and construction of the sword scabbard and the quiver containing the arrows; the exotic suite of sand grains trapped in the boat caulking; and the insects which colonised the grave after it had been sealed.

In the end, though, the Scar burial has left us with as many questions as answers—and perhaps that is also part of its enduring appeal. The excavation and survey of the area indicated that other archaeological features occur nearby, and it may be that the answers to some of these vexed questions are still to be found beneath the sand dunes at Scar. In the meantime, we can only marvel at the wealth and variety of the Viking graves, and the strength and strangeness—at least to us—of the pagan beliefs which underpinned them.

What are the lessons for the future?

What at first appeared to be a fairly insignificant burial by the beach turned out to be a major archaeological discovery. The site was only rescued thanks to the vigilance of local archaeologists who quickly realised the potential of the site, and to the quick response of the authorities who at short notice made funds available for its excavation. The Scar burial highlights the importance of constant monitoring of areas at risk from coastal erosion, and the need for swift action when important new sites are discovered. The vicinity of the burial site has now been protected as a monument of national importance.

ACKNOWLEDGEMENTS:

Excavation of the boat burial would not have been possible without the enthusiastic co-operation and many kindnesses of Mrs Caroline Deerness of Scar and her family, to whom we owe a deep debt of gratitude. We are also grateful to the many other islanders of Sanday who gave us such a warm welcome, took such an interest in the project and provided accommodation, practical help and encouragement throughout. In particular, we wish to acknowledge Rod Thorne and his family for all their help, especially during the last hectic week; Leslie Cooper and Karl Cooper; Ian and Irene Brown; and Bernie Flett.

Scar was originally identified as the site of a Viking burial by Julie Gibson and Raymond Lamb, whose support and guidance throughout the project has been invaluable. The success of the field project was due in large measure to the great skill and dogged determination, sometimes in atrocious weather conditions, of our marvellous excavators: Lennard Anderson, Alan Duffy, Hazel Moore and Graeme Wilson; it would not have been possible without them. We also thank visiting specialists, Richard Welander, Anne Allen and Jacqui Marwick for all their help on site; and we are very indebted to the various photographers who visited and produced such a high quality record of the work, especially Michael Brooks of Historic Scotland and Richard Welsby of Stromness, Orkney.

The project was funded throughout by Historic Scotland, with practical support and equipment provided by Orkney Islands Council, including site accommodation and lighting. We are especially pleased to acknowledge the help of the staff of Orkney Islands Council Planning Department.

Our debt to the specialists and conservators who worked on the materials in post-excavation must already be obvious. As well as the named contributors to this volume, we wish to acknowledge the help of AOC (Scotland) Ltd, particularly Coralie Mills who managed the post-excavation programme. We are very grateful to Sylvia Stevenson (artefacts) and Christina Unwin (plans and reconstruction drawing) for their excellent illustrations, and to Michael Brooks for the photography of artefacts. We also acknowledge with gratitude the considerable editorial help of Ann MacSween, the general assistance of Melissa Seddon, and the advice on illustrations of Christina Unwin and Matt Ritchie. The first full draft was kindly read by Barbara Crawford, James Graham-Campbell and Caroline Paterson, to all of whom we offer grateful thanks.

Olwyn Owen wishes to thank the many friends and colleagues in Scandinavia and Britain who have so freely offered information, advice and encouragement on aspects of the material assemblage. She is deeply indebted to all of them, but especially grateful to Ingmar Jansson (University of Stockholm) for help with the Swedish comparanda (brooch and plaque); to Björn Ambrosiani and Kenneth Svensson (Birka Project, Stockholm), and Claus Fevejle and the late Stig Jensen (Ribe Museum) for useful discussions and for access to unpublished information about finds from recent excavations.

She is also very grateful to the following individuals and institutions for other information: Gerd Stamsø Munch (Tromsø Museum); Oddmunn Farbregd (Vitenskapsmuseet, Trondheim); Jenny-Rita Næss and Åsa Dahlin Hauken (Arkeologisk Museum i Stavanger); Birthe Weber (Universitetets Oldsaksamling, Oslo); Helge Sørheim (Sunnmøre Museum); Sten Tesch (Sigtuna Museums); Ann Pedersen (National Museum of Denmark, Copenhagen); Pat Wallace (National Museum of Ireland, Dublin); Leslie Webster and Barry Ager (British Museum); James Graham-Campbell (University College, London); Susan Kruse (SCRAN, National Museums of Scotland); Christopher Chippindale (Cambridge University Museum of Archaeology and Anthropology); Trevor Cowie and Alison Sheridan (National Museums of Scotland, Edinburgh); Ann Brundle (Tankerness House Museum, Orkney); Colleen Batey (Kelvingrove Museum, Glasgow); and Euan MacKie (Hunterian Museum, Glasgow).

She wishes to thank Finbar McCormick and Jerry Harman for attempting to identify the whalebone used for the decorated plaque; Amanda Clydesdale and Richard Welander for discussion of the technology and other aspects of the brooch; Barbara Crawford for drawing her attention to the likely connection between the plaque and the goddess Freyja; Caroline Paterson for discussion of early Viking art styles and equal-armed brooches, and for other information on the Scottish graves; Sigrid Kaland for drawing her attention to the unpublished plaques in Historisk Museum, Bergen; Kjersti Schanche for information about a new north Norwegian plaque; and Gill Walsh for research assistance. Finally, she wishes to thank those friends and colleagues who kindly commented on earlier drafts of reports on individual objects: Ingmar Jansson and Björn Ambrosiani (the brooch and the plaque); Claus Fevejle (the plaque); Susan Kruse and Pat Wallace (the lead weights); and Anna Ritchie (the gaming pieces).

Dr Stephen Carter offers his thanks to Dr Andrew Kitchener of the Royal Museum of Scotland, Edinburgh and to Dr Hans Kruuk of the Institute for Terrestrial Ecology, Banchory, for their useful comments on otter's habits.

Michél Carlsson wishes to thank Mary Macleod for help with translation of his original draft from Swedish into English, and Andrea Smith for providing additional information.

Kim Nissan would like to thank the following colleagues for their invaluable help and interest: Phil Clogg (Durham University), Dr R Janaway (Bradford University), Dr J McDonnell (Bradford University), Richard Welander (Historic Scotland) and Paul Wilthew (National Museum of Scotland); and Esther Cameron, Russell Scott and Jacqui Watson for replying to queries and supplying references.

Thea Gabra-Sanders would like to thank Dr Margareta Nockert for her help.

Daphne Home Lorimer is very grateful to Dr Theya Mollison for her constructive advice and suggestions; Dr Raymond Lamb for information on Pictish and Viking equestrian practices; the entire staff of the Physiotherapy Department, Balfour Hospital, Kirkwall, for their help in interpreting muscle action; and Joy Livet for a demonstration of spinning techniques.

Dianne Dixon wishes to thank Dr J E Dixon, of the Department of Geology and Geophysics, University of Edinburgh, whose help and advice were invaluable; Dr S Elphick and Dr S Kearns for technical and analytical help; and Professor B Upton and Dr S Harley for helpful discussion about potential areas of suitable rocks in Scandinavia.

Anne Allen extends thanks to all who helped in the preparation of her report on the boat: Jan Bill and Ole Crumlin-Pedersen, The Danish National Maritime Museum; Arne Emil Christensen, University of Oslo; Dr Emeleus, Department of Geology, University of Durham; Dr H Hamerow and Dr M Millett, Department of Archaeology, University of Durham; Peter Marsden, Museum of London; Sean McGrail, Institute of Archaeology, University of Oxford; and Dr R Prescott, Scottish Institute of Maritime Studies, University of St Andrews.

William Thomson acknowledges the help of Brian Tulloch whose knowledge of Burness was of great assistance; William Ward who made available the maps of Burness; and Dr Barbara Crawford who read a first draft of the report.

All illustrations are the copyright of Historic Scotland, except where otherwise indicated in the captions to the figures. Thanks are due to the following organisations and individuals for permission to reproduce their copyright illustrations:

Historic Scotland (Crown Copyright); The Royal Commission on Ancient and Historical Monuments of Scotland (Crown Copyright); The Trustees of the National Museums of Scotland; The Trustees of the National Library of Scotland; David Simon; Richard Welsby Photography, Stromness; Professor Mick Aston (and Channel 4's *Time Team*); Shetland Museum (Shetland Islands Council); Universitetets Oldsaksamlingen med Vikingskipshuset, Oslo, Norway; Tromsø Museum, Norway; Historisk Museum, Bergen Universitetet, Norway; Statens Historiska Museet, Stockholm, Sweden; Sigtuna Museums, Sweden; Nationalmuseet, Copenhagen, Denmark; Manx Museum and National Trust; National Museum of Ireland, Dublin; Cambridge University Museum of Archaeology and Anthropology; and Manchester City Art Galleries.

The finds from the Scar boat burial are on display in Tankerness House Museum, Broad Street, Kirkwall, Orkney; and the site archive has been deposited in the National Monuments Record of Scotland, 16 Bernard Terrace, Edinburgh.

APPENDICES

APPENDIX 1. CATALOGUE OF BOX FRAGMENTS AND RELATED FINDS

Andrea Smith

Find no 95/920025, F39
Iron band fragment with nail stump, L 32 mm, W 26 mm, wood grain on underside oriented parallel to short axis. This piece was found 60 cm west of the main concentration of fragments.

Find no 99/920026, F40
Nail, shank incomplete L 17 mm, head round Dia 12 mm. Wood grain 5 mm thick under head has grain parallel to head, on shank wood grain runs parallel to shank. Found close to the sickle handle and brooch, 30 cm north-west of the main concentration.

Find no 102/920028, F40
Iron band fragment, right-angled from corner fitting. W 20 mm, L (longest side) 18 mm, wood grain on underside oriented parallel to short axis. This piece lay 70 cm west of the main group.

Find no 120/920029, F40
Iron band fragment with nail stump in centre. Larger than others, 57 x 22–28 mm, with wood grain on underside running parallel to long axis. There is a clean break in the line of the wood grain possibly indicative of a split or join in the wood. The outer surface was covered in textile remains, identified by Gabra-Sanders as a brocaded textile. Found in the area where the woman's head might have been, 30 cm to the north of the main group.

Find no 125/920031, F40
Staple, L 24 mm T 6 mm, with wood cast on underside of centre bar.

Find no 144/920033, F40
Iron band, L 75 mm, W 20 mm, with two nail stumps 55 mm apart. Wood grain on underside parallel with short axis. Found 30 cm north-west of main concentration.

Find no 146/911512, F40
This find number covers a group of six objects, found between the shears and the weaving batten. These were lifted together in a sand lump, which also contained a large quantity of small fishbones. Found in the area of the boat burial disturbed by otters.

A. Tapering or shouldered iron band, L 77 mm, width on wider part 20 mm, on narrower part 12 mm, crossed by two staples, one 48 mm long, other 15 mm long. Wood grain on underside of band runs parallel to long axis. Probably represented remains of sliding bar closing mechanism, or even a proper lock.

B. Iron band fragment, angled from corner fitting. Longest side W 24 mm, L 34 mm with nail stump. Wood grain on underside runs parallel with short axis. There are two small patches of textile remains on the outer surface.

C. Iron band fragment, very similar to and probably broken off B above. 15 x 15 mm with nail stump and wood grain on underside.

D. Iron band fragment, very similar to B and C and probably part of same. 21 x 22 mm with nail stump and wood grain on underside.

E. Nail fragment, L 13 mm, head rounded 11 x 13 mm, true outline obscured by textile remains. Wood cast below head had grain running parallel to head.

F. Small irregular right-angled fragment, possibly broken off smaller staple attached to tapering bar A.

Find no 153/920080, F40
Iron band with nail stump, L 52 mm, W 22 mm, with wood grain on underside running parallel to short axis. This item is very similar to Find 155 below, and is probably from the same piece, although without the corrosion drips, indicating that the pieces may have been separated early in their depositional history. Textile remains on outer surface, identified by Gabra-Sanders (*infra*) as a repp weave with ribbed effect. Found 4 cm to the north-east of the shears, and immediately to the south of Find no 155.

Find no 155/920081
Iron band with three sides intact, L 60 mm, W 23 mm, and two nail stumps on underside 39 mm apart. Conservation report noted that its smooth surface was unusual, suggesting that there had been no solid material in contact with it during the early stages of burial and corrosion; possibly it had been lying in water or air in a void. Corrosion drips on one of the long sides indicate that it had originally been positioned with the long axis in the horizontal plane. Wood remains on the underside have the grain running parallel with the short axis. This item is very similar to Find 155 above, and may have belonged to the same piece. Found 6 cm to the north-east of the shears and immediately to the north of Find no 153.

Find no 156/920082, F40
a. Nail fragment L 20 mm, round head Dia 12 mm, with wood cast under head, grain running parallel with head. Found 5 cm to the north-east of the shears, between Finds 153 & 161.

b. Nail fragment, L 16 mm, head round, Dia 10 mm. Mineralised wood below head with grain running parallel to head. Found almost touching the blade end of the shears on the side with the whorl.

Find no 157/920083, F40
Nail fragment L 22 mm, round head Dia 10 mm, with wood casts under head and on shank with grain running in opposite directions. Found 3 cm away from the end of the shears.

Find no 158/920023, F37

Iron corrosion blister, found during sieving, with convex surface, 45 x 28 mm. On convex surface there are casts of organic remains, identified in the conservation laboratory as a piece of skin or leather and a small hand of fibre, possibly fur or carded fleece. This does not resemble any of the other fragments found anywhere near the area of the box, but it is impossible to say whether something like this belongs to the box or not.

Find no 161/920039, F40
This find number covers a group of four objects which were found together close to the blade end of the shears. Amongst these was the needle tidy which is discussed separately (Chapter 5), and which may have formed part of the contents of the box. A loose fragment of unidentifiable textile was also found amongst these objects.
A. Iron band fragment with nail stump, L 19 mm, W 21 mm, with wood grain on underside running parallel to short axis (21 mm side). Textile casts on the outer surface have been identified by Gabra-Sanders (*infra*) as a 2/1 twill weave.
B. Nail, possibly complete, L 35 mm, head irregular oval 10 x 17 mm, with mineralised wood 6.5 mm deep under the head with grain running parallel to the head, and wood remains on the shank with grain running parallel to the shank.
C. Nail, L 22 mm, with irregular oval head 9 x 13 mm, and wood remains under head and down shank with grain all running parallel to head.

Find no 162/920084, F40
Nail, L 22 mm, head much obscured but c. 12 mm dia from X-ray. Cast of wood under head has grain running parallel to head, and on shank grain runs parallel to shank. Found 5 cm south-east of the blade end of the shears.

Find no 163/920085, F40
Nail, L 14 mm, head (from X-ray) round, Dia 13 mm . Mineralised wood under head with grain running parallel to head. Found 12 cm south-east of the blade end of the shears.

Find no 166/920087, F40
Nail, L 26 mm, head round, Dia 10 mm. Mineralised wood on shank and in thin layer over top of head, grain all runs parallel to head. Found on top of the shears where the heels of the blades met.

Find no 167/920088, F40
Nail, L 15 mm, head round, Dia 11 x 13 mm. Mineralised wood below head with grain running parallel to head. Found 4 cm north-east of the handle end of the shears.

Find no 168/920089, F40
Two fragments of iron band, probably from same piece. Found 5 cm south-west of the handle end of the shears.
A. L 65 mm, W 17–20 mm, with nail stump 20 mm from one (true?) end. Wood preserved on underside has grain running parallel with short axis. Conservation laboratory has identified casts of hair or fur fibres on outer surface, randomly oriented as if from slightly twisted hank or pelt.
B. L 26 mm, W 18 mm, with nail stump on one end. Wood preserved on underside has grain running parallel with short axis.

Find no 204/920112, F40
Group of objects and fragments of iron corrosion, from which the following can be recognised:
A. Iron band fragment with nail stump, 27 x 17 mm, no real edges. Conservation laboratory identified two layers of textile (twill?) on the outer surface, and there is mineralised wood on the underside.
B. Nail, L 23 mm, with rounded head 10 x 12 mm, mineralised wood under head 5 mm thick with grain running parallel to head, wood also on shank with grain running parallel to shank.
C. Nail, L 20 mm, round head, Dia 12 mm.
D. Fragment of nail shank L 8 mm, with area of mineralised wood attached to one end 18 x 22 mm, but no trace of head or other metal.

Find no 241/920154, F40
Nail, L 27 mm, head distorted by corrosion blister. The conservation report records that there is some kind of fibre wrapped around the shank 8 mm from the head, but this is very difficult to distinguish from the wood cast. Found 20 cm south-east of the blade end of the shears.

APPENDIX 2. CATALOGUE OF TEXTILES

Thea Gabra-Sanders

Dimensions are given to the maximum length and width in cm. *Side A indicates the side visible when found and side B the reverse side.* The direction of the spin of the yarn is indicated by Z (for clockwise, if a yarn is held vertically, the twisted fibres slope in the same direction as the centre of the portion of the letter Z) and S (for anti-clockwise, if a yarn is held vertically, the twisted fibres slope in the same direction as the centre portion of the letter S). The systems are designated 1 and 2 as the warp and the weft cannot be differentiated. The thread-count is the number of threads per cm, one figure for the warp and one for the weft. The colour describes the mineralised textile, not the textile itself.

Equal armed brooch
Find 141 FNo 40 LabNo 911511
Around pin fastener a fragment 1.5 x 1.0 cm of red/brown partly mineralised ? fibre, ? tabby weave. System (1), Z-spun, ? thread/cm. System (2), ? spun, ? threads/cm. Textile impression on back of the brooch. Weave: herringbone twill, spin: ?, 30–35 x ? threads/cm.

Sickle
Find 145 FNo 40 LabNo 920037
Side B
Fragment, 16.0 x 0.5 cm of brown mineralised ? fibre, tabby weave. System (1), Z-spun, 17 threads/cm. System (2), Z-spun, 15 threads/cm.

Weaving batten
Find 142 FNo 40 LabNo 920036
Side A
Three fragments, 1.3 x 1.0 cm, an area of ± 2.6 cm and 1.0 cm of reddish brown mineralised ? fibre textile remains. Weave: ?; Spin: Z x Z, ? x Z, Z x Z; thread-count: ?.

Side B
Fragment A
5.5 x 3.5 to 4 cm of brown mineralised ? fibre self-patterned tabby weave (5–span warp or weft floats in plain weave). System (1), Z-spun, 22 threads/cm. System (2), Z-spun, 14 threads/cm.
Fragment B
1.3 x 1.0 cm of reddish brown mineralised ? fibre ? weave. System (1), Z-spun, ? threads/cm. System (2), Z-spun, ? threads/cm.

Fragment C
± 2.6 x 2.6 cm of reddish brown mineralised ? fibre ? weave. System (1), ? spun, ? threads/cm. System (2), ? Z-spun, ? threads/cm.

Fragment D
± 1.0 x 1.0 cm of reddish dark brown mineralised ? fibre ? weave. System (1), Z-spun, ? threads/cm. System (2), Z-spun, ? threads/cm.

Iron shears
Find 154 FNo 40 LabNo 911515
Side A
Fragment A
4.0 x 3.0 cm of crumpled brown mineralised ? fibre tabby weave. System (1), Z-spun, 17–20 threads/cm. System (2), Z-spun, 12 threads/cm.

Fragment B
± 5.0 x 1.2 cm of brown mineralised ? fibre tabby weave. System (1), Z-spun, 10 threads/cm. System (2), Z-spun, 8 threads/cm.

Side B
Fragment A
3.0 x 2.5 cm of folded brown mineralised ? fibre tabby weave. System (1), Z-spun, 16 threads/cm. System (2), Z-spun, 14 threads/cm.

Fragment B
4.0 x 2.0 cm of brown mineralised ? fibre tabby weave. System (1), Z-spun, 14 threads/cm. System (2), Z-spun, 10 threads/cm.

Needle tidy
Find 161 FNo 40 LabNo 920039
S-plied light brown ? fibre string, 2.5 mm wide, wound around wooden needlecase 14–15 times.

Box
Iron fragment with wood adhering
Find 120 FNo 40 Lab No 920029
Fragment, ± 4.5 x 4.5 cm of brown mineralised ? fibre with brocaded effect on a repp weave ground. Warp, Z-spun, 18–20 threads/cm. Weft, Z-spun 10 threads/cm. Brocaded weft, ? fibre, S-plied.
Iron band fragment with nail stump
Find 146 FNo 40 Lab No 911512
Adhering to the iron band fragment are two small reddish-brown mineralised ? fibre, textile fragments in a ? weave, with ? threads/cm. Only one yarn could be identified as Z-spun. The nail stump also has a small reddish-brown mineralised textile fragment in a ? weave, woven from ? spun, ? fibre, with ? threads/cm adhering to it.

Iron fragment with pin
Find 153 FNo 40 Lab No 920080
Fragment, 3.0 x 1.5 cm of brown mineralised ? fibre repp weave. System (1), Z-spun, 16 threads/cm. System (2), Z-spun, 6 threads/cm.

Iron corrosion blister
Find 158 FNo 37 LabNo 920023
The convex surface of the blister is covered with brown mineralised fibres, probably a fragment of haired skin.

Stud
Find 161 FNo 40 LabNo 920039
Fragment, 2.0 x 0.5 cm of brown mineralised ? fibre 2/1 twill weave. System (1), Z-spun, 20 threads/cm. System (2), Z-spun, ? threads per cm.

Loose metal fragment
Find 161 FNo 40 LabNo 920039
Fragment, 1.0 x 0.5 cm of brown mineralised ? fibre, ? weave. System (1), Z–spun, 15 threads/cm. System (2), Z–spun, 10 threads/cm.

Iron band fragment with nail stump
Find 168 FNo 40 LabNo 920089
Fragment, 4.0 x 1.5 cm of reddish brown mineralised fibres which are lying parallel and could be hair or fur.

Iron band fragment with nail stump
Find 204 FNo 40 LabNo 920112
Top layer. Fragment ± 2.0 x 1.5 cm of reddish-dark brown mineralised ? fibre, ? 2/1 twill weave. System (1), Z–spun, ? threads/cm. System (2), Z–spun, ? threads/cm.
2nd layer. Fragment 1.5 x 0.3 cm (visible) of reddish- brown mineralised ? fibre, 2/1 twill weave. System (1), Z–spun, 23 threads/cm. System (2), Z–spun, 12 threads/cm.

Iron nail, head distorted by corrosion blister
Find 241 FNo 40 Lab No 920154
Wrapped around the shank of the nail just under the head is a reddish-brown plied yarn, ? fibre, ? spun.

Iron band
Find 155 FNo 40 LabNo 920081
Fragment, 0.6 x 0.6 cm of brown mineralised ? fibre ? tabby weave. System (1), Z–spun, ? threads/cm. System (2), ? spun, ? threads/cm.

Sword

Find 137 FNo 40 LabNo 911518
Side A Part 2
Fragment A
Under wood (quiver), 3.5 x 2.0 cm of light brown mineralised plant fibre tabby weave. System (1), Z–spun, 15 threads/cm. System (2), Z–spun, 12 threads/cm.

Fragment B
3.0 x 1.2 cm of mineralised plant fibre ? weave. System (1), ? spun, ? threads/cm. 1.0 x 0.5 cm of brown hair (?haired skin).

Side A Part 3
Fragment A
2.5 x 1.7 cm of mineralised light brown plant fibre tabby weave. System (1), Z–spun, 14 threads/cm. System (2), Z–spun, 12 threads/cm.

Fragment B
Partly under wood (quiver), 4.0 x 2.2 cm of mineralised light brown tabby weave. System (1), Z–spun, 15 threads/cm. System (2), Z–spun, 14 threads/cm. The textile goes round the edge of the sword.

Side A Part 4
Fragment, 2.5 x 1.4 cm of mineralised plant fibre ? weave. System (1), ? spun, 15 threads/cm. System (2), ? spun, 14 threads/cm. ± 3.0 x 2.5 cm of light brown hair (? haired skin).

Side B Part 1
Fragment, 2.5 x 2.0 cm of mineralised plant fibre ? tabby weave. System (1), ? spun, ? threads/cm. System (2), ? spun, ? threads/cm.

Side B Part 2
Fragment A
3.5 x 2.5 cm of mineralised light brown plant fibre tabby weave. System (1), Z–spun, 14 threads/cm. System (2), Z–spun, 12 threads/cm.

Fragment B
3.0 x 1.2 cm of mineralised plant fibre tabby weave. System (1), ? spun, ? threads/cm. System (2), ? spun, ? threads/cm.

Side B Part 3
Fragment A
5.6 x 1.2 cm of light brown mineralised plant fibre tabby weave. System (1), Z–spun, 15 threads/cm. System (2), Z–spun, 14 threads/cm.

Fragment B
± 5.0 x 3.0 cm of light brown mineralised plant fibre tabby weave. System (1), Z–spun, 14 threads/cm. System (2), Z–spun, 12 threads/cm.

Side B Part 4
Fragment B
0.5 x 0.4 cm of mineralised light brown plant fibre tabby weave. System (1), Z–spun, 15 threads/cm. System (2), Z–spun, 15 threads/cm.

Fragment C
2.0 x 0.5 cm of mineralised light brown plant fibre tabby weave. System (1), Z–spun, ? threads/cm. System (2), Z–spun, ? threads/cm.

Fragment D
± 3.5 x 2.0 cm of mineralised light brown plant fibre tabby weave. System (1), Z–spun, 13 threads/cm. System (2), Z–spun, 12 threads/cm. Some roots.

Side B Part 5
± 3.0 x 2.5 cm of light brown hair (? haired skin).

Hilt
Side A
Fragment, 1.5 x 1.5 cm of mineralised brown ? fibre tabby weave. System (1), Z–spun, ? threads/cm. System (2), ? spun, ? threads/cm.

Side B
Fragment A, 4.5 x 2.3 cm of brown mineralised ? fibre tabby weave. System (1), Z–spun, 16 threads/cm. System (2), Z–spun, 14 threads/cm.

Fragment B, 3.0 x 2.0 cm of brown mineralised ? fibre tabby weave. System (1), Z–spun, 15 threads/cm. System (2), Z–spun, 15 threads/cm.

Comb

Find 136 FNo 40 LabNo 920002

Most of the rivets on side A and three rivets on side B of the comb have very small remains of mineralised yarn or fibres adhering to them.

Side A

Rivet 1: fragment 0.5 x 0.4 cm of mineralised brown plant fibre ? weave. System (1), Z-spun, ? threads/cm. System (2), ? spun, ? threads/cm.

Rivet 2–3–4–5: some very small fragments of mineralised yarn, ? fibre, ? spun.

Rivet 6: a few mineralised ? fibres.

Rivet 7: ± 0.3 x 0.2 cm of light brown mineralised plant fibre ? tabby weave. System (1), Z-spun, 15 threads/cm. System (2), Z-spun, ? threads/cm.

Rivet 10: a few light brown mineralised plant fibres.

Side B

Rivet 1: a few mineralised plant fibres.

Rivet 2: very small fragment of brown mineralised plant fibre ? tabby weave. System (1), Z-spun, ? threads/cm. System (2), ? spun, ? threads/cm.

Rivet 6: very small fragment of brown mineralised plant fibre ? tabby weave. System (1), 20 threads/cm. System (2), Z-spun, ? threads/cm.

Rivet 8: fragment, 0.8 x 0.6 cm of brown mineralised plant fibre tabby weave. System (1), Z-spun, 25 threads/cm. System (2), Z-spun, 15 threads/cm.

The following small mineralised fragments were retrieved from sieving –

Lab No	Weave	Fibre	Thread-count	Spin
930418	?	?	?	Z/Z
930420	? 2/1 twill	?	15 x 13/cm	Z/?Z
930421	?	?	?	one S-plied yarn
930422	tabby	?	15 x 10/cm	Z/Z
930422	tabby	?	15 x 13/cm	Z/Z
930422	tabby	?	20 x 12/cm	Z/Z
930423	tabby	?	12 x 10/cm	Z/Z

APPENDIX 3. XRF ANALYSIS OF THE BROOCH

Paul Wilthew

Summary

A total of 16 qualitative analyses of samples of gilding, the shell and the fill of bosses were confirmed to be silver sheet filled with a lead-tin alloy. The brooch was a copper alloy containing zinc and probably also tin and lead. It had been mercury gilded. It was also found that detectable gold remained even in areas in which the surface consisted of a dark green corrosion layer.

Introduction

The aim of the analysis was to answer certain questions which had been raised by Amanda Clydesdale of the conservation department at AOC (Scotland) Ltd, during examination of the gilt copper alloy equal-armed brooch. The analyses were aimed to determine -

1. The composition of the shells from the hemispherical bosses.
2. The composition of the fill of the bosses.
3. The method used to gild the brooch.
4. The extent of the remaining gilding.
5. The composition of the copper alloy.

Analytical method

All analyses were carried out by energy-dispersive X-ray fluorescence. The analysed areas were irradiated with a primary X-ray beam produced by a Rhodium target X-ray tube run at 46 KV with an anode current of 0.30 mA. The primary beam was collimated to give an elliptical irradiated area of *c* 1.5 mm by 1 mm. Secondary X-rays were detected using a silican (lithium) solid state detector. The samples remained in gelatine capsules during analysis, but as only qualitative data was required, this should not have affected the results significantly.

Results and discussion

The elements detected in each analysis are listed in Table 5.

Boss shells
The shells of bosses 3, 10 and 12 are all silver. The silver may have contained copper, zinc, lead or tin, but it is also possible that these elements were detected as a result of contamination from corrosion product from the fill of the bosses or the copper alloy base metal of the brooch itself.

Boss fill
Each of the samples of the fill was found to be rich in both lead and tin, suggesting that the bosses had been filled with an alloy rather than pure lead.

Gilding method
The fragment of gilding contained quite high levels of mercury, indicating that mercury gilding had been used.

Extent of the gilding
Two corroded areas on the front surface of the brooch fragment were analysed. No gilding was visible in either area, but fairly high levels of gold were nevertheless detected, suggesting that gilding remains under or within part of the corrosion layer, although it may not be in a condition which would allow it to be revealed.

Copper alloy
Copper and zinc were detected in all the samples and fragments analysed, suggesting that the copper alloy contained significant levels of zinc. Analysis of a fracture surface confirmed this, but lead and tin were also detected. It is impossible to be certain of the original composition on the basis of a surface analysis of a corroded object, particularly as a lead-tin alloy was present, but the metal was probably a quaternary copper-zinc-tin-lead alloy, the nearest modern equivalent of which would be a gunmetal.

Table 5: Significant elements detected in each area analysed.

Analysis	Sample	Major elements	Minor elements	Trace elements
F5331b	Frag of gilding	Au Cu Hg	Zn	Ag
F5332B	Boss 3, shell	Ag	Cu Pb Sn	Zn Br
F5333B	Boss 4, fill	Sn Pb Cu	Zn	Ag
F5334B	Boss 7, fill	Sn Pb Cu	Zn Ag	
F5335B	Boss 10, shell (prob)	Ag	Pb Sn Cu	Zn
F5336B	Boss 10, fill	Pb Sn	Cu Zn Ag	
F5337B	Boss 11, fill	Sn Pb	Cu Ag Zn	
F5338B	Boss 11, fill	Sn Pb	Ag Cu Zn	
F5339B	Boss 12, fill	Sn Pb	Cu Ag Zn	
F5340B	Boss 12, outer shell	Ag	Pb Sn Cu	Zn
F5341B	Boss 12, inner shell	Sn Pb	Ag Cu Zn	
F5342B	Boss 13, fill	Pb Sn	Cu Zn Ag	
F5343B	Boss 14, fill	Sn Pb	Cu Zn	Ag
F5344B	Brooch frag, dark green	Cu	Zn Au Pb Sn	Ag Hg
F5345B	Brooch frag, pale green	Cu Zn	Pb Sn Au	Ag Hg
F5346B	Brooch frag, cross-section	Cu Zn	Zn Sn Pb	

Notes: Traces of iron and calcium were detected in most analyses, but may be due to contamination. Bromine was detected in the analysis of the shell of Boss 3 (F5332B), presumably because of the presence of bromide in the silver corrosion products.

APPENDIX 4. LIST OF KNOWN VIKING PERIOD CARVED WHALEBONE PLAQUES

Olwyn Owen

Abbreviations
C = Universitetets Oldsaksamlingen, Oslo; B = Bergen Historisk Museum; T = Vitenskapsmuseet, Universitetet I Trondheim; Ts = Tromsø Museum; BM = British Museum; SHM = Statens Historiska Museet, Stockholm; SM = Sigtuna Museum; SS = Stockholms Stadsmuseum; NMS = National Museums of Scotland, Edinburgh; TH = Tankerness House; HM = Hunterian Museum, Glasgow; NMI = National Musuem of Ireland, Dublin; CUM = Cambridge University Museum of Archaeology and Anthropology; na = not allocated

Norway
Nos. 1–34 follow Petersen's (1951) list. Museum numbers in brackets.

1. Ommestad, Hof, Hedmark (C 22536)
2. Toranger, Austvoll, Sund, Hordaland (B 5874 i)
3. Folkedal, Granvin, Ulvik, Hordaland (B 7114 b)
4. Seim, Granvin, Ulvik, Hordaland (B 8635 p)
5. Hopperstad, Vik, Sogn og Fjordane B 4637 l)
6. Haugateig av Hopperstad, Vik, Sogn og Fjordane (B 906 t)
7. Grande, Ørlandet, Sør-Trøndelag (T 1074)
8. Dombu, Meldalen, Sør-Trøndelag (T 2450)
9. Trondheim, Sør-Trøndelag (T 5634)
10. Vikestad, Vikna, Nord-Trøndelag (C 1738)
11. Halsan, Levanger, Nord-Trøndelag (T 504)
12. Nedre Eggen, Alstahaug, Skogn, Nord-Trøndelag (T 1340)
13. Dun, Fosnes, Nord-Trøndelag (T 4960)
14. Stor-Skomo, Ranem, Overhalla, Nord-Trøndelag (T 7693)
15. Stor-Skomo, Ranem, Overhalla, Nord-Trøndelag (T7717)
16. Melhus, Ranem, Overhalla, Nord-Trøndelag (T 8145)
17. Klinga, Namsos, Nord-Trøndelag (T 10929)
18. Hestmannen, Lurøy, Nordland (B 274)
19. Hov, Dønnes, Nesna, Nordland (B 1042)
20. Meløy, Nordland (B 5293 h)
21. Åkvik, Herøy, Nordland (T 2150)
22. Tommeide, Dønnes, Nesna, Nordland (T 8318)
23. Alsøy, Nesna, Nordland (T 13189 f)
24. Myre, Dverberg, Nordland (Ts 769)
25. Grytøy, Trondenes, Troms (B 272)
26. Gåre, Kvæfjord, Troms (Ts 48)
27. Gåre, Kvæfjord, Troms (Ts 49)
28. Gåre, Kvæfjord, Troms (Ts 50)
29. Gåre, Kvæfjord, Troms (Ts 51)
30. Krøttøy, Sands, Bjarkøy, Troms (Ts 73)
31. Tisnes, Tromsøysund, Troms (Ts 802)
32. Åkerøy, Trondenes, Troms (Ts 1377)
33. Engstad, Ranem, Overhalla, Nord-Trøndelag (T 15833)
34. Staulosen, Nord-Nesøy, Rødøy, Nordland (Ts 4217 a)
35. Utakleiv, Birksnes, Lofoten, Nordland (Ts 3497 k)
36. Utakleiv, Birksnes, Lofoten, Nordland (Ts 3497 l)
37. Nordheim u. Sommarøy, Hillesøy, Lenvik, Troms (Ts 4052 f)
38. Vik, Buksnes, Vestvågøy, Nordland (Ts 5685)
39. Vik, Buksnes, Vestvågøy, Nordland (Ts 6334)
40. Loppasanden, Loppa, Finnmark (Ts 6360 h)
41. Enge, Sømna, Nordland (T 17596)
42. Føre, Bø, Vesterålen, Nordland (Ts 8698)
43. Åkerøy, Tjøtta, Nordland (T 18209)
44. Hagbartholmen, Steigen, Nordland (Ts 5281 d)
45. Lilleberge, Namdalen, Nord-Trøndelag (BM)
46. Villa, Vestnes, Romsdalsfjord, Møre og Romsdal (BM)
47. Solvoll av Huseby øver/nedre, Kvæfjord, Troms (Ts 6696)
48. Slägstad, Bjarkøy, Troms (Ts 10904 b)

Sweden
49. Birka, Uppland (SHM)
50. Birka, Uppland (SHM)
51. Birka, Uppland (SHM)
52. Sigtuna, Uppland (SM)
53. Hjulsta, Norra Spånga, Uppland (SS)

Denmark
54. Ribe (na)
55. Ribe (na)

Scotland
56. King's Cross Point, Arran (NMS)
57. Saevar Howe, Birsay, Orkney (TH)
58. Scar, Sanday, Orkney (TH)
59. Bernera, North Uist, Western Isles (HM)
60. Bornish, South Uist, Western Isles (na)

Ireland
61. Kilmainham/Islandbridge, Dublin (NMI)

England
62. Ely, Cambridgeshire (CUM)

Unprovenanced (Lesley Webster pers comm)
63. Sold in a London auction house in 1981
64. Sold in a London auction house in 1990
65. Sold in a London auction house in 1992

APPENDIX 5. THE IDENTIFICATION OF MINERALISED WOOD FROM PARTS OF THE BOAT AND FROM ARTEFACTS

R P J McCullagh

Introduction
The aims of the analyses were as follows:

1. to establish the range of species present within the boat timbers and to examine the correlation of species to particular components of the craft. A supplementary aim is to identify possible repairs or funerary additions made to the craft;

2. to identify the species of wood used in the manufacture of various artefacts, selected by specialists.

The boat timbers
Selection of timbers
It has been possible (see Chapter 3) to use the excavation record to reconstruct with a considerable degree of certainty, the positions of the five strakes on the southern side of the boat, much of the first (lowest) strake on the northern side and the keel. The ribs on the northern side have also been located with slightly less certainty. In addition, it has been possible to suggest the locations of the rowlocks. There remains a considerable doubt about precise locations of boat components, funerary additions and grave goods towards the eastern end of the boat.

Strakes
The programme of identification was targeted at two rivets from each strake, ideally located as far from each other as possible. The purpose was to test for the presence of single continuous timbers within each strake and thereby to locate any repairs made to the boat and to assess its seaworthiness at the time of burial.

Find	Lab No	Component Number
328	920240	Strake 1
400	920308	Strake 1 east end
401	920309	Strake 1 east end
104	920017	Strake 2
218	920133	Strake 2 west end
392	920300	Strake 3 east end
416	920053	Strake 3
332	920244	Strake 4
340	920252	Strake 4
352	920263	Strake 4
410	920047	Strake 4
248	920159	Strake 5
385	920293	Strake 5 with rivet east end

Keel
Three types of specimen were available. The keel itself survived as a mass of organic material which was sampled as a block and is now frozen. Nails or rivets have been identified which seem to represent attachments of the first strake to the keel – with the potential for mineralised wood from both elements. Finally, rivets or nails have been identified which appear to secure the keel to the stem.

Again, identification was intended to test the unity of the keel and also the form of the attachments to other components.

Find	Lab No	Component Number
336	920248	Keel and Strake 1 east end
470	92000	Keel

Ribs
All the ribs were located, but there were only three nails to which two distinct pieces of wood are still attached, indicating the presence of both rib and strake wood. Unfortunately all were at the eastern end of the boat, lying amongst the densest cluster of ironwork and some doubt on their identification remains.

Find	Lab No	Component Number
339	920251	Rib and Strake 2
359	920273	Rib and Strake 5
384	920292	Possible rib east end
391	920299	Possible rib rivet east end

Rowlocks
Several potential rowlock fixing nails have been identified. These were longer than the rivets and lacked the characteristic fixing plate of the rivets. It was anticipated that these specimens would retain wood from the uppermost strake (Strake 5) and a more robust (possibly contorted) timber that had formed the rowlock.

Find	Lab No	Component Number
251	920161	Strake 5 nail possible rowlock

Washrail
It was thought possible that some of the nails were derived from the fixing of a wooden rail to the boat.

Find	Lab No	Component Number
255	920181	Strake 5 nail
283	920196	Strake 5 nail

Specimens chosen as back-ups but not identified
236	920150
272	920173
289	920202
304	920207
338	920250
411	920048
436	920073
437	920074

Species identification
Mineralised wood can be identified using low to medium magnification (x 30 to x 200). The identification has to proceed along similar routes to that of charcoal, but with mineralised wood the exposure of the specimen to obtain views of the necessary sections is even less predictable. In addition, the cell

structure is frequently preserved only as a negative cast of the original. Despite these difficulties, identification is possible in most cases. In this report, identifications were compared to photomicrographs (Schweingruber 1978) and to the AOC (Scotland) Ltd reference collection of thin sections. All the identifications are listed in Table 6.

Strakes

Strake 1 and accessories
Find 328   Lab No 920240   Strake 1
Species: *Quercus* sp (Oak)
The identification was made on one elongate fragment, which represents a small amount of wood mineralised around a part of the shaft. This would represent the timber furthest from the head of the nail; it is uncertain whether this would be the timber of Strake 1, Strake 2 or the keel.

Find 400   Lab No 920308   Strake 1 east end
Species: *Quercus* sp (Oak)
The specimen consisted of two fragments of mineralised wood, immediately behind the head and at the other end of the shank. The head was rectangular. Both areas of wood were *Quercus*. The wood was mature with tyloses throughout the early growth vessels. Neither the X-ray nor visual examination could determine whether parts of two separate strakes were present.

Find 401   Lab No 920309   Strake 1 east end
Species: *Quercus* sp (Oak)
From the X-ray it is plain that the complete rivet is present, but this was not apparent from surface examination. Samples were taken from behind the head and from a large mass of material at the other end of the shank. Both samples were identified as *Quercus* sp. Both timbers were from mature wood with tyloses present throughout the larger vessels. If the X-ray does demonstrate the presence of both head and plate, then the shank length was approximately 3 cm.

Strake 2
Find 104   Lab No 920017   Strake 2
Species: *Quercus* sp (Oak)
The specimen appeared to be formed from two fused masses of mineralised wood, each one associated with a rivet terminal (it was not clear which was the head or plate). Samples were taken from both masses and both were identified as *Quercus* sp. It was clear that the long axis of each mass correlated to the longitudinal axis of the timber. Such observations were made in an attempt to detect the manner by which the roundwood was converted to timbers. Unfortunately, there was insufficient cross-sectional detail to support such an interpretation.

Find 218   Lab No 920133   Strake 2 west end
Species: *Quercus* sp (Oak)
The specimen consisted of two small fragments of mineralised wood adhering to the separated head and plate of the rivet. Both pieces were identified as *Quercus* sp. Both pieces represented mature wood.

Strake 3
Find 392   Lab No 920300   Strake 3 east end

Species: *Quercus* sp (Oak)
The specimen consisted of two fragments, the larger one containing the rectangular plate. Only the wood around the plate could be identified: that surviving around the head was too poorly preserved to permit identification.

Find 416   Lab No 920053   Strake 3
Species: *Quercus* sp (Oak)
The nail or rivet survived as three small fragments. Mineralised wood was identified on two of these fragments; in both cases it was *Quercus* sp.

Strake 4
Find 332   Lab No 920244   Strake 4
Species: *Quercus* sp (Oak)
There was insufficient wood preserved within the corrosion products of the small nail/rivet to allow for full identification. Those characters that were observed were closest to those of *Quercus* sp, but this identification could not be substantiated.

Find 340   Lab No 920252   Strake 4
Species: *Quercus* sp (Oak)
The circular head and the rectangular plate were both preserved on this specimen: the largest mass of mineralised wood lay behind the head. The shank itself can be seen in X-ray to have been bent. The space between head and plate was 3.0 cm. Almost central along the shank was a zone of non-woody material measuring 0.2 cm broad. This material was rich in large grains of quartz and other rock types – possibly mica. Only the wood immediately behind the head could be identified: *Quercus* sp.

Find 352   Lab No 920263   Strake 4
Species: *Quercus* sp (Oak)
Only the plate remained attached to this single mass of mineralised wood. On the other side, the shank was exposed and measured 0.2 cm by 0.2 cm. The wood split along what may have been a real join between separate timbers. Both pieces were identified as *Quercus* sp.

Find 410   Lab No 920047   Strake 4
Species: *Quercus* sp (Oak)
A single mass of mineralised wood transfixed by the shank of a short rivet. Both head and plate appeared to be rectangular and the shank separating them was 2.3 cm long. The wood was identified as *Quercus* sp The timber was seen to be straight grown with annual growth increments of 0.2 cm. The timber had been split radially, with the rivet penetrating the radial section.

Strake 5
Find 248   Lab No 920159   Strake 5
Species: *Quercus* sp (Oak)
The metal component represented a long nail, measuring at least 5 cm. No plate was attached and the shank did not appear broken. A possible join between two components was noted close to the distal end of the shank. Wood from either side of this join was identified and in both cases found to be *Quercus* sp. Possible caulking material was observed between these two areas of mineralised wood. The timber was from mature oak with tyloses throughout the larger vessels.

Find 385   Lab No 920293   Strake 5 with rivet east end
Species: *Quercus* sp (Oak)
The specimen consisted of two pieces of wood sandwiched between the head and plate of a short rivet. The plate and head were indistinguishable as both were sub-rectangular, each measuring approximately 1.5 cm across. The two pieces of wood were initially cemented together but a slight pressure was sufficient to part them. Both pieces were identified as *Quercus* sp.

The length of the shank was 2.2 cm. The width of each piece of wood, taken to represent individual planks, was 1.0 cm, leaving a zone approximately 0.2 cm in width in which the absence of wood fibres and the presence of large quartz grains indicates that the caulking survived between the planks.

Keel

Find 336   Lab No 920248   Keel and Strake 1 east end
Species: cf *Quercus* sp (Oak)
The wood was very distorted and blistered by the formation of the iron corrosion products, making identification difficult. The material bore the closest resemblance to Quercus, but not all the necessary traits (eg no massive medullary rays were seen) were visible.

The metal appears both in the X-ray and visually to be a rivet with a head and plate. This may cast some doubt on the interpretation, based on location, that this specimen represents the keel. The space between head and plate was 3.2 cm. A slight gap within the wood structure at 1.5 cm from the head, may represent the junction between two separate timbers.

Find 470   Lab No 92000   Keel
Species: *Quercus* sp
This specimen was extracted as a block from a mass of possible organic matter from the region of the keel. On site it was thought possible that this material represented waterlogged wood from this component. A sample from a similar location was retrieved within a Kubiena tin and was the subject of a thin-section slide examination (Carter, Appendix 11).

The mid-brown matter bore a close resemblance to poorly preserved waterlogged wood, but on microscopic inspection this was shown to be a mass of filaments. Although bearing a strong resemblance to the mineralised wood found elsewhere on site, it was thought to be possible that the unconsolidated state of these filaments may indicate an alternative form of preservation. It is possible that the iron salts had invaded waterlogged wood, infilling the vessels. Then, at some time after the supply of iron salts had diminished, the water table had shifted, causing the wood to decay. Another scenario which was considered was that the filaments were not the result of iron infiltration but instead owed their survival to the accumulation of wood resins within a semi-waterlogged environment.

To establish whether the surviving keel material would be suitable as a radiocarbon date source, a test was undertaken to determine its organic content. It was thought possible that some of the complex cellular structures in the material did not consist solely of solidified, translocated iron salts and that some woody resins may still be present. The test was based on the comparison of the keel with one of the rivets as they were first oven-dried,

then steeped in an organic solvent (Acetone) for 8 hours. Both samples were then placed in a furnace for 4 hours at 400°C, to ignite any remaining combustible material.

	Lab No	Pre-solvent wt	Post-solvent wt	Wt (g)
Keel	92000	7.43	7.25	5.99
Rivet	920133	8.26	8.19	7.08

The keel clearly consisted of a small amount of combustible material (c. 17% of its post-solvent weight), but it is not certain what the material was. The ambiguous nature and source of this material forestalled its further consideration as a dating source.

Ribs

Find 339   Lab No 920251   poss Rib and Strake 5
Species: *Pinus silvestris* (Scots pine)
         Quercus sp (Oak)
Mineralised wood was located in two places on the shaft of this long (5 cm) nail or rivet (no plate is apparent on the X-ray). The larger of the two masses of wood, located behind the head, was identified as *Pinus silvestris*, the smaller piece was *Quercus*.

An arrangement of the timbers whereby the rib, which was made from Scots pine, was attached to an oak strake by means of a long nail hammered from the inside of the boat is suggested. It is of course possible that the provenance of the wood and the nail has been mis-attributed and that the specimen represents a piece of Scots pine attached to the upper surface of the strake.

It was not possible to identify any morphological features in either piece of mineralised wood to permit the reconstruction of the form of either components.

Find 359   Lab No 920273   Rib and Strake 5
Species: *Pinus silvestris* (Scots pine)
         Quercus sp (Oak),
The wood was concentrated in two places along the shank of this rivet. The larger mass of wood was located behind a sub-rectangular plate measuring 2.0 cm by 1.5 cm. The smaller mass lay at the other end of the shank. It was unclear whether the head had survived. In the X-ray, a slight tapering of the shank towards the putative plate confirms these designations. The wood at the plate end was Pinus silvestris, the other wood was *Quercus* sp. It would seem that the rivet was hammered through the strake into the rib from the outside of the boat.

The shank measured at least 5 cm long and was 0.8 cm across close to the head end.

Find 384   Lab No 920292   Possible rib east end
Species: *Quercus* sp (Oak)
The specimen was small and amorphous, no recognisable element of either a rivet or a nail was visible. The X-ray shows a very vague outline which could be the head of the nail, but this is far from certain. The wood was identified with some uncertainty as *Quercus* sp: the uncertainty arose from the absence of a clear transverse section, although the presence of large, tyloses filled vessels and massive multi-seriate rays argue strongly in favour of oak.

Find 391   Lab No 920299   Possible rib rivet east end
Species: *Quercus* sp (Oak)
Mineralised wood survived on the lower part of the shank away from the large head. The wood seems to have been split or cut tangentially – the easiest form of conversion when using oak – and the nail has been hammered in at right angles to this plane. The absence of wood from the shank closer to the head, suggests that some other timber has failed to survive. The shank is neither as long nor as robust as other nails recorded from rib location within the boat.

Rowlocks

Find 251   Lab No 920161   Strake 5 nail possible
                                              rowlock
Species: *Quercus* sp (Oak)
Prior to identification this piece was known to be a possible fixing for a rowlock to the upper surface of the gunwale or to Strake 5. The mineralised wood was located at two points along the shank of this long nail, the shank of which measured 6 cm. The shank measured 0.4 cm by 0.4 cm.

The mineralised wood was sampled from a small mass close to the head of the nail and from the much larger mass at the end of the shank. Both samples were identified as *Quercus* sp.

The nail had pierced the wood radially and most probably had transfixed the strake through its narrow side. If the location and interpretation of the nail are correct then it most probably was hammered down through the greatest thickness of the plank.

Washrail

Find 255   Lab No 920181   Strake 5 with nail
Species: not identifiable
Although a considerable length of the shaft of this nail survived and appeared to retain mineralised wood, it proved impossible to obtain any interpretable material and what little wood fibres were present could not be identified.

Find 283   Lab No 920196   Strake 5 nail possible
                                              washrail
Species: *Pinus silvestris* (Scots pine)
This piece consisted of a small amount of mineralised wood attached to the rounded head of a small nail. The wood was identified as *Pinus silvestris*. The shank of the nail measured 0.2 cm by 0.2 cm.

The location of this specimen in the grave was interpreted as evidence for a washrail (Chapter 3).

GENERAL OBSERVATIONS

Strakes

Although it is likely that some shrinkage and distortion occurs in the process by which iron salts invest and ultimately replace the cellular structure of wood, the presence of some rivets with both head and plate *in situ* allows for minimum measurements to be made in some of the dimensions of wooden components of the boat. It seems probable that the strakes were seldom much greater than 1.5 cm thick and that the ribs were not massive, with measurements ranging from 5 cm to 3 cm for the depth.

The timbers for the strakes seem to have been manufactured from well grown, mature oak. It has been neither possible to examine variation along the length of individual strakes nor between strakes. Where it was possible to make the observation, it seems that the rivets pierced the timbers without opening shakes or splits: this may reflect the use of green (ie freshly converted) timbers.

Keel

The timber used in the keel was oak, but the timber was poorly mineralised and no further observations were possible.

Ribs

In two of the four cases examined (Finds 339 & 359), long nails (5 cm minimum length) had been used to join timbers of Scots pine and oak. If the provenance of the specimens were correct, then the oak component derives from Strake 5 and it is possible to determine from which side of the strake the nail had been hammered. In one piece (Find 359), the nail was struck through the strake from the exterior. In the second piece, the nail passed through the rib first. The two other putative ribs contained a single species (oak) – it is therefore possible that the interpretation of provenance was incorrect. If correct, however, and the identification has not been limited by poor preservation, the presence of oak ribs in addition to Scots pine is implied.

Rowlocks

The one possible rowlock fragment (Find 251) consisted of a long nail which had been hammered though oak. One mass of mineralised oak was pierced in a manner consistent with a narrow plank nailed through one of its shorter sides. The space between this identified material and the head of the nail was almost devoid of wood remains, but some very small fragments, located close to the head, were also shown putatively to be oak.

Canopy

Two specimens with nails rather than rivets were identified from Strake 5. This and their position suggested that they might be part of the putative canopy. No wood structure survived on one (Find 255), but the remaining specimen (Find 283) was identified as a piece of Scots pine transfixed by a small nail. The size of the nail is less than the only other fitment to Strake 5, the possible rowlock (Find 251). The presence of a simple canopy is thus made more probable.

ARTEFACTS

Wooden components of artefacts were mineralised within the iron corrosion products of most artefacts and also of many of the fragments of artefacts. The identification to species had two purposes, firstly to complete the catalogue of component materials, and secondly to help reassemble fragmentary remains of artefacts.

The identification of wooden components has not been undertaken routinely throughout the assemblage of artefacts, but has progressed in response to enquiries posed by various specialists working on the project. The material was inherently fragile and unstable and in certain cases the necessary conservation measures have precluded identification. In general, there was sufficient mineralised wood or casts of cell structure adhering to each object to permit identification. Unlike the boat components, the artefacts have retained some value in their conserved state and much more care has been required in the course of identification. In most cases, destruction of the object, the surest means of getting access to the minute exposures of wood cell structure, was not encouraged and thus identification was achieved by the accumulation of numerous observations of fragments of diagnostic features. The items that were selected for identification are listed in Table 6.

The scabbard
Find 137 Lab No 911518
The sword was recovered during excavation as a large elongated mass of intensively corroded metal. Attached to the upper surface was a smaller mass, which was initially interpreted as separate elongate object, possibly a knife. In the course of conservation it became apparent that not only had the form of the sword been preserved to a remarkable degree but the corroded mass had also retained the form and structure of the scabbard. The attached smaller mass was shown to be a bundle of arrows within a quiver (see below).

At low magnification it was possible to distinguish the casts of both the cloth and wooden components of the scabbard. Samples were taken from the mass of corroded material that included the hilt and a fragment of the proximal part of the upper humerus. Further samples were examined from the corroded material close to the tip of the blade of the sword.

Small fragments of the cast material (c 1 mm^2 in cross-section) were removed. In the few transverse sections that were available the wood appeared to be ring- or semi-ring porous. The pores were often paired and at high magnification (x 400) smaller vessels, filled entirely with metallic precipitates, were seen in the later wood. Around the spring growth pores, dense iron precipitates formed slightly raised annuli. These were interpreted as casts of circumvascular tissue.

In the radial sections, only simple perforation plates were observed. The rays were generally homogenous and large bordered pits were visible in the larger vessels. In some cases what appeared to be slight spiral thickening was visible, but at high magnification this appeared to be an effect of slight sculpturing of the inner cell surface by helical ridges rather than actual thickening of the cell wall. In the tangential section, it was clear that the rays were more than uniseriate and ranged between eight and ten cells high. These various traits suggest that the original wood was *Fraxinus excelsior* (ash). The timber was split radially into thin laths and thus provided alight weight, flexible and durable means of supporting the softer furnishings of the scabbard.

The shears
Find 154 Lab No 911515
Small fragments of cast wood were removed from corroded material adhering to the iron shears. It was thought that this material represented the remains of a wooden box that had once contained the shears as well other objects (Chapter 5).

The identification represents the same degree of coalesced observation as the sword, but in this case the wood was identified as *Acer sp* (maple). Initially the wood was identified as *Fraxinus excelsior* (ash), but after more of the box had been identified, the specimens from the shears were re-examined. It thus seems likely that the shears were not boxed separately – as was originally thought, but had been wrapped in cloth and placed within the large maple-wood box that was identified from the iron fittings.

The needle tidy
Find 161 Lab No: 920039
This object was the most fragile item in the assemblage and although identification was sought for the wooden material surrounding the putative needles, it was not possible to remove fragments of corrosion products without endangering the whole object. Identification was based upon the surface examination of the fibrous cellular which are exposed at one end of the object.

From a minute exposure of the radial structure, fenestriform pits were observed. From a similarly minute example of the transverse structure the infilled cast of an irregular pore was interpreted as a resin canal. Other observations confirmed the general coniferous form to the wood. Although not conclusive these observations indicate that the original wood was of the genus *Pinus* and most probably *P. silvestris* (Scots pine).

The arrow shafts
Find 137 Lab No 920334
The arrows were identified within the mass of corroded metal attached to the upper surface of the sword. After conservation they appeared as a group of lanceolate metal heads with narrow cylindrical shafts. Some binding was visible around the head of the shaft where the tang had been secured.

Two cylindrical fragments were examined from a possible total of nine arrows. Both of these specimens were undoubtedly *Pinus silvestris*. In both cases the curvature of the annual rings was less than that of the shaft itself; the shafts were therefore converted from some larger piece of Scots pine.

The quiver
Find 137 Lab No 920334
Fragments of the putative quiver were noted in the course of conservation work. These fragments formed thin sheets of mineralised wood adhering to the outer surface of both arrow heads and shafts. These small patches were clearly different in form from either the wooden shafts or the adjacent scabbard, hence their interpretation as the remains of a wooden quiver.

Unfortunately, all of these fragments were too thin and too heavily mineralised to permit identification to species. The wood was clearly dicotyledonous and the rays were between four and six cells wide; the wood was also possibly ring-porous, but further refinement was not possible. The attempted identification has thus confirmed that this wooden artefact was made from a different material to the arrow shafts. It was also possibly different from the species used in the scabbard. This exercise has not confirmed the identification of the artefact as the quiver.

The putative spacer
Find 137 Lab No 920334
In the course of conservation work, a cylindrical void was noted, slightly off-centre within the bundle of arrows (measurements for

this feature are supplied with the conservation report in the archive). In some places, thin concave sheets of mineralised wood formed the vestigial wall to this void and indicated that it resulted from an organic object around which the arrows had been arranged. One obvious interpretation was that this void represented the last remains of the bow.

Samples of the mineralised wood were particularly difficult to obtain because of the fragility of the mineralised arrow bundle and because of the very poor preservation of the wood. Few fragments measured more than 0.5 mm thick and all were heavily encrusted with a pale precipitate. A weak solution of hydrochloric acid was used to test for calcium carbonate; this test proved positive. It was noteworthy that the mineralised wood looked to be very abraded or weathered and the calcium carbonate deposits were present only on the surface and were absent from the interiors of the larger vessels. It seems likely that the deposit occurred late in the sequence of decay.

Despite the removal of these obscuring deposits, the identification was unsuccessful. The wood was certainly different from that of the arrow shafts (identified as Scots pine), but beyond being possibly ring-porous no greater refinement was possible.

The identification to just this most general of classes must argue against the reconstruction of the lost artefact as the bow. In almost all cases, European bows have been either simple carved structures made from yew (*Taxus baccata* L) or composites which contained lathes of bone. One alternative explanation might be that there was a wooden rod within the quiver to act as a spacer.

Box fitting

Find 99   Lab No 920025

This specimen was on three, oval-headed nails associated with the putative box. In conservation the shape of the wood preserved over the shaft had been interpreted as the remains of a possible dowel.

By breaking the nail longitudinally it was possible to observe that the appearance of dowelling was the result of two separate pieces of wood preserved upon the nail. The wood attached to the head of the nail was set perpendicular to the shaft material, conforming to the expected arrangement for a simple butt joint which would have suited the construction of a box. The wood attached to the nail head was 7 mm deep and although some distortion will have occurred in the preservation process, the original dimensions of the timber can be assumed to have approximated to this measurement. The very sharply defined discontinuity between the head wood and the shaft wood indicated that the box was manufactured from carefully prepared timber and with a high degree of craftsmanship. The nail shaft was square in cross-section.

The wood was identified as *Acer* sp. (maple). Although it is possible to distinguish between *A. campestre* L (Field Maple), *A. pseudoplatanus* L (Great Maple) and *A. platanoides* L (Norway Maple) using anatomical criteria, it requires well preserved specimens in thin-section. In this case it was not possible to be absolutely certain that the identification to *Acer* was correct and it was considered impossible to attempt further refinement.

Box fitting

Find 163 Lab No 920085

This particular nail was chosen because it was one of the furthest distant from the findspot of Find 99. The same observations as Find 99 were repeated in Find 163 and the wood was identified as *Acer* sp. (maple).

Box fitting

Find 204 Lab No 920112

Find 204 included a small nail, a fragment of mineralised wood pierced by a nail hole, a metal plate or a strap fragment with cloth attached, and some amorphous fragments of mineralised wood. The metal plate is remarkable for the quality of preservation of the cloth. The nail again repeated the form of Find 99, but provides a broader surface area for both pieces of butted wood. The juxtaposed surfaces appear to have been prepared to a high degree of smoothness.

The species of both pieces of wood attached to the nail were again *Acer* sp. and the spiral thickening on the few negative casts of larger vessels attached to the plate also indicate the presence of maple.

It seems likely that these three specimens represent the fixing nails of a butt-jointed box of finely cut and prepared maple. If the metal plate also functioned as a fixing, then the presence of cloth on opposite side of the plate from the wood must indicate that the box was cloth-covered.

Large iron handle

Find 150 Lab No 911516

Although not closely located to the recognisable box fittings it was thought possible that this large handle may have been attached to the box. A large piece of mineralised wood was attached by a nail or rivet to one end of the handle; a second large fragment may once also have been attached. Both pieces were examined and identified as *Pinus silvestris* (Scots pine).

This identification does not preclude the attachment of the handle to the box but makes it unlikely. The apparent absence of cloth from what ought to have been a component of the lid or side walls reinforces the unlikelihood of the proposed provenance. Although some of the boat timber was also Scots pine, it is not feasible at present to re-interpret Find 150 as a boat fitting. No satisfactory alternative is proposed and further evidence must be sought.

Band fragment

Find 120 Lab No 920029

This specimen, which consists of a large rectangular plate, was found furthest from the site of the putative box than the other fittings. The mineralised wood was attached to one face, from which projected a boss. Mineralised cloth, possibly the remains of a brocaded fabric was attached to the other face. The mineralised wood survived as no more than a very thin skin and identification proved difficult.

Nevertheless, it was possible to demonstrate that the wood was again *Acer* sp (maple). It is almost certain that this specimen does represent some element of the fittings or fixings of the box.

Table 6. Mineralised wood

Boat component	Find no	Side of keel	End	Species
Strakes				
Strake 1:	400	South	East	*Quercus* sp (Oak)
	401	South	East	*Quercus* sp (Oak)
Strake 2	104	South	East	*Quercus* sp (Oak)
	218	South	West	*Quercus* sp (Oak)
Strake 3	392	South	East	*Quercus* sp (Oak)
	416	South	East	*Quercus* sp (Oak)
Strake 4	332	South	Middle	*Quercus* sp (Oak)
	340	South	Middle	*Quercus* sp (Oak)
	352	South	Middle	*Quercus* sp (Oak)
	410	South	East	*Quercus* sp (Oak)
Strake 5	248	South	West	*Quercus* sp (Oak)
	385	South	East	*Quercus* sp (Oak)
Keel				
Strake 1	328	North	East	*Quercus* sp (Oak)
Strake 1	336	North	East	*Quercus* sp (Oak)
Rib				
Strake 5	339	South	Middle	*Pinus silvestris* (Scots Pine)
				Quercus sp (Oak)
Strake 5	359	South	Middle	*Pinus silvestris* (Scots Pine)
				Quercus sp (Oak)
Strake ?	384		North	East *Quercus* sp (Oak)
Strake ?	391		South	East *Quercus* sp (Oak)
Rowlock				
Strake 5	251	South	West	*Quercus* sp (Oak)
Canopy				
Strake 5	255	South	West	not identifiable
Strake 5	283	South	West	*Pinus silvestris* (Scots Pine)

Artefacts	Find No	Lab Code	Species
Scabbard	137	911518	*Fraxinus excelsior* (Ash)
Shears	154	911515	*Acer* sp (Maple)
Needle case	161	920039	cf *P. silvestris* (Scots Pine)
Arrows	137	920334	*Pinus silvestris* (Scots Pine)
Quiver	137	920334	not identified
Bow(?)	137	920334	not identified
Box fitting	99	920025	*Acer* sp. (Maple)
Box fitting	163	920085	*Acer* sp. (Maple)
Box fitting	204	920112	*Acer* sp. (Maple)
Fe handle	150	911516	*Pinus silvestris* (Scots Pine)
Band frag.	120	920029	*Acer* sp. (Maple)

APPENDIX 6. INVENTORY OF HUMAN BONES

Daphne Lorimer

SKELETON Find 134 (male)

Skull: missing but a few fragments found

Cranium

Occiput (Find 96): One fragment with part of lambdoid suture, fossa for the occipital lobe of the cerebrum and the lateral sinus; one very small fragment with part of lambdoid suture.
Parietal bone (Find 76): Small fragment – side unknown.
Petrous-temporal bone (found with Find 124): Fragment of right petrous portion.

Mandible

Right gonial angle with socket for the lower third molar and foramen for the mandibular artery (Find 71).

Teeth

3| roots only partially formed
|6 roots complete.
|2 root not quite closed
|5 root only half complete
e̲ resorption of roots just started.
d̲

Vertebrae

Lumbar:
1st: missing
2nd (Find 8): body and separate posterior part of neural arch with inferior articular facets.
3rd (Find 134): left side of body and transverse process damaged.
4th (Find 134): complete.
5th (Find 134): complete except for right side of lower margin.
Sacrum: Partially reconstructed but right lateral portion of the 3rd to 5th segments and part of left auricular surface missing. Inferior margin of 5th segment missing.

Measurements:
Width of body of 1st segment = 47.0 mm.
Width of ala = 33.2 mm.

Thorax

Ribs

Right side (Find 119): Head, neck, tuberosity and small fragment of shaft of a mid-rib. chondral ends of 2 ribs and 1 fragment of shaft.
Left side (Find 134): Chondral ends of 2 ribs.
Side unknown: Chondral ends of 2 ribs; 15 fragments of shaft; 2 fragments of shaft wall

Sternum

(Find 134): Proximal 3 segments of gladius or body.
(Find 119): Lower 2 segments of gladius.

Scapula:

Right side (Find 18): Piriform shaped glenoid fossa only.
Measurements:
Max length of glenoid fossa = 42.0 mm.
Max width of glenoid fossa = 32.0 mm.

Upper extremity

Clavicle:

Right side (from Find 119): Acromial end only.
Side unknown (from Find 201): Fragment of shaft.

Humerus

Right side: Distal half of shaft and lower end.

Radius

Right side: Attached to iron corrosion from sword – head damaged.
Measurements: Max length = 277.0 mm.
Left side: Distal quarter of shaft and lower end.

Ulna

Right side: Attached to iron corrosion from sword. Upper end broken.
(Note: The ulna was rotated over the radius, thus indicating that right arm had been placed palm down by the body on top of the sword).
Left side: Distal one/quarter shaft and lower end.

Carpal bones

Right side: Find 134: navicular; Find 201: lunate, triquetral, pisiform, greater multangular and hamate; Find 134: lesser multangular.
Left side: Find 134: navicular, lunate, triquetral, greater multangular, lesser multangular; Find 201: pisiform.

Metacarpal bones

Right side: Find 134 1st, 2nd, 3rd, 4th and (Find 119) 5th in two parts. *Left side:* Find 134 1st, 2nd, 3rd, 4th and (Find 201) 5th in two parts).

Phalanges

*Right side:*1st row: (Find 134) 1st, 2nd, 3rd; (Find 119) 4th, 5th.
2nd row: (Find 119) ///, 2nd, 3rd, 4th, 5th.
3rd row: (Find 119) —, —, —, —, 5th
Left side:
1st row: (Find 134) 1st, 2nd, 3rd, 4th, 5th.
2nd row: (Find 119) ///, 2nd, 3rd; (Find 201) 4th, 5th.
3rd row: (Find 201) —, —, —, 4th, —.
[Note: Find 119 also contained a child's manubrium sternum and the epiphysis of a right ulna and eight very small fragments of bone. Also found were a fragment of os pubis and two fragments of an acetabulum (side unknown).]

Pelvic girdle

Os innominatum: *Right side:*

Ilium: Anterior portion of body with acetabular portion complete but posterior portion of body, iliac crest and auricular surface

fragmented and reconstructed.
Ischium: Complete.
Os pubis: Complete.
Left side: Reconstructed.
Ilium: Anterior half of body and iliac crest missing.
Ischium: Reconstructed but complete.
Os pubis: Reconstructed from one large fragment and one small, but complete.

Lower extremity

Femur
Right side: Head, neck, trochanters (broken) and proximal three-quarters shaft.
Measurements:
Max diam of head = 49.0 mm
Sub-trochanteric A-P diam = 30.1 mm
Sub-trochanteric Medio.lat.diam = 29.5 mm
Platymeric index = $\frac{29.5 \times 100}{30.1}$

(No platymeria) =98
Left side: Head, neck, trochanter and proximal one-third shaft.
Measurements:
Max diam of head = 49.5 mm
Sub-trochanteric A-P diam = 38.0 mm
Sub-trochanteric medio-lat.diam = 31.6 mm
Platymeric index = $\frac{31.6 \times 100}{38}$

(Platymeria present) = 83.15

Tibia
Right side: Reconstructed from two parts but complete except for lower end of shaft and part of wall.
Measurements:
Max length = 450.0 mm
A.P. diam at nutrient foramen = 34.4 mm
Medio.lat. diam at nutrient foramen = 27.8 mm
Circumference at nutrient foramen = 104.0 mm
Platycnemic index = $\frac{27.8 \times 100}{34.4}$

(Platycnemia not present) = 80.8
Left side: Complete.
Measurements:
Max length = 420.0 mm
A.P. diam at nutrient foramen = 31.6 mm
Medio.lat. diam at nutrient foramen = 28.0 mm
Circumference nutrient foramen = 103.0 mm.
Platycnemic index = $\frac{28.6 \times 100}{31.6}$

(Platycnemia not present) = 90.5

Fibula
Right side: Reconstructed from two parts but complete.
Measurements: Max length = 406.0mm
Left side: Complete.
Measurements: Max length = 410.0mm

Tarsal bones
Right side: Talus, calcaneus, 1st cuneiform and navicular.

Left side: Talus, calcaneus, cuboid, 1st, 2nd and 3rd cuneiforms and navicular.

Metatarsal bones
Right side: 1st, 2nd only.
Left side: 1st, 2nd, 3rd, 4th, 5th.

Phalanges:
Right side: ———
Left side:
1st row: 1st, 2nd, 3rd, 4th, —.
2nd row: ///, —, —, —, 5th.
3rd row: 1st, —, —, —, 5th.
+ 3 sesamoid bones.
[**Note:** Find 100 possibly animal and Find 61 part of head of humerus possibly animal.]

SKELETON Find 133 (female)

Skull
Small part only.

Cranium
Parietal bone:
Right side: Complete.
Left side: Anterior portion fragmented and partially reconstructed (bones very thin and the sutures open).

Thorax

Ribs
3 fragments of shaft and 3 fragments of shaft wall (side unknown)

Upper extremity

Metacarpals
Right side: 2nd (head and shaft), 4th and 5th only.

Phalanges
Right side:
1st row: 1st (broken), 2nd, —, 4th, —.
2nd row: ///, 2nd, 3rd, 4th (distal end only),—.
3rd row: —, 2nd, —, —, —.

Pelvic girdle

Os innominatum
Right side:
Ilium: Complete except for slight damage to auricular surface.
Ischium: Complete except for damage to tuberosity.
Os pubis: Separatd from acetabulum but complete and reconstructed.

Lower extremity

Femur
Right side: Head neck, trochanters and shaft (gluteal ridge marked); lower end fragmented (11 pieces).
Measurements:
Max diam of head = 42.4 mm
Sub-trochanteric A.-P.diam = 25.4 mm
Sub-trochanteric medio-lat diam = 33.6 mm

Platymeric index = $\dfrac{25.4 \times 100}{33.6}$ = 75.59

(Platymeria present) = 75.59

Left side: Abraided distal extremity and distal two-thirds of the shaft only (rivet adhering to posterior surface of lower end of shaft) + 14 very small fragments of bone – some possibly corroded).

Patella

Right side: Complete (+ small fragment of possible proximal end of tibia).
Left side: Complete.

Tibia

Right side: Large fragment comprising superior surface of head and anterior wall of neck and shaft with tuberosity; shaft with distal extremity missing.
+ 1 fragment of shaft wall.
Left side: Two fragments of head; shaft including the tuberosity and the distal extremity (where there was post mortem damage).

Fibula

Right side: Large fragment of shaft and one small fragment of shaft wall.
Left side: Shaft only.

Tarsal bones

Right side: Talus, anterior portion of calcaneus, cuboid, 1st, 2nd and 3rd cuneiforms and navicular (with *post mortem* damage).
+ 8 very small fragments of bone.
Left side: Talus and anterior part of calcaneus.
+ 3 small fragments of calcaneus.
+ 8 very small fragments of bone and 1 rivet.

Metatarsals

Right side: 1st, 2nd, 3rd, 4th and 5th (*post mortem* damage to 1st, 4th and 5th).
Left side: 1st and shaft with distal end of one metatarsal.

Phalanges

Right side: 1st row: 1st, 2nd, 3rd, 4th, 5th only.
Left side: 1st row: 1st (damaged *post mortem* – proximal end and fragment of shaft only).

SKELETON Find 135 (child)

Skull

Cranium

Frontal bone: Vertical portion complete; horizontal portion missing except for small part of orbital plates.
Petrous-temporal bone:
Right side: Squamous portion present (*post mortem* hole in centre) zygomatic process broken and separate; mastoid process missing; possible small fragment of petrous portion (separate).
Sphenoid:
Left side: Possible part of lesser wing.

Facial bones

Maxilla: Left side: anterior surface of the body complete but the posterior wall of the antrum was missing; the frontal process was present, but the only part of the alveolar border present lay in the region of the upper left second deciduous molar.
+ 7 small fragments of possible alveolar border.
Malar bone:
Left side: Complete.

Teeth: 5
⊥ 3̲ 4̲ e̲ 6̲ 7̲
[**Note:** 2 possible fragments of wood found with teeth.]

Lower extremity

Femur

Right side: Fragment of medial side of distal epiphysis.

Tibia

Right side: Both diaphyses, shaft and proximal epiphysis complete; distal epiphysis damaged.
Left side: Two fragments of distal end of shaft.

Fibula

Right side: Shaft and proximal diaphysis complete except for *post mortem* damage to shaft; 1 fragment of distal diaphysis and fragment of proximal epiphysis.
Left side: 8 large and 3 very small fragments of shaft wall.
[**Note:** 2 possible fragments of metal found with right tibia and fibula.]

Patella

Right side: Eroded *post mortem*.
Tarsal bones:
Right side: Talus, calcaneus only.
Left side: Possible fragment of talus and fragment of calcaneus
+ 7 possible fragments of tarsal bones

Metatarsal bones

2 shafts and diaphyses (side unknown)
+ 2 fragments of shafts.
[**Note:** 'Rivet attached to big toe'- rivet broken into two pieces and big toe unidentifiable except for a possible small fragment of bone.]
Also with bones of right foot of skeleton 135 were:-
(1) an adult left lesser multangular carpal bone and 2nd and 5th phalanges from an upper extremity.
(2) a tibia and fibula belonging to a small mammal and a fragment of shell

HUMAN BONES EXTRACTED FROM OSSEOUS MATERIAL FOUND IN SOIL SAMPLES

(1) From bag labelled:191/Rt/04 – 58Hts – F40 sf large mammal A:
   1 1st terminal phalanx (upper extremity). 1 upper right first molar with roots half developed (no wear, so probably unerupted).

(2) From bag labelled: 191/R7/05 Sq.14 F47 A:
    1 left capitate
    1 5th terminal phalanx (extremity).
(3) From bag labelled 191/Rt/04 (1/8 Rt) 50Htrs Bag11 57
    F40 (Bones found in soil samples)
    large mammal:
    1 proximal end of phalanx of proximal row, possibly 4th.
(4) from bag labelled: 191/Rt/01 F32 Bone/sm. mammal 3.5g
    1 possible radial proximal epiphysis (side unknown).
(5) from bag labelled 191/Rt/03 16Htrs F49 large mammal:
    1 capitate.
(6) From bag labelled: 191/Rt/05 F47 Sample 8 Bag 6 large
    mammal bone:
    1 crown of upper right third molar.
    2 proximal ends of juvenile ribs with diaphyses for heads and
    tubercles.

APPENDIX 7. BIRD BONE REPORT

Tanya O'Sullivan

The bulk of the bird bone sample from Scar consists of undiagnostic fragmentary splinters. Two bones are identifiable to species, a Scolopacidae tarso-metatarsus with a mid shaft break and distal end intact, and a complete Corvidae ulna.

The ulna is similar in size and morphology to that of either a chough (*Pyrrhocorax pyrrhocorax*) or jackdaw (*Corvus monedula*). The chough inhabits cliffs and inland outcrops and quarries, nesting on ledges in crevices or caves (Kirkman & Jourdain 1966), and is common within the limits of rocky coasts with short turf and mountain sheep walks. The modern range and distribution of the chough tends to be confined to western Scotland, Islay, Jura, Colonsay and the tip of Kintyre (Harrison 1988). It is not on record as having nested on Orkney, although stray birds may have ventured to the islands. The jackdaw, primarily a grassland bird, is known to have begun colonising Orkney by the 1880s. The jackdaw is susceptible to climate change and its numbers decreased in Britain between the fourteenth and nineteenth centuries (Harrison 1988). There was an overall increase, particularly strong at its northern limits in Scotland, during the warmer temperatures of the late eighteenth and early nineteenth century. It is possible that prior to the fourteenth century, warmer climes may also have encouraged nesting.

The tarso-metatarsus displays the diagnostic features of the Scolopacidae family and can possibly be linked in terms of size to the whimbrel (*Numenius phaeopus*). For most of the British Isles it comes as a passage migrant. In the north of Scotland and in Orkney and Shetland it may be a breeding bird (Kirkman & Jourdain 1966). It tends to nest on rough open moorland. The whimbrel was noted breeding in Scotland in 1769 (Harrison 1988) but very little information exists on its past status. It appears, like the jackdaw, to have responded to climate changes but the pattern would suggest that breeding occurred in larger numbers and with a greater range in cooler periods. The presence of this bone in the collapse and fill inside the boat may have been due to otter disturbance as fish remains in the same context have indicated. It seems likely that this bone is intrusive from a later era because, as Harrison (1988) has suggested, this species may have been widespread between the fourteenth and nineteenth centuries.

There was no evidence on any of the bone fragments to suggest that the birds did not die naturally. In a tenth century Norse grave from Buckquoy, Orkney (Ritchie 1977), there was no indication that bird bones were recovered although 54 species were recovered from the excavation of the associated Viking Age farmstead. In conclusion it can be said that the bird bones found at Scar (as may be the case on other contemporary grave sites) are incidental to the burial itself, and consist of stray birds possibly brought in by otters or other mammals.

APPENDIX 8. REPORT ON THE FISH BONES

Ruby Ceron-Carrasco

Introduction

All contexts containing fish bone were examined. The samples were processed and the retents and flots sorted. F38 was hand processed and a percentage of the resulting 2 mm and 1 mm seived material was examined: the vast amount of the material was fish bone with only a few small marine molluscs and egg shell fragments.

All diagnostic elements were separated and identified where possible to species level or to the representative family group. Identification was carried out using the modern fish bone reference collection at AOC (Scotland) Ltd.

Results

The following contexts contained fish bone remains:

Contexts pre-dating the boat burial

F5: pale brown shell sand, possibly an old A horizon
Very few fish remains (0.2 g) were recovered from the retent. The species identified were eel, very small saithe, and sandeels.

F7: wind blown shell sand
This context contained only a minimal amount (less than 1 g) of fish remains. The only species tentatively identified was Gobiidae, from a vertebrae.

F49: tumble from stone wall
A very small quantity of material (2 g) was recovered from the retent. The species identified were bull-rout, eel, butterfish, small saithe (approximately 20 cm), and a large quadrate from the upper jaws of a Gadidae species.

Collapse and fill inside the boat

F26: upper sand layer over stones in west end
A small amount of fish bone (0.7 g) was recovered from retent sorted material. The species identified were small saithe (20 cm total length), a possible vertebrae from a large Salmonidae (?), butterfish and Gobiidae.

F27: lower sand layer inside chamber
Very little fish bone (0.5 g) was recovered from retent sorted material. The species identified were sea scorpion and small saithe (20 cm total length).

F33: upper sand layer inside chamber
Fish remains (32.9 g) were recovered from the retent and flot. Eel, butterfish, very small saithe and pollack, rockling and other small unidentified Gadidae were represented.

F38: layer of fish bone
This context was bulk sampled and manually seived. The layer was 1.06 m in length and up to 5 cm deep, comprising mainly fish bone with some sand deposits, also containing very small marine molluscs and egg shell. The total weight of the whole processed and seived sample was 3.5 kg.

An eighth of the 2mm retent material was examined as well as a quarter of the 1 mm retent.

The species represented in this context were eel, sandeel, rocklings, small saithe, small pollack, small cod (?), and other

unidentified small Gadidae, sea scorpion, bull-rout, butterfish and flatfish, possibly from the Pleuroctenidae family.

F40: sand layer overlying finds in boat
This context was quite rich in fish remains, mostly retent-recovered material and some flot. The total weight of the fish bone sample was 191.1 g. The species represented were small saithe, small pollack, small cod, rockling and other unidentified small Gadidae, eel, sandeel, sea scorpion, bull-rout, butterfish, wrasse and small flatfish, possibly from the Pleuroctenidae group.

F42: rooty shell sand inside chamber
This contained some fish remains (3.2 g) recovered from retent sorted material. The species identified were eel, sea scorpion, small saithe and rockling. A small denticle from a skate or ray was also present.

F43: rooty shell sand inside chamber
10.7 g of fish bone were recovered, mainly from retents. The species identified were eel, sea scorpion, bull-rout, small saithe, rockling and small flatfish.

Contexts with fish bone later than the boat burial

F8: west fill of shallow ditch
Very little fish bone (0.2 g) was present in this context. All was retent recovered material.
The identified species from this context were eel, sandeel, butterfish, very small Gadidae, and possible mackerel.

F9: old A horizon on eroded slope.
Less than 0.1 g of fish bone was recovered from the retent. The species identified were bull-rout, butterfish and possible sticklebacks.

F11: upper fill of shallow ditch
0.2 g of fish bone was recovered from the retents. The species identified were bull-rout, small saithe (approx 15 cm total length), eel, butterfish, and sandeel.

F12: lower fill of shallow ditch
This context contained 1.4 g of retent recovered material. The species identified were small saithe (15–20 cm total length), rockling , small Gadidae, eel, Gobiidae, and bull-rout.

F20: general layer of mottled sand
Very little fish bone (0.5 g) was recovered from retent sorted material. Species identified were eel, sandeel, very small Gadidae and a medium-size abdominal vertebrae, possibly belonging to a gadid.

F32: layer of shell sand with small stones
This layer produced both retent and flot recovered material, with a total weight of 1.2 g. The species identified were sea scorpion, eel, butterfish, very small saithe, sandeel, and very small Gadidae.

F50: fill of shallow wide trench
A few fish remains (2 g) were retrieved from retent sorted material. The species identified were bull-rout, eel, butterfish and very small Gadidae.

Conclusions

There is every indication that the fish bone remains from Scar derived from animal activity. There is no indication whatsoever that any of these fish specimens had been caught and eaten by man. All the species identified fall into the category of the coastal otter's *(Lutra lutra)* favourite food (Gormally & Fairley 1982,

Murphy & Fairley 1985, Watt 1992, Kruuk pers comm): small species, inshore rock-dwellers and bottom feeders. The nature of F38, with such a high concentration of fish bone, further supports this view. The site is within close proximity to the sea and to fresh water streams, (otters prefer to stay close to fresh water, Kruuk pers comm), and so provides ideal territory for otters. It is concluded that F38 was used as otters' 'holts' and that the fish remains, of which a vast amount was flattened and distorted (an indication that they had gone through process of digestion), must be the product of otters' faeces. The latter are different to 'spraints' which are mainly territory markers and are found in open air (Kruuk & Hewson 1978).

List of all species and family groups identified, with their English and Latin names

Gadidae (cod family)

Gadus morhua (cod)

Pollachius pollachius (pollack)

Pollachius virens (saithe)

Gaidropsaurus sp (rockling)

Ammoditae (sandeels)

Anguillidae

Anguilla anguilla (eel)

Pholidae

Pholis gunnellus (butterfish)

Pleuroctenidae (right-eyed flatfish)

Cottidae (sculpins)

Myoxocephalus scorpius (bull-rout)

Taurulus bubalis (sea scorpion)

Labridae (wrasses)

Scombridae (mackerels and tunnies)

Scomber scomber (mackerel)

Rajidae (skates, rays and dogfish)

Gasterosteidae (sticklebacks)

Gasterosteus aculeatus (stickleback)

Gobiidae (gobies)

APPENDIX 9. REPORT ON THE LAND SNAILS

Stephen Carter

Summary

Twenty land snail assemblages from Scar, spanning the four site context groups, were briefly examined and quantified. Assemblages that pre-dated the boat grave (Groups A and B) indicated an open environment of short vegetation with more sheltered habitats probably provided by stone walls or rubble. The boat grave fill (Group C) contained assemblages similar to those recorded from calcareous crevices and caves, which confirms the existence of a burial chamber. The more diverse contexts of Group D contained the same small group of species seen in Groups A and B and a similar environment is indicated. Snails from the fills of two shallow gullies included many recently dead individuals suggesting that these features filled in within the last few decades.

Introduction

Although the shells are abundant and well preserved, most derive from contexts that have not conventionally been used in land snail studies. Land snails are seen as a source of palaeoenvironmental information (primarily vegetation reconstruction) and suitable source sediments include buried soils and natural accumulated sediments. At Scar, most of the assemblages derive from the sand filling the boat grave and sediments associated with later human activity.

Methods

Land snails were extracted from bulk sample residues after flotation and sieving through a 500 m mesh; only apical fragments were collected. The shells were identified using the author's reference collection of fossil material; shells of *Cochlicopa*, *Vertigo* and *Oxychilus* were identified to genus only, as considerable effort is required to split these genera into species.

The approximate total number of shells in each assemblage was assessed using volume and assigned to one of three categories after standardising the results to 10 litres of sample: few (1–100), frequent (100–1000) and abundant (1000+). The relative abundance of the species present in each assemblage was estimated and assigned to one of three categories: few (0–5 %), frequent (5–30 %) and abundant (30–100%).

Given the limited time available for this exercise, it is inevitable that these categories are approximate and that rare species are under-represented in the species lists.

Results

The results are summarised in Table 7 below. They have been divided into four context groups and contexts are listed in stratigraphic order within the groups.

Key to the table

Total numbers of shells (10 litres of sediment):	Relative proportions of each species:
★ 0–100	+ 0–5%
★★ 100–1000	++ 5–30%
★★★ 1000+	+++ 30–100%

Table 7

Group A

Context	F17	F16
Total shells	★	★★
Species		
Cochlicopa spp.	+	++
Vertigo spp.		
Lauria cylindracea	+	++
Vallonia excentrica	+	++
Punctum pygmaeum		+
Discus rotundatus		
Vitrina pellucida		
Vitraea contracta		+
Nesovitraea hammonis		+
Oxychilus spp.		
Clausilia bidentata	+	++

Group B

Context	F49	F7	F5
Total shells	★★★	★	★★
Species			
Cochlicopa spp.	++		++
Vertigo spp.			+
Lauria cylindracea	++		+++
Vallonia excentrica			++
Punctum pygmaeum			+
Discus rotundatus	+++		+
Vitrina pellucida			
Vitraea contracta	++		
Nesovitraea hammonis			
Oxychilus spp.	++		
Clausilia bidentata	++		++

Group C

Context	F40	F39	F42	F43	F33	F27	F26
Total shells	?	★★★	★★	★★★	★★★	★	★
Species							
Cochlicopa spp.	++	++	++	++	++	++	++
Vertigo spp.							
Lauria cylindracea	++	++	++	++	++	++	++
Vallonia excentrica	++	+	++	+	+	+++	++
Punctum pygmaeum		+		+	+		
Discus rotundatus	+++	+++	++	+++	+++	++	++
Vitrina pellucida		+	+	+			
Vitraea contracta	++	++	++	++	++		
Nesovitraea hammonis							
Oxychilus spp.	++	++	++	++	++	+	+
Clausilia bidentata	++	++	++	++	++	+++	++

Group D

Context	F20	F32	F9	F12	F8	F11	F50	F3
Total shells	★★	★	★★	★★	★	★	★★	★★
Species								
Cochlicopa spp.	++	+	+++	++	+	++	++	++
Vertigo spp.					+	+	++	+
Lauria cylindracea	+++	+	+++	++	+	++	+++	++
Vallonia excentrica	++	+	++	++			+	+
Punctum pygmaeum	+		++	++	+		++	
Discus rotundatus		+			+	+	+	++
Vitrina pellucida								+
Vitraea contracta			+				+	+
Nesovitraea hammonis								
Oxychilus spp.		+	+			+		++
Clausilia bidentata		+	+	+	+		+	++

Discussion

Group A (Natural post-glacial deposits)
The two assemblages in this group are from layers of wind-blown sand. F16 was interpreted as a bA horizon and the higher shell concentration relative to F17 agrees with this. The short species list for F16 is paralleled in modern coastal sand sites in Orkney (Evans & Vaughan 1983) with the exception of *Clausilia bidentata*. In this situation, *C. bidentata* probably reflects the existence of stone walls or rubble nearby offering crevices for the snails.

Group B (Contexts pre-dating the boat burial)
Of the three assemblages from this group, F7 contained so few shells that a species list was not recorded, while F5 is similar to F16 but with two additional species. The high concentration and assemblage composition of F49 (wall tumble) compares closely with the boat grave fills (Group C), which emphasises the fact that all of these contexts (burial chamber and wall tumble) are essentially crevice habitats. The Group B assemblage is consistent with the shell sand and rubble habitat offered by the three contexts.

Group C (Collapse and fill inside the boat)
All of the Group C assemblages come from the collapse and fill inside the boat. Two types of assemblage can be distinguished: the main fills of the boat (F40, F39, F42, F43 & F33) contain high concentrations of shells dominated by *Discus rotundatus,* with *Vitraea contracta* and *Oxychilus spp.* notably common; while two sand layers over the east end of the boat (F27 & F26) contain few shells.

The relatively high diversity of the main boat fill assemblages is probably a result of the high shell concentration making rare species more apparent. The dominance of *D. rotundatus* and relative abundance of *Vitraea* and *Oxychilus* create assemblages similar to those from calcareous crevice and cave habitats (Evans & Jones 1973). This is appropriate for an underground buried chamber in shell sand and indicates that snails had access to the chamber as it gradually filled with sand.

The contrast between F27 and F26 and the other Group C assemblages reflects the fact that these contexts do not form part of the burial chamber fill. Their snail assemblages are probably largely derived from existing surface sediments and therefore reflect the local environment.

Group D (Later contexts)
Group D includes a variety of contexts associated with rubble, sand accumulations and buried land surfaces. In general, shell concentrations are not high. F20, F32 and F9 are sand layers with assemblages dominated by species typical of open ground and the crevice species are only present in low numbers (possibly derived from earlier sediments). The relative rarity of *Clausilia bidentata* makes a notable contrast with the Group A and B assemblages, which are otherwise similar.

The latest group of assemblages are those from the shallow ditches or gullies F13 and F52. The lower fill (F12) is similar to the earlier Group D assemblages but the others are distinguished by the consistent presence of *Vertigo spp.* (probably all *V. pygmaea*)

and relative rarity of *Vallonia excentrica*. Such differences are typical of open shell sand habitats and appear to reflect small-scale and short-term patterns in snail abundance. Both F12 and F50 (the fill of F52) contained a high proportion of shells that, judging by their lack of re-crystallisation, must have been alive within the last few decades. It is clear from this result that the gullies and all stratigraphically higher contexts are recent in origin.

Conclusion
Overall, the assemblages display characteristics and patterns of variation that are consistent with the current interpretation of the site stratigraphy. Group A and B contexts were barely excavated and are therefore poorly understood. Although they are a type of context often used for land snail analysis, detailed study cannot be justified in this case. The composition of the assemblages from the fill of the boat grave (Group C) confirms that a burial chamber existed for some time after the construction of the grave. The recent origin of the shell assemblages in gullies F13 and F52 is a significant finding for the phasing of these features.

APPENDIX 10. INSECT AND OTHER MACROFOSSIL REMAINS ASSOCIATED WITH THE COPPER ALLOY BROOCH

F D Large, H K Kenward & A R Hall

Summary
Macrofossil remains from a series of sediment samples from around the equal-armed brooch from the boat burial have been extracted and examined. Plant remains were extremely rare and poorly-preserved; most plant matter appears to have become completely humified. Invertebrate macrofossils were present in moderate numbers, although the less robust material was poorly preserved and not easily identifiable. Some flies and beetles appear to have become established within the burial, with a food chain perhaps based on decomposer fungi utilising wood and other plant matter. Flesh-feeding flies and other insects associated with corpses were not recognised.

Introduction
Fourteen small sediment samples were submitted for analysis. They represented the cleanings from both surfaces of the gilt copper alloy brooch (Lab No 911511) found in the Viking boat burial.

Methods
All the samples bore the code 911511. While the various sample containers (polythene bags, plastic boxes and gelatin capsules) generally were accompanied by descriptions indicating the position from which they had been removed from the brooch, individual numbers had not been assigned and so, for ease of record-keeping during processing, the letters A – N have been used here. The descriptions are appended in brackets in the results section.

Sample N consisted of material from a gelatin capsule only, while samples B and G included material in addition to that in the capsules. With the exception of material in the capsules, the samples were transferred to 75 x 25 mm specimen tubes, covered with 50 g/l sodium pyrophosphate solution and set to disaggregate in an ultra-sound bath for two hours. A few drops of the liquid fraction were placed on slides for parasite analysis following the rapid method of Dainton (1992). The samples were then washed on a 300 m sieve, and the retent stored in IMS in 120 ml glass jars for subsequent examination under the binocular microscope following the scan technique of Kenward *et al* (1980; 1986) and Kenward (1992). Arthropod remains were temporarily transferred to damp filter paper for study.

Results
None of the prepared slides contained any parasite eggs. Insect preservation was not very good. The more robust remains (such as most of the beetles) were somewhat pale, but preservationally labile fossils were usually fragmentary, with identification characters difficult to make out. Small numbers of plant fragments were generally present, but these were very decayed and, although plant matter appears originally to have been present, and indeed probably plentiful, most of it had humified almost completely.

The samples produced arthropod remains as follows. Insects were adults unless otherwise stated. M – many (probably 10 or more); S – several (probably between 4 and 9).

Sample A [A single lump of material in an unlabelled box]
The sample consisted mostly of very fine amorphous organic material, some of which remained in lumps after processing. There were traces of fine sand and some well-rotted plant fragments, none identifiable more closely. Some fungal cleistothecia (probably Gymnoascaceae) were noted. Very few insects were found, and these were extremely poorly preserved.

1	*Quedius* sp. pronotum (very 'filmy')
2	very fragmentary fly puparia
1	mite

Sample B [Loose fragments from initial cleaning round rivet area]
The gelatin capsule contained shell sand with some plant tissue fragments and tiny pieces of metal. Most of the processed sample consisted of shell sand with lumps of dark brown amorphous organic material and rotted orange-coloured wood fragments. There were a few ?Gymnoascaceae cleistothecia, some seed fragments of *Stellaria* sp. and a few rootlets. Some metallic fragments were also present.

2	*?Heterodera* sp. cysts
S	larval fragments (probably fly or beetle)
1	*Aphodius* sp. leg

Sample C [Loose soil etc from vicinity of boss 10. Found with boat rivet/wood]
Mainly rotted orange-coloured wood and lumps of fine, amorphous organic matter with some shell sand, a piece of poorly-preserved moss and pieces of copper corrosion product. Fungal cleistothecia were abundant.

S	*?Heterodera* sp. cysts
M	larval heads, perhaps *Cryptophagus scutellatus*
1	*Aleocharinae* sp.
1	?fly larval head
2	mites

Sample D [Sand etc from back of brooch]
After processing the retent was predominantly shell sand with some plant fibres, rootlets, soft lumps of amorphous organic material and rotted wood fragments. There were also fragments of metal, small lumps of copper corrosion product and a piece of mineralised textile. Some evidence of possible iron staining.

1	*Heterodera* sp. cyst
S	insect larval fragments
1	Staphylininae sp. abdominal segment

Sample E [Black organic material and good section of yellow fibrous material]
The retent consisted of small compressed lumps of amorphous

organic material, some unidentified plant fibres and lumps of copper corrosion product. Traces of fungal cleistothecia were recorded.

2 *?Heterodera* sp. cysts
M larval heads, perhaps of *Cryptophagus scutellatus*
M other larval fragments
M mite

Sample F [Soil lumps with yellow (?bone/wood) and ?peat]
The sample disaggregated to give a retent consisting mostly of fine plant fragments and lumps of amorphous organic/peaty material with some shell sand.

S unidentified larval fragments
S larval heads, perhaps *?Cryptophagus scutellatus*
3 fly puparia
1 Nematode cyst, probably *Heterodera* sp.
2 mites
1 weevil, undiagnostic tibia and elytral fragment with scales
1 *Xylodromus concinnus*
M (10+) *Cryptophagus scutellatus*
1 *Anobium punctatum*
2 Aleocharinae sp.

Sample G [Cleaning top debris from broken-off piece]
The capsule contained a few plant fibres, some shell sand and lumps of copper corrosion product.
After sieving there were lumps of peaty/amorphous organic material, plant fragments and shell sand with pieces of copper corrosion product, a little rotted bone and a small quantity of fungal cleistothecia (?Gymnoascaceae). Also some fragments of metal – some apparently fused – and tiny pieces of mineralised textile.

1 *?Heterodera* sp. cyst
M larval heads, perhaps *?Cryptophagus scutellatus*
3 *Cryptophagus scutellatus*
S mites
M unidentified insect larval fragments

Sample H [Soil from back of large piece]
After processing the sample consisted mainly of a mixture of rotted wood and other fine organic material together with shell sand, copper corrosion products and fragments of metal (?iron). There was possible iron staining – sometimes cementing clumps of sand grains. There were also a small piece of mineralised textile and a few tiny fragments of rotted bone. Small amounts of fungal cleistothecia from ?Gymnoascaceae were also identified.

4 *?Heterodera* sp. cysts
1 *Cryptophagus scutellatus*
1 *Anobium punctatum*
1 weevil (an undiagnostic femur)
1 *Cercyon* sp.
M insect larval fragments
M fragmentary fly puparia

Sample I [Black organic soil(?) from above boss 6]
The retent consisted of some shell sand, particles of copper corrosion products and a couple of metal fragments with some plant fibres, but was mostly undisaggregated fine amorphous organic material.

1 *?Heterodera* sp. cyst
M larval heads, possibly *?Cryptophagus scutellatus*
S undiagnostic insect larval fragments
M mites
M (17+) *Cryptophagus scutellatus*
2 *Xylodromus concinnus*
1 Aleocharinae sp.
1 fly (crumpled head)

Sample J [No description of sample]
Most of the processed sample consisted of fine, amorphous organic matter (?well-rotted wood) with some lumps of rotted wood, rootlets, fungal cleistothecia (?Gymnoascaceae), a piece of moss, some rotted spongy bone fragments and a few *Stellaria* sp. seed fragments. Some shell sand, pieces of copper corrosion product, metal flakes and slag-like metallic lumps were noted.

S *?Heterodera* sp. cysts
M fly puparium fragments
S *Cryptophagus scutellatus*
2 mites

Sample K [Black organic material from detached piece of rim]
Processing produced a retent largely consisting of fine, amorphous organic lumps with some well-rotted plant tissue fragments and rootlets. There were also a little shell sand and a small piece of rotted rib bone.

M mites
1 insect larval head capsule
1 larval head, possibly *?Cryptophagus scutellatus*
M (10+) *Cryptophagus scutellatus*
1 *Xylodromus concinnus*

Sample L [Black organic layer from above boss 13]
A few peaty/fine amorphous organic lumps and rotted plant fragments, with some fungal cleistothecia. The prepared slide gave a single ?moss spore.

1 weevil (joined femur and tibia)
1 *Cryptophagus scutellatus*
M larval heads, perhaps *?Cryptophagus scutellatus*
M fragments of indeterminate insect immatures
1 mite
1 fragmentary pupa, probably of Coleoptera or Lepidoptera

Sample M [Soil cleaned from top surface main piece]
A few plant fibres, a piece of moss, some shell sand, copper corrosion product fragments, flakes of metal and slag-like metallic lumps. No insects were found.

Sample N [Yellow fibrous material above central boss (capsule only)]

A very small quantity of shell sand, copper compound lumps and plant fibres were present in the capsule. No insect remains were found.

Discussion

A summary of the arthropod remains recorded from the samples is given in Table 8. The quantification is an approximate minimum number of individuals for all the remains amalgamated.

It appears that the beetle *Cryptophagus scutellatus* bred inside the burial chamber; the large number of individuals recorded cannot have arrived accidentally and there were larval head capsules which may also have been this species. *C. scutellatus* is a typical component of assemblages of archaeological insects from deposits formed within wooden buildings, and is frequently referred to in the literature of stored products insects. It is almost certainly a fungus feeder. Doubtless it found ample food within the burial chamber, in fungi growing on decaying timber and clothing. The predatory staphylinid *Xylodromus concinnus* is also a typical insect of archaeological 'house' assemblages and frequently found in buildings and stored products. The absence of other species typically associated with these two beetles is probably a result of difficulty of invasion, i.e. the sealed nature of the chamber (and perhaps a limited local fauna), rather than the lack of suitable habitats within it. If the beetles invaded naturally, then the burial may have taken place in the warmer part of the year, but importation through human agency from within an artificially warm structure at any time of the year certainly cannot be ruled out. The beetles may well have crawled on to one of the bodies while they lay in a building, or have been brought in with timber or cut plants.

The *Quedius* sp. did not appear to be the rather subterranean *mesomelinus*. Of the other beetles, *Anobium punctatum*, the woodworm, is very common in deposits on archaeological occupation sites. The specimen(s) found may have just strayed into the chamber or, more probably, have originated in the timber within it. The remaining beetles may also have been strays; they were too infrequent to allow any speculation as to their origin in material brought into the chamber.

The flies may have been attracted to rotting flesh or to other organic matter near the body. The puparia were very poorly preserved, and not identifiable within the constraints of the present project; the other insect immatures, similarly, could not be identified without unacceptable expenditure of time.

Nothing was recorded which corresponded with the 'worms' recorded in the conservation report, and the 'lemon-shaped capsules' appear to have been the cysts of *Heterodera* sp., which are, however, at least an order of magnitude larger than the eggs of intestinal parasitic nematodes. *Heterodera* is a nematode parasitic upon plant roots, and it quite possibly infested the roots represented by rootlets in the samples. It is also worth noting that closer inspection of the organic sediment suggests that it was not 'adipocere' but had an organic origin in plant matter, perhaps largely wood. The close proximity of the brooch to the sickle handle may explain the presence of the wood.

Table 8. *Arthropod taxa recorded from the samples of material associated with the Scar brooch, with an approximate indication of abundance. S = several; M = many.*

Taxon	Abundance
Heterodera sp. cysts	S
Acarina spp.	M
Diptera sp. (adult)	1.00
Diptera spp. (puparium)	M
Cercyon sp.	1.00
Xylodromus concinnus	S
Quedius sp.	1.00
Staphylininae sp.	1.00
Aleocharinae sp.	2.00
Anobium punctatum	1.00
Cryptophagus scutellatus	M>50
Curculionidae sp.	1.00
Coleoptera sp?p. larvae (perhaps including *C.scutellatus*)	M

APPENDIX 11. REPORT ON THE SOIL THIN SECTIONS

Stephen Carter

Introduction

The floor of the burial chamber, beneath the skeletons and artefacts, was covered in a thin spread of a distinctive dark brown sediment (F53). This was sampled using two 8 cm x 5 cm Kubiena tins (blue samples 17 & 20), with the aim of identifying the nature of the sediment; the tins were pushed into the upper surface of the spread. The sediment blocks were impregnated with resin and thin sections produced by the Department of Environmental Science, University of Stirling. The sections were cut in a vertical plane along the long axis of the block.

A preliminary examination of the sections showed that the dark sediment only occupied the top 1 cm to 2 cm of the sections. It overlay thin bands of residues forming the remains of wood boat strakes almost totally destroyed by biological decay. The strakes rested on clean shell sand.

The boat strakes

The locations of the thin section samples were plotted onto a plan of the boat rivets in order to determine the position of the sections in relation to the boat. Sample 17 lies across the junction between the first and second strakes, at right angles to the keel. This junction is immediately apparent in the section (Fig. 34). Sample 20 lies within the first strake, also at right angles to the keel.

The first strake

This is present across the full width of sample 20 and half of sample 17. It consists of a band of residues not more than 1 mm thick that is more or less continuous in sample 17 but frequently broken in sample 20. The band has a pale yellowish brown amorphous organic groundmass with a dotted appearance caused by frequent fine silt-sized fragments of darker amorphous organic matter. There is a discontinuous layer (200 m thick) of more structured brown organic matter at the base of the band. It consists of parallel laminations of highly decomposed plant tissue. Partially within and above this layer there is a concentration of objects interpreted as resin filled casts of cells. The resin is yellow brown and only slightly birefringent. There are two size ranges of cast: discrete clusters of 200 m to 300 m diameter objects occur 1 mm to 3 mm apart, and a more continuous layer of 10 m to 100 m diameter objects between and around them. They all appear to be rod-shaped but in sample 17 most have been cut in transverse section and therefore are circular or oval. This indicates a strong preferred orientation parallel to the boat keel. In sample 20 the orientation of the resin casts is more variable with many oblique sections probably resulting from disturbance of the band of residues. The larger resin casts tend to be hollow or only partially infilled. There are also a few unicellular and multicellular fungal spores present throughout the band.

The second strake

This is only present in half of sample 17. It is represented by a band no more than 400 m thick which occurs more or less continuously across the section. The band consists of parallel layers of brown amorphous organic matter showing slight traces of plant tissue structure. These lie in a matrix of pale yellow brown amorphous organic matter. A diffuse layer of rod-shaped resin objects overlies the layered organic matter; it contains rods less than 100 m in diameter with very few larger examples. There are frequent unicellular and multicellular fungal spores throughout the whole band.

The strake overlap (Fig. 34)

In sample 17 the two strakes overlap by 17 mm with the first overlying the second strake. The end of the second strake is abrupt but the first disintegrates into an irregular band of resin-rich amorphous organic matter after 4 mm of overlap. The strakes are separated by 1 mm and the gap is filled with quartz-rich sand, lacking siltstone fragments but containing a suite of unusual minerals. These are concentrated in a band roughly 600 m thick immediately over the second strake.

The sand

Sand within the boat (F53)

The sand within the boat (i.e. above the strakes in the thin section) consists of well-sorted quartz and siltstone in the size range 200 to 400 m. The packing voids between the sand grains are largely filled with a fine yellow/brown organo-mineral groundmass containing silt-sized mineral grains, fragments of amorphous organic matter, frequent fungal tissue and a few resin fragments. In sample 20 there are occasional yellow impregnative nodules. These are of unknown composition but may be phosphatic.

Sand outside the boat

The sand outside the boat consists of well sorted marine shell fragments, quartz and siltstone in the size range 200 m to 400 m. The packing voids between the sand grains are largely empty and there is little fine groundmass. The boundary between the calcareous sand outside the boat and the de-calcified sand within does not lie precisely at the strakes. In sample 20 it is 1 to 5 mm below and in sample 17 it is 10 mm below the junction of the strakes.

Discussion

The bands of material in the former positions of the boat strakes contain very little of the original wood. The last vestiges of this are represented by the layered brown organic matter in both strakes. The two strakes differ in the quantity of rod-shaped resin objects that they contain. The size, shape, orientation and internal morphology of these objects matches the resin and gum infillings found in the heartwood of some hardwoods trees. If they are vessel infillings, the clustered distribution of large resin infillings in the first strake probably indicates that this was made from a ring-porous wood (possibly oak). The rarity of large infillings in the second strake either indicates that there were few large vessels in the wood or that this was not heartwood and large vessels were still open.

The remarkable mineralogy of the sand trapped between the strakes merits further research and will not be discussed further here (see also pages 44-5 & Appendix 12). The survival of this small band of sand, and the overall clarity of the bands of residues that represent the strakes, indicate that there has been only limited small-scale disturbance since the strakes decayed. Modern roots were noted in both thin sections and these could have caused all of the disruption to the strake residues.

The approximate coincidence of the limit of sand decalcification and the boat strakes indicates that decalcification took place within the boat whilst the strakes were still a substantial barrier to the movement of liquids. A likely context for this is the initial decomposition of the three corpses in the boat, creating a large volume of acidic fluids that were contained by the boat. Shell sand could have entered the boat during the burial or immediately after. The deeper decalcification noted below the strake junction could be the result of fluid leaking out of the boat at this point.

The distinctiveness of the sand in the base of the boat (F53) is due to the loss of shell fragments by decalcification and the presence of significant quantities of amorphous organic matter and pigment. Given the advanced state of decomposition, it is not possible to identify these organic components morphologically.

APPENDIX 12. THE PETROLOGICAL INVESTIGATION OF MINERAL GRAINS TRAPPED BETWEEN CAULKING AND TIMBERS OF THE BOAT REMAINS AT SCAR

Dianne Dixon

Petrography

Detailed optical examination of the linear group of grains indicated the deep-green, prismatic, amphibole crystals which display a preferred orientation (lying with long axes in the plane between the boat timbers) were accompanied by a suite of less obvious minerals, pale green and pinkish grains including olivine, possible orthopyroxene, clinopyroxene, epidote, garnet, spinel, and probably other phases.

This complex assemblage eliminates all Orcadian beaches from being the source of the sand grains which became incorporated. Sand derived from the Old Red sedimentary rocks which form most of the Orkney Islands would contain a simple suite of grains dominated by quartz and shell fragments. Although the small outcrops of amphibolite-bearing, 'basement' rocks in the Stromness area could have contributed amphiboles, they certainly do not include olivine- and pyroxene-bearing rocks.

To produce sand containing fresh grains of minerals characteristic of both basic igneous rocks (e.g. basalt) and metamorphic rocks (e.g. amphibolite) requires the juxtaposition of the two rock types at the coast. No such suitable juxtaposition occurs on Shetland or the northern Scottish mainland coasts. To pursue the possibility that the sand could have become incorporated during construction of, or repairs to, the boat on the Scandinavian coast, it was essential to confirm the identity of all the mineral grains (not just those petrographically identifiable), and determine their chemical compositions, by electron-microprobe.

Four microfine slices were cut from the resin block (thin section sample 17: see Appendix 11) and polished sections prepared for microprobe analysis. Each slice contained a trail of minerals more numerous than in the original thin section. Initial exploratory analyses were obtained as economically as possible by running overnight using the automated stage. The trails were first scanned for several elements, to confirm the identity of known phases, to establish if there was a range of compositions within each phase, to identify any other minerals present and to set coordinates for analysis points. The elements measured were Si, Ti, Al, Fe, Mn, Mg, Ca, Cr, K, Na and Zn.

The analyses have revealed several characteristics and some unusual compositions, which enhance the possibility of locating parent rock-types and make more definite any comparison with sand and/or rock samples from suitable locations. Unfortunately, though not unexpectedly, from a computer search of the literature, it would appear that there are no publications with comparable mineral analyses of beach sands. The scanning also revealed a surprising feature: zinc, unexpected except as a trace element in mineralogical analysis, is concentrated in a zone which appears to separate the remains of the boat timbers from the heavy mineral trail (Stephen Carter, personal communication). This is consistent with Zn from brass objects within the grave being redeposited. A Ca-Zn phosphate was noted, forming pale brown crystals, unstable under the electron beam, which would require sophisticated techniques to analyse properly; but it may be Scholzite: $Ca_3ZnP_2O_8(OH)_2.H_2O$.

Mineralogy
The minerals confirmed and identified by microprobe analysis may be divided into three groups.

Basic Igneous Association

Olivines. Indicative of basic igneous rocks, probably olivine-rich, alkali basalts.

Pyroxenes. All pyroxenes turned out to be clinopyroxenes, consistent with the occurrence of basic igneous rock. Two suites may be present, one alkaline and one tholeiitic.

Feldspars. Both K-feldspar and plagioclase. The plagioclase is intermediate (labradorite), in keeping with the basalt minerals. The K-feldspar is probably associated with granitic gneiss. A granitic rock-fragment occurs amongst the grains.

Spinel. An unusual Ti-Fe-Cr composition is present, as well as more normal Ti-bearing magnetites which are common associates of olivine and pyroxene in basalts.

Ilmenite. An ore mineral, $(Fe,Mg)TiO_3$, found in basic igneous and metamorphic rocks.

Metamorphic Association

Amphiboles. The pleochroic green hornblendes have a range of compositions. Many are aluminous and consistent with medium to high-grade amphibolites.

Garnets. Almandines, with CaO content varying from 3 to 12% and MgO from 2 to 4%, characteristic of medium to high grade metamorphic rocks (schists).

Epidote. A calcium- and aluminium-bearing metamorphic mineral, consistent with the presence of amphiboles and garnet in other suitable compositions.

Sphene. A durable accessory mineral, common in amphibolites.

Haematite. Opaque, especially ferric oxide, Fe_2O_3. Common.

Miscellaneous

Phosphate. Calcium-zinc bearing phosphate, probably hydrous.

Unknown A. Si-Al-Fe-Mg-P-Ca bearing, probably hydrous.

Discussion
Since this exotic suite of minerals cannot be sourced in Orkney, Shetland or the northern Scottish mainland, and given that the boat contained an elaborate Viking burial and is likely to have been brought to Orkney from Scandinavia, the obvious inference is that the sand became trapped in the caulking when the boat was built or repaired in Scandinavia. It follows that, if we could locate an area or areas in coastal Scandinavia where petrological examination of the sand grains reveals a similar or identical assemblage to that found trapped in the boat remains at Scar, we would have narrowed down the list, and perhaps identified, the Scandinavian location(s) where the boat might have been built or repaired. This, in turn, might offer a clue as to the origins of the people buried at Scar.

Unfortunately, no comprehensive overview of mineral analyses of Scandinavian beach sands is presently available. The search for areas where high grade metamorphic rocks outcrop in close association with basaltic rock identified the Skåne peninsula of southern Sweden as one promising locality. Some 75 km north of Lund, a promontory forms the southern lip of a prominent bay, Skälderviken. It is composed of Precambrian gneisses with amphibolites, intruded by a swarm of Permo-Carboniferous basaltic dykes, which is a very suitable combination of rocks to produce the trapped mineral assemblage. There is also a known Viking boat-building site on a rock ledge (presumably a raised wave-cut platform) at the base of a 30 m cliff (Crumlin-Pedersen 1984).

All that can be said at this stage of the enquiry, though, is that this site is a possible candidate for the source of the sand trapped in the caulking of the Scar boat. To confirm its candidacy, it would be necessary to undertake petrographical examination of sand grains from the site, and then, if they revealed a similar asemblage to those from Scar, microprobe analysis. For a more convincing 'confirmation', it would be important to analyse the same minerals in rocks from the vicinity to establish the parent associations of minerals contributing to the sand. Other possibly suitable locations along the Scandinavian coastline should also be sought. This issue therefore merits further research, and might offer opportunities for an international research project, but unfortunately falls outwith the scope of the present project.

REFERENCES

Aagård, G-B 1984 'Gleicharmige spangen', *in* Arwidsson, G (ed) *Systematische analysen der gräberfunde*, 95–110. Stockholm: Birka II:1.

Almgren, B 1966 *The Viking*. London.

Almquist, B & Greene, D (eds) 1976 *Proceedings of the seventh Viking Congress*. Ireland.

Ambrosiani, B & Clarke, H (eds) 1992 *Early investigations and future plans*. Stockholm: Birka Studies 1.

Ambrosiani, K 1981 'Viking age combs, comb making and combmakers in the light of finds from Birka and Ribe', *Stockholm Studies in Archaeology*, 2. Stockholm.

Andersen, H H *et al* 1971 'Århus Søndervold. En byarkaeologisk undersøgelse', *Jysk Archaeologisk Selskabs Skrifter*, 9. København.

Anderson, J 1870–2 'Notes on the evidence of spinning and weaving in the brochs or Pictish towers, supplied by the stone whorls and the long-handled broch combs found in them', *Proc Soc Antiq Scot*, 9, 548–61.

Anderson, J 1874 'Notes on the relics of the Viking period', *Proc Soc Antiq Scot*, 10, 536–94.

Anderson, J 1880 'Notes on the contents of two Viking graves in Islay, discovered by William Campbell, Esq, of Ballinaby; with notices of the burial customs of the Norse sea-kings, as recorded in the sagas and illustrated by their grave-mounds in Norway and in Scotland', *Proc Soc Antiq Scot*, 14, 51–89.

Anderson, J 1907 'Notice of bronze brooches and personal ornaments from a ship burial of the Viking time in Oronsay, and other bronze ornaments from Colonsay', *Proc Soc Antiq Scot*, 41, 437–50.

Andersson, B, Damell, D & Norrmen, J (eds) 1991 *Fornsigtuna: en kungsgårds historia*. Tierp.

Angel, L 1964 'The reaction area of the femoral neck', *Clinical Orthopaedics*, 32, 130–42.

Arbman, H 1940 & 1943 *Birka I. Die Gräber*. Tafeln (1940). Text (1943). Kunglige Vitterhets Historie och Antikvitets Akademien. Stockholm.

Arne, T J 1911–12 'Ein persisches Gewichtssystem in Schweden', *Orientalisches Archiv*, 2, 122–7.

Arne, T J 1914 *La Suède et l'Orient. Études archéologiques sur les relations de la Suède at de l'Orient pendant l'age des Vikings*. Uppsala. (=Archives d'études Orientales 8).

Arne, T J 1934 *Das Bootgräberfeld von Tuna in Alsike, Uppland*. Kunglige Vitterhets Historie och Antikvitets Akademien. Stockholm.

Arwidsson, G (ed) 1984 *Systematische Analysen der Gräberfunde*. Stockholm: Birka II:1.

Arwidsson, G (ed) 1989 *Systematische Analysen der Gräberfunde*. Stockholm: Birka II:3.

Arwidsson, G & Thorberg, H 1989 'Kästen und Schachteln', *in* Arwidsson G (ed), *Systematische Analysen der Gräberfunde*, 113–121. Stockholm: Birka II:3.

Aykroyd, R G, Lucy, D, Pollard, A M & Roberts, C A 1999 'Nasty, brutish, but not necessarily short: a reconsideration of the statistical methods used to calculate age at death from adult human skeletal and dental age indicators', *American Antiquity*, 64(1), 55–70.

Bacon, G E 1990 'The dependence of human bone texture on life style', *Proc Roy Soc Lond*, B240, 363–70.

Balfour, J A 1908–9 'Notice of a Viking grave-mound, Kingscross, Arran', *Proc Soc Antiq Scot*, 20, 371–5.

Barclay, R S 1977 *Orkney testaments and inventories, 1573–1615*. Scottish Record Society (new ser). Edinburgh.

Barry, G 1805 (1975) *The history of the Orkney Islands*. (Facsimile 1975, Edinburgh).

Bass, W M 1987 *Human Osteology: A Laboratory and Field Manual*. Missouri Archaeological Society.

Batey, C E 1993 'The Viking and late Norse graves of Caithness and Sutherland' *in* Batey, C E, Jesch, J & Morris, C D (eds), *The Viking Age in Caithness, Orkney and the North Atlantic*, 148–64. Edinburgh. (= Proceedings of the eleventh Viking Congress).

Batey, C E, Jesch, J & Morris, C D (eds) 1993 *The Viking Age in Caithness, Orkney and the North Atlantic*. Edinburgh. (= Proceedings of the eleventh Viking Congress).

Batey, C E 1994–5 'A Viking whalebone plaque fragment and linen smoother', *Glas Arch Jour*, 19, 109–13.

Bencard, M, Jörgensen, L B & Madsen, H B (eds) 1991 *Ribe excavations 1970–1976*, 4. Esbjerg.

Bender Jørgensen, L 1984 'North European textile production and trade in the 1st millenium AD: a research project', *Jour Danish Archaeol*, 3, 124–34.

Bender Jørgensen, L 1992 *North European textiles until AD 1000*. Aarhus.

Bersu, G & Wilson, D M 1966 *Three Viking graves in the Isle of Man*. London. (= Soc Medieval Archaeol Monograph 1).

Bertelsen, R 1979 'Farm mounds in north Norway: a review of recent research', *Norw Arch Rev*, 12, 48–56.

Bessinger, J B & Creed, R P (eds) 1965 *Medieval and linguistic studies in honour of Francis Peabody Magoun Jr*. London.

Biddle, M & Kjølby-Biddle, B 1986 'A parcel of pennies from a mass-burial associated with the Viking wintering at Repton 873–4' *in* Blackburn, M A S (ed) *Anglo-Saxon monetary history*. Leicester.

Bill, J 1994 'Iron nails in Iron Age and medieval shipbuilding', *in* Westerdahl, C (ed) *Crossroads in ancient shipbuilding*. Oxford. (= Oxbow Monograph No 40).

Biuw, A 1992 *Norra Spånga, bebyggelse och samhälle under järnåldern*, Stockholmsmonografier, 76. Stockholm.

Blackburn, M A S (ed) 1986 *Anglo-Saxon monetary history*. Leicester.

Blindheim, C Heyerdahl-Larsen, B & Tollnes, R L 1981 *Kaupang-funnene*, Norske Oldfunn xi. Universitetets Oldsaksamlingen, Oslo.

Bøe, J 1940 'Norse antiquities in Ireland', *in* Shetelig, H (ed) *Viking antiquities in Great Britain and Ireland*. Oslo, vol 3, 48–69.

Boddington, A, Garland, N & Janaway, R (eds) 1987 *Death, decay and reconstruction: approaches to archaeology and forensic science*. Manchester.

Bojko, A M 1982 Technical report on the metalwork from a pagan Saxon cemetery. University of Durham (Dip in Arch Cons), unpublished thesis.

Bond, J, Dockrill, S, Gibson, J & Owen, O forthcoming 'The Styes of Brough, Sanday, Orkney, re-examined for Channel 4's *Time Team*'.

Bonde, N 1989 'Dendrokronologiske dateringer på Nationalmuseet 1988', *Arkæologiske udgravninger i Danmark 1988*, 229–41.

Bonde, N, Bartholin, T, Christensen, K, Eriksen, O H & Havemann, K 1990 'Dendrokronologiske dateringsundersögelser på Nationalmuseet 1989', *Arkæologiske udgravninger i Danmark 1989*, 245–64.

Bonde, N, Daly, A, Eriksen, O H & Havemann, K 1992

'Dendrokronologiske dateringsundersögelser på Nationalmuseet 1991', *Arkæologiske udgravninger i Danmark 1991*, 255–71.

Bonde, N & Christensen A E 1993 'Dendrochronological dating of the Viking Age ship burials at Oseberg, Gokstad and Tune, Norway', *Antiquity*, 67, 256, 576–83.

Bone, P 1989 'The development of Anglo-Saxon swords from the fifth to the eleventh century', *in* Chadwick Hawkes (ed) *Weapons and warfare in Anglo-Saxon England*, 63–70. Oxford.

Bourke, C 1994 'Finds from the River Blackwater', *Current Archaeology*, 134, 63–4.

Bowman, A 1992 'Boats in medieval Orkney'. National Maritime Museum, Greenwich. Unpublished report.

Brogger, A W, Falk, H & Shetelig, H (eds) 1917–18 *Osebergfundet I*. Kristiania.

Brogger, A W 1921 *Ertog og øre: den gamle Norske vegt*. Kristiania. Videnskapsselskapets Skrifter ii. Hist.-Filos. Klasse, 1921, no 3.

Brogger, A W 1929 *Ancient emigrants*. Oxford.

Brothwell, D 1972 'Palaeodemography and earlier British populations', *World Archaeology*, 4 (1972), 75–87.

Brothwell, D 1981 *Digging up bones*. Oxford.

Bruce-Mitford, R L S 1972 *The Sutton Hoo ship-burial: a handbook*. London.

Bruce-Mitford, R L S 1975 *The Sutton Hoo ship burial. Vol 1: Excavations, background, the ship, dating and inventory*. London.

Burness map (no date), in the possession of William I Ward, Holm, Orkney.

Cant, R G 1984 'Settlement, society and church organisation in the Northern Isles', *in* Fenton, A & Pálsson, H (eds) *The Northern and Western Isles in the Viking World: survival, continuity and change*, 169–79. Edinburgh.

Carlsson, M forthcoming 'The combs and other artefacts of antler and bone from the Birka excavation 1990–1995'.

Carver, M O H (ed) 1992 *The age of Sutton Hoo: the seventh century in north-western Europe*. Woodbridge.

Chadwick Hawkes, S (ed) 1989 *Weapons and warfare in Anglo-Saxon England*. Oxford (= Oxford University Committee for Archaeology Monograph, 21).

Christensen, A E 1959 'Færingen fra Gokstad', *Viking*, 23, 57–69.

Christensen, A E Ingstad, A S & Myhre, B 1992 *Oseberg Dronningens grav: vår arkeologiske nasjonalskatt i nytt lys*. Oslo.

Christensen, K 1991 'Wood-anatomical and dendrochronological studies', *in* Bencard, M, Jörgensen, L B & Madsen, H B (eds) *Ribe excavations 1970–1976*, 4, 169–81. Esbjerg.

Clarke, C & Fraser, W 1946 'Excavation of pagan burial mounds: Ingleby, Derbyshire', *Derbyshire Arch Jour*, 66, 1–23.

Clarke, C & Munslow, F W 1949 'Ingleby: Second report', *Derbyshire Arch Jour*, 69, 78–81.

Clouston, J Storer 1923–4 'The Orkney Lands', *Proc Orkney Antiq Soc*, 2, 61–8.

Coffey, G & Armstrong, E C R 1902 'Scandinavian objects found at Island-Bridge and Kilmainham', *Proc Roy Irish Acad*, XXIV C, 107–122.

Coffey, G & Armstrong, E C R 1910 'Scandinavian objects found at Islandbridge and Kilmainham', *Proc Roy Irish Acad*, 28, 107–22.

Cowen, J D 1934 'A catalogue of objects of the Viking period in the Tullie House Museum, Carlisle', *Trans Cumberland and Westmorland Antiq and Archaeol Soc* (second series), 34, 166–87.

Cowen, J D 1948 'Viking burials in Cumbria', *Trans Cumberland and Westmorland Antiq and Archaeol Soc* (second series), 48, 73–6.

Cowie, T G, Bruce, M & Kerr, N 1993 'The discovery of a child burial of probable Viking-Age date on Kneep headland, Lewis 1991: interim report', *in* Batey, C E, Jesch, J & Morris, C D (eds) *The Viking age in Caithness, Orkney and the North Atlantic*, 165–72. Edinburgh.

Craven, J B 1897 *History of the Church in Orkney 1558–1662*. Kirkwall.

Crawford, B E 1987 *Scandinavian Scotland*. Leicester.

Cronyn, J, Pye, E & Watson, J 1985 'The recognition and identification of traces of organic materials in association with metal artefacts', *in* Phillips, L (ed) *The archaeologist and the laboratory*, 24–27. (= CBA Research Report No 58).

Crowfoot, G M 1949 'Textiles from a Viking grave at Kildonan, on the Isle of Eigg', *Proc Soc Antiq Scot*, 83, 26–28.

Crumlin-Pedersen, O 1984 *Pugna Forensis. Arkeologiska undersökningar kring Foteviken, Skåne, 1981–3*. Malmö.

Crumlin-Pedersen, O & Munch Thye, B (eds) 1995 *The ship as symbol in prehistoric and medieval Scandinavia*. Copenhagen.

Crumlin-Pedersen, O 1995 'Boat-burials at Slusegaard and the interpretation of the boat-grave custom', *in* Crumlin-Pedersen, O & Munch Thye, B (eds) *The ship as symbol in prehistoric and medieval Scandinavia*, 87–99. Copenhagen.

Cubbon, A M 1971 *The art of the Manx crosses*. Douglas.

Cubbon, A M 1982 'Find of a Viking sword, spear and shield at Claghbane, Ramsey, Isle of Man', *Proc Isle of Man Nat Hist and Antiq Soc*, 8:4, 439–57.

Cubbon, A M 1983 'The archaeology of the Vikings in the Isle of Man', *in* Fell, C et al (eds) *The Viking Age in the Isle of Man*, 13–26. London. (= Proceedings of the ninth Viking Congress, Isle of Man, 1981).

Curle, C L 1982 *Pictish and Norse Finds from the Brough of Birsay*. Edinburgh. (= Soc Antiq Scot monog ser no 1).

Dainton, M 1992 'A quick, semi-quantitative method for recording nematode gut parasite eggs from archaeological deposits', *Circaea, the Journal of the Association for Environmental Archaeology* 9 (2), 58–63.

Dasent, G W 1894 *The Orkneyingers' Saga* (Rolls Series). London.

Davenport, P (ed) 1991 *Archaeology in Bath 1976–1985*. Oxford. (= Oxford University Committee for Archaeology, monog no 28).

Davidan, O 1982 'Om hantverkets utveckling i Staraja Ladoga', *Fornvännen*, 170–9.

Davidan, O 1992 'Kunsthandwerkliche Gegenstände des 8. bis 10. Jahrhunderts aus Alt-Ladoga', (Die sammlung der Staatlichen Ermitage in St Petersburg), *in Zeitschrift für Archäologi des Mittelalters, Jahrgang 20, 1992*. Köln.

Davidson, D A, Lamb, R & Simpson, I 1983 'Farm mounds in north Orkney: a preliminary report', *Norw Arch Rev*, 16: 1, 39–44.

Davidson, D A, Harkness, D D & Simpson, I A 1986 'The formation of farm mounds on the island of Sanday, Orkney', *Geoarchaeology*, 1:1, 45–60.

Davidson, H R 1962 *The Sword in Anglo-Saxon England*. Oxford.

Dodwell, C R (ed) 1961 *Theophilus—de diversis artibus*. London.

Dommasnes, L H 1979 'Et gravmateriale fra yngre jernalder brukt til å belyse kvinners stilling', *Viking*, 95–114.

Dommasnes, L H 1982 'Late Iron Age in western Norway. Female roles and ranks as deduced from an analysis of burial customs', *Norw Arch Rev*, 15, 70–84.

Drotz, M & Ekman, T 1995 'Kumla Ättebacke—1000 år i Härads Kumla.

Södermanland, Härads socken, RAÄ 15'. *Rapport UV* 1995:32. Stockholm.

Dunning, G & Evison, V 1961 'The Palace of Westminster Sword', *Archaeologia*, 98, 123–158.

Dunwell, A J, Cowie, T G, Bruce, M F, Neighbour, T & Rees, A R 1995 'A Viking Age cemetery at Cnip, Uig, Isle of Lewis', *Proc Soc Antiq Scot* 125, 719–52.

Edge, A G & Williams, J 1863 in 'Exhibitions and donations', *Proc Soc Antiq London*, 2 ser, ii, 229.

Edlin, H E 1985 *Broadleaves*. Forestry Commission Booklet no 20, HMSO, London.

Edwards, A J H 1927 'Excavations of graves at Ackergill and of an earth house at Freswick Links, and a discovery of a Viking grave at Reay, Caithness', *Proc Soc Antiq Scot*, 62, 196–209.

Edwards, A J H 1929 'Excavations at Reay Links and at a horned cairn at Lower Dounreay, Caithness', *Proc Soc Antiq Scot*, 63, 138–50.

Edwards, A J H 1934 'A Viking cist-grave at Ballinaby, Islay', *Proc Soc Antiq Scot*, 67, 74–8.

Edwards, B J N 1992 'The Vikings in north-west England: the archaeological evidence' in Graham-Campbell, J (ed) *Viking Treasure from the North West: the Cuerdale Hoard in its Context 43-62*. Liverpool. (= Liverpool Museum Occasional Paper no 5).

Eldjárn, K 1984 'Graves and grave goods: survey and evaluation' in Fenton, A & Pálsson, H (eds) *The Northern and Western Isles in the Viking World: survival, continuity and change*, 2–11. Edinburgh.

Elfstrand, B & Fernholm, R 1986 'En vikingagrav på Stafsund. Fornlämning 24, Ekerö socken, Uppland', Riksantikvarieämbetet och Statens historiska museer, *Rapport UV* 1986:13. Stockholm.

Ellis Davidson, H R 1982 *Scandinavian Mythology*. Middlesex.

Evans, J G & Jones, H 1973 'Subfossil and modern land-snail faunas from rock rubble habitats', *Journal of Conchology* 28, 103–129.

Evans, J G & Vaughan, M 1983 'The molluscs from Knap of Howar, Orkney', *in* Ritchie A 'Excavation of a Neolithic farmstead at Knap of Howar, Papa Westray, Orkney'. *Proc Soc Antiq Scot* 113, 40–121.

Fanning, T 1983 'Some aspects of the bronze ringed pin in Scotland', *in* O'Connor, A & Clarke, D V (eds) *From the Stone Age to the 'forty-five*, 324–42. Edinburgh.

Fell, C et al (eds) 1983 *The Viking Age in the Isle of Man*, London. (= Proceedings of the ninth Viking Congress, Isle of Man, 1981).

Fellows-Jensen, G 1984 'Viking Settlement in the Northern and Western Isles' *in* Fenton, A & Pálsson, H *The Northern and Western Isles in the Viking World'*, 148–68. Edinburgh.

Fenton, A & Pálsson (eds) 1984 *The Northern and Western Isles in the Viking World: survival, continuity and change*. Edinburgh.

Freke, D 1986 'Peel Castle', *Current Archaeology*, 99, 102–5.

Freke, D 1987 'Pagan lady of Peel', *Archaeology Today*, Feb 1987, 40–45.

Freke, D 1995 *The Peel Castle dig*.

FVTC 1992 *From Viking to Crusader, the Scandinavians and Europe 800–1200*. Udevalla. (= Nordic Council of Ministers in collaboration with the Council of Europe, the 22nd Council of Europe exhibition).

Gabra-Sanders, T 1998 'A review of Viking-Age textiles and fibres from Scotland: an interim report', *in* Jørgensen, L & Ranaldo, K (eds) *Textiles in European archaeology*, 177–85. Göteborg.

Gabriel, I 1988 'Hof- und Sakralkultur sowie Gebrauchs- und Handelsgut im Spiegel der Kleinfunde von Starigard/Oldenburg', *Bericht der Römisch-Germanischen Kommission*, 69, 103–291.

Geijer, A 1938 *Birka III: Die Textilfunde aus den Gräbern*. Kungl. Vitterhets Historic och Antikvitets Akademien. Uppsala.

Gjessing, P 1939 'Noen nordnorske handelsproblemer i jernalderen', *Viking*, 3, 37–54.

Gordon, K 1990 'A Norse Viking-age grave from Cruach Mhor, Islay', *Proc Soc Antiq Scot*, 120, 151–60.

Gormally, M G & Fairley, J S 1982 'Food of Otters *(Lutra lutra)* in a Freshwater Lough and an Adjacent Brackish Lough in the West of Ireland', *Jour Zool Lond* 197, 313–321.

Gourlay, R, Low, D & Batey, C E forthcoming 'The Viking grave at Balnakeil, Durness, Sutherland', *in* Baldwin, J R (ed) *Strathnaver and the Northlands of Sutherland*. (Scottish Society for Northern Studies).

Graham-Campbell, J A 1975 'Two Scandinavian brooch-fragments of Viking-age date from the Outer Hebrides', *Proc Soc Antiq Scot*, 106, 212–14.

Graham-Campbell, J A 1976 'The Viking-age silver hoards of Ireland', *in* Almquist, B & Greene, D (eds) *Proceedings of the seventh Viking Congress*, 39–74. Ireland.

Graham-Campbell, J 1980 *Viking Artefacts*. London.

Graham-Campbell, J (ed) 1992 *Viking Treasure from the North West: the Cuerdale Hoard in its Context*. Liverpool (= Liverpool Museum Occasional Paper no 5).

Graham-Campbell, J A 1995 'The Irish Sea Vikings: raiders and settlers', *in* Scott, T & Starkey, P (eds) *The Middle Ages in the north-west*, 59–83. Oxford.

Graham-Campbell, J A et al 1995 *The Viking-Age Gold and Silver of Scotland*. Edinburgh.

Graham-Campbell, J A & Batey, C E 1998 *Vikings in Scotland: an archaeological survey*. Edinburgh.

Graham-Campbell, J A & Paterson, C forthcoming *The pagan Norse graves of Scotland*. Edinburgh.

Gräslund, A-S 1973 'Barn i Birka', *Tör*, 14, 161–79.

Gräslund, A-S 1980 *The Burial Customs: a study of the graves on Björkö*. Birka IV. Kungl Vitterhets Historie och Antikvitets Akademien, Stockholm.

Gray, H 1977 *Anatomy Descriptive and Applied*. Revised American edition from fifteenth English edition (Pickering, T). New York.

Grieg, S 1928 *Kongsgaarden*. Oslo: Osebergfundet II.

Grieg, S 1940 'Viking Antiquities in Scotland', *in* Shetelig, H (ed) *Viking antiquities in Great Britain and Ireland*, vol 2. Oslo.

Grieg, S 1947 *Gjermundbufunnet: en høvdingegrav fra 900–årene fra Ringerike*. Oslo: Norske Oldfunn VIII.

Grieve, S 1914 'Note upon Carn Nan Bharraich or Carn of the men of Barra or burial mound of the Viking time on the island of Oronsay', *Proc Soc Antiq Scot*, 48, 272–91.

Hævernick, T E & Haberey, W 1963 'Gättsteine aus glas', *Jahrbuch des Römisch-Germanischen Zentralmuseums Mainz*, 10, 130–8.

Hägg, I 1971 *Mantel och Kjortel; vikingatidens dräkt*. Fv 66. Stockholm.

Hägg, I 1991 *Die Textilfunde aus der Siedlung und aus den Gräbern von Haithabu*. Neumünster. (Berichte über die Ausgrabungen von Haithabu, 29).

Hald, M 1980 *Ancient Danish Textiles from Bogs and Burials*. The National Museum of Denmark, Copenhagen.

Hall, R 1984 *The Excavations at York: The Viking Dig*. London.

Hamilton, J R C 1956 *Excavations at Jarlshof, Shetland*. Edinburgh.

Harrison, C 1988 *The History of the Birds of Britain*. London.

Hedges, J W 1980 'Textiles and textile production in Dark Age Britain', Unpublished MPhil thesis, University of Southampton.

Hedges, J W 1983 'Trial excavations on Pictish and Viking settlements at Saevar Howe, Birsay, Orkney', *Glas Arch Jour*, 10, 73–124.

Hedman, A 1991 'Platåhusen', *in* Andersson, B, Damell, D & Norrmen, J (eds) *Fornsigtuna: en kungsgårds historia*, Tierp.

Hencken, H O'N 1936 'Ballinderry Crannog, no. 1', *Proc Royal Irish Academy*, 43, 103–240.

Hencken, H 1950 'Lagore Crannog: An Irish Royal residence of the 7th to 10th centuries AD', *Proc Royal Irish Academy*, 53, 203–224.

Henshall, A S 1952 'Early textiles found in Scotland: part I' *Proc Soc Antiq Scot*, 86, 1–29.

Hill, P 1997 *Whithorn and St Ninian: the excavation of a monastic town*. Stroud.

Hunter, J R & Dockrill, S J 1982 'Some Norse sites on Sanday, Orkney', *Proc Soc Antiq Scot*, 112, 570–76.

Hunter, J R, Bond, J M & Smith, A M 1993 'Some aspects of early Viking settlement in Orkney', *in* Batey, C E, Jesch, J & Morris C D M (eds) *The Viking age in Caithness, Orkney and the North Atlantic*, 272–84. Edinburgh. (= Proceedings of the eleventh Viking Congress).

Hunter, J R, Dockrill, S J, Bond, J M & Smith, A N forthcoming *Archaeological investigations on Sanday*.

Huntly, B & Birks, H J B 1983 *An atlas of past and present pollen maps for Europe: 0–13,000 years ago*. Cambridge.

Hvass, S 1986 'Vorbasse – eine Dorfsiedlung während des 1. Jahrtausends n. Chr. in Mitteljutland, Dänemark', *Bericht der Römisch-Germanischen Kommission*, 67, 529–42.

Ingstad, AS 1988 'Textiles from Oseberg, Gokstad and Kaupang', *Archaeological Textiles: Report from the 2nd NESAT Symposium*, 133–48. Copenhagen.

Janaway, R C 1983 'Textile fibre characteristics preserved by metal corrosion; the potential of SEM studies', *The Conservator* 7, 48–52.

Janaway, R C 1985 'Dust to dust: the preservation of textile materials in metal artefact corrosion products with reference to inhumation graves', *Science and Archaeology* 27, 29–34.

Janaway, R C 1987 'The preservation of organic materials in association with metal artifacts deposited in inhumation graves', *in* Boddington, A, Garland, N & Janaway, R (eds) *Death, Decay and Reconstruction: Approaches to Archaeology and Forensic Science*, 127–48. Manchester.

Janaway, R C 1989 'Corrosion preserved textile evidence: mechanisms, bias and interpretation', *in* Janaway, R & Scott, B (eds), *Evidence Preserved in Corrosion Products: New Fields in Artifact Studies*, 21–9.

Janaway, R & Scott, B (eds) 1989 *Evidence Preserved in Corrosion Products: New Fields in Artifact Studies*. UKIC Occasional Papers.

Jansson, I 1972 'Till dateringen av vikingatidens ovala spännbucklor. En granskning av fyndkombinationerna', *Tör*, 14, 62–88.

Jansson, I 1981 'Economic aspects of fine metalworking in Viking Age Scandinavia', *in* Wilson, D M & Caygill, M L (eds), *Economic Aspects of the Viking Age*, 1–20. London. (= British Museum Occasional Paper No 30).

Jansson, I 1985a *Ovala Spännbucklor: en studie av vikingatida standardsmycken med utgångspunkt från Björkö-fynden*. Uppsala: Archaeological Studies,

Uppsala University, Institute of North European Archaeology, Aun 7.

Jansson, I 1985b *in Islam konst och kultur: en utställning i samproduktion mellan Statens historiska museum, Kungl. Myntkabinettet och Medelhavsmuseet*. Stockholm.

Jensen, S 1987 'Pre-Viking and early Viking Age Ribe: excavations at Nicolajgade 8, 1985–6', *Jour Danish Arch*, 6, 175–89.

Jensen, S 1991 *The Vikings of Ribe*. Ribe.

Jesch, J 1991 *Women in the Viking Age*. Woodbridge.

Johannessen, F 1940 'Båtene fra Gokstadskibet', *Viking* 4: 125–30.

Kaland, S H H 1973 'Westnessutgravningene på Rousay, Orknøyene', *Viking*, 37, 77–102.

Kaland, S H H 1981 'Westness', *Discovery and Excavation in Scotland 1980*, 25. Edinburgh.

Kaland, S H H 1993 'The settlement of Westness, Rousay', *in* Batey, C E, Jesch, J & Morris, C D (eds) *The Viking Age in Caithness, Orkney and the North Atlantic*, 308–17. Edinburgh. (= Proceedings of the eleventh Viking Congress).

Keepax, C 1975 'Scanning electron microscopy of wood replaced by iron corrosion products', *Journal of Archaeological Science* 2, 145–150.

Kennedy K A R 1989 'Skeletal markers of occupational stress', *in* Iscan, M Y & Kennedy, K A R (eds) *Reconstruction of life from the skeleton*, 129–60. New York.

Kenward, H K 1992 'Rapid recording of archaeological insect remains – a reconsideration', *Circaea, the Journal of the Association for Environmental Archaeology* 9 (2), 81–8.

Kenward, H K, Engleman, C, Robertson, A & Large, F 1986 'Rapid scanning of urban archaeological deposits for insect remains', *Circaea* 3, 163–72.

Kenward, H K, Hall, A R & Jones, A K G 1980 'A tested set of techniques for the extraction of plant and animal macrofossils from waterlogged archaeological deposits', *Science and Archaeology* 22, 3–15.

Kermode, P M C 1928 'Ship burial in the Isle of Man, *Antiquity*, 2, 91–3.

Kermode, P M C 'A ship-burial in the Isle of Man', *Antiq Jour*, 10, 126–33.

Kirkman, F B & Jourdain, F C R 1966 *British Birds*. London.

Krogman, W M & Iscan, M Y 1986 *The Human Skeleton in Forensic Medicine*. Springfield Illinois USA

Kruse, S E 1988 'Ingots and weight units in Viking Age silver hoards', *World Archaeology*, 20, (2), 285–301.

Kruse, S E 1992 'Late Saxon balances and weights from England', *Medieval Archaeology*, 36, 7–95.

Kruse, S E 1993 'Silver storage and circulation in Viking Age Scotland. The evidence of silver ingots', *in* Batey, C E et al (eds), *The Viking Age in Caithness, Orkney and the North Atlantic*, 187–203. Edinburgh. (= Proceedings of the eleventh Viking Congress).

Kruuk, H & Hewson, R 1978 'Spacing and Foraging of Otters *(Lutra lutra)* in a Marine Habitat', *J Zool Lond*, 185, 205–212.

Kyhlberg, O 1971 *Birka. De vikingatida vikterna*. Stockholm.

Kyhlberg, O 1980 *Vikt och värda*. Stockholm. (= Stockholm Studies in Archaeology, 1).

Lamb, G 1992 Naggles of Piapittem (*The Placenames of Sanday*). Published privately.

Lamb, R G 1980 *The archaeological sites and monuments of Sanday and North Ronaldsay, Orkney*. Edinburgh.

Lamb, R G 1993 'Carolingian Orkney and its transformation' *in* Batey, C E, Jesch, J & Morris, CD (eds), *The Viking Age in Caithness, Orkney and the North Atlantic*, 260-71. Edinburgh. (= Proceedings of the eleventh Viking Congress).

Lang, J (ed) 1978 *Anglo-Saxon and Viking Age Sculpture and its Context*. Oxford. (=BAR Brit Ser no 49).

Lang, J & Ager, B 1989 'Swords of the Anglo-Saxon and Viking Periods in the British Museum: A Radiographic Study', *in* Chadwick Hawkes, S (ed), *Weapons and Warfare in Anglo-Saxon England*, 85–122. Oxford. (= Oxford University Committee for Archaeology Monograph No 21).

Lewis, A R 1958 *The Northern Seas*. Princeton.

Linklater, E 1980 *Orkney and Shetland*. London.

Logan, F D 1983 *The Vikings in History*. London.

Lovejoy, C O Meindl, R S Prysbeck, T R & Barton, T J 1985 'Chronological metamorphosis of the auricular surface of the ilium: A new method for the determination of age at death', *Amer Jour Phys Anthrop*, 68, 15–28.

Lowe, C E 1998 *St Boniface Church, Orkney: Coastal erosion and archaeological assessment*. Stroud.

McDonnell, J 1989 'Iron and its alloys in the fifth to eleventh centuries AD in England', *World Archaeology*, 20, (2), 373–382.

McGrail, S 1987 *Ancient Boats in NW Europe: the archaeology of water transport to AD 1500*. London.

McGrail, S 1993 *Medieval boat and ship timbers from Dublin. Medieval Dublin Excavations 1962–81,* Series B, 3. Royal Irish Academy, Dublin.

Mackenzie, M 1750 *Orchades*.

McKern, T W & Stewart, T D 1957 'Skeletal age changes in young American males, analyzed from the standpoint of identification', *Headquarters QM Res and Dev Command,* Tech Rep EP-45. Natick, Mass.

MacLaren, A 1974 'A Norse house on Drimore machair, South Uist', *Glas Arch Jour*, 3, 9–18.

MacLeod, D J *et al* 1916 'An account of a find of ornaments of the Viking time from Valtos, Uig, in the island of Lewis', *Proc Soc Antiq Scot*, l, 181–9.

McNeill, M 1891 'Notice of excavations in a burial mound of the Viking time in Oronsay', *Proc Soc Antiq Scot*, 25, 432–5.

Malmer, M 1992 'Weight systems in the Scandinavian Bronze Age', *Antiquity*, 66, 377–88.

Marshall, D N 1964 'Report on excavations at Little Dunagoil', *Trans Buteshire Nat Hist Soc*, 16, 1–69.

Marwick, E W 1975 *The Folklore of Orkney and Shetland*. London.

Marwick, H 1923 'Antiquarian notes on Sanday', *Proc Orkney Antiq Soc*, 1, 21–9.

Marwick, H 1952 *Orkney Farm-Names*. Kirkwall.

Marwick, J G 1927–8 'Notes on some relics from Orkney exhibited before the Society', *Proc Soc Antiq Scot*, 62, 121–2.

Maryon, H 1971 *Metalworking and Enamelling*. (= Dover facsimile edition of the 1959 (4th) edition).

Maxwell, H 1913 'Notes on a hoard of personal ornaments, implements, and Anglo-Saxon and Northumbrian coins from Talnotrie, Kirkcudbrightshire', *Proc Soc Antiq Soc*, 47, 12–16.

Miller & Hebden 1872 *Plan of Estate of Westove* (in possession of William I Ward).

Montelius, O 1877 'Om de ovala spännbuckorna 2', *Kungl. Vitterhets Historie och Antikvitets Akademien*, månadsblad, 64–6.

Montelius, O 1892 'Öfversigt öfver den nordiska forntidens perioder intill kristendomens införande', *Svenska fornminnesföreningens tidskrift*, 8:2.

Morris, C D M 1985 'Viking Orkney: a survey' *in* Renfrew, C (ed) *The prehistory of Orkney 4000 BC – 1000 AD*, 210–42. Edinburgh.

Morris, C D M 1989 *The Birsay Bay project I: Brough Road excavations 1976–82*, Durham. (= Department of Archaeology, University of Durham, monog 1).

Müller-Wille, M 1970 'Bestattung im Boot. Studien zu einer nordeuropäischen Grabsitte', *Offa*, 25/26.

Müller-Wille, M 1974 'Boat graves in northern Europe', *International Journal of Nautical Archaeol*, 3, 187–204.

Müller-Wille, M 1976 *Das Bootkammergrab von Haithabu*. Berichte über die Ausgrabungen in Haithabu, viii.

Müller-Wille, M 1995 'Boat-graves, old and new views', *in* Crumlin-Pedersen, O & Munch Thye, B (eds) *The ship as symbol in prehistoric and medieval Scandinavia*, 101–9. Copenhagen.

Murphy, K P & Fairley, J S 1985 'Food of Otters *(Lutra lutra)* on the South Shore of Galway Bay', *Proceedings of the Royal Irish Academy,* Section B- Biological, Geological and Chemical Science. 85B(4), 40–55.

Murray, H J R 1952 *A History of Board Games Other than Chess*. Oxford.

Näsström, B-M 1995 *Freyja—the Great Goddess of the North*. (= Lund Studies in History of Religions, vol 5). Lund.

Nerman, B 1969 *Die Vendelzeit Gotlands. II Tafeln*. Kungl. Vitterhets Historie och Antikvitets Akademien. Stockholm.

Niclasen, B (ed) 1968 *Proceedings of the fifth Viking Congress*. Torshavn.

Nordahl, E 1982 *Sigtuna under medeltiden*, Sigtuna. (= Sigtuna Museer Skriftserie 1).

Nordal, S 1944 *Flateyjarb 19*. Akranes.

NSA = 1842 *New Statistical Account of Scotland,* Orkney Islands. Edinburgh.

Oakeshott, R E 1960 *The Archaeology of Weapons*. London.

Olsen, M 1954 'Runic inscriptions in Great Britain, Ireland and the Isle of Man', *in* Shetelig, H (ed) *Viking Antiquities in Great Britain and Ireland*, vol 6, Oslo, 153–233.

Olsen, S L (ed) 1988 *Scanning Electron Microscopy in Archaeology*. Oxford. (= BAR Int Ser no 452).

O & S Recs = 1907–1913 *Orkney and Shetland Records*, 2, London, (= Viking Society for Northern Research, 2).

Ortner, D J & Aufderheide, A C (eds) 1991 *Human Palaeopathology*. Washington & London.

Owen, O A 1999 *The sea road: a Viking voyage through Scotland* (The Making of Scotland series, Canongate). Edinburgh.

Owen, O A & Smith, B 1988 'Kebister, Shetland: an armorial stone and an archdeacon's teind barn?', *Post-medieval Arch*, 22, 1–20.

Owen, O A & Lowe, C E 1999 *Kebister. The four-thousand-year-old story of one Shetland township*. Edinburgh (= Society of Antiquaries of Scotland Monograph Series, 14).

Page, R I 1983 'The Manx rune-stones' *in* Fell, C et al (eds) *The Viking Age in the Isle of Man*, 133–46. London. (= Proceedings of the ninth Viking Congress, Isle of Man 1981).

Paulsen, P 1933 *Studien zur Wikinger-Kultur*, Neumünster. (= Forschungen zur Vor- und Frühgeschichte aus dem Museum vorgeschichtlicher Altertümer in Kiel 1).

Pearson, G W, Pilcher, J R, Baillie, M G L, Corbett, D M & Qua, F 1986 'High-precision ¹⁴C measurement of Irish oaks to show the natural ¹⁴C variations from AD 1840-5210 BC', in Stuiver, M & Kra, R S (eds) *Proceedings of the 12th International ¹⁴C Conference.* (=Radiocarbon 28 (2B)), 911-34.

Peterkin, A 1820 *Rentals of the Ancient Earldom and Bishoprick of Orkney*. Edinburgh.

Petersen, J 1914 'Bretspillet i forhistorisk tid', *Oldtiden*, 4, 75–92.

Petersen, J 1919 *De norske vikingesverd. En typologisk-kronologisk studie over vikingetidens vaaben*. Kristiania. (= Videnskapsselskapets skrifter, II, hist.-filos. klasse 1919, no 1).

Petersen, J 1928 *Vikingetidens smykker i Norgen*. Stavanger.

Petersen, J 1951 *Vikingetidens Redskaper*. Oslo. (= Skrifter utgitt av Det Norske Videnskaps-Akademi i Oslo, II. Hist-filos Kl, 1951, no 4).

Petré, B 1984 *Arkeologiska undersökningar på Lovö*. Del 2 & Del 4 Stockholm. (= Acta Universitatis Stockholmiensis. Studies in North-European Archaeology, 8 & 10).

Phillips, L (ed) 1985 *The Archaeologist and the Laboratory* (= CBA Research Report no 58).

Price, N S 1989 *The Vikings in Brittany*. London: Saga-Book XXII:6, 319–440.

Ramskou, T 1954 'Lindholm Høje. En gravplads fra yngre jernalder og en boplads fra tidlig middelalder', *Nationalmuseets Arbejdsmark*, 37–48.

Ramskou, T 1965 'Vikingerne ofrede mennesker', *Nationalmuseets Arbejdsmark*, 79–86.

Ramskou, T 1976 *Lindholm Høje. Gravpladsen*, Copenhagen. Nordiske Fortidsminder B2.

Renfrew, C (ed) 1985 *The prehistory of Orkney 4000 BC – 1000 AD*. Edinburgh.

Resi, H G 1986 Gravplassen Hunn i Ostfold. *Norske Oldfunn XII*. Universitetets Oldsaksamling. Oslo.

Richards, J D 1991 *Viking Age England*. London.

Richards, J D, Jecock, M, Richmond, L & Tuck, C 1995 'The Viking barrow cemetery at Heath Wood, Ingleby, Derbyshire', *Medieval Archaeology*, 39, 51–70.

Ritchie, A 1977 'Excavation of Pictish and Viking-age farmsteads at Buckquoy, Orkney', *Proc Soc Antiq Scot*, 108, 174–227.

Ritchie, A 1993 *Viking Scotland*. London.

Ritchie, J N G 1981 'Excavations at Machrins, Colonsay', *Proc Soc Antiq Scot*, 111, 263–81.

Robertson, W N 1969 'A Viking grave found at the Broch of Gurness, Aikerness, Orkney', *Proc Soc Antiq Scot*, 101, 289–90.

Roes, A 1963 *Bone and Antler Objects from the Frisian Terp-mounds*. Haarlem.

Roes, A 1965 *Vondsten van Dorestad*. Archaeologica Traiectina, VII. Groningen.

Roesdahl, E 1977 *Fyrkat En jysk vikingeborg II. Oldsagerne og gravpladsen*, Nordiske Fortidsminder Serie B, Bind 4, Copenhagen.

Rygh, O 1885 *Norske Oldsager*. Christiana.

Schanche, K 1991 'En båtbegravelse i Føre, Bø i Vesterålen', *Ottar*, 188 (May 1991), 13–20.

Schweingruber, F H 1978 *Microscopic Wood Anatomy*. Swiss Federal Institute of Forestry Research, Birmensdorf.

Scott, T & Starkey, P (eds) 1995 *The Middle Ages in the north-west*, 59–83. Oxford.

Sephton, J 1899 *The Saga of King Sverri of Norway*. London.

Sharples, N, Webster, J & Parker-Pearson, M 1995 The Viking Age settlement at Bornish, South Uist. Interim report on the 1995 excavations. University of Sheffield, unpublished report.

Shetelig, H 1910 'Traces of the custom of suttee in Norway during the Viking Age', *Saga-Book of the Viking Club*, 6, 180–208.

Shetelig, H 1917–18 in Brogger, A W, Falk, H & Shetelig, H (eds) *Osebergfundet I*, Kristiania.

Shetelig, H 1920 *Vestfoldskolen*, Kristiania. (= Osebergfundet III).

Shetelig, H (ed) 1940–54 *Viking antiquities in Great Britain and Ireland*, 1-5 (1940) and 6 (1954). Oslo.

Sjøvold, T 1971 'Whale-bone tools in the Iron Age of north Norway', *Actes du VII Congrès International des sciences préhistoriques et protohistoriques*, II, Prague, 1200–4.

Sjøvold, T 1974 *The Iron Age settlement of arctic Norway, II. Late Iron Age*, Oslo. (= Tromso Museums Skrifter, 10:2).

Small, A 1968 'A Viking longhouse in Unst, Shetland' in Niclasen, B (ed) *Proceedings of the fifth Viking Congress*, 62–70. Torshavn.

Smith, J 1907 *The Church in Orkney*. Kirkwall.

Smyth, A P 1979 *Scandinavian York and Dublin*. II. New Jersey & Dublin.

Soil Survey of Scotland, Orkney, the Northern Isles (map).

Sperber, E 1993 'Establishing weight systems in Bronze Age Scandinavia', *Antiquity* 67, 613–19.

Steinnes, A 1959 'The 'huseby' system in Orkney', *Scot Hist Rev*, 38, 36–46.

Stephens, H 1850 *The Book of the Farm*, II. Edinburgh & London.

Steuer, H 1973 'Gewichte aus Haithabu', *Berichte über die Ausgrabungen in Haithabu*, 6, 9–22.

Stevenson, R B K 1968 'The brooch from Westness, Orkney', in Niclasen, B (ed) *Proceedings of the fifth Viking Congress*, 25–31. Torshavn.

Stevenson, R B K 1989 'The Celtic brooch from Westness, Orkney, and hinged pins', *Proc Soc Antiq Scot* 119, 239–70.

Stirland, A 1991 'Diagnosis of occupationally related palaeopathology: can it be done?' in Ortner, D J & Aufderheide, A C (eds) *Human Palaeopathology*. Washington & London.

Stjernquist, B 1951 'Vä under järnåldern', *Kunglige Humanistiska Vetenskapssamfundet i Lund*, xlvii. Lund.

Stumann-Hansen, S 1988 'The Norse landnam in the Faroe Islands in the light of recent excavations at Toftanes, Leirvik', *Northern Studies*, 25, 58–84.

Taylor, A B 1938 *The Orkneyinga Saga*. Edinburgh.

Tempel, W-D 1969 *Die Dreilagenkämme aus Haithabu*. Studien zu den Kämmen der Wikingerzeit im Nordseeküstengebiet und Skandinavien. Göttingen.

Thomson, W P L 1990 'Settlement Patterns at Tuquoy, Westray, Orkney', *Northern Studies*, 27, 35–49.

Thomson, W P L 1993 'Some Settlement Patterns in Medieval Orkney', in Batey, C E, Jesch, J & Morris, C D (eds) *The Viking Age in Caithness, Orkney and the North Atlantic*, 340–8. Edinburgh.

Thomson, W P L 1995 'Orkney Farm-names; a re-assessment of their chronology', *in* Crawford, B E (ed) *Scandinavian Settlement in Northern Britain,* 42–63. Leicester.

Thomson, W P L 1996 *Lord Henry Sinclair's 1492 Rental of Orkney.* Kirkwall.

Thorsteinsson, A 1968 'The Viking burial place at Pierowall, Westray, Orkney' *in* Niclasen, B (ed) *Proceedings of the fifth Viking Congress,* Torshavn, 150–73.

Thunmark-Nylén, L 1995 'Vendeltid eller vikingatid? Om datering av Gotländska fornfynd kring år 800', *Tor,* 27:2. Societas Archaeologica Upsaliensis.

Traill, W 1883 *A Genealogical Account of the Traills of Orkney.* Kirkwall.

Tschan, F J (ed) 1959 *Adam of Bremen: History of the Archbishops of Hamburg-Bremen.* New York.

Tulloch, B W 1995 'The Burness Crofters', *in* Thomson, W P L (ed) *The Making of Modern Orkney,* 38–47. Aberdeen.

Ulbricht, I 1978 Die Geweihverarbeitung in Haithabu. *Die ausgrabungen in Haithabu,* 7. Neumunster.

Wainwright, F T (ed) 1962 *The Northern Isles.* Edinburgh.

Wallace, P F 1987 'The economy and commerce of Viking Age Dublin', *Der handel der Karolinger- und Wikingerzeit,* Göttingen. Untersuchungen zu handel und verkehr der vor- und frühgeschichtlichen zeit in Mittel- und Nordeuropa, Part IV.

Wallace, P F 1992 *The Viking Age Buildings of Dublin.* Dublin: Medieval Dublin Excavations 1962–81, Ser A, Vol 1, parts 1–2. Dublin.

Wamers, E 1994 'König im Grenzland. Neue Analyses des Bootkammergrabes von Haiðaby', *Acta Archaeologica,* 65, 1–56.

Wamers, E 1995 'The symbolic significance of the ship-graves at Haiðaby and Ladby', *in* Crumlin-Pedersen, O & Munch Thye, B (eds) *The ship as symbol in prehistoric and medieval Scandinavia,* 149–59. Copenhagen.

Warmind, M L 1995 'Ibn Fadlan in the context of his age', in Crumlin-Pedersen, O & Munch Thye, B (eds) *The ship as symbol in prehistoric and medieval Scandinavia,* 131–7. Copenhagen.

Warner, R 1975–6 'Scottish silver arm-rings: an analysis of weights', *Proc Soc Antiq Soc,* 107, 136–43.

Watkins, S 1991 Fiche 1 A:2–5 *in* Davenport, P (ed) *Archaeology in Bath 1976–1985,* Oxford. (= Oxford University Committee for Archaeology, monograph no 28).

Watson, J 1988 'The identification of organic materials preserved by metal corrosion products', *in* Olsen, S L (ed) *Scanning Electron Microscopy in Archaeology,* 65–76. (=British Archaeological Report International Series 452).

Watson, P 1993 'The conservation and recording of the boat rivets and nails from Scar'. AOC (Scotland) Ltd. Unpublished report.

Watt, J 1992 'The Diet of Otters *(Lutra lutra)*', Unpublished PhD, Department of Zoology, University of Aberdeen.

Wegraeus, E 1973 'Pilspetsar under vikingatid', *Tor,* 15, 191–208.

Welander, R, Batey, C & Cowie, T G 1987 'A Viking burial from Kneep, Uig, Isle of Lewis', *Proc Soc Antiq Scot,* 117, 149–74.

Westerdahl, C (ed) 1994 *Crossroads in ancient shipbuilding.* Oxford. (= Oxbow Monograph No 40).

Wheeler, Sir R 1927 *London and the Vikings.* London.

Wilde, Sir W 1866 'On the Scandinavian antiquities lately discovered at Islandbridge, near Dublin', *Proc Roy Irish Acad,* 10, 13–22.

Wilson, D M 1965 'Some neglected late Anglo-Saxon swords', *Medieval Archaeology,* 9, 32–54.

Wilson, D M 1970 'An Anglo-Saxon playing piece from Bawdsey', *Proc Suffolk Inst Arch,* 32, 38–42.

Wilson, D M 1974 *The Viking age in the Isle of Man: the archaeological evidence,* Odense. (= C C Rafn Lecture, no 3).

Wilson, D M 1978 'The dating of Viking art in England' *in* Lang, J (ed) *Anglo-Saxon and Viking Age Sculpture and its Context,* 135–144. Oxford. (= BAR Brit Ser no 49).

Wilson, D M & Caygill, M L (eds) 1981 *Economic Aspects of the Viking Age,* London. (= British Museum Occasional Paper No 30).

INDEX

Västerhus, Jämtland, Sweden 154
Vestfold 90
Vig, Norway 107
vík (bay) 3
Vik, Buksnes, Lofoten-Vesterålen
  85
Vikestad, Nœro, Nord-Trøndelag
  84
Viking Age
  boats in Orkney 46-7
  Sanday in the 3-16
  weight systems 120-3
Volga River 157
"Volunes" 5

walrus ivory 130
Waterford 168
weapons 114-15, 137-8, *see also*
  arrowheads; sword
weaving 77, 143, 153
weaving batten 30, 35, 91-3, 142
weight systems
  Bronze Age 123
  Isle of Man 122
  markings 123-4
  Roman 123
  Scandinavian 121, 123
  Scotland 122
weights
  lead bullion 1, 23, 31, 118-26,
    137, 138, 139-40, 150, 160
    context of 121
    description and technology
    118-20
  typology, distribution and
    dating 124-6
  Viking Age 120-1
West Seaton, Workington, Cumbria
  166
Westbrough 12
Western Isles 47, 83, 169
  Viking graves in 172, 179-82,
    184
Westminster, Palace of 111
Westness, Rousay 1, 43, 46, 50, 83,
  90, 92, 130, 135, 139, 145-6,
  149, 154, 155, 172
  importance of 174-6, 178, 183,
    184
Westove, Sanday 8, 10, 11
Westray 8, 46, 92, 125
Wexford 168
whalebone 74, 80, 81, 127
Whithorn 125
wick (ON *vík*: a bay) 3
Wigmund, Archbishop of York 83
willow 111
woman's equipment 30, 60-102,
  142-8
wood
  fragments from keel 27, 28
  identification of the 28, 43
  mineralised 114
  scarcity of 49

X-Ray Fluorescence Spectroscopy
  (XRF) 39, 63, 95, 104, 105

yew (*Taxus baccata L*) 114
York 122, 167
  York Minster 166
Ytre Arne, Haus, Hordaland,
  Norway 123, 124